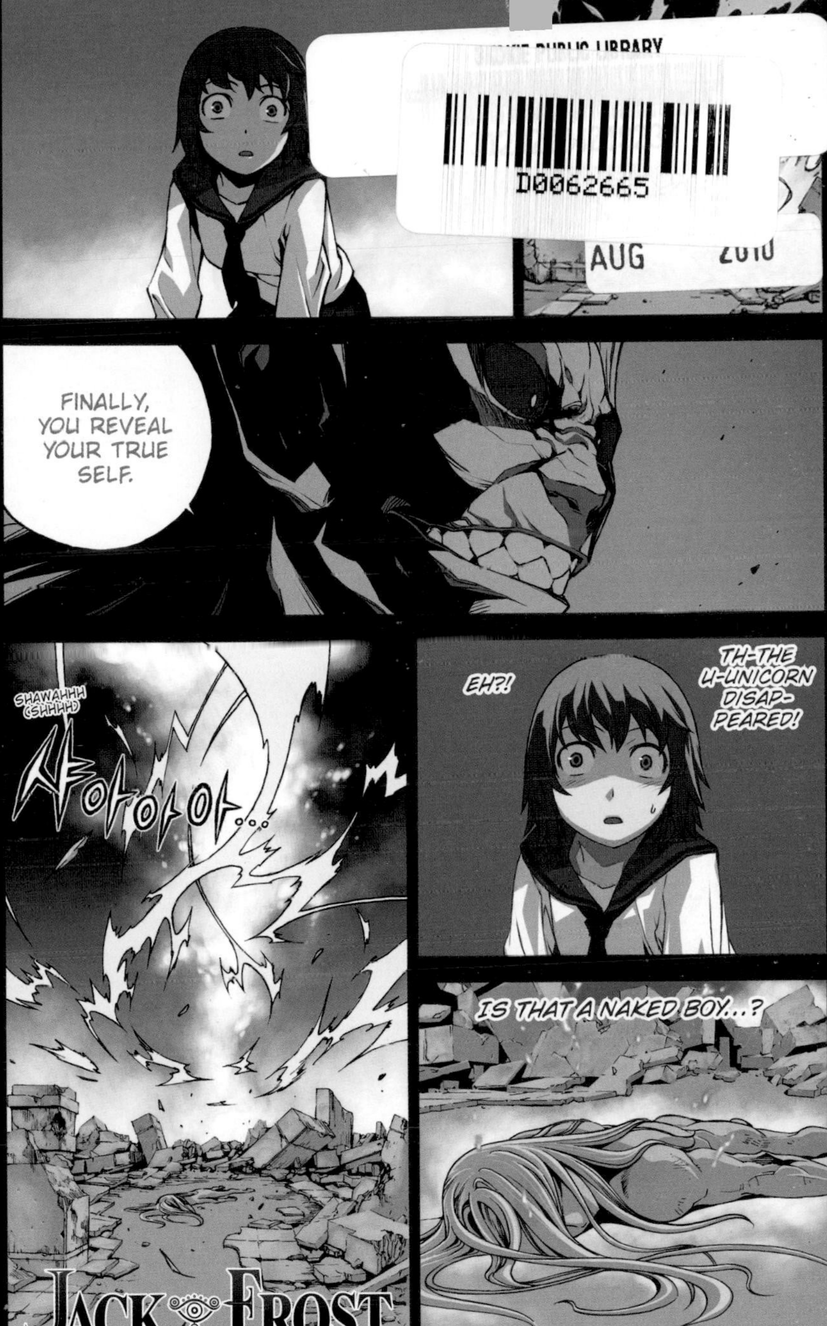
FINALLY, YOU REVEAL YOUR TRUE SELF.
SHAWAHHH (SHHHH)
EH?!
TH-THE U-UNICORN DISAP-PEARED!
IS THAT A NAKED BOY...?
JACK FROST
The Amityville

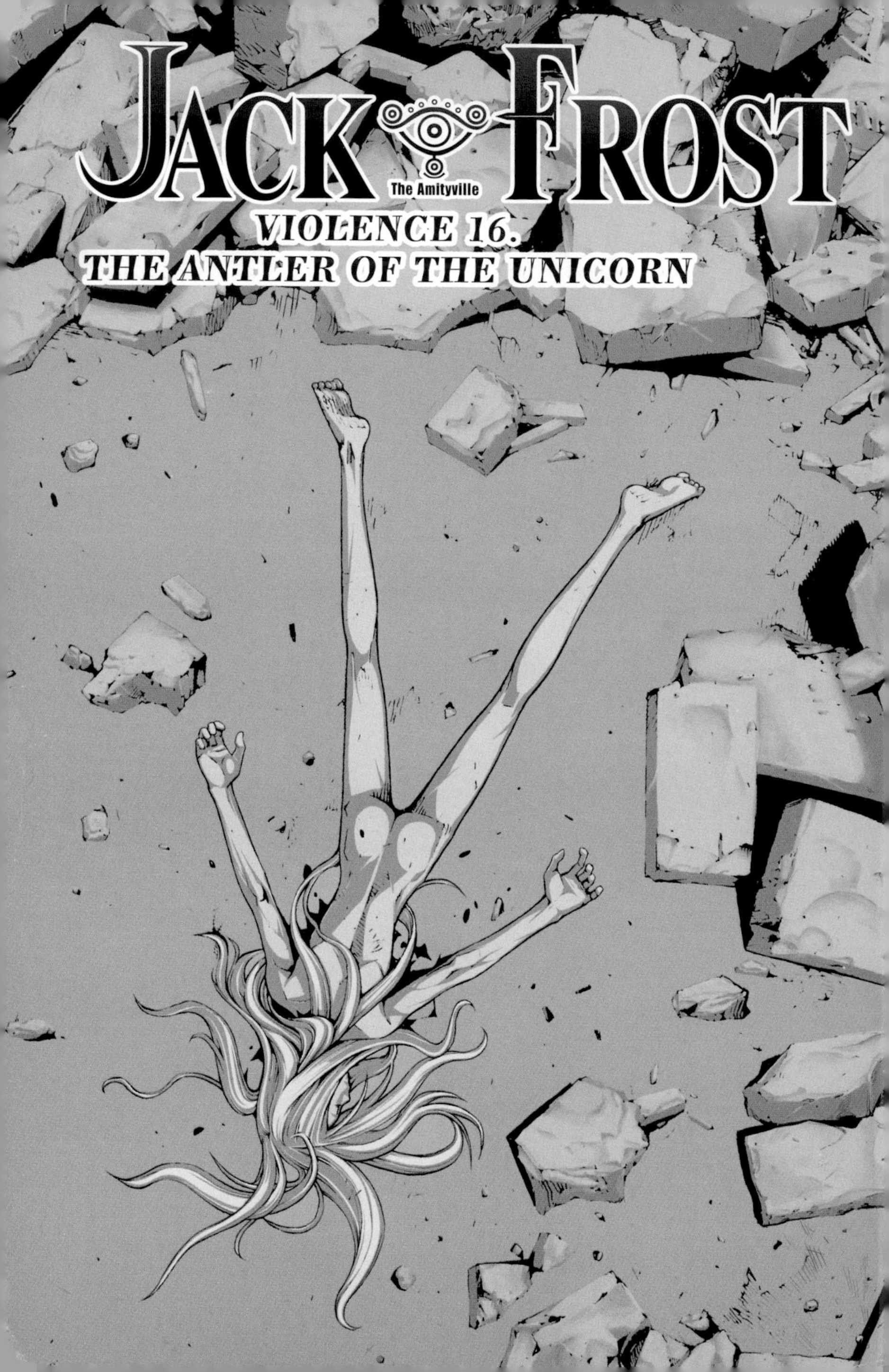
JACK FROST
The Amityville
VIOLENCE 16.
THE ANTLER OF THE UNICORN

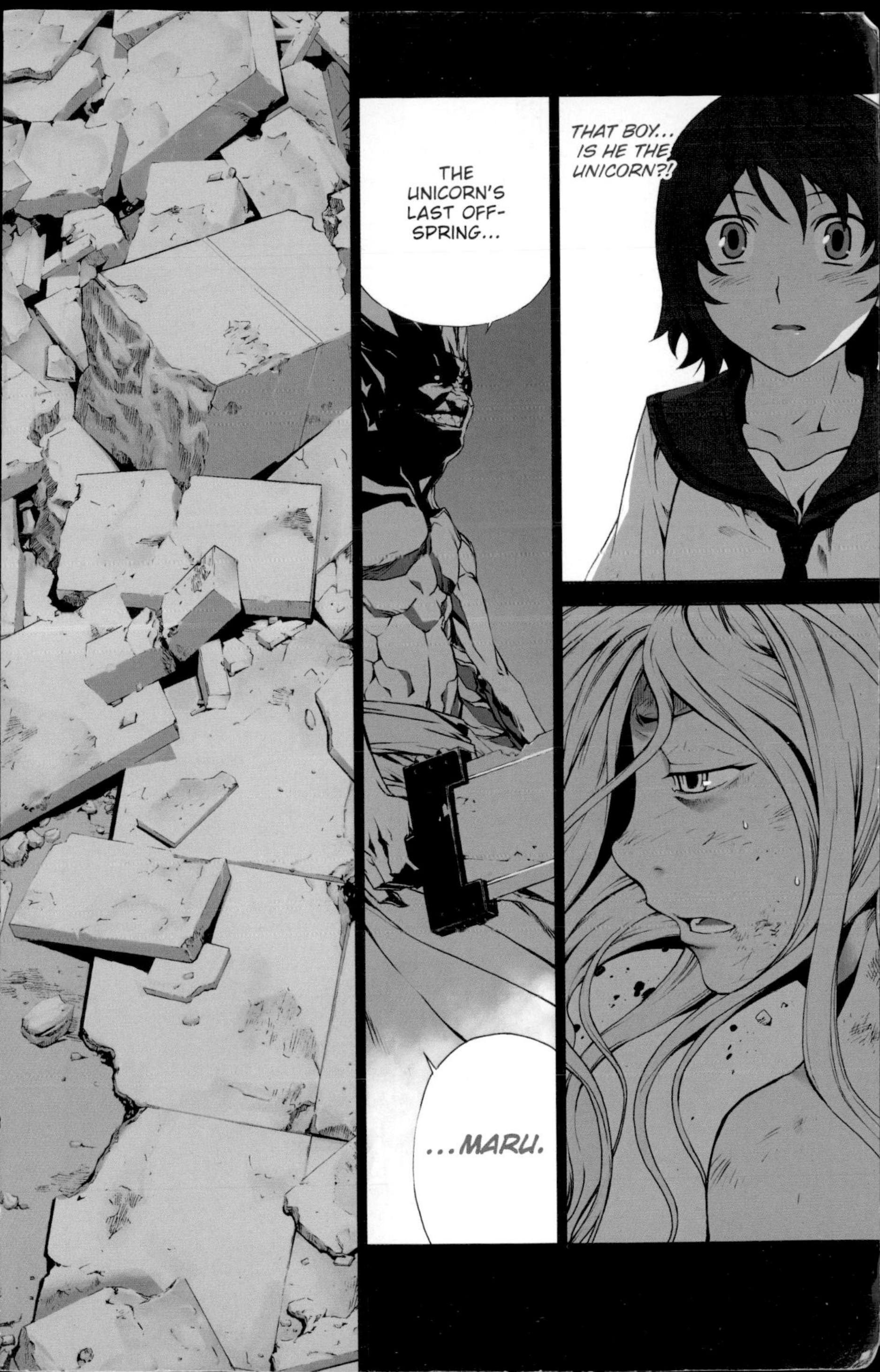
THE UNICORN'S LAST OFF-SPRING...
...MARU.
THAT BOY... IS HE THE UNICORN?!

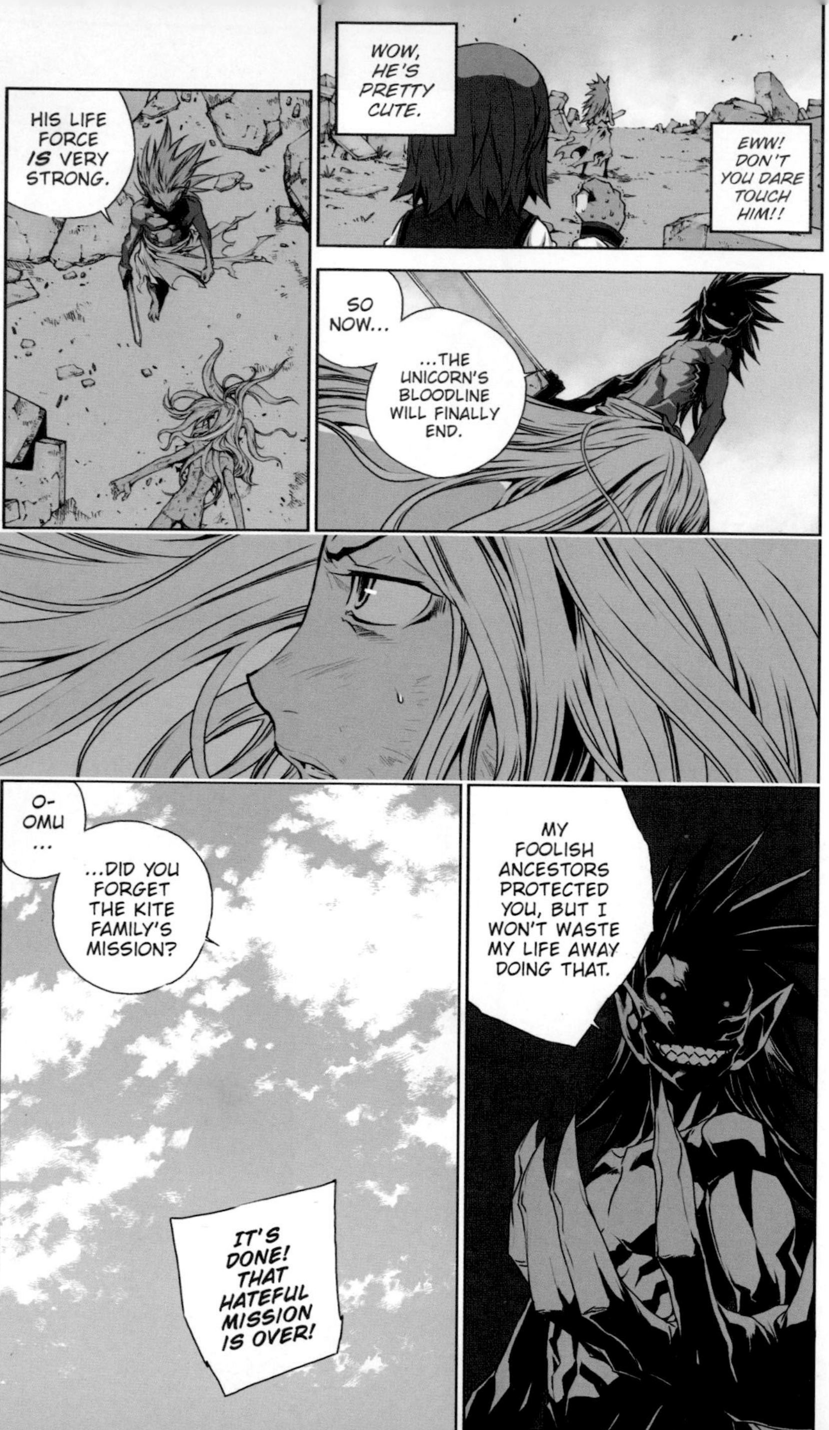
HIS LIFE FORCE IS VERY STRONG.
WOW, HE'S PRETTY CUTE.
EWW! DON'T YOU DARE TOUCH HIM!!
SO NOW...
...THE UNICORN'S BLOODLINE WILL FINALLY END.
O-OMU...
...DID YOU FORGET THE KITE FAMILY'S MISSION?
IT'S DONE! THAT HATEFUL MISSION IS OVER!
MY FOOLISH ANCESTORS PROTECTED YOU, BUT I WON'T WASTE MY LIFE AWAY DOING THAT.

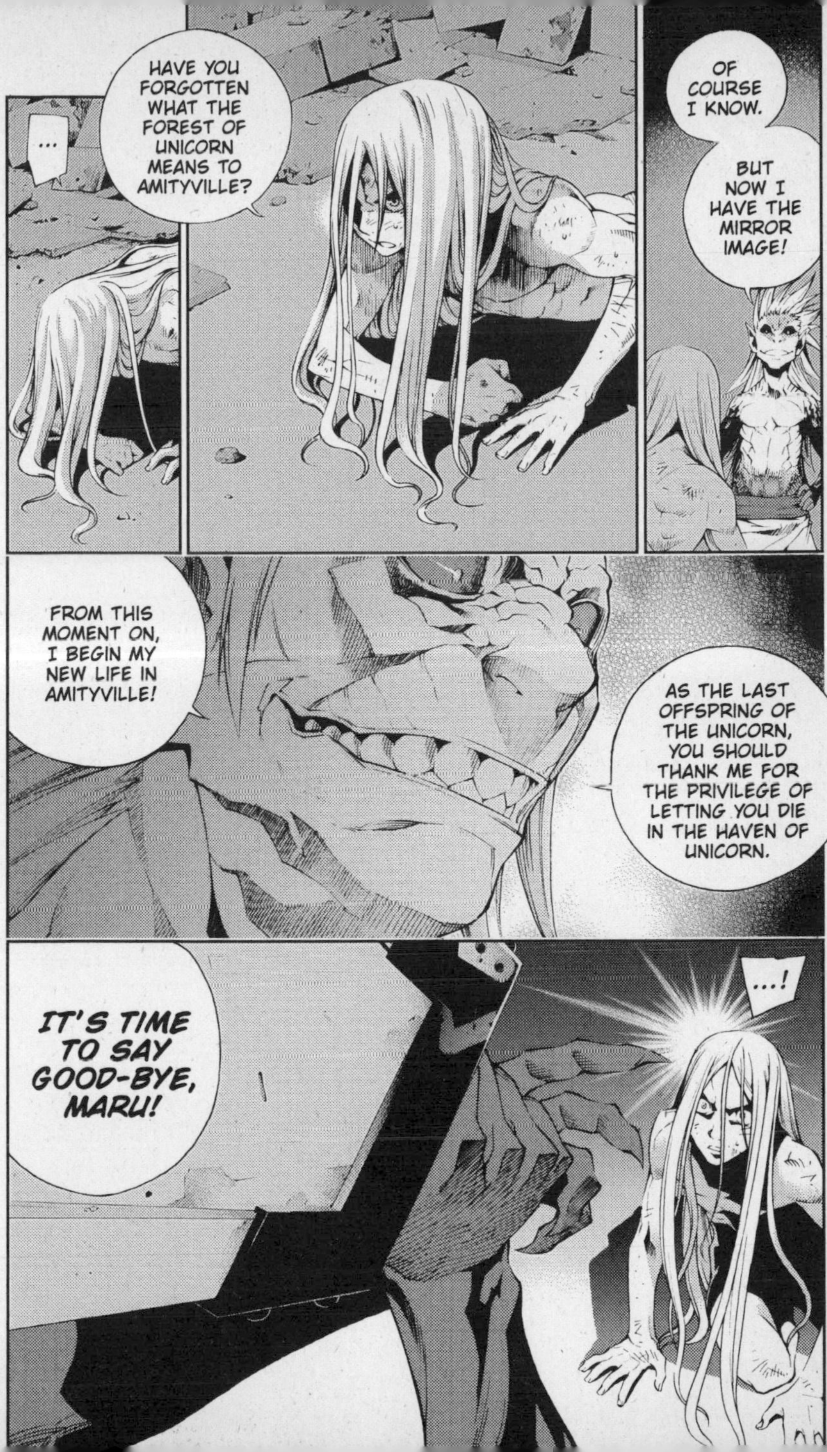
...
HAVE YOU FORGOTTEN WHAT THE FOREST OF UNICORN MEANS TO AMITYVILLE?
OF COURSE I KNOW.
BUT NOW I HAVE THE MIRROR IMAGE!
FROM THIS MOMENT ON, I BEGIN MY NEW LIFE IN AMITYVILLE!
AS THE LAST OFFSPRING OF THE UNICORN, YOU SHOULD THANK ME FOR THE PRIVILEGE OF LETTING YOU DIE IN THE HAVEN OF UNICORN.
IT'S TIME TO SAY GOOD-BYE, MARU!
...!

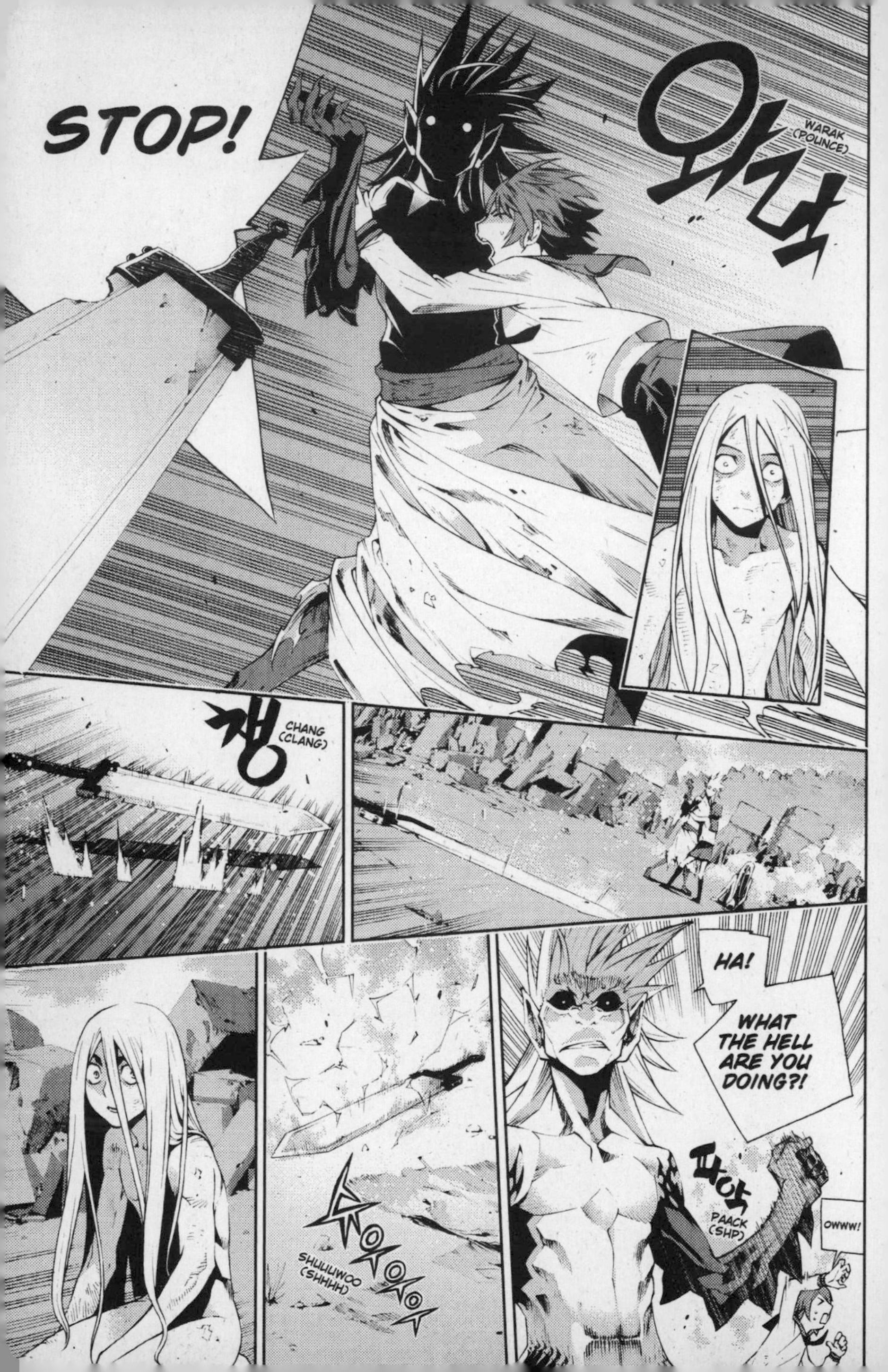
STOP!
와락
WARAK (POUNCE)
쟁
CHANG (CLANG)
HA!
WHAT THE HELL ARE YOU DOING?!
파악
PAACK (SHP)
OWWW!
슈우우우
SHUUUWOO (SHHHH)

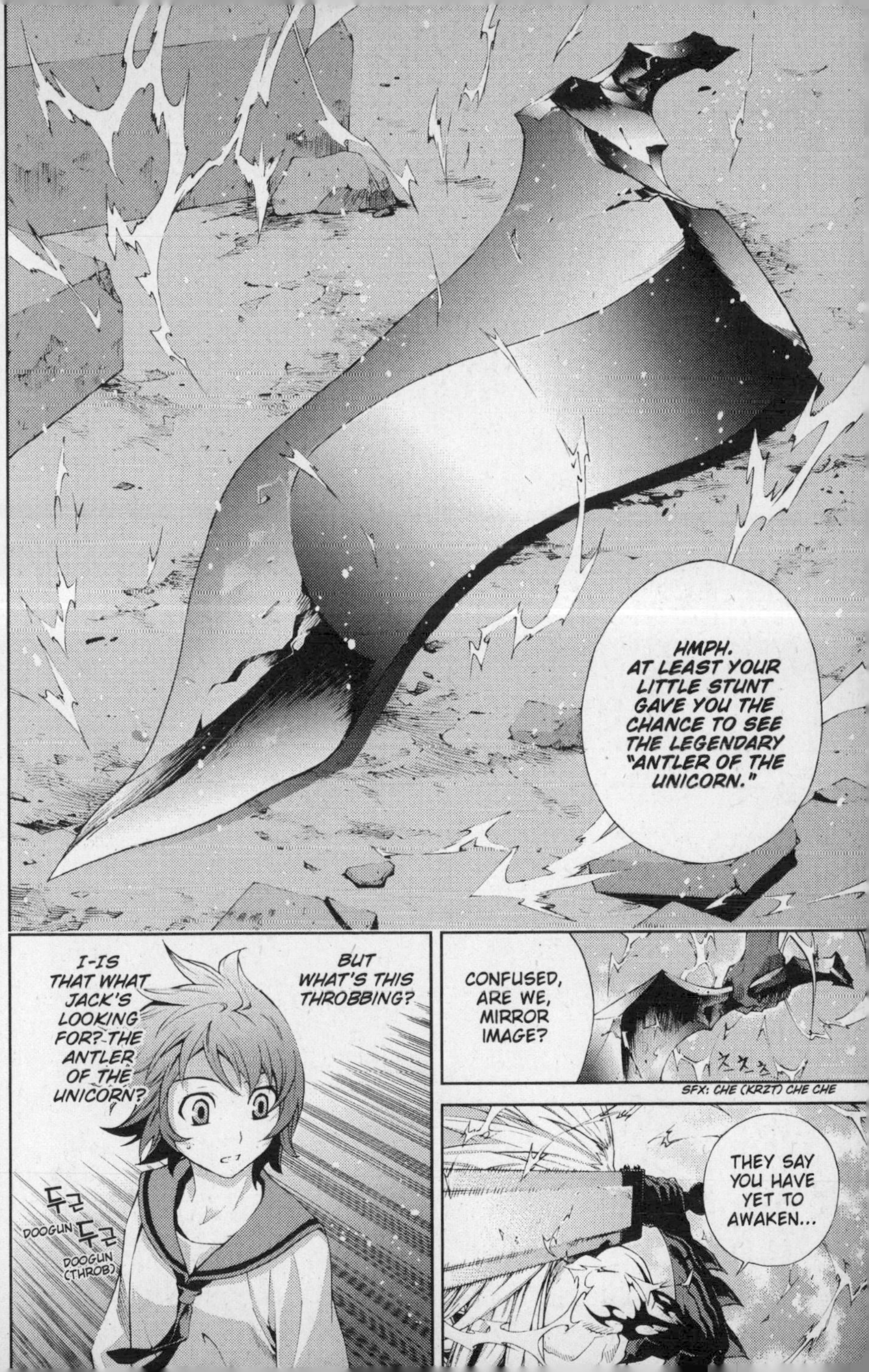
HMPH. AT LEAST YOUR LITTLE STUNT GAVE YOU THE CHANCE TO SEE THE LEGENDARY "ANTLER OF THE UNICORN."
I-IS THAT WHAT JACK'S LOOKING FOR? THE ANTLER OF THE UNICORN?
BUT WHAT'S THIS THROBBING?
두근 두근
DOOGUN
DOOGUN (THROB)
CONFUSED, ARE WE, MIRROR IMAGE?
SFX: CHE (KRZT) CHE CHE
THEY SAY YOU HAVE YET TO AWAKEN...

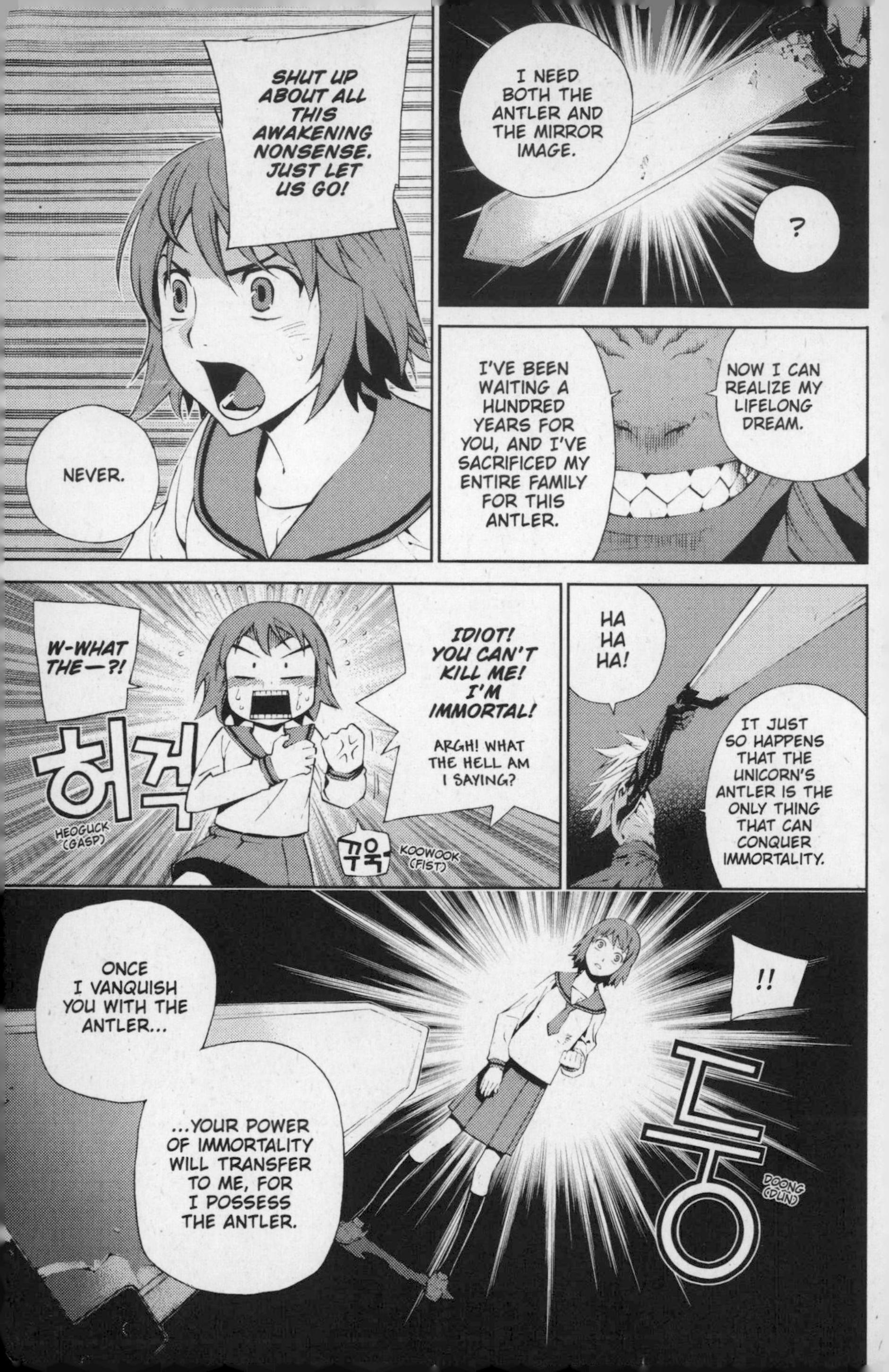
SHUT UP ABOUT ALL THIS AWAKENING NONSENSE. JUST LET US GO!
NEVER.
I NEED BOTH THE ANTLER AND THE MIRROR IMAGE.
?
I'VE BEEN WAITING A HUNDRED YEARS FOR YOU, AND I'VE SACRIFICED MY ENTIRE FAMILY FOR THIS ANTLER.
NOW I CAN REALIZE MY LIFELONG DREAM.
W-WHAT THE—?!
허걱
HEOGUCK (GASP)
IDIOT! YOU CAN'T KILL ME! I'M IMMORTAL!
ARGH! WHAT THE HELL AM I SAYING?
꾸욱
KOOWOOK (FIST)
HA HA HA!
IT JUST SO HAPPENS THAT THE UNICORN'S ANTLER IS THE ONLY THING THAT CAN CONQUER IMMORTALITY.
ONCE I VANQUISH YOU WITH THE ANTLER...
...YOUR POWER OF IMMORTALITY WILL TRANSFER TO ME, FOR I POSSESS THE ANTLER.
!!
둥
DOONG (DUN)

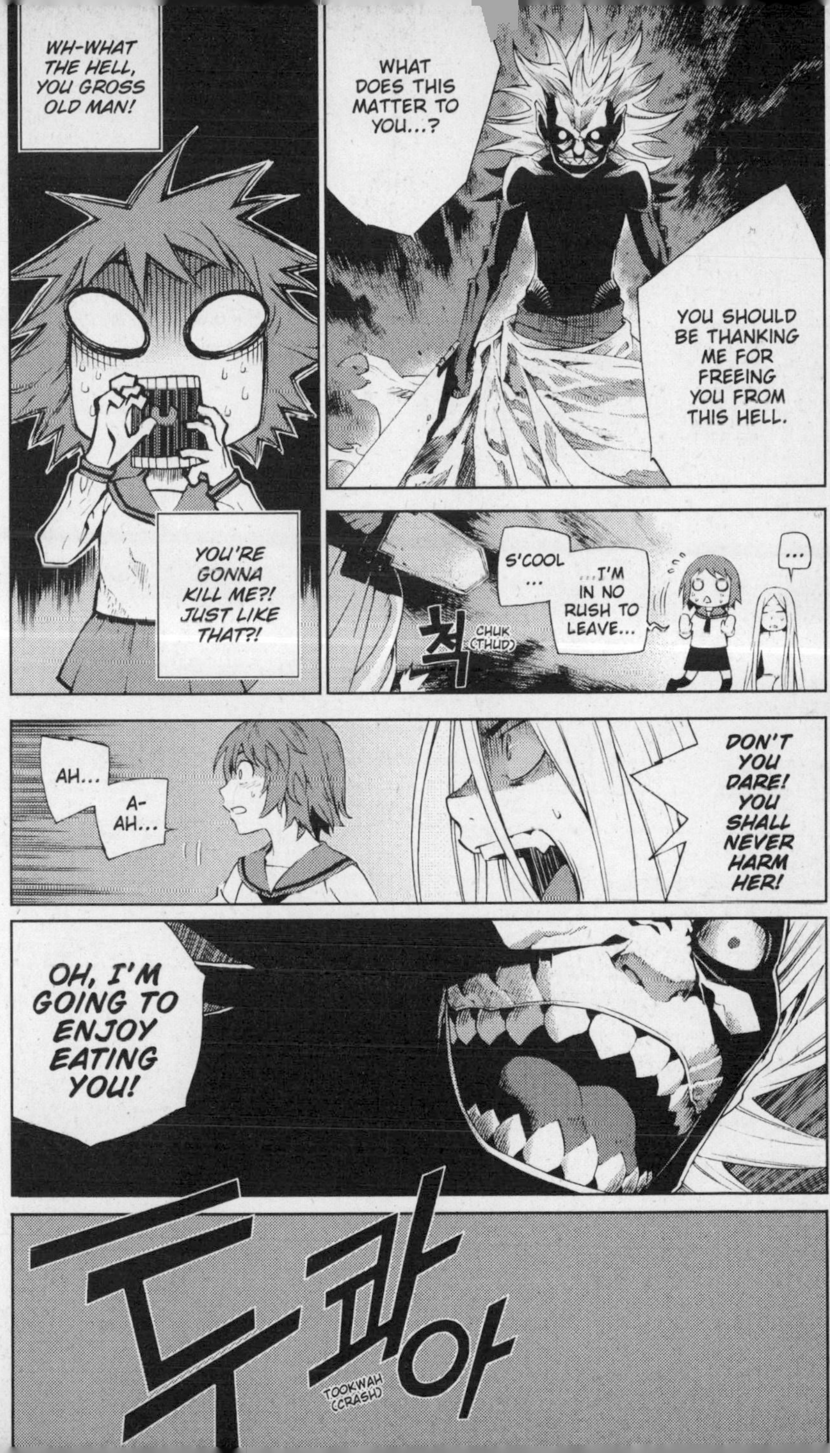
WH-WHAT THE HELL, YOU GROSS OLD MAN!
YOU'RE GONNA KILL ME?! JUST LIKE THAT?!
WHAT DOES THIS MATTER TO YOU...?
YOU SHOULD BE THANKING ME FOR FREEING YOU FROM THIS HELL.
척
CHUK (THUD)
S'COOL ...
...I'M IN NO RUSH TO LEAVE...
...
AH...
A-AH...
DON'T YOU DARE! YOU SHALL NEVER HARM HER!
OH, I'M GOING TO ENJOY EATING YOU!
두콰아
TOOKWAH (CRASH)

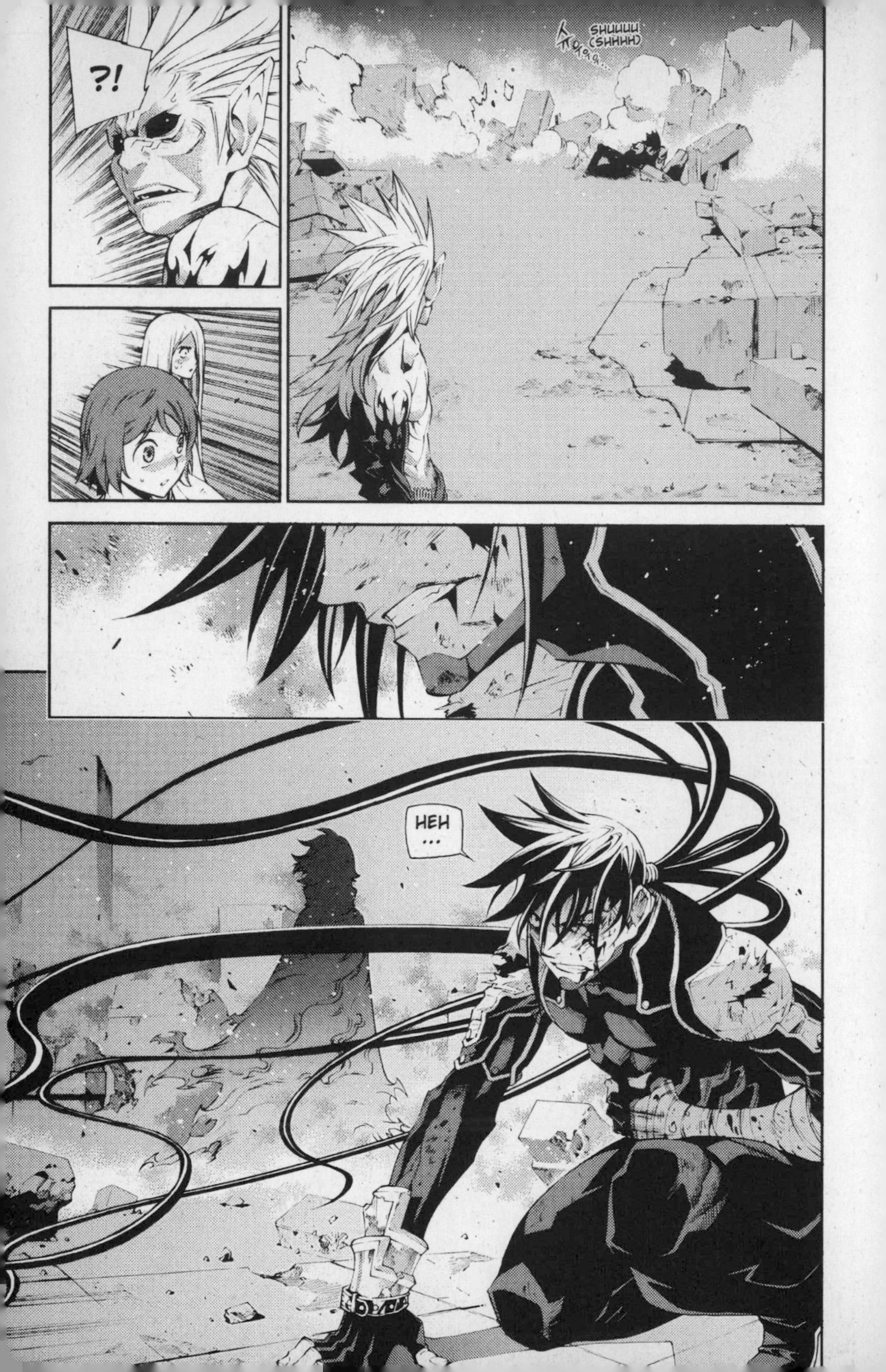
?!
스아아아...
SHUUUU (SHHHH)
HEH ...

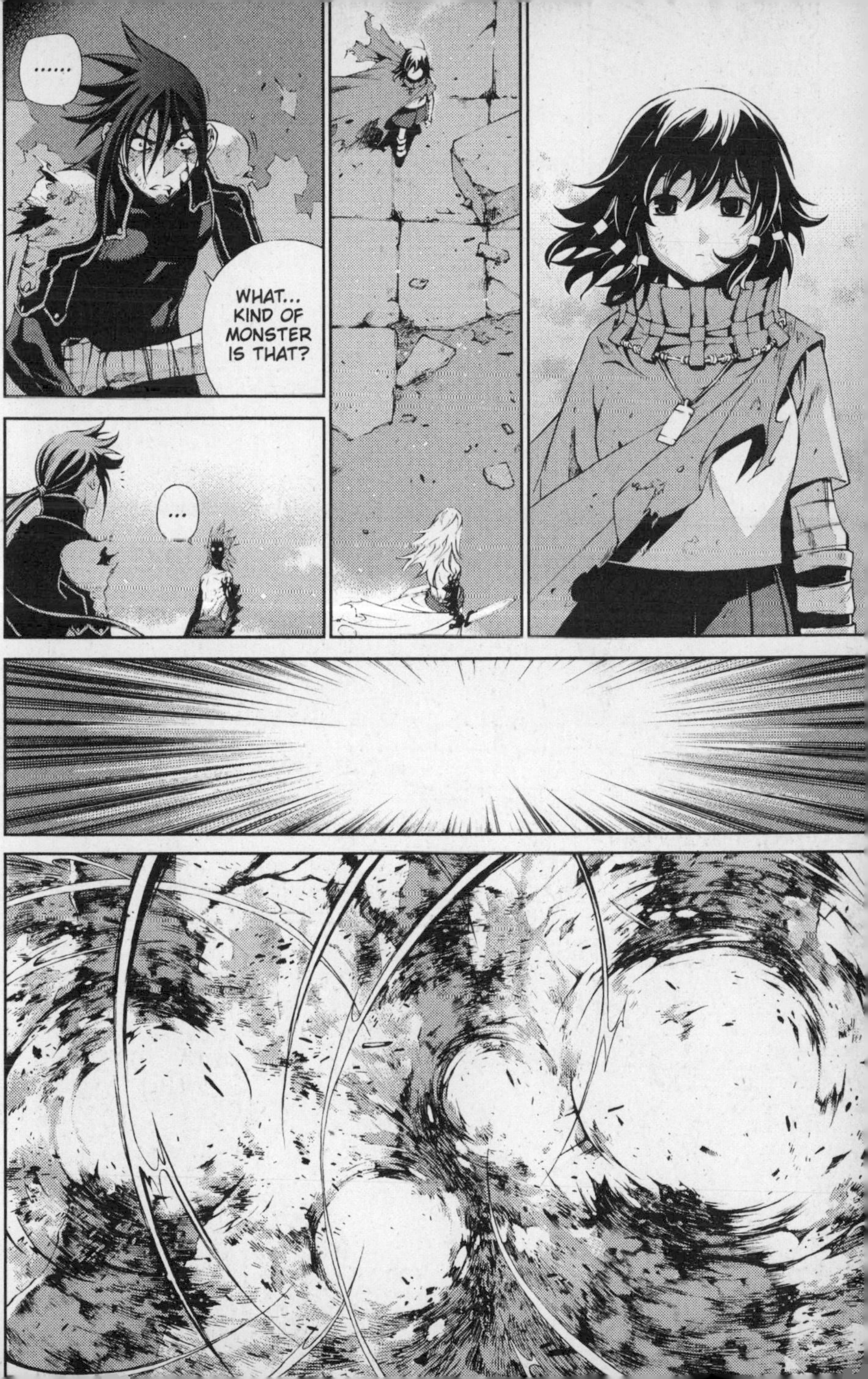
......
WHAT... KIND OF MONSTER IS THAT?
...

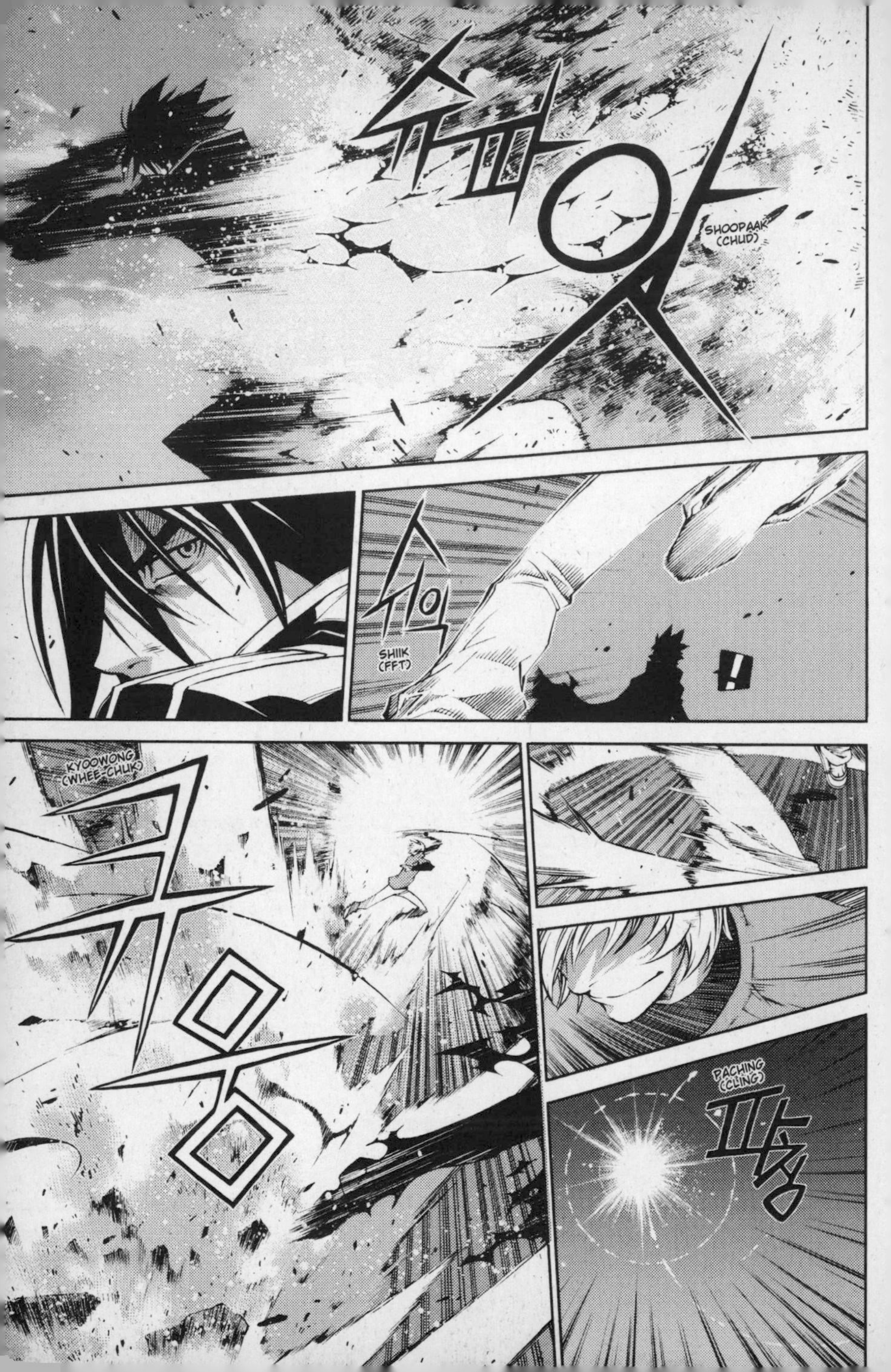
SHOOPAAK (CHUD)
SHIIK (FFT)
!
KYOOWONG (WHEE-CHUK)
PACHING (CLING)

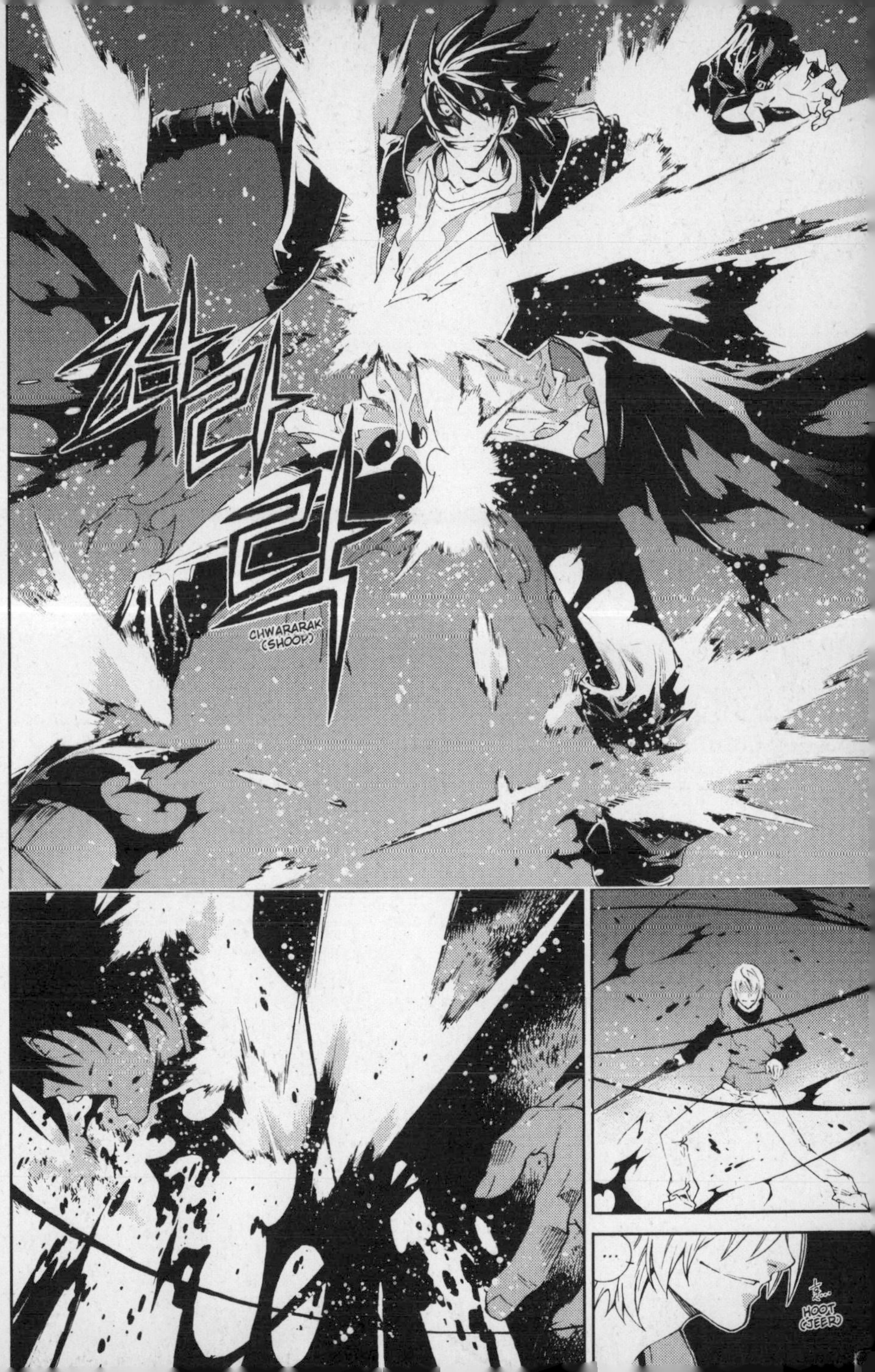
CHWARARAK
(SHOOP)
...
HOOT
(JEER)

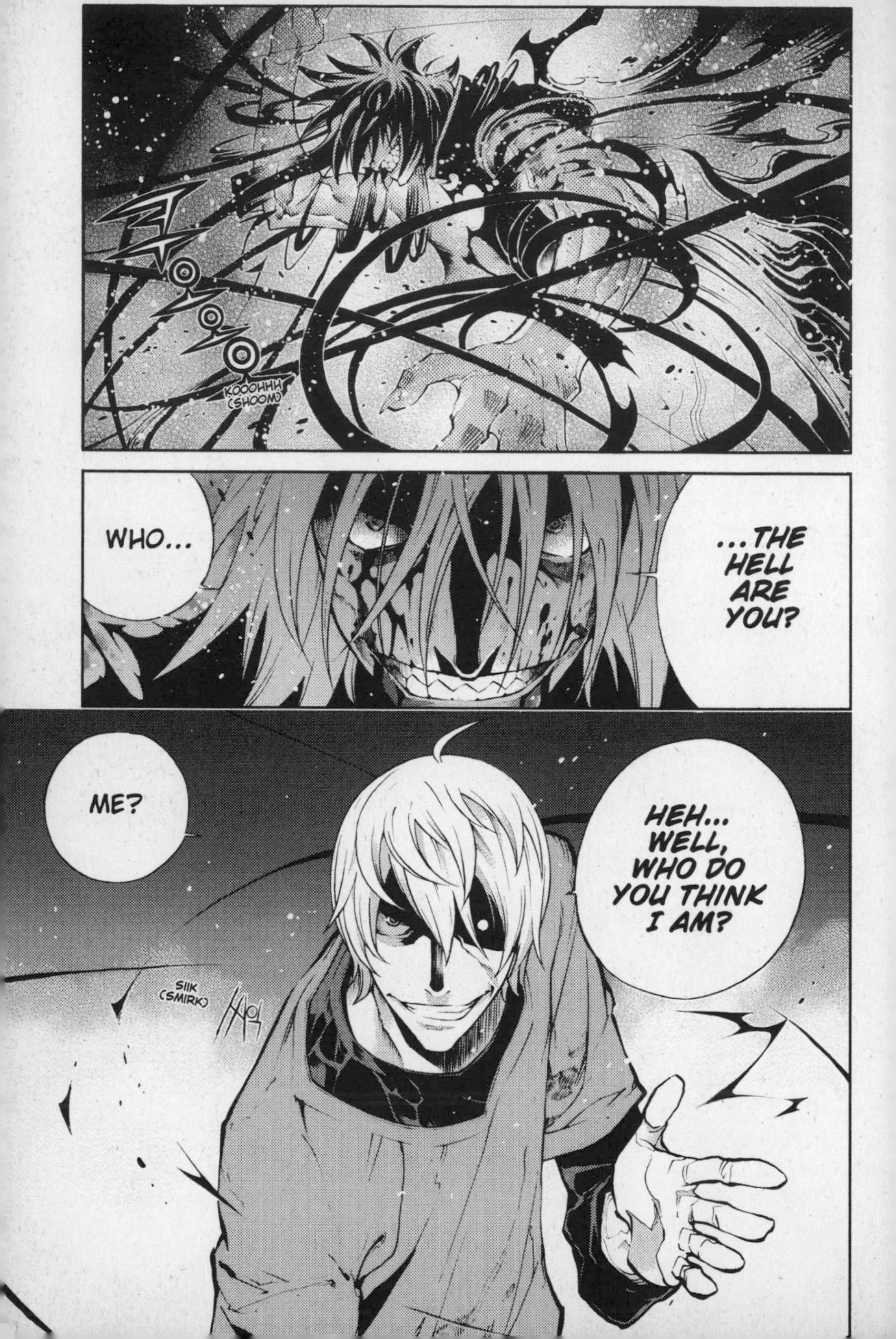
KOOOHHH (SHOOM)
WHO...
...THE HELL ARE YOU?
ME?
HEH... WELL, WHO DO YOU THINK I AM?
SIIK (SMIRK)

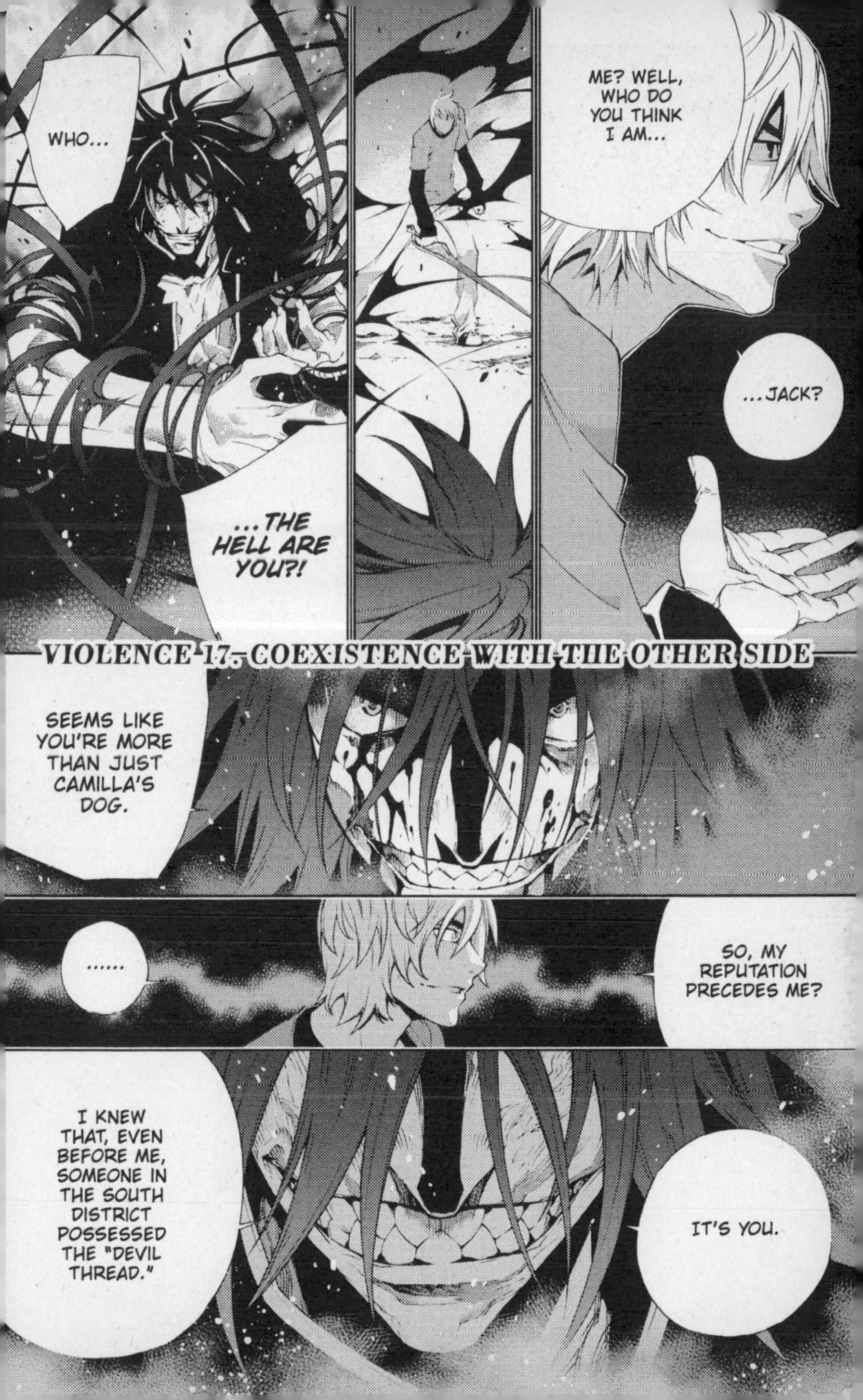
WHO...
...THE HELL ARE YOU?!
ME? WELL, WHO DO YOU THINK I AM...
...JACK?
VIOLENCE 17. COEXISTENCE WITH THE OTHER SIDE
SEEMS LIKE YOU'RE MORE THAN JUST CAMILLA'S DOG.
......
SO, MY REPUTATION PRECEDES ME?
I KNEW THAT, EVEN BEFORE ME, SOMEONE IN THE SOUTH DISTRICT POSSESSED THE "DEVIL THREAD."
IT'S YOU.

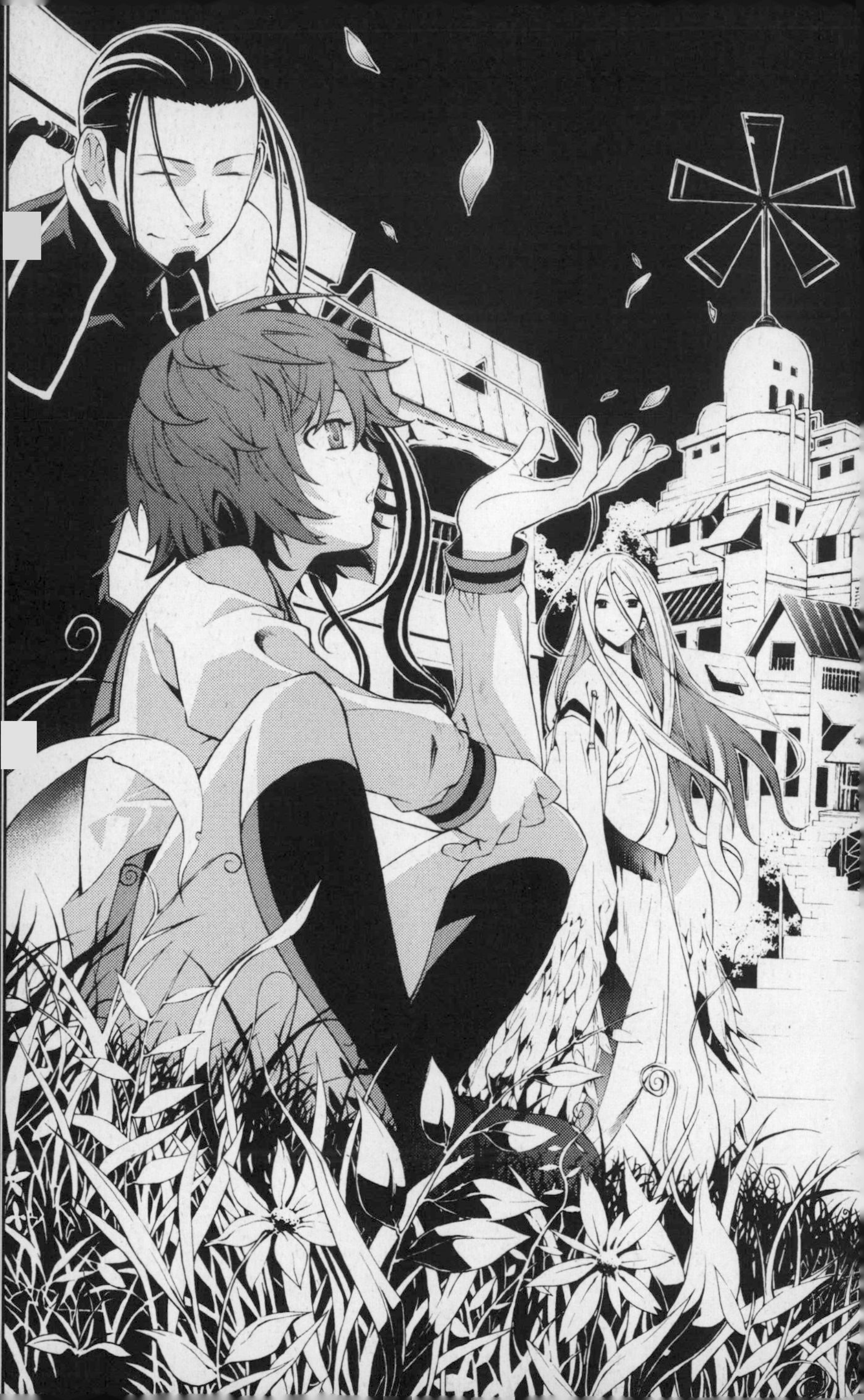

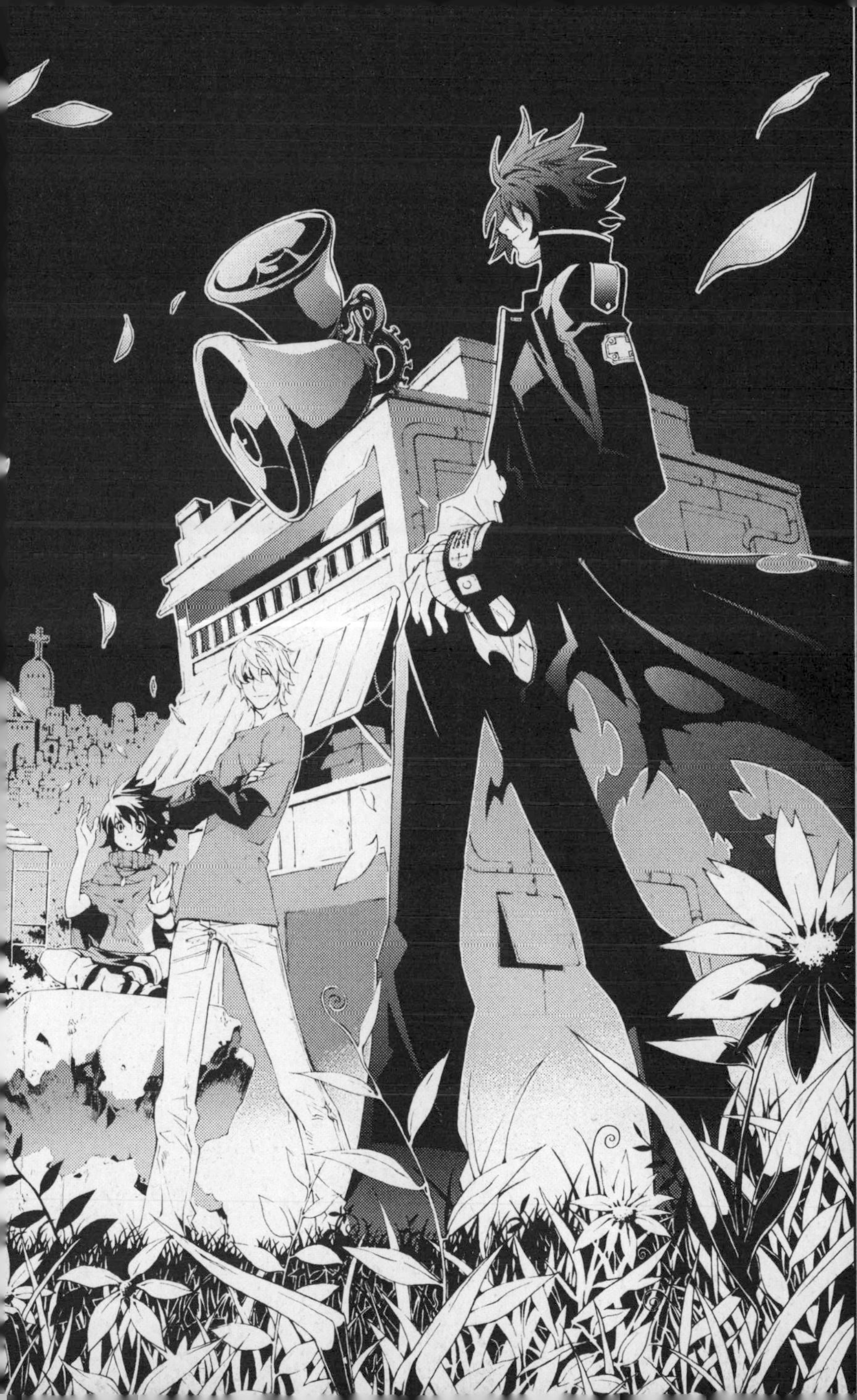

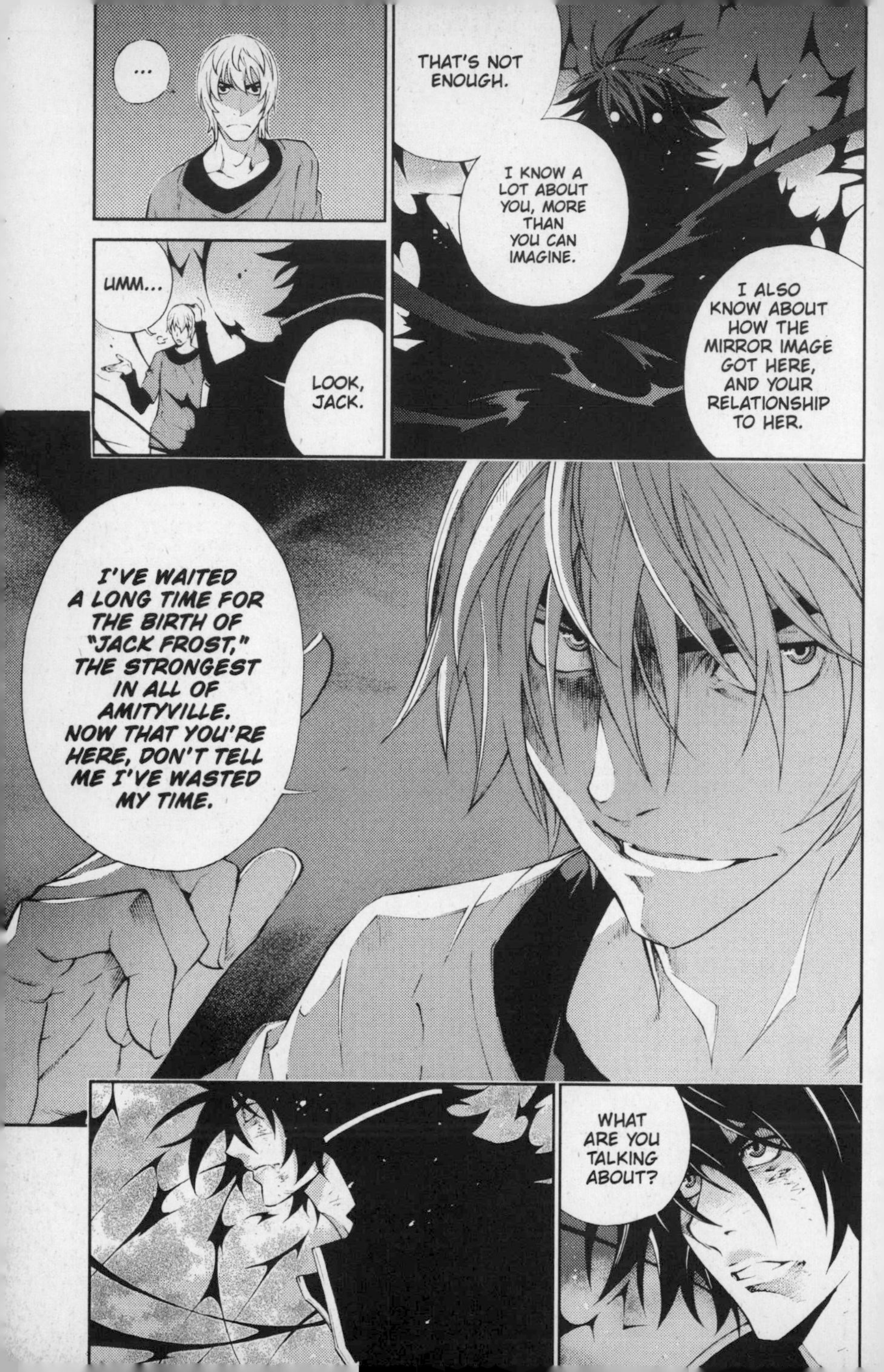
...
UMM...
LOOK, JACK.
THAT'S NOT ENOUGH.
I KNOW A LOT ABOUT YOU, MORE THAN YOU CAN IMAGINE.
I ALSO KNOW ABOUT HOW THE MIRROR IMAGE GOT HERE, AND YOUR RELATIONSHIP TO HER.
I'VE WAITED A LONG TIME FOR THE BIRTH OF "JACK FROST," THE STRONGEST IN ALL OF AMITYVILLE. NOW THAT YOU'RE HERE, DON'T TELL ME I'VE WASTED MY TIME.
WHAT ARE YOU TALKING ABOUT?

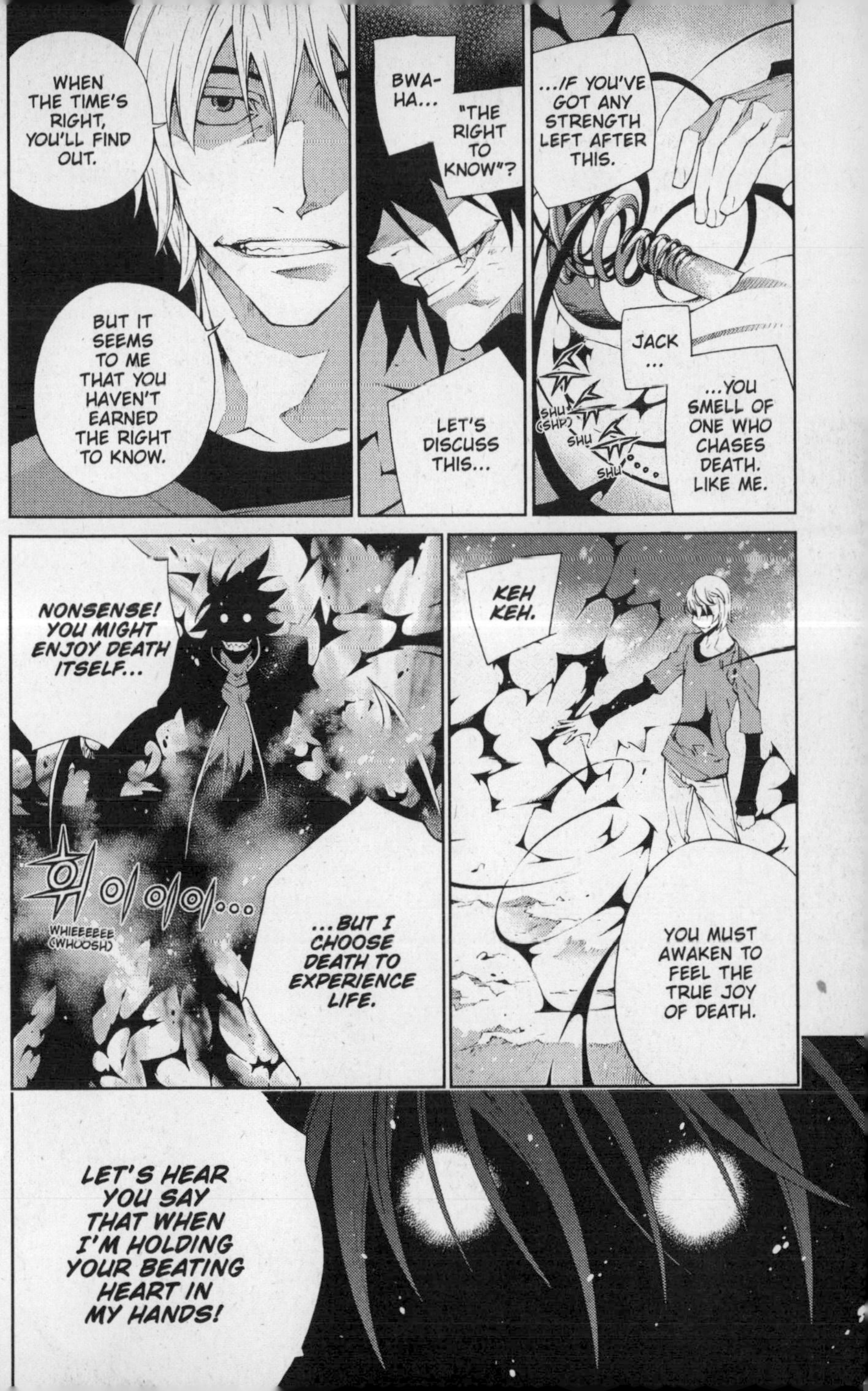
WHEN THE TIME'S RIGHT, YOU'LL FIND OUT.
BUT IT SEEMS TO ME THAT YOU HAVEN'T EARNED THE RIGHT TO KNOW.
BWA-HA...
"THE RIGHT TO KNOW"?
LET'S DISCUSS THIS...
...IF YOU'VE GOT ANY STRENGTH LEFT AFTER THIS.
SHU (SHP) SHU SHU....
JACK...
...YOU SMELL OF ONE WHO CHASES DEATH. LIKE ME.
NONSENSE! YOU MIGHT ENJOY DEATH ITSELF...
휘 이 이이...
WHIEEEEEEE (WHOOSH)
...BUT I CHOOSE DEATH TO EXPERIENCE LIFE.
KEH KEH.
YOU MUST AWAKEN TO FEEL THE TRUE JOY OF DEATH.
LET'S HEAR YOU SAY THAT WHEN I'M HOLDING YOUR BEATING HEART IN MY HANDS!

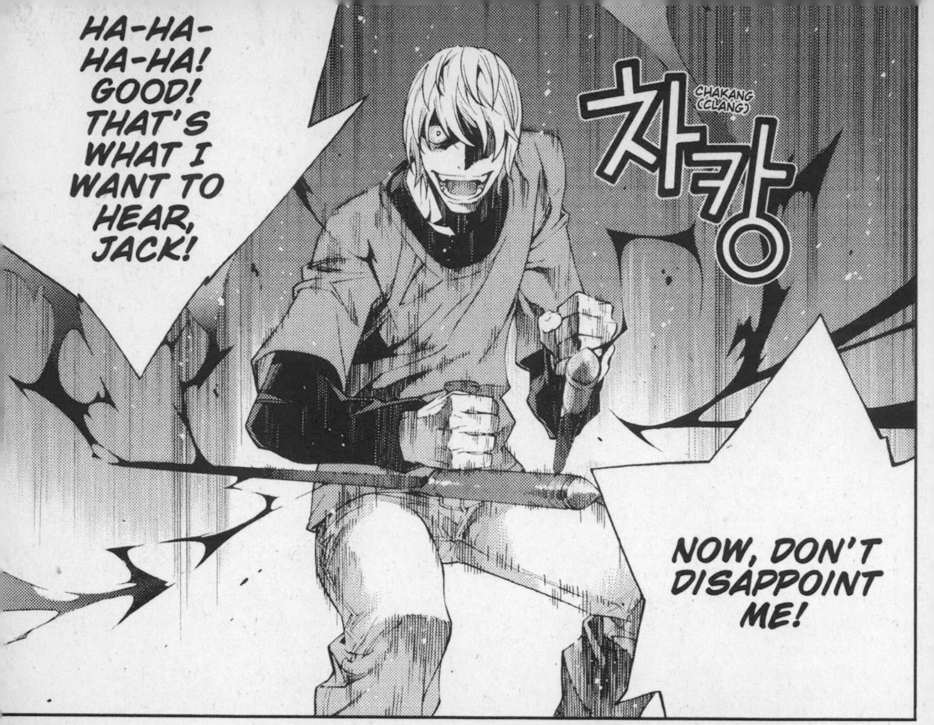
HA-HA-HA-HA! GOOD! THAT'S WHAT I WANT TO HEAR, JACK!
차캉
CHAKANG (CLANG)
NOW, DON'T DISAPPOINT ME!
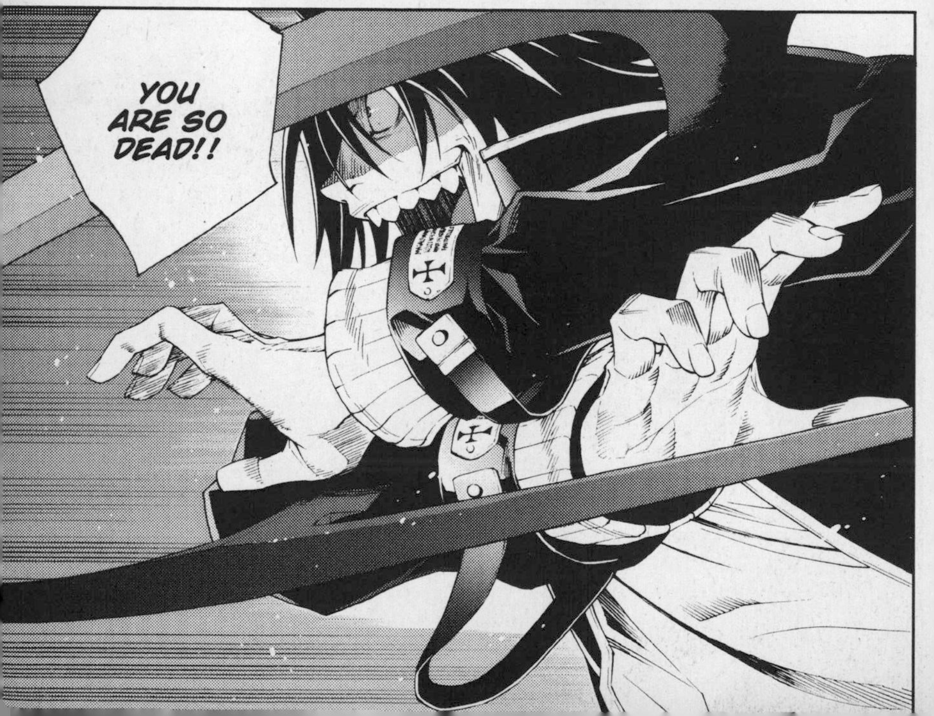
YOU ARE SO DEAD!!

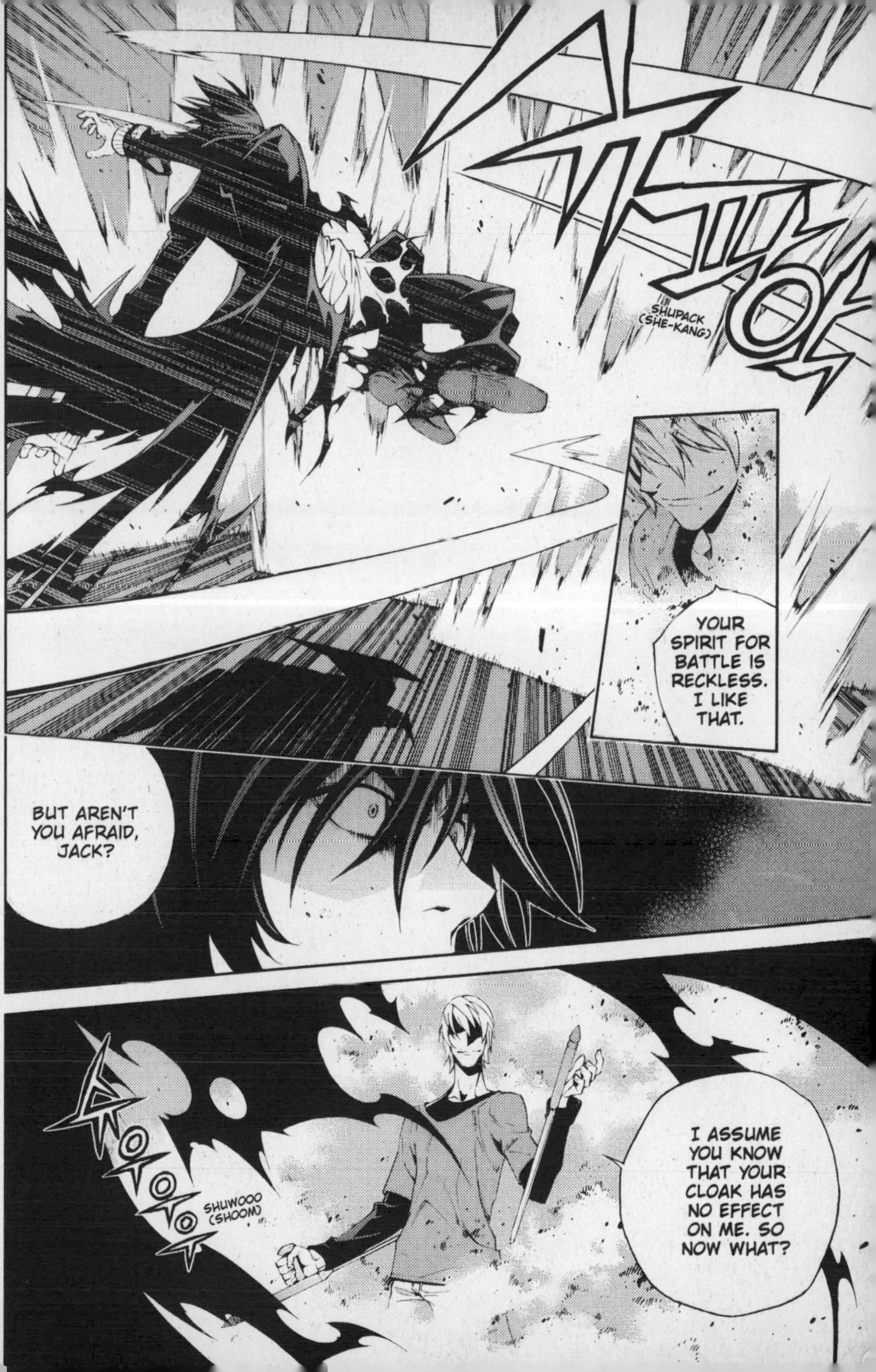
SHUPACK (SHE-KANG)
YOUR SPIRIT FOR BATTLE IS RECKLESS. I LIKE THAT.
BUT AREN'T YOU AFRAID, JACK?
SHUWOOO (SHOOM)
I ASSUME YOU KNOW THAT YOUR CLOAK HAS NO EFFECT ON ME. SO NOW WHAT?

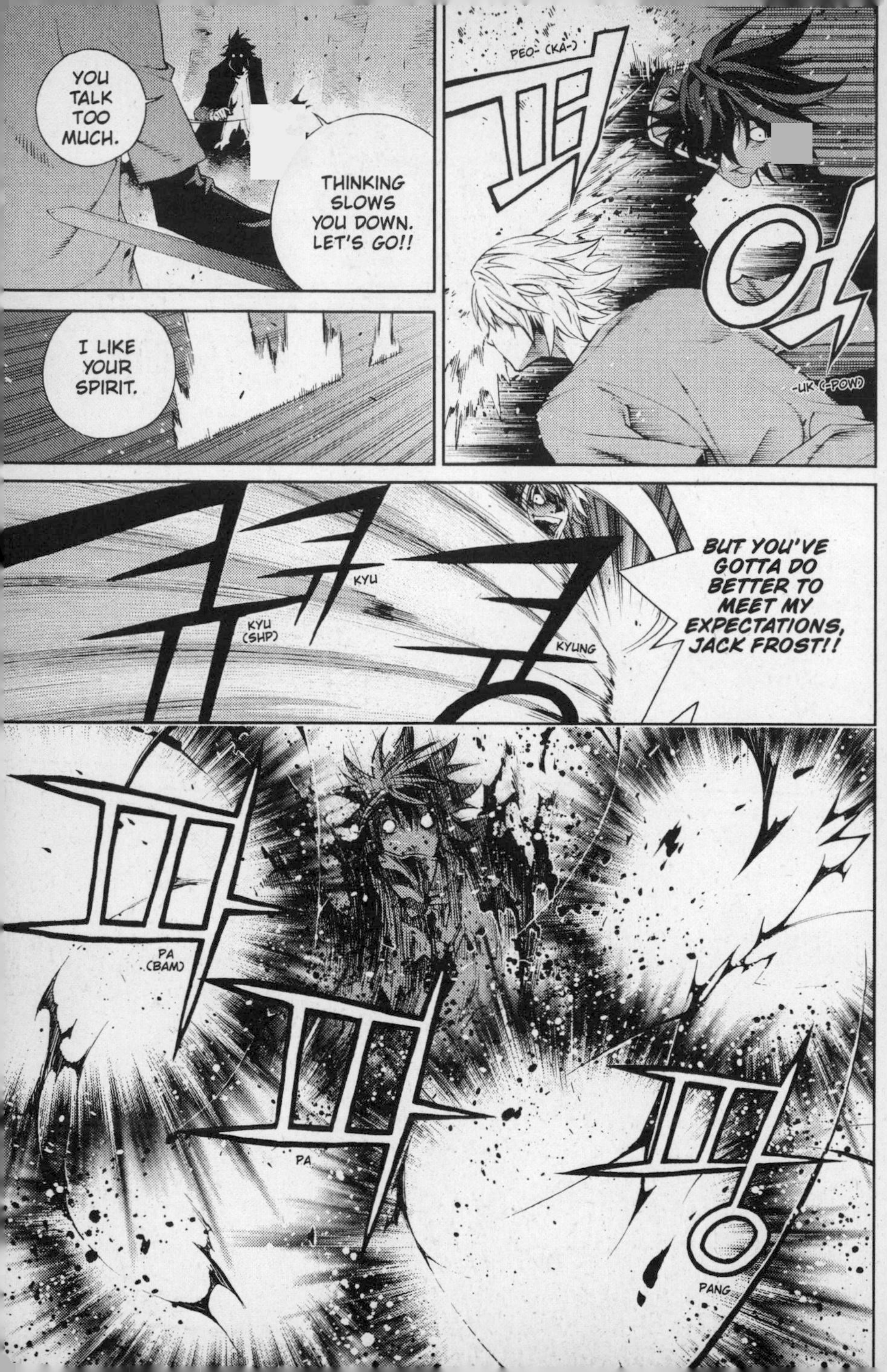
YOU TALK TOO MUCH.
THINKING SLOWS YOU DOWN. LET'S GO!!
I LIKE YOUR SPIRIT.
PEO- (KA-)
-UK (-POW)
KYU (SHP)
KYU
KYUNG
BUT YOU'VE GOTTA DO BETTER TO MEET MY EXPECTATIONS, JACK FROST!!
PA (BAM)
PA
PANG

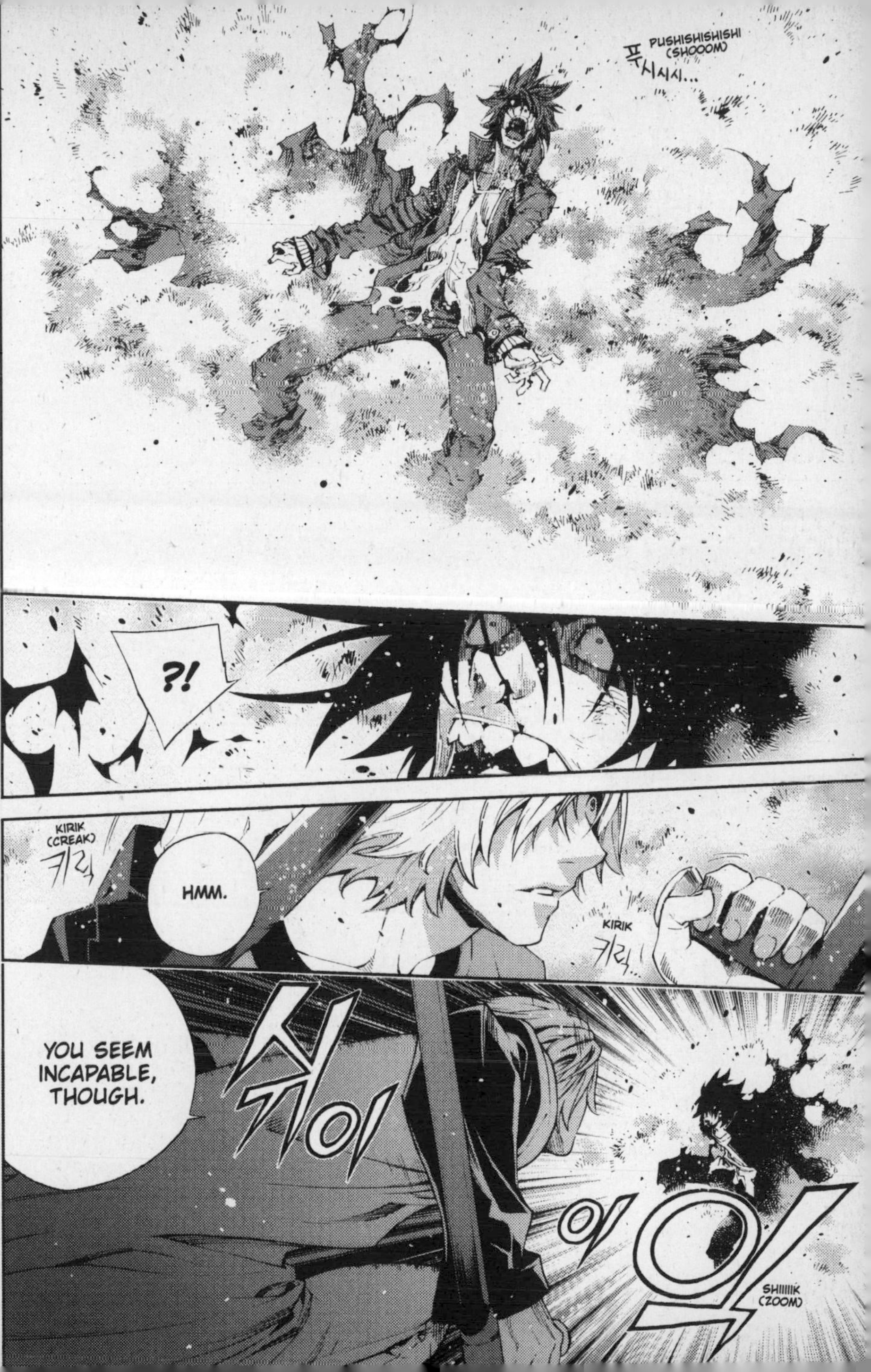
PUSHISHISHISHI (SHOOOM)
푸시시시...
?!
KIRIK (CREAK)
키릭
HMM.
KIRIK
키릭...
YOU SEEM INCAPABLE, THOUGH.
SHIIIIK (ZOOM)

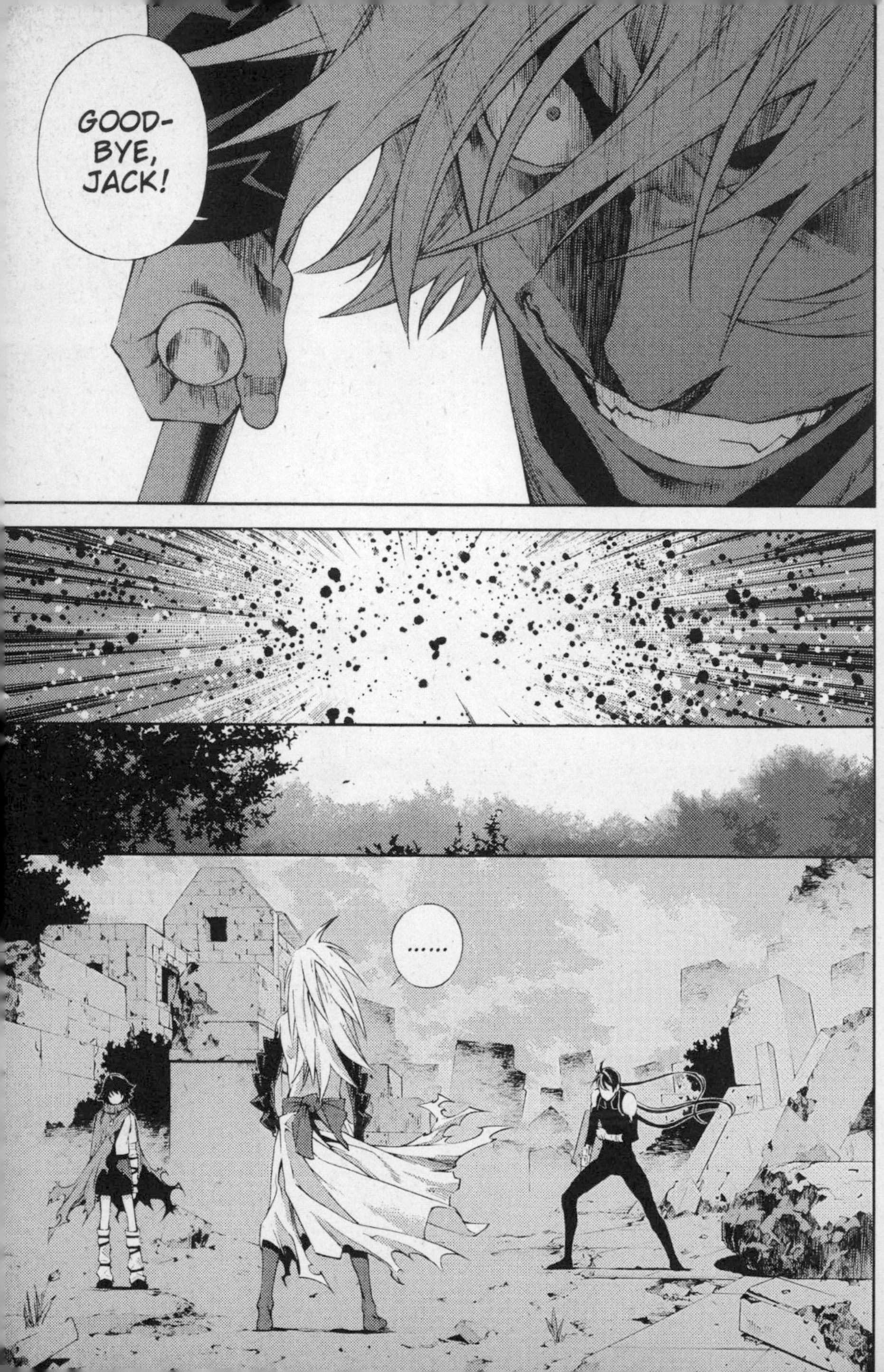
GOOD-BYE, JACK!
......

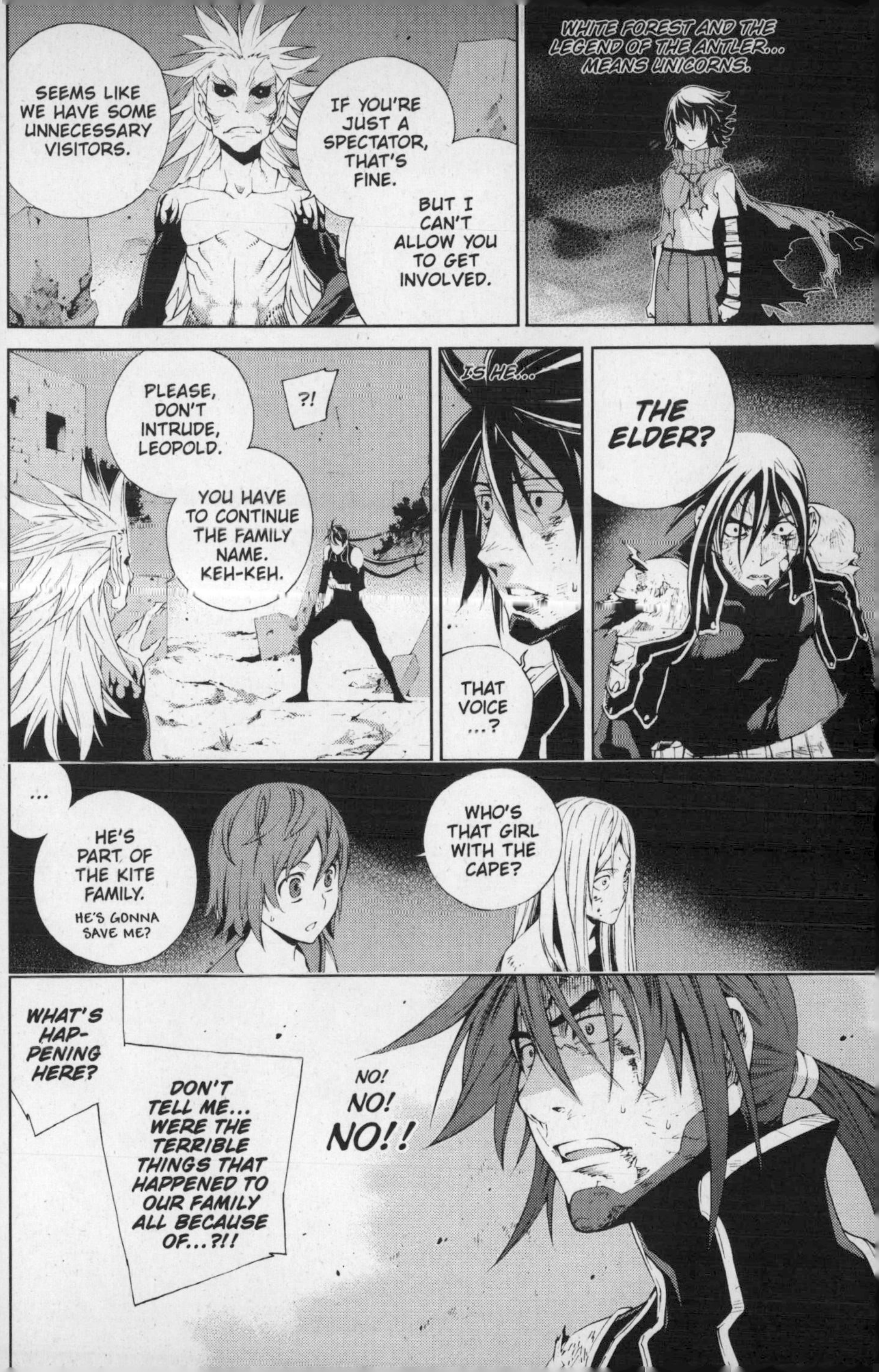
SEEMS LIKE WE HAVE SOME UNNECESSARY VISITORS.
IF YOU'RE JUST A SPECTATOR, THAT'S FINE.
BUT I CAN'T ALLOW YOU TO GET INVOLVED.
WHITE FOREST AND THE LEGEND OF THE ANTLER... MEANS UNICORNS.
PLEASE, DON'T INTRUDE, LEOPOLD.
?!
YOU HAVE TO CONTINUE THE FAMILY NAME. KEH-KEH.
IS HE...
THAT VOICE ...?
THE ELDER?
...
HE'S PART OF THE KITE FAMILY.
HE'S GONNA SAVE ME?
WHO'S THAT GIRL WITH THE CAPE?
WHAT'S HAP-PENING HERE?
DON'T TELL ME... WERE THE TERRIBLE THINGS THAT HAPPENED TO OUR FAMILY ALL BECAUSE OF...?!!
NO! NO! NO!!

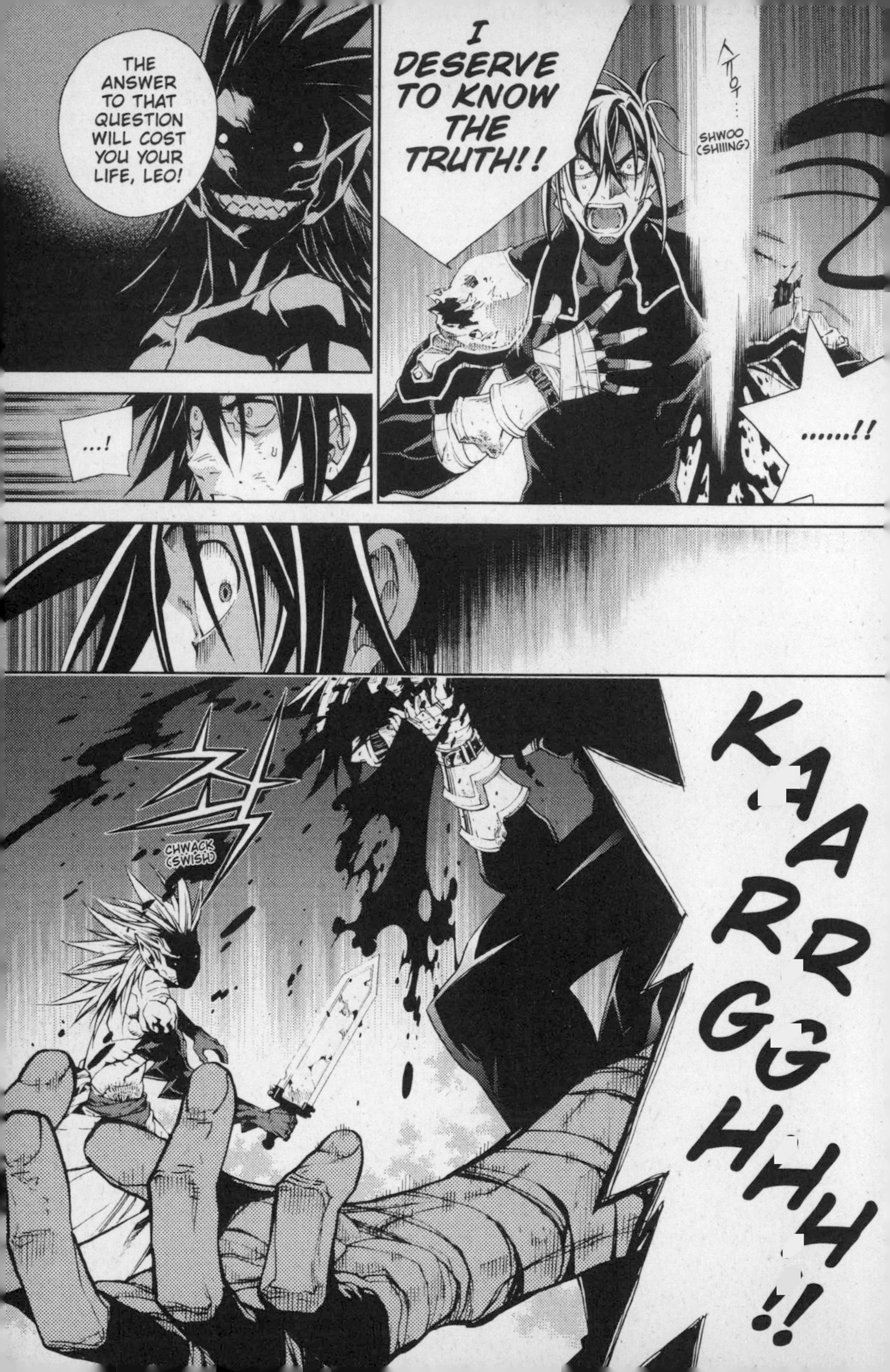
THE ANSWER TO THAT QUESTION WILL COST YOU YOUR LIFE, LEO!
...!
I DESERVE TO KNOW THE TRUTH!!
SHWOO (SHIIING)
......!!
CHWACK (SWISH)
KAARRGGHHHH!!

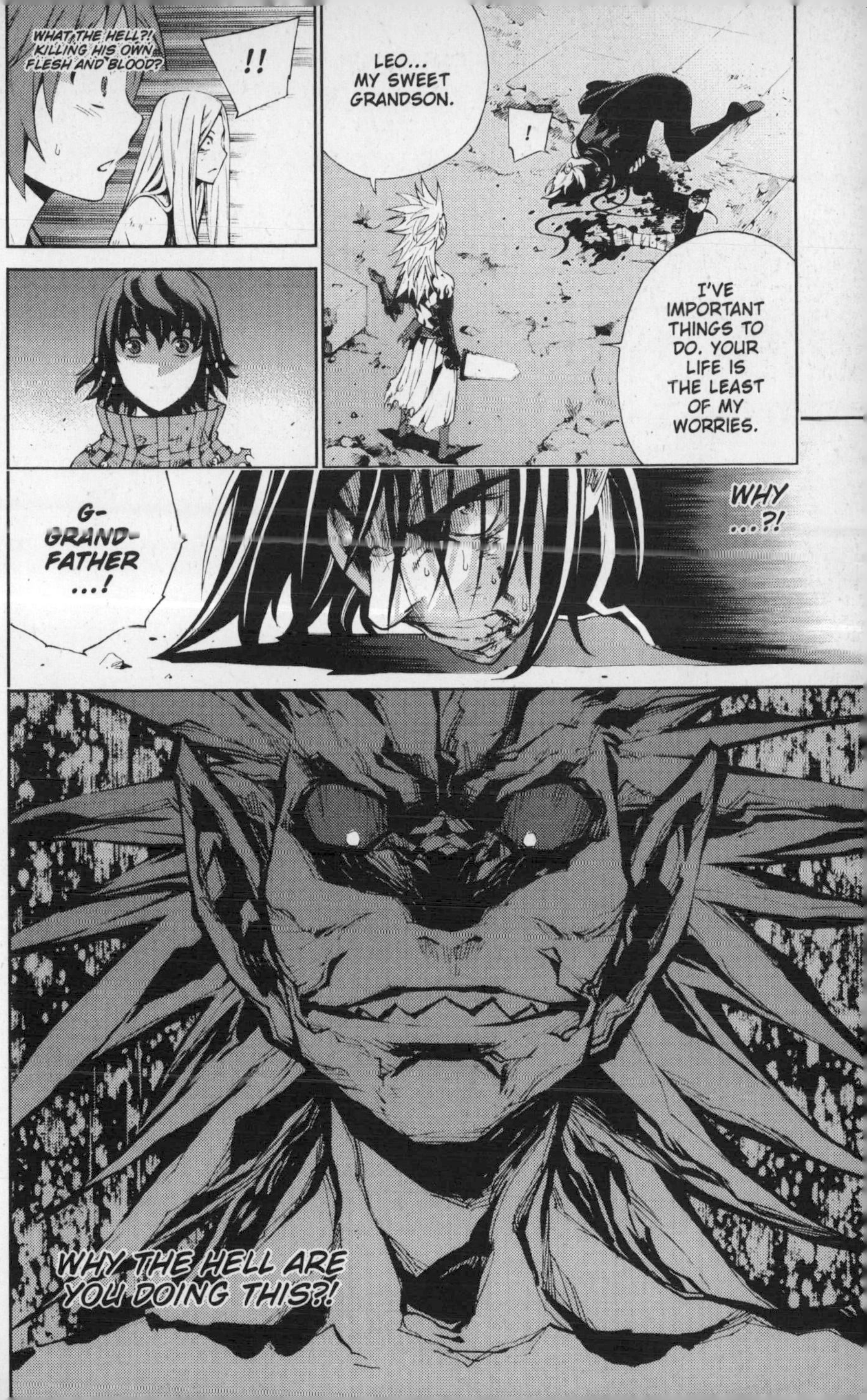
WHAT THE HELL?! KILLING HIS OWN FLESH AND BLOOD?
!!
LEO... MY SWEET GRANDSON.
!
I'VE IMPORTANT THINGS TO DO. YOUR LIFE IS THE LEAST OF MY WORRIES.
G-GRAND-FATHER...!
WHY...?!
WHY THE HELL ARE YOU DOING THIS?!

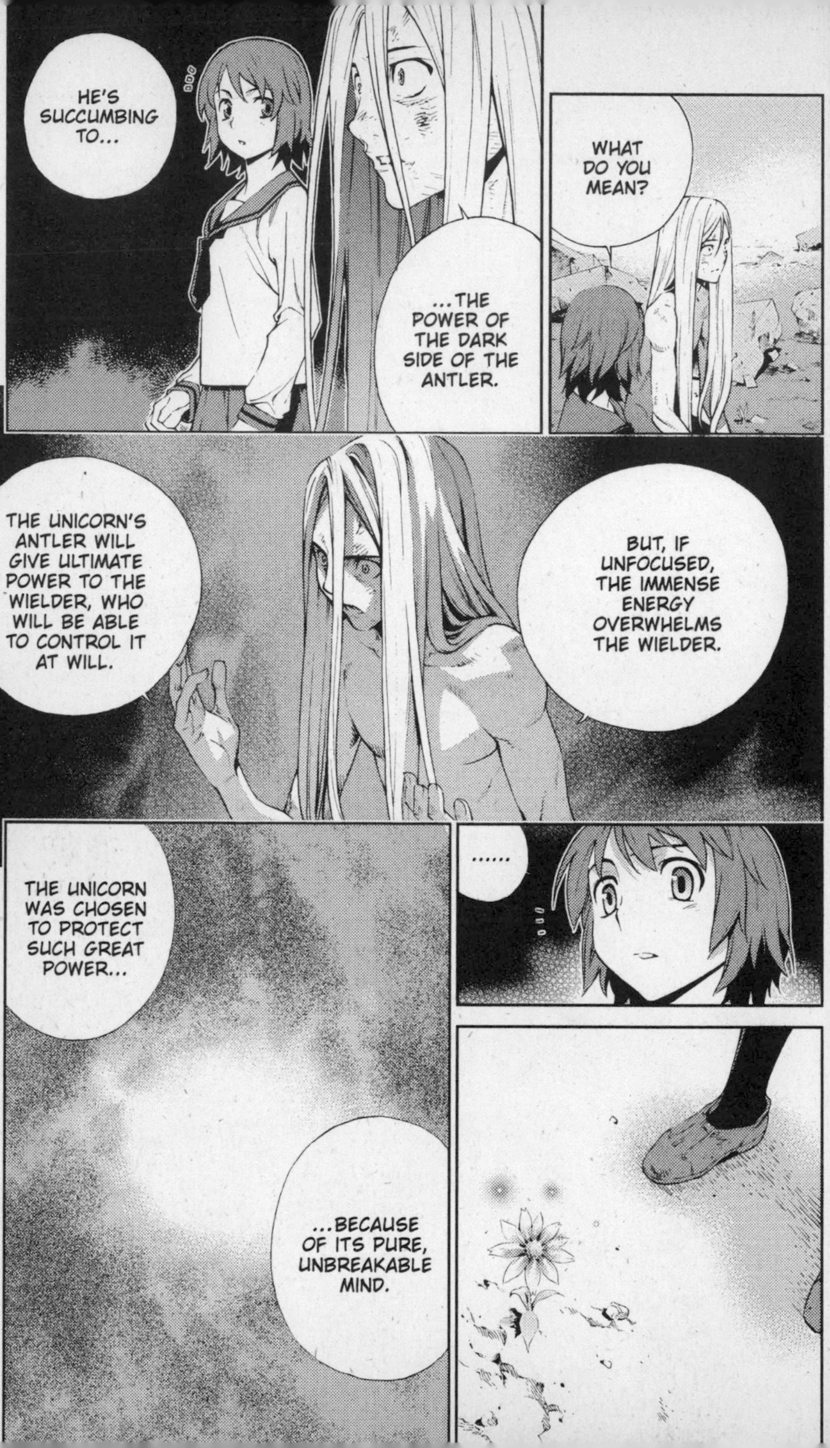
HE'S SUCCUMBING TO...
...THE POWER OF THE DARK SIDE OF THE ANTLER.
WHAT DO YOU MEAN?
THE UNICORN'S ANTLER WILL GIVE ULTIMATE POWER TO THE WIELDER, WHO WILL BE ABLE TO CONTROL IT AT WILL.
BUT, IF UNFOCUSED, THE IMMENSE ENERGY OVERWHELMS THE WIELDER.
THE UNICORN WAS CHOSEN TO PROTECT SUCH GREAT POWER...
...BECAUSE OF ITS PURE, UNBREAKABLE MIND.
......

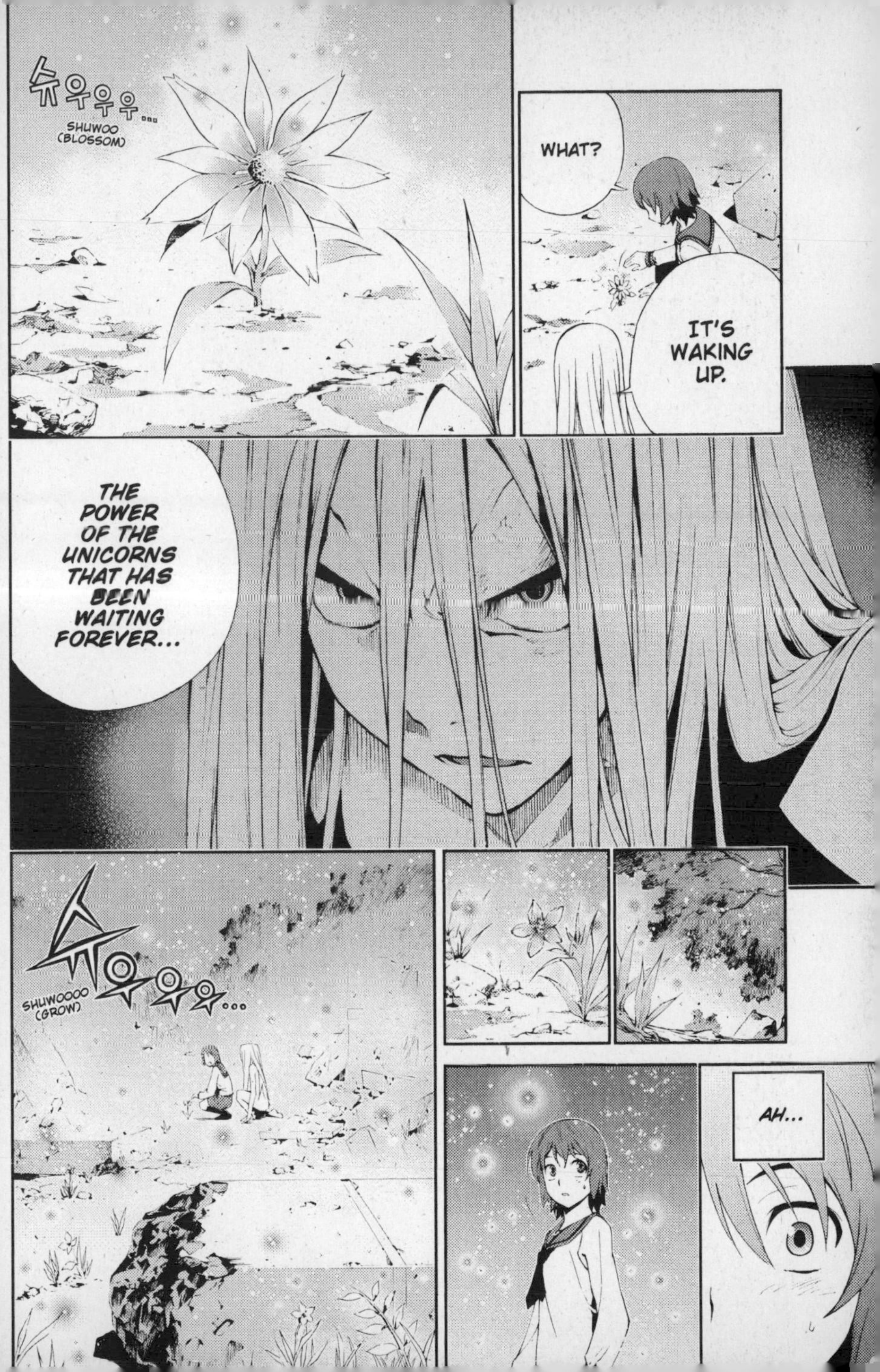
슈우우우...
SHUWOO (BLOSSOM)
WHAT?
IT'S WAKING UP.
THE POWER OF THE UNICORNS THAT HAS BEEN WAITING FOREVER...
SHUWOOOO (GROW)
AH...

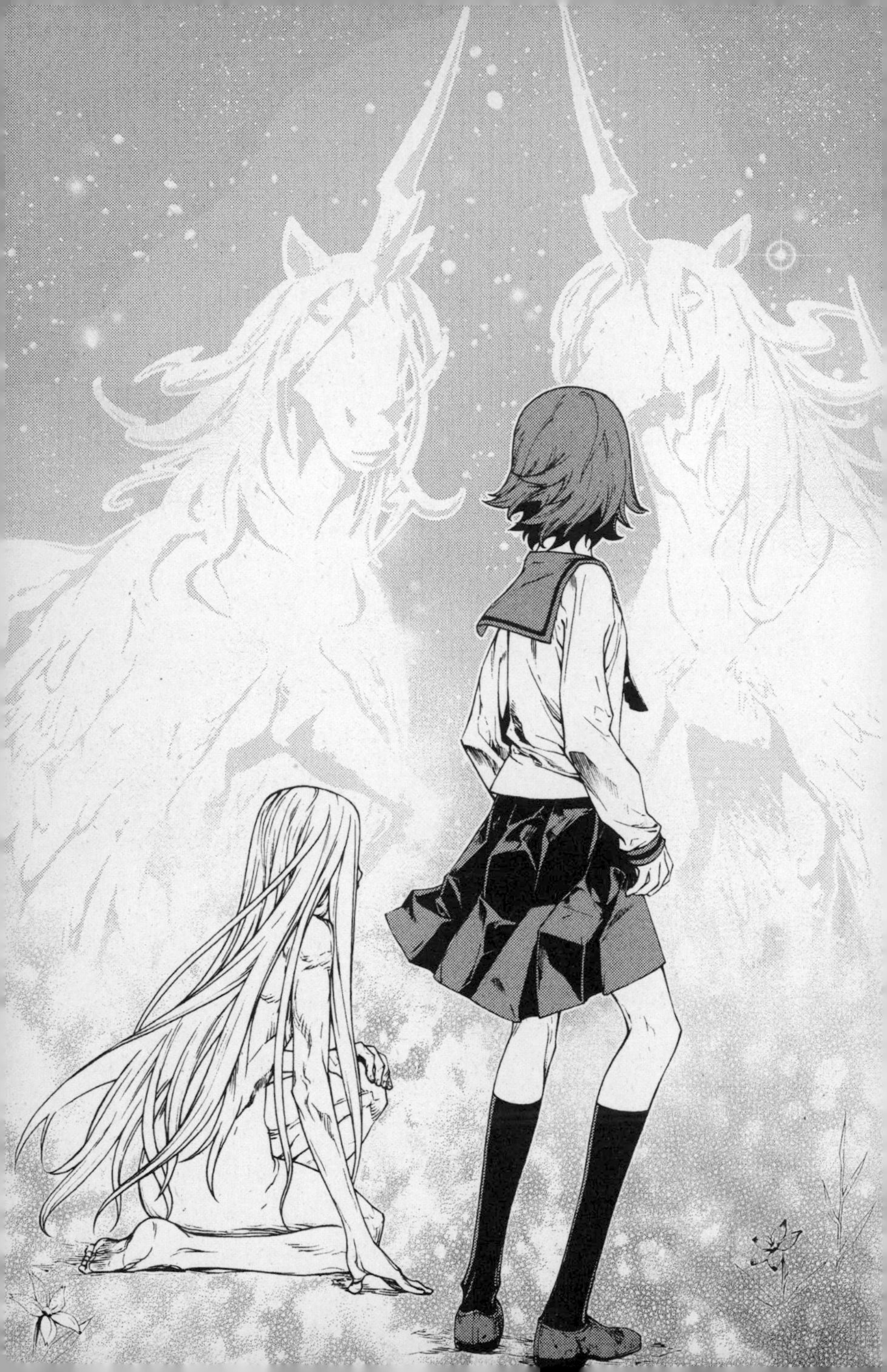

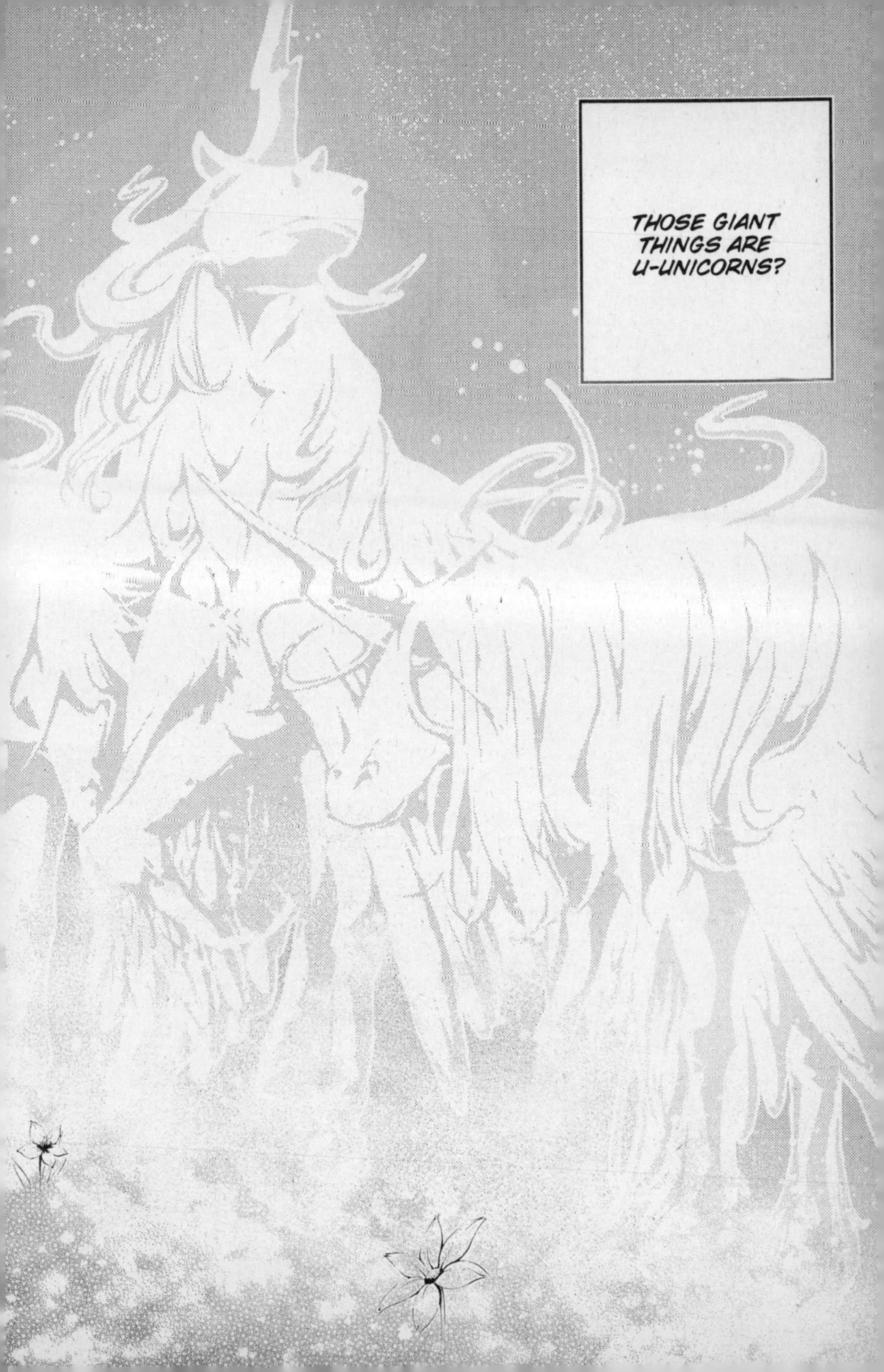
THOSE GIANT THINGS ARE U-UNICORNS?

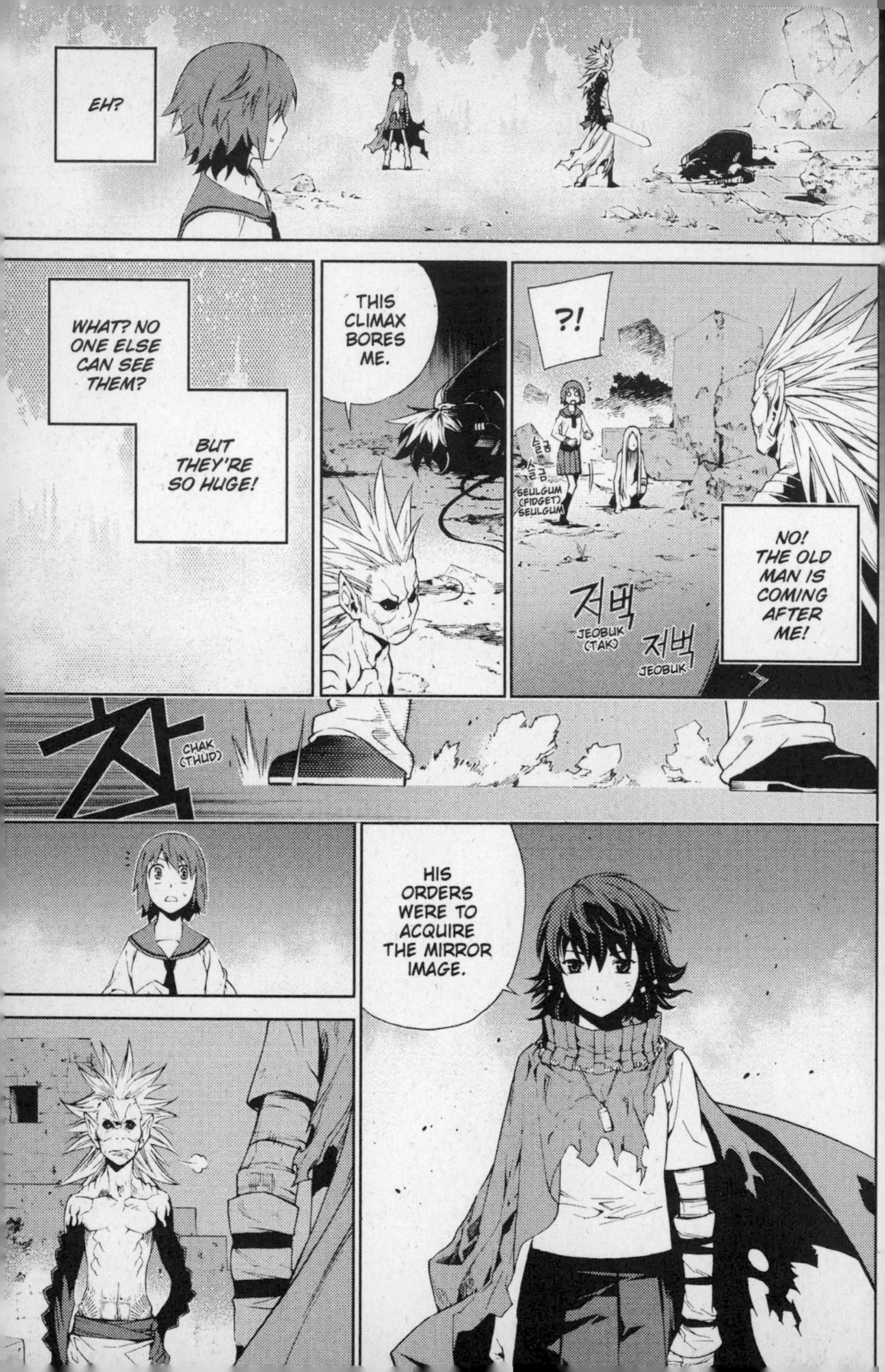
EH?
WHAT? NO ONE ELSE CAN SEE THEM?
BUT THEY'RE SO HUGE!
THIS CLIMAX BORES ME.
?!
슬금
슬금
SEULGUM (FIDGET) SEULGUM
저벅
JEOBUK (TAK)
저벅
JEOBUK
NO! THE OLD MAN IS COMING AFTER ME!
착
CHAK (THUD)
HIS ORDERS WERE TO ACQUIRE THE MIRROR IMAGE.

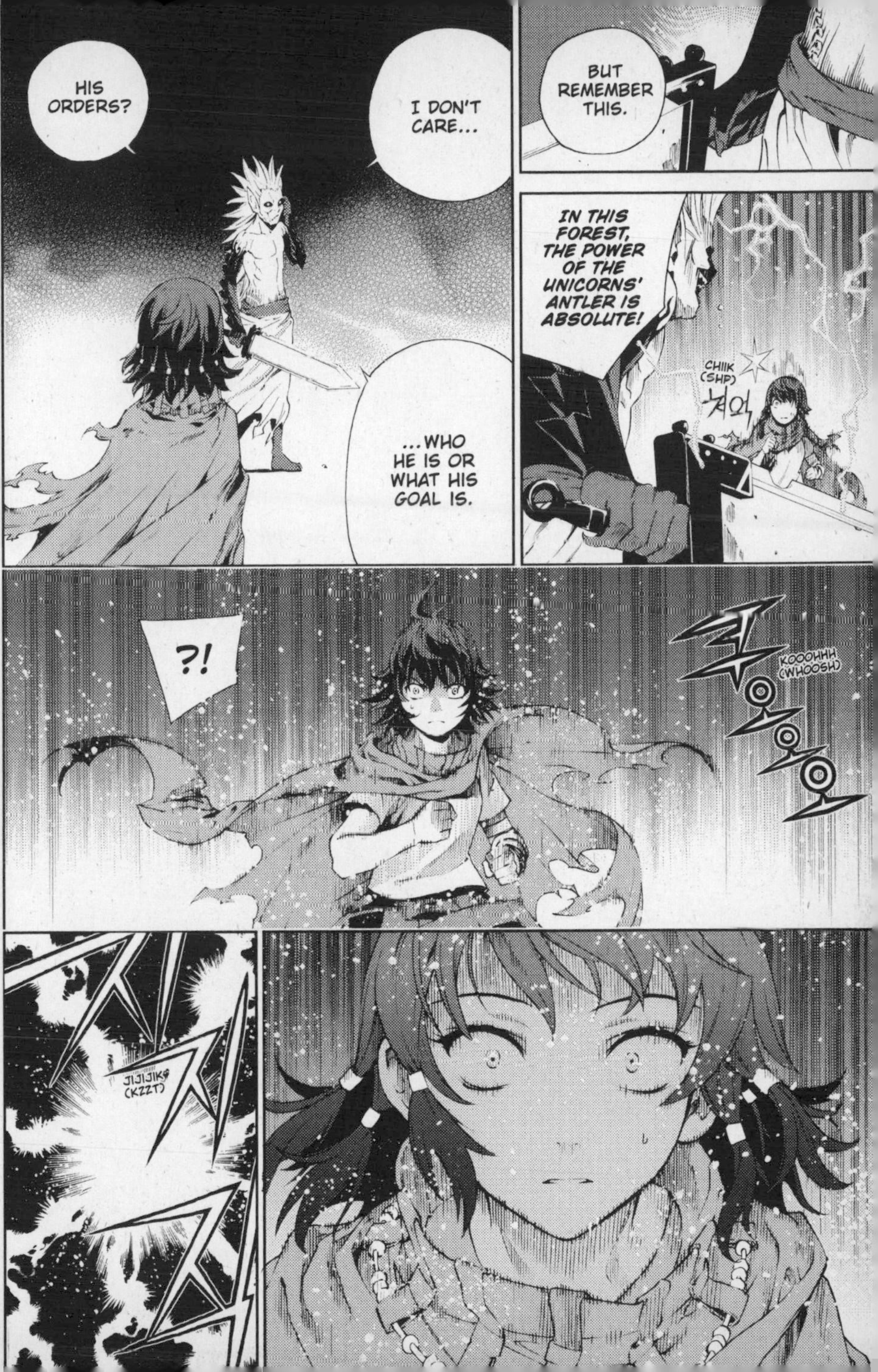
HIS ORDERS?
I DON'T CARE...
...WHO HE IS OR WHAT HIS GOAL IS.
BUT REMEMBER THIS.
IN THIS FOREST, THE POWER OF THE UNICORNS' ANTLER IS ABSOLUTE!
CHIIK (SHP)
?!
KOOOHHH (WHOOSH)
JIJIJIK (KZZT)

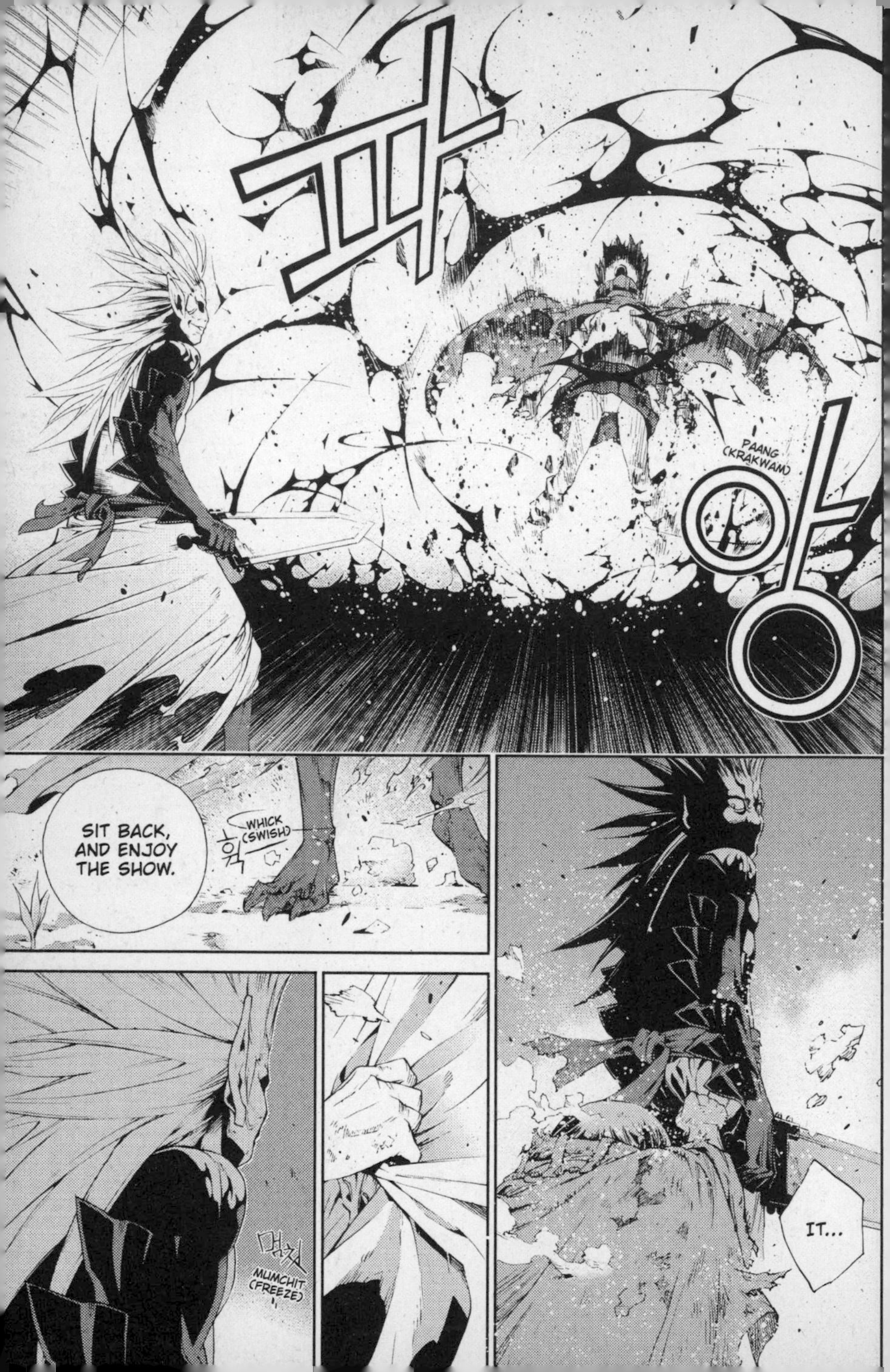
PAANG (KRAKWAM)
SIT BACK, AND ENJOY THE SHOW.
휙
WHICK (SWISH)
멈칫
MUMCHIT (FREEZE)
IT...

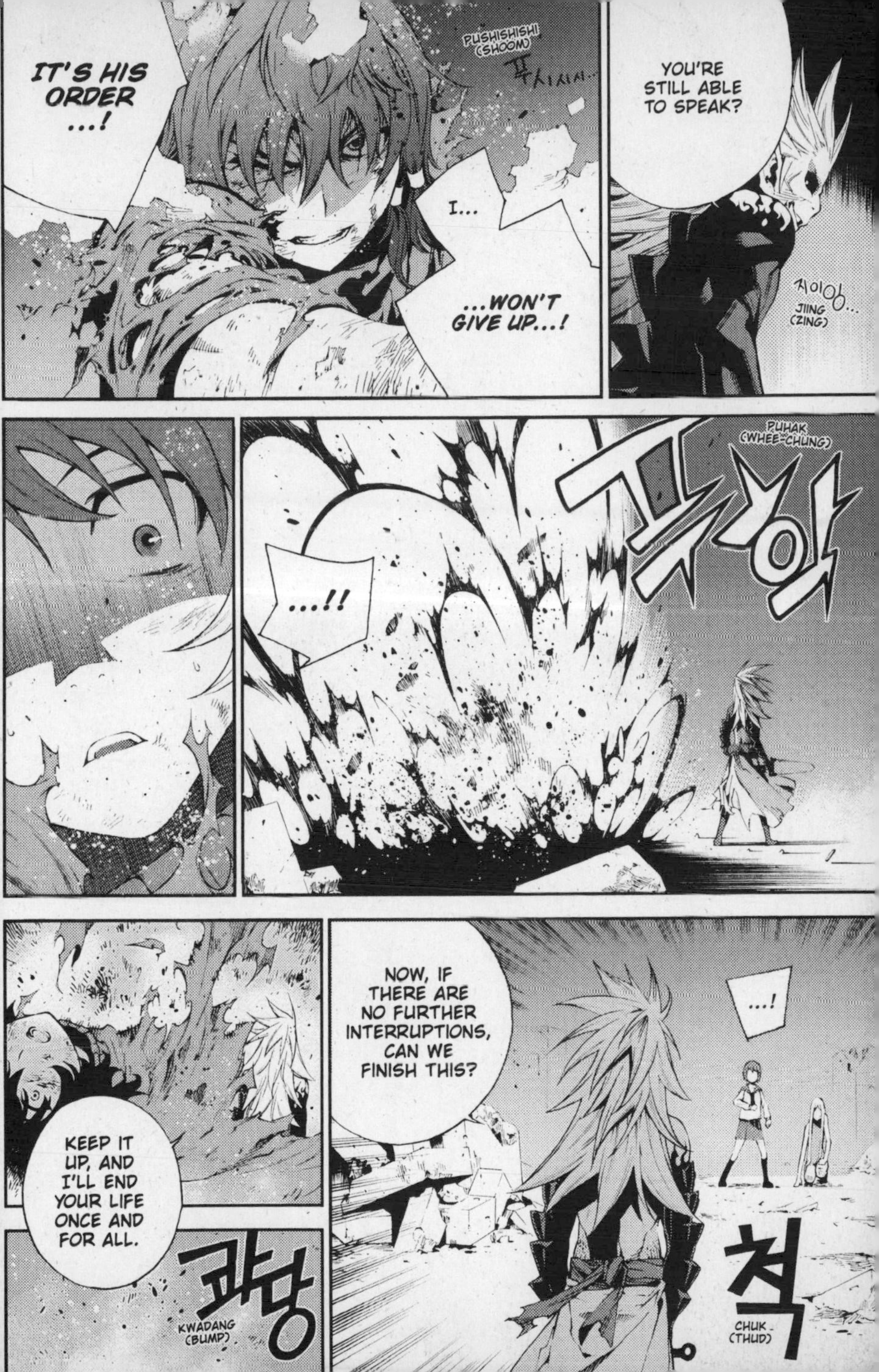
IT'S HIS ORDER ...!
PUSHISHISHI (SHOOM)
I...
...WON'T GIVE UP...!
YOU'RE STILL ABLE TO SPEAK?
JIING (ZING)
...!!
PUHAK (WHEE--CHUNG)
KEEP IT UP, AND I'LL END YOUR LIFE ONCE AND FOR ALL.
콰당
KWADANG (BUMP)
NOW, IF THERE ARE NO FURTHER INTERRUPTIONS, CAN WE FINISH THIS?
...!
척
CHUK (THUD)

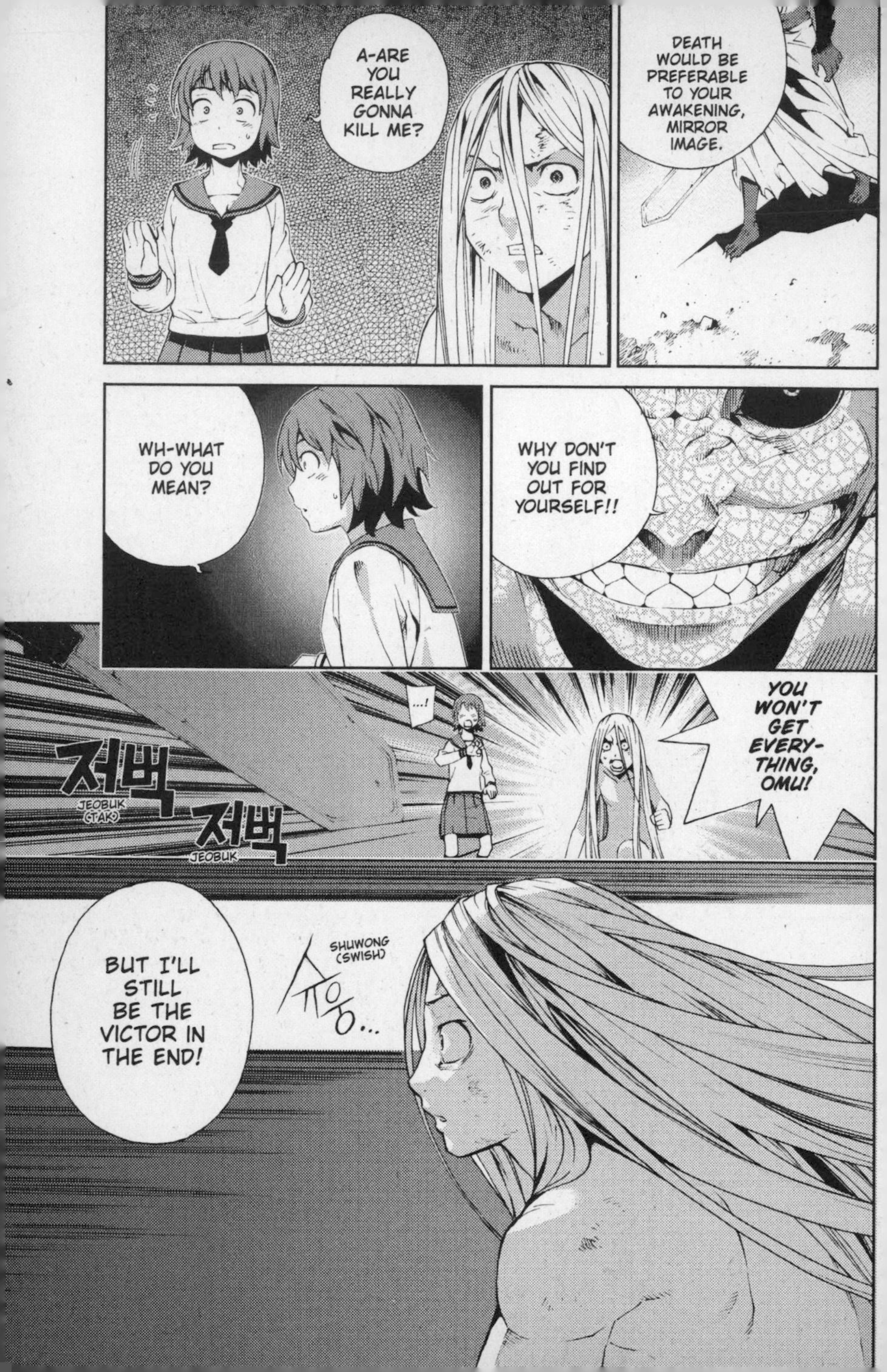
A-ARE YOU REALLY GONNA KILL ME?
DEATH WOULD BE PREFERABLE TO YOUR AWAKENING, MIRROR IMAGE.
WH-WHAT DO YOU MEAN?
WHY DON'T YOU FIND OUT FOR YOURSELF!!
저벅
JEOBUK (TAK)
저벅
JEOBUK
...!
YOU WON'T GET EVERY-THING, OMU!
BUT I'LL STILL BE THE VICTOR IN THE END!
SHUWONG (SWISH)
슈웅...

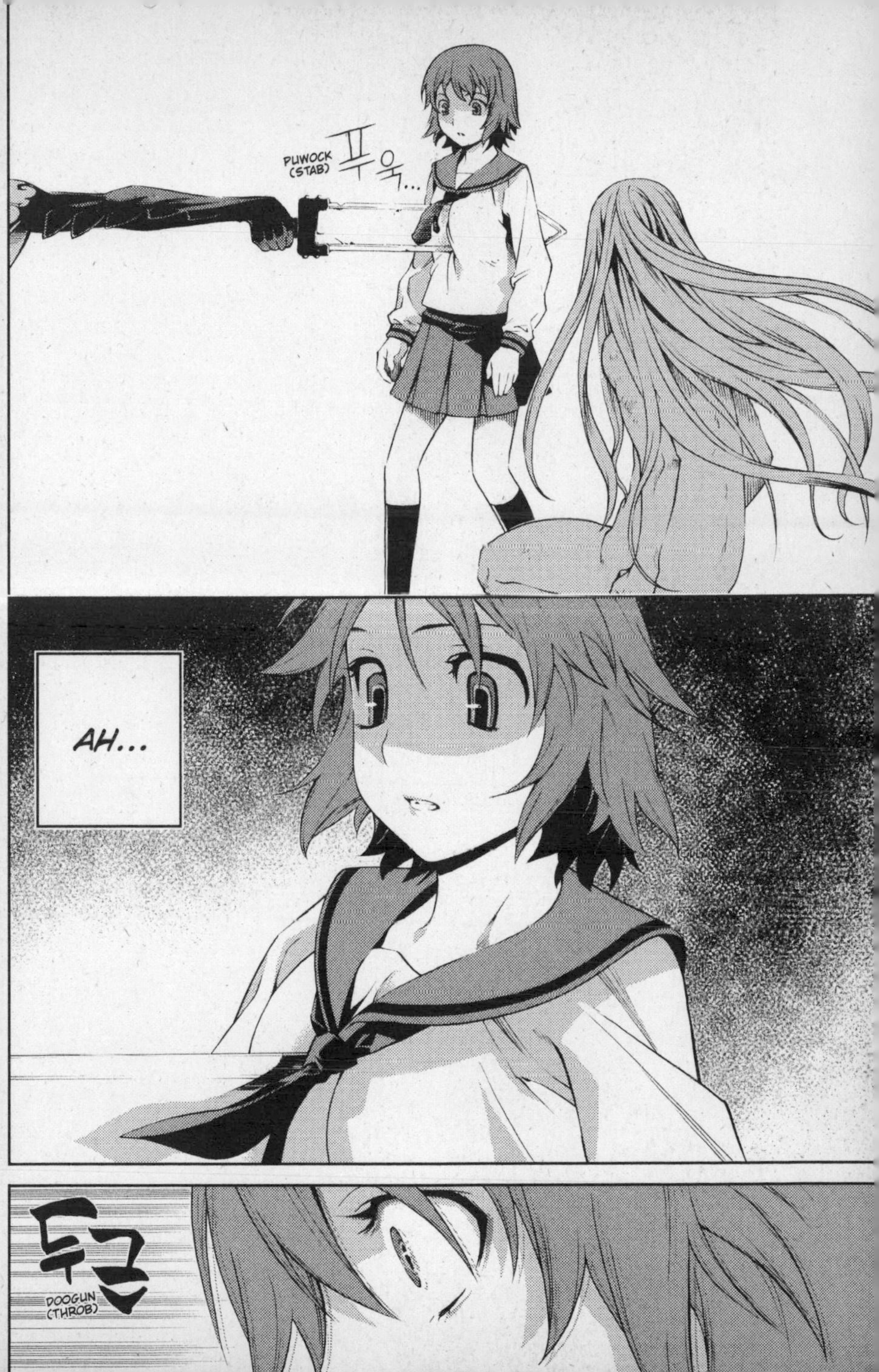
푸욱...
PUWOCK
(STAB)
AH...
두근
DOOGUN
(THROB)

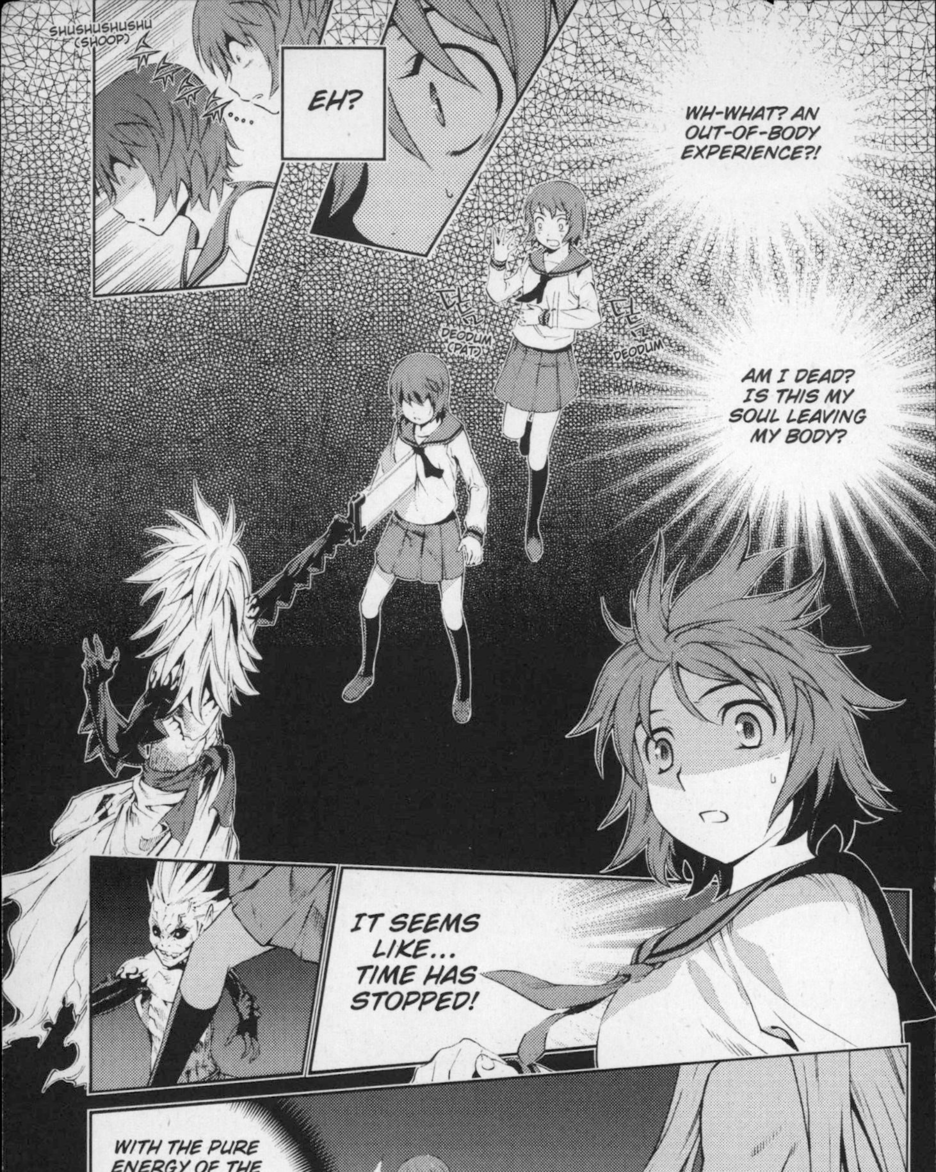
SHUSHUSHUSHU (SHOOP)
...
EH?
WH-WHAT? AN OUT-OF-BODY EXPERIENCE?!
DEODUM (PAT)
DEODUM
AM I DEAD? IS THIS MY SOUL LEAVING MY BODY?
IT SEEMS LIKE... TIME HAS STOPPED!
WITH THE PURE ENERGY OF THE UNICORNS' ANTLER FLOWING THROUGH THE MIRROR IMAGE'S HEART, A NEW WORLD IS MADE.
SSUK (SSK)

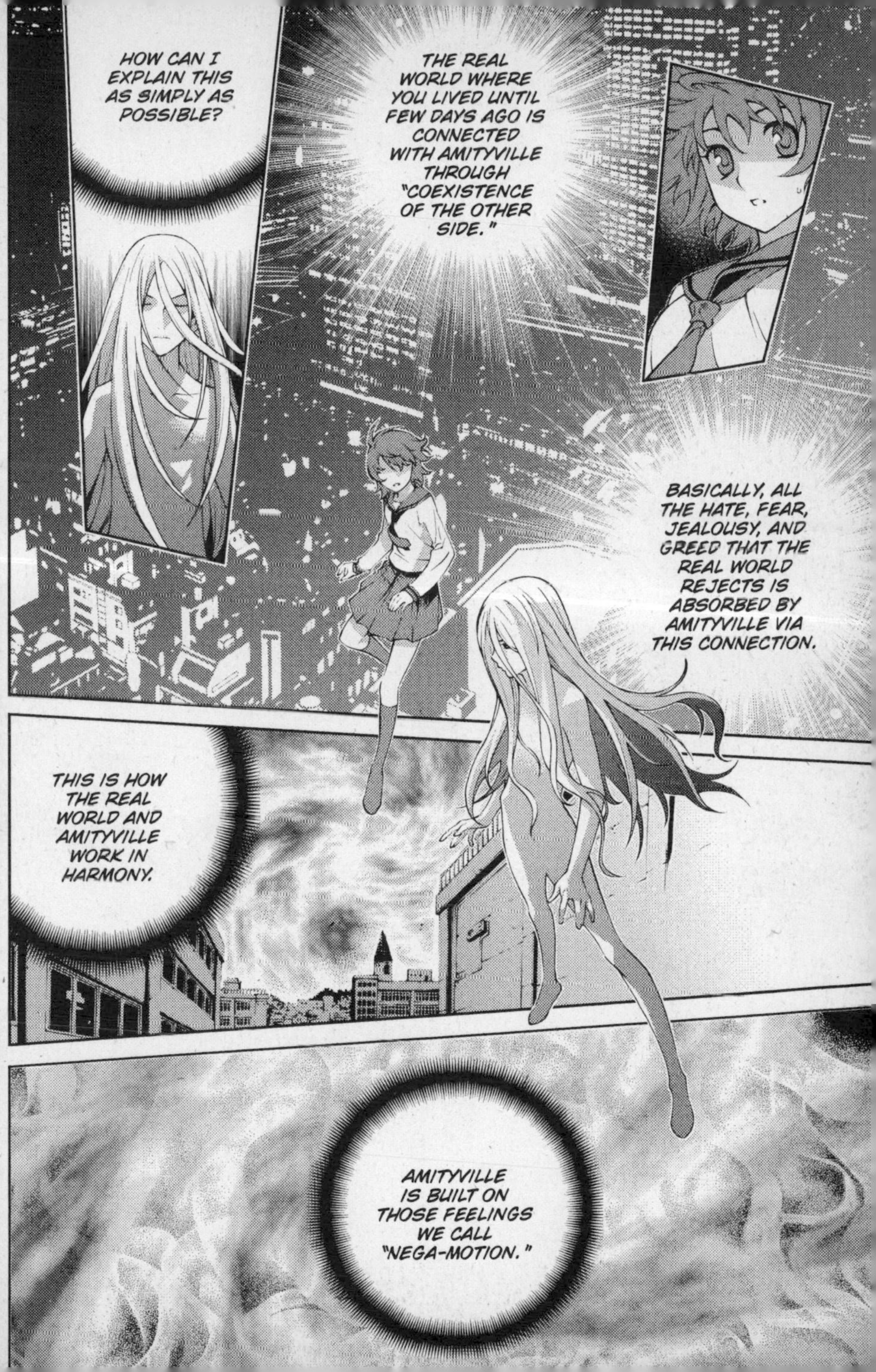
HOW CAN I EXPLAIN THIS AS SIMPLY AS POSSIBLE?
THE REAL WORLD WHERE YOU LIVED UNTIL FEW DAYS AGO IS CONNECTED WITH AMITYVILLE THROUGH "COEXISTENCE OF THE OTHER SIDE."
BASICALLY, ALL THE HATE, FEAR, JEALOUSY, AND GREED THAT THE REAL WORLD REJECTS IS ABSORBED BY AMITYVILLE VIA THIS CONNECTION.
THIS IS HOW THE REAL WORLD AND AMITYVILLE WORK IN HARMONY.
AMITYVILLE IS BUILT ON THOSE FEELINGS WE CALL "NEGA-MOTION."

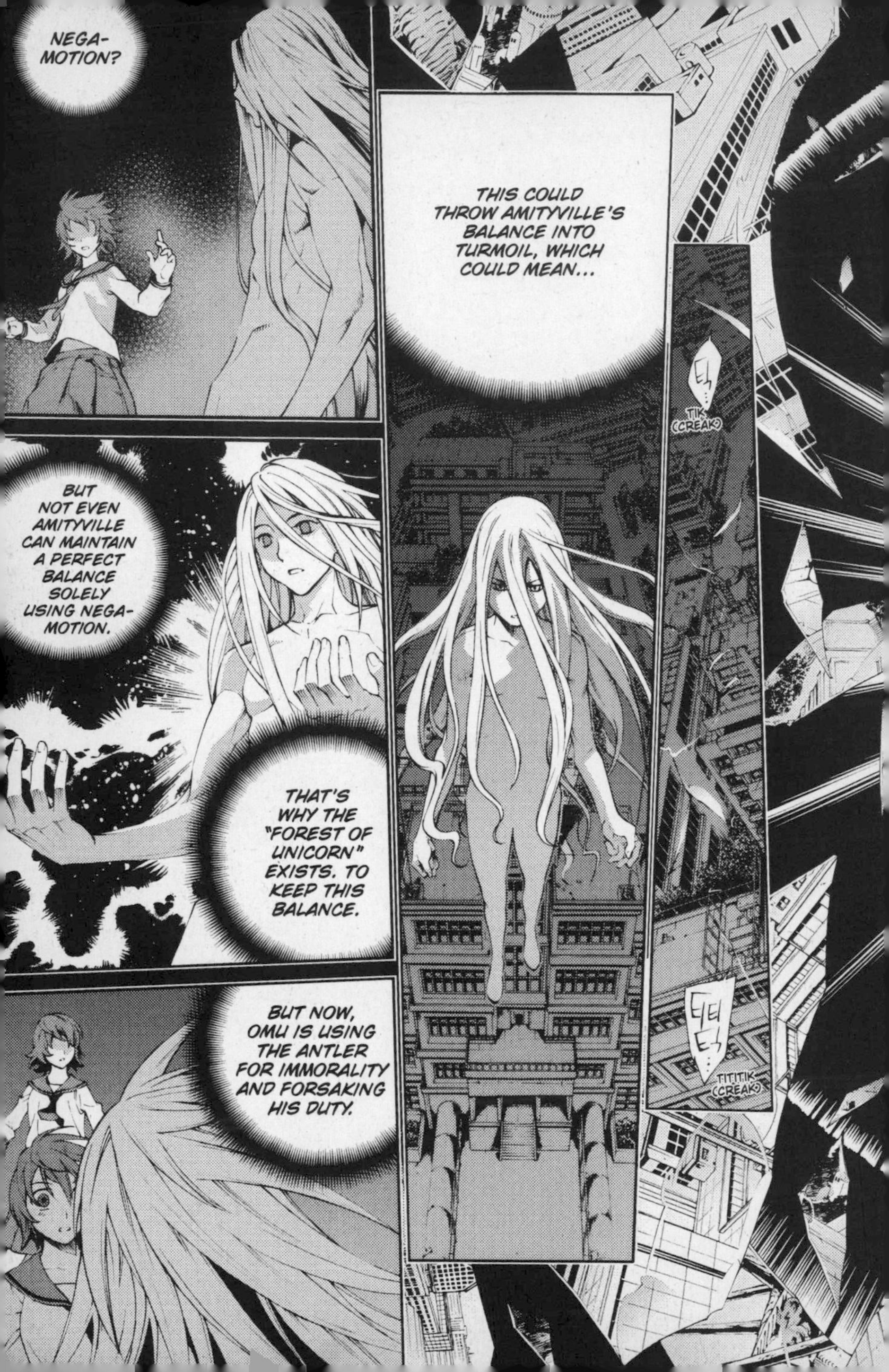
NEGA-MOTION?
BUT NOT EVEN AMITYVILLE CAN MAINTAIN A PERFECT BALANCE SOLELY USING NEGA-MOTION.
THAT'S WHY THE "FOREST OF UNICORN" EXISTS. TO KEEP THIS BALANCE.
BUT NOW, OMU IS USING THE ANTLER FOR IMMORALITY AND FORSAKING HIS DUTY.
THIS COULD THROW AMITYVILLE'S BALANCE INTO TURMOIL, WHICH COULD MEAN...
틱...
TIK (CREAK)
티티틱...
TITITIK (CREAK)

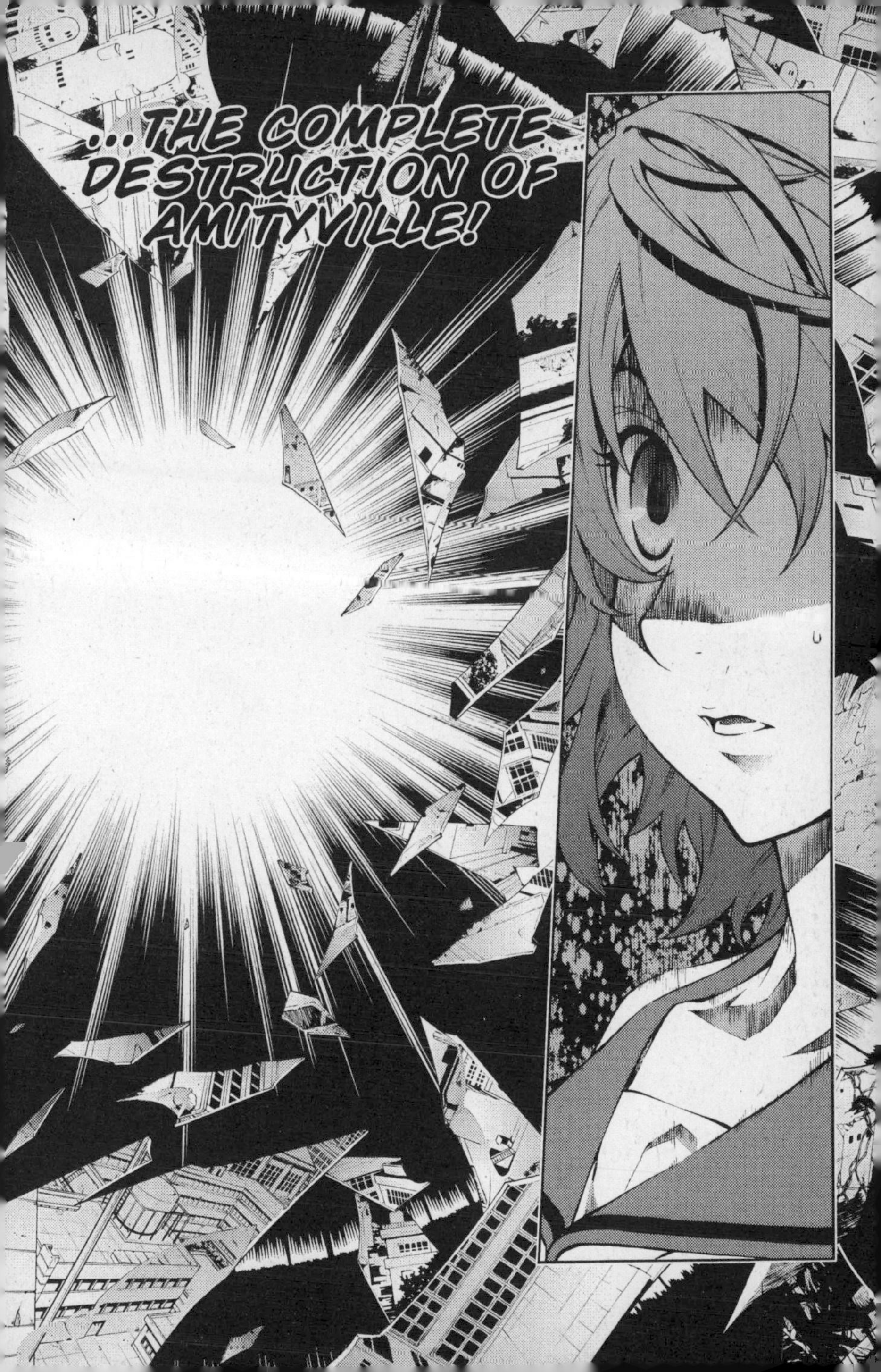
...THE COMPLETE DESTRUCTION OF AMITYVILLE!

JACK FROST

FROST

The Amityville

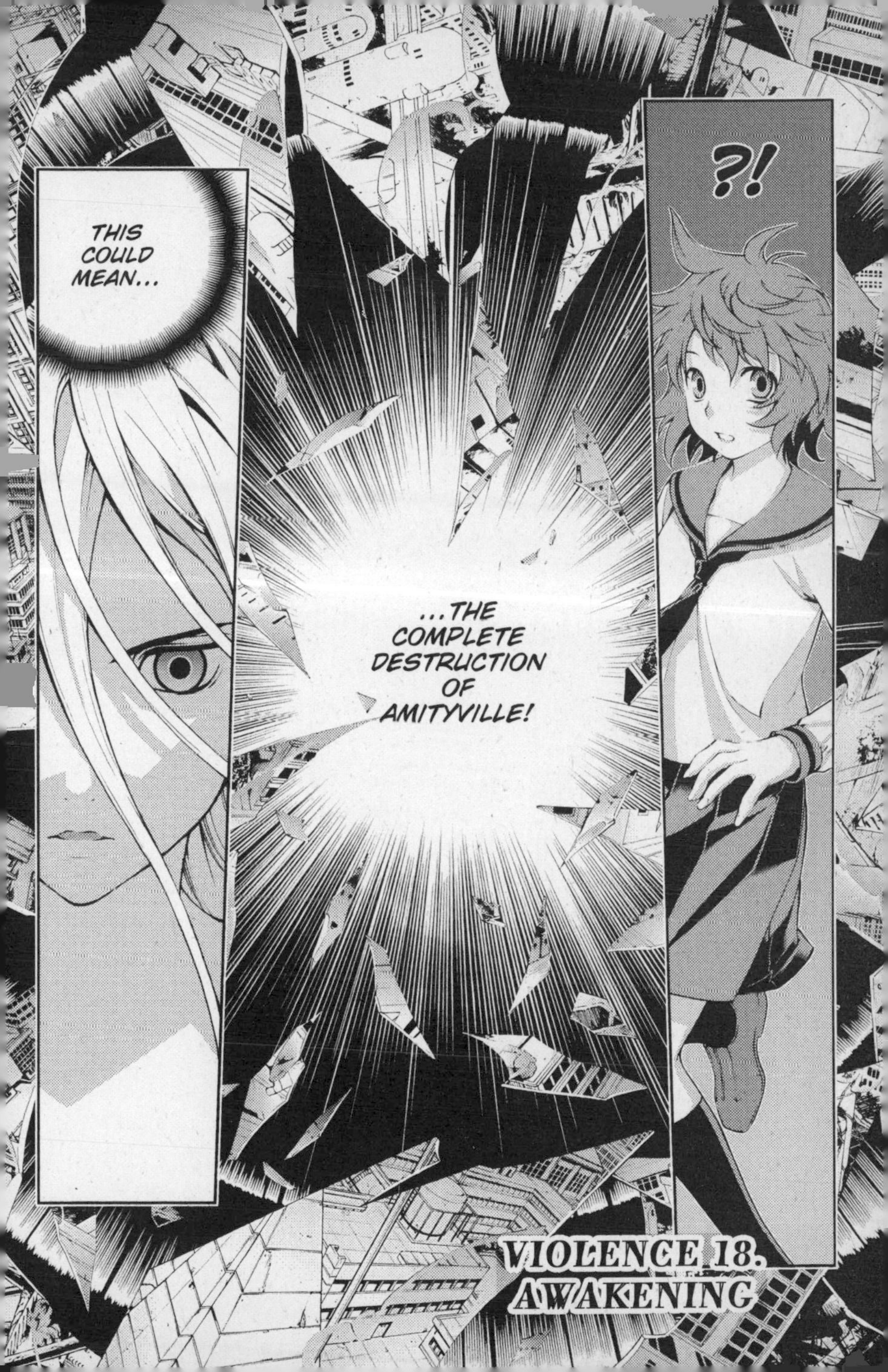
THIS COULD MEAN...
?!
...THE COMPLETE DESTRUCTION OF AMITYVILLE!
VIOLENCE 18. AWAKENING

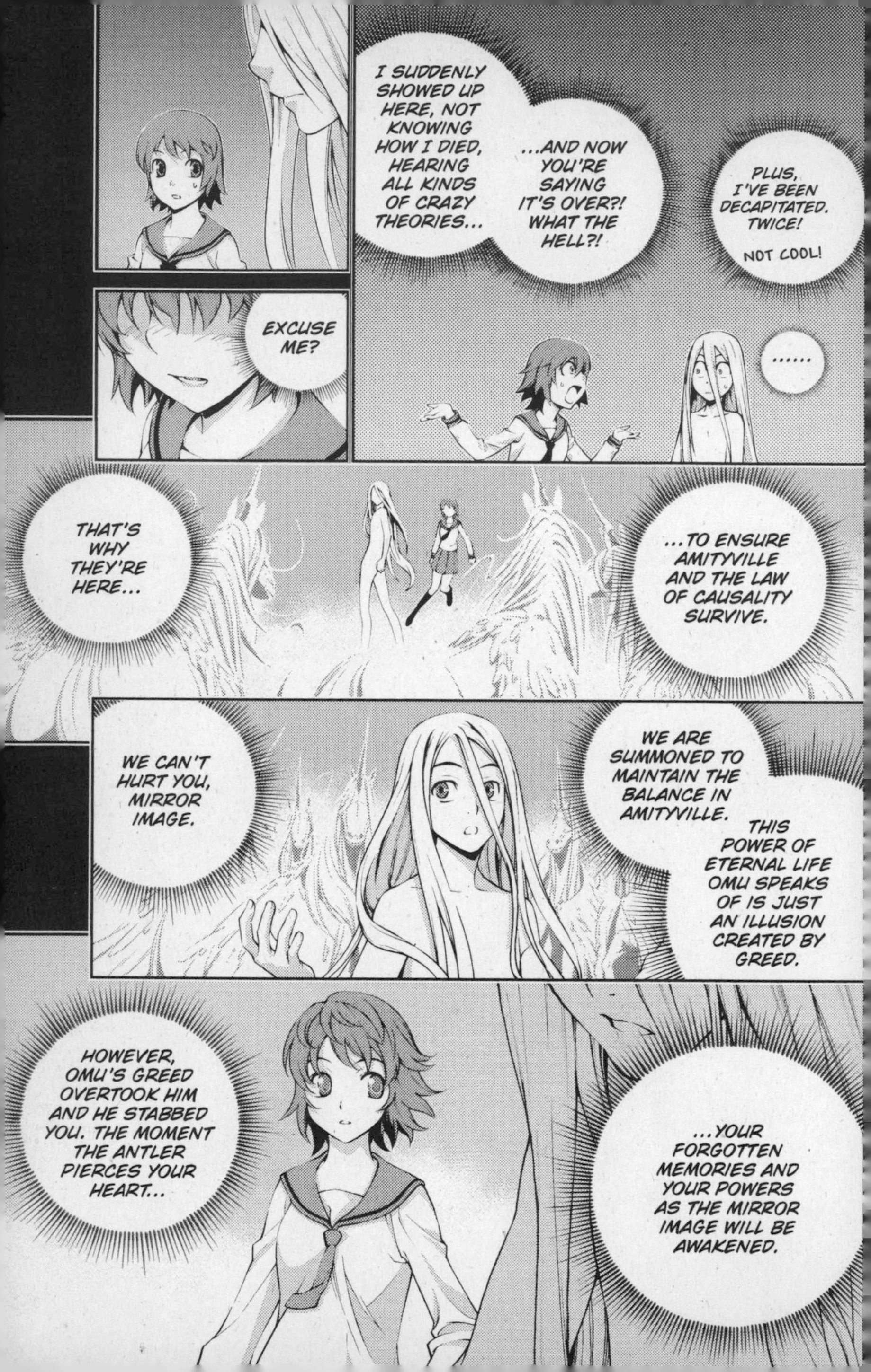
EXCUSE ME?
I SUDDENLY SHOWED UP HERE, NOT KNOWING HOW I DIED, HEARING ALL KINDS OF CRAZY THEORIES...
...AND NOW YOU'RE SAYING IT'S OVER?! WHAT THE HELL?!
PLUS, I'VE BEEN DECAPITATED. TWICE!
NOT COOL!
......
THAT'S WHY THEY'RE HERE...
...TO ENSURE AMITYVILLE AND THE LAW OF CAUSALITY SURVIVE.
WE CAN'T HURT YOU, MIRROR IMAGE.
WE ARE SUMMONED TO MAINTAIN THE BALANCE IN AMITYVILLE.
THIS POWER OF ETERNAL LIFE OMU SPEAKS OF IS JUST AN ILLUSION CREATED BY GREED.
HOWEVER, OMU'S GREED OVERTOOK HIM AND HE STABBED YOU. THE MOMENT THE ANTLER PIERCES YOUR HEART...
...YOUR FORGOTTEN MEMORIES AND YOUR POWERS AS THE MIRROR IMAGE WILL BE AWAKENED.

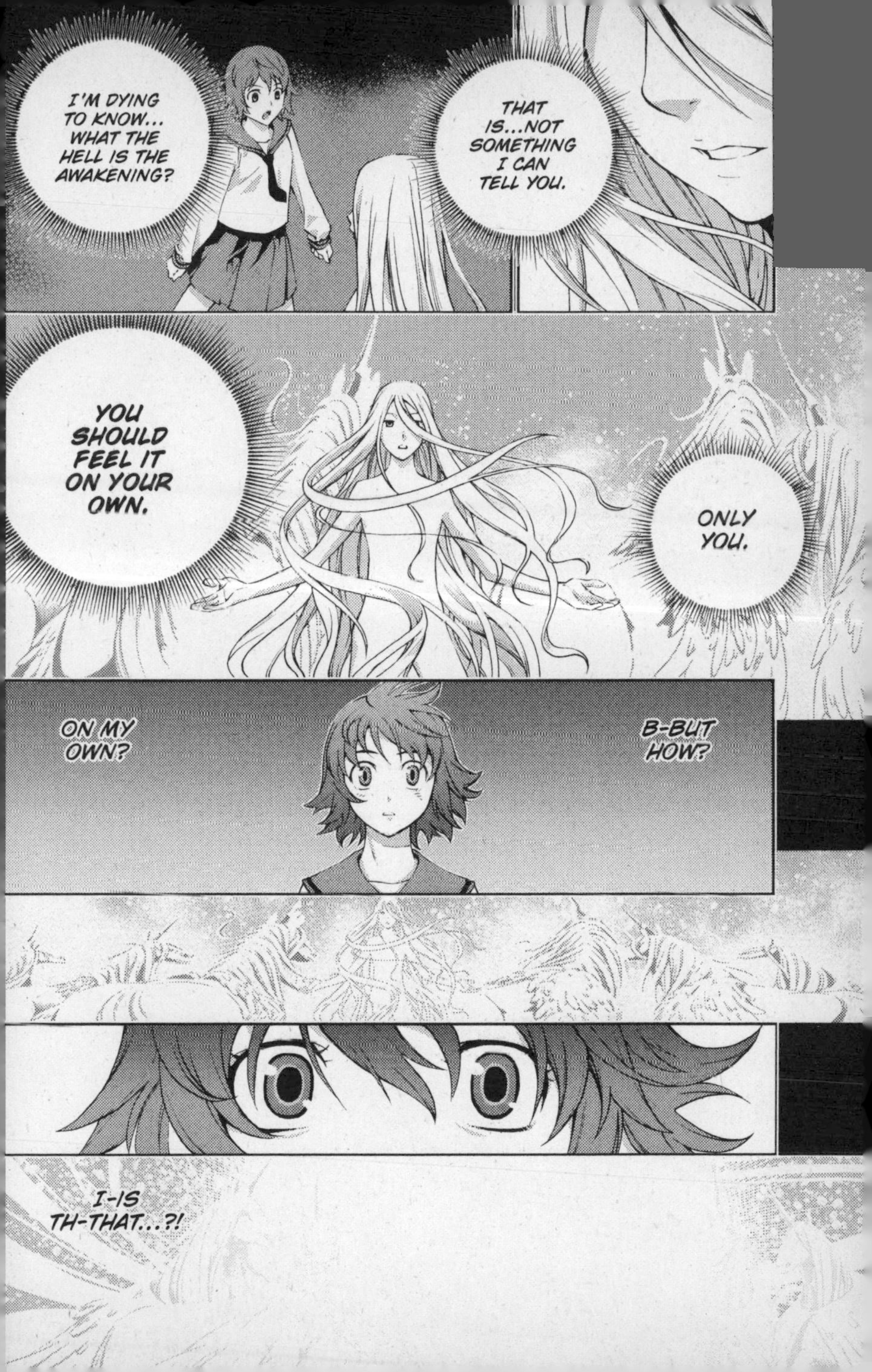
I'M DYING TO KNOW... WHAT THE HELL IS THE AWAKENING?
THAT IS...NOT SOMETHING I CAN TELL YOU.
YOU SHOULD FEEL IT ON YOUR OWN.
ONLY YOU.
ON MY OWN?
B-BUT HOW?
I-IS TH-THAT...?!

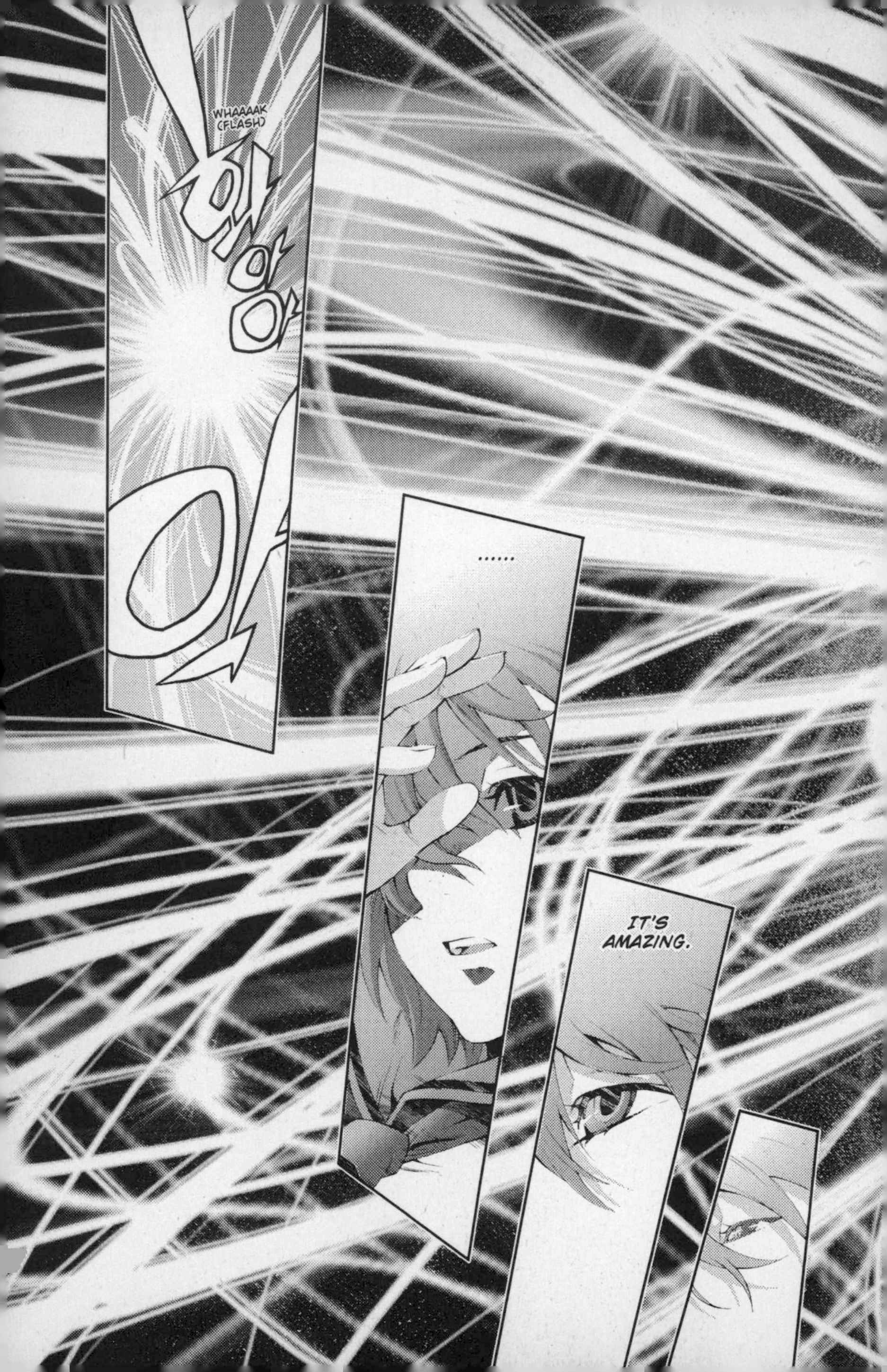
WHAAAAK
(FLASH)
......
IT'S AMAZING.

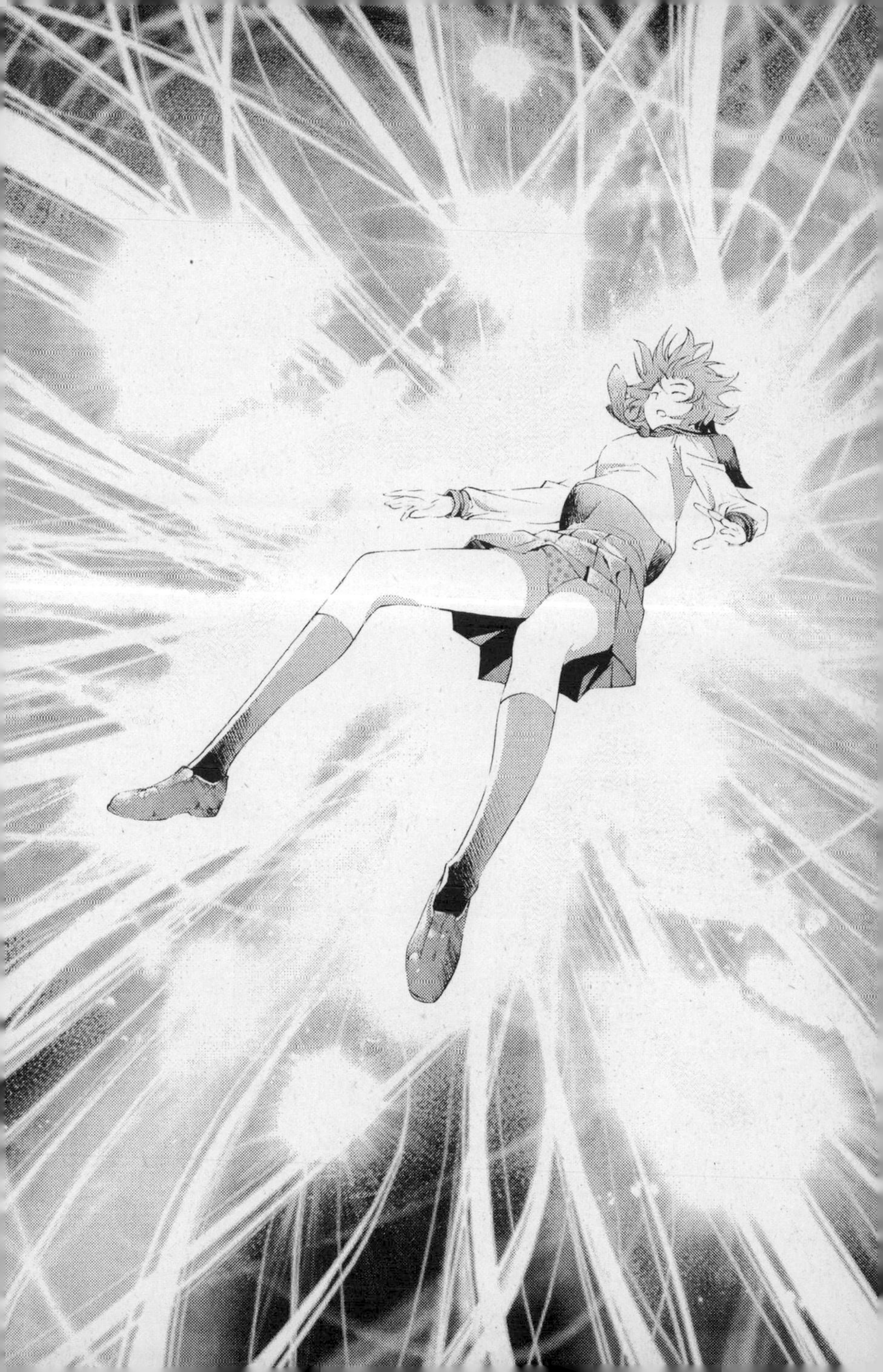

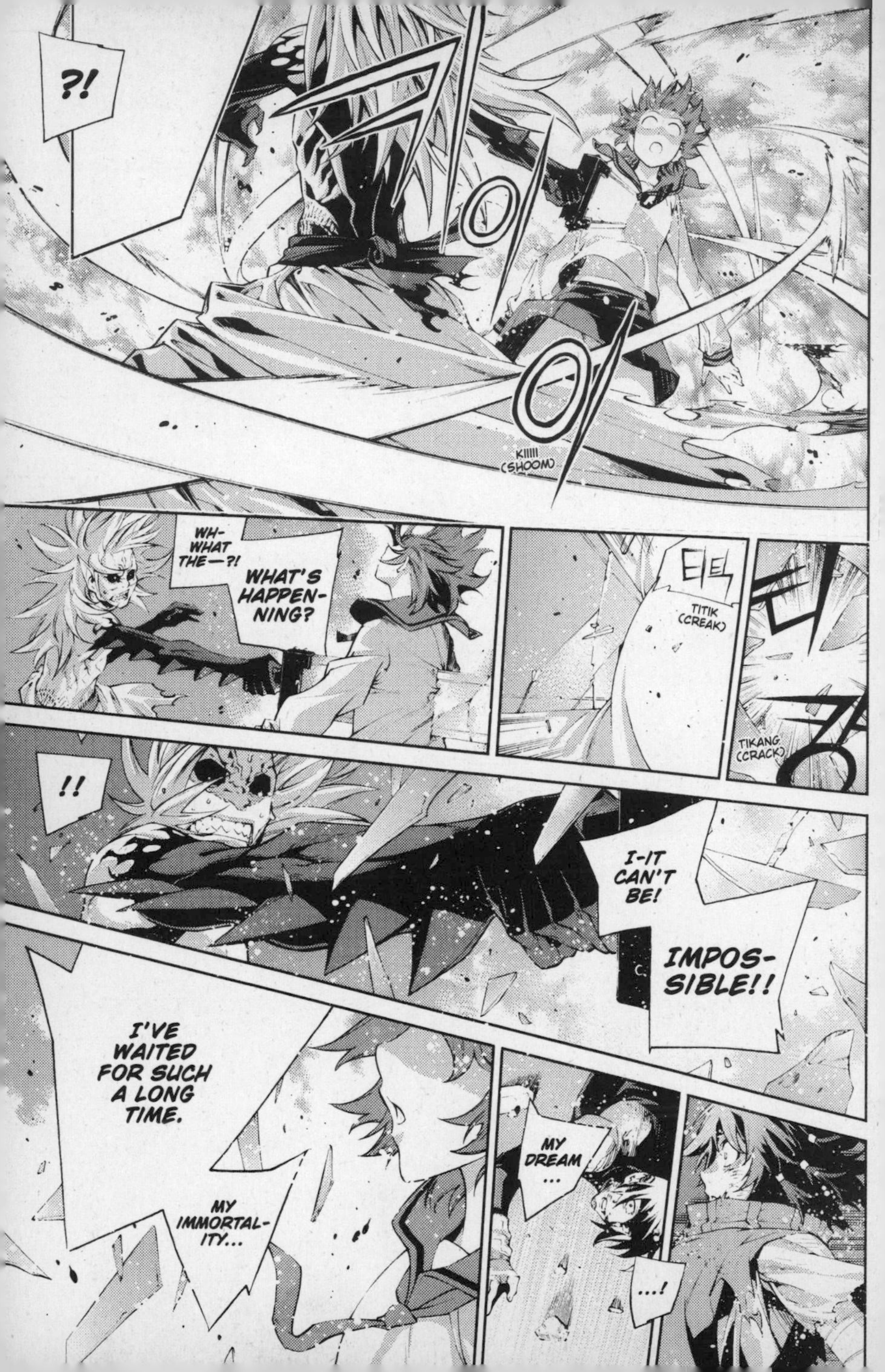
?!
KIIIII (SHOOM)
WH- WHAT THE—?!
WHAT'S HAPPENNING?
TITIK (CREAK)
TIKANG (CRACK)
!!
I-IT CAN'T BE!
IMPOSSIBLE!!
I'VE WAITED FOR SUCH A LONG TIME.
MY IMMORTALITY...
MY DREAM...
...!

KOOWHAACK
(SHOOM)

I'M DISAPPOINTED, JACK.

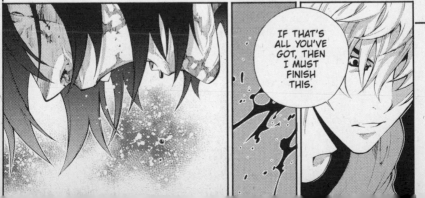

IF THAT'S ALL YOU'VE GOT, THEN I MUST FINISH THIS.

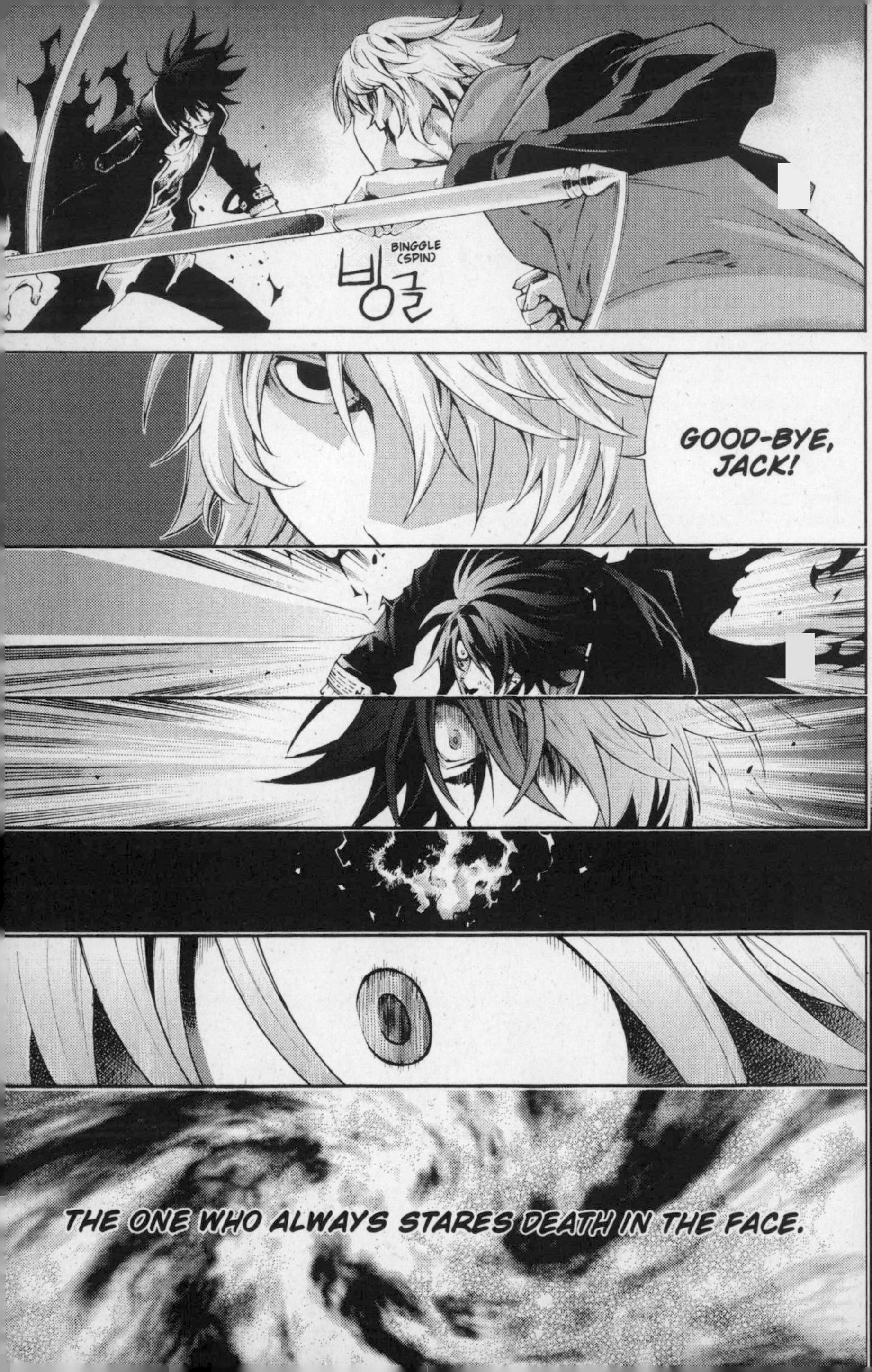

BINGGLE (SPIN)
빙글
GOOD-BYE, JACK!
THE ONE WHO ALWAYS STARES DEATH IN THE FACE.

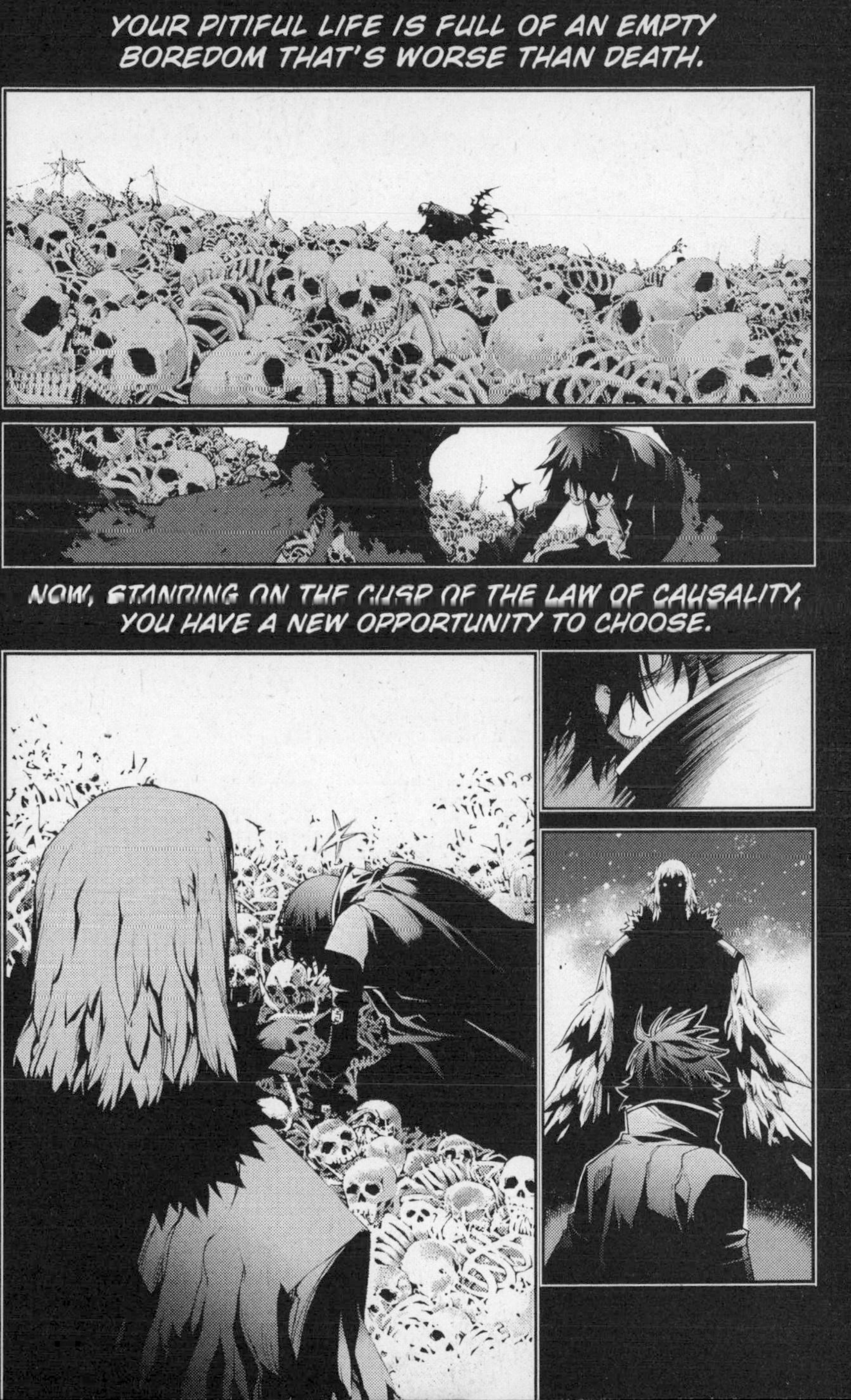
YOUR PITIFUL LIFE IS FULL OF AN EMPTY BOREDOM THAT'S WORSE THAN DEATH.
NOW, STANDING ON THE CUSP OF THE LAW OF CAUSALITY, YOU HAVE A NEW OPPORTUNITY TO CHOOSE.

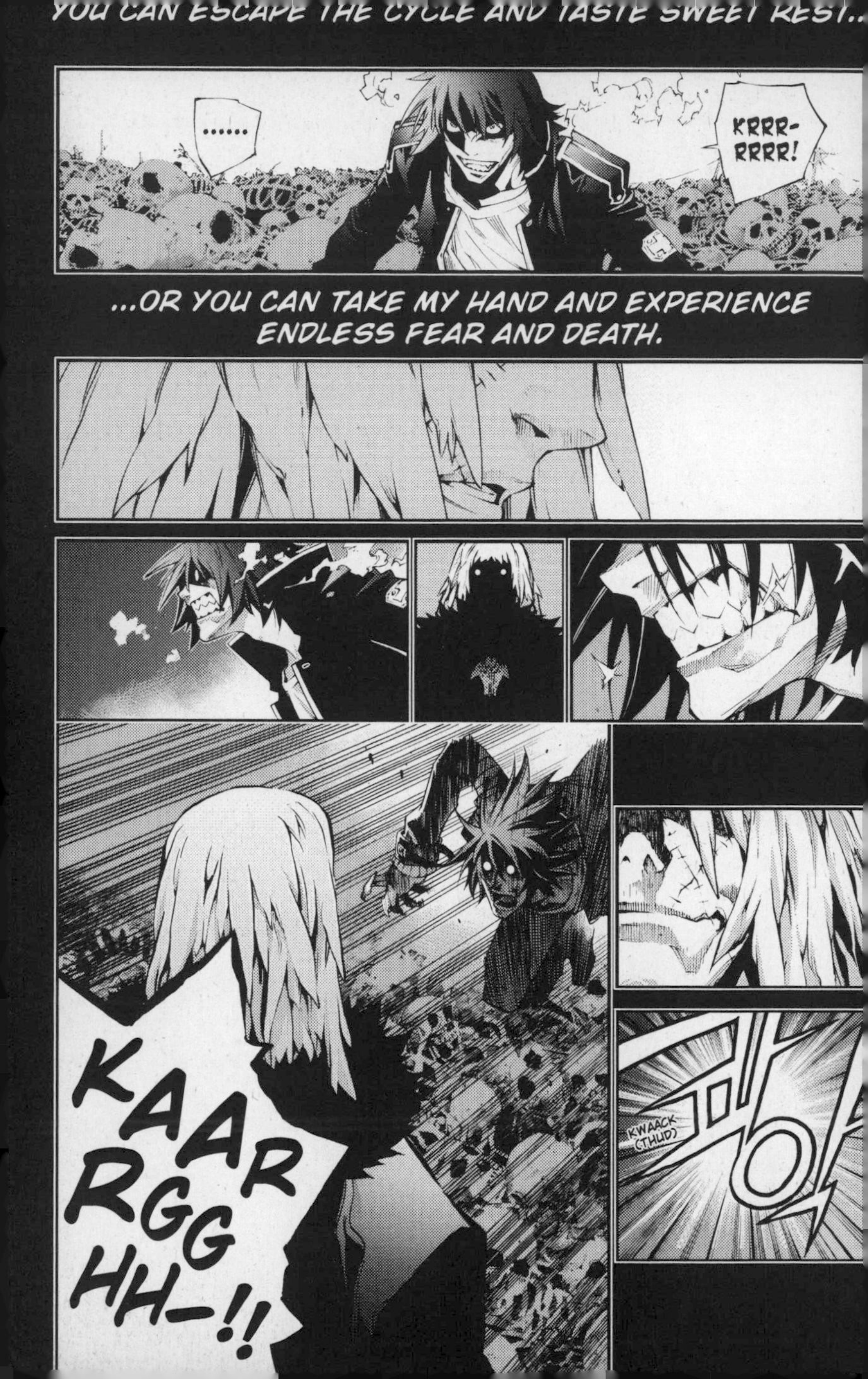
YOU CAN ESCAPE THE CYCLE AND TASTE SWEET REST...
......
KRRR-RRRR!
...OR YOU CAN TAKE MY HAND AND EXPERIENCE ENDLESS FEAR AND DEATH.
KAARRGGHH-!!
KWAACK (THUD)

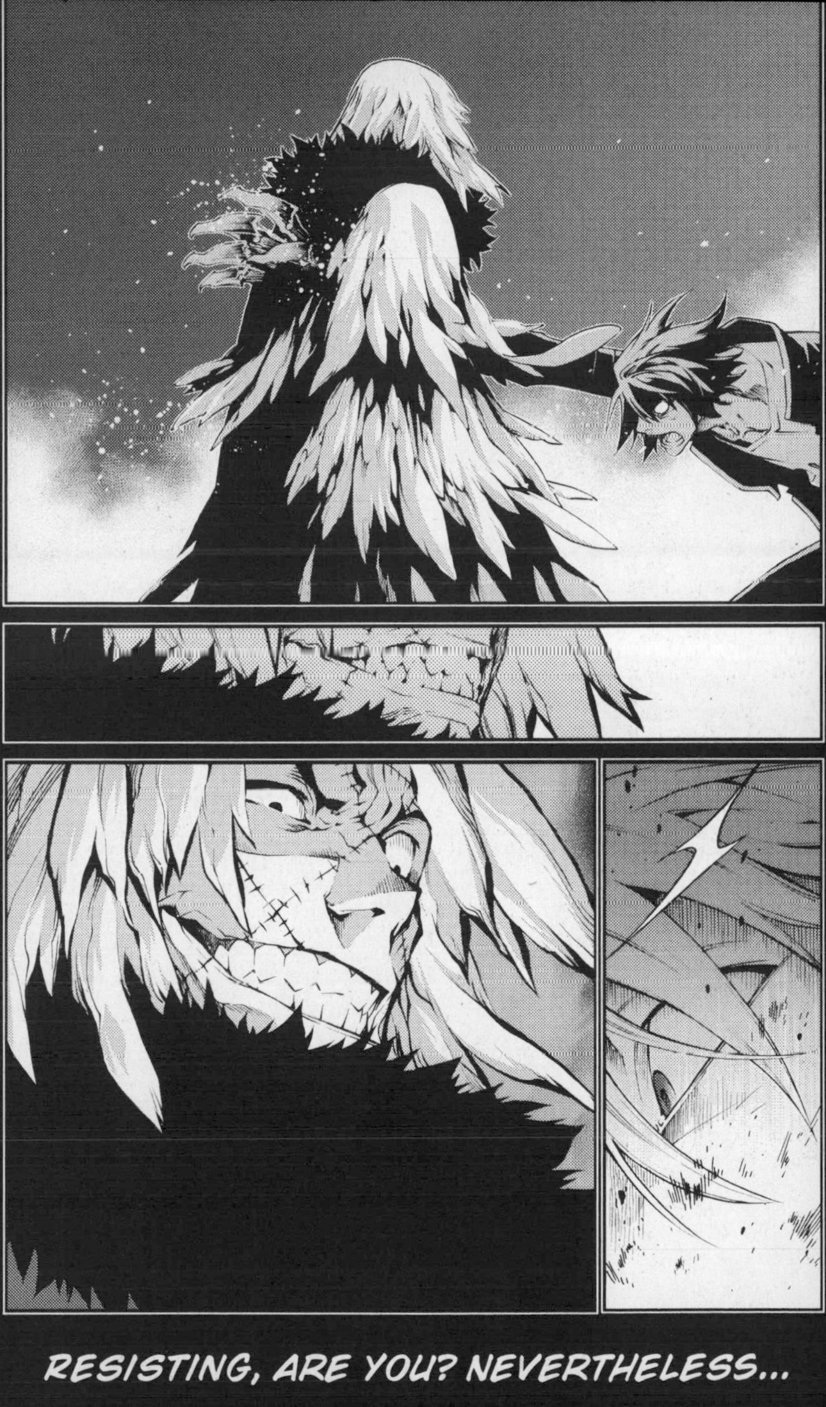
RESISTING, ARE YOU? NEVERTHELESS...

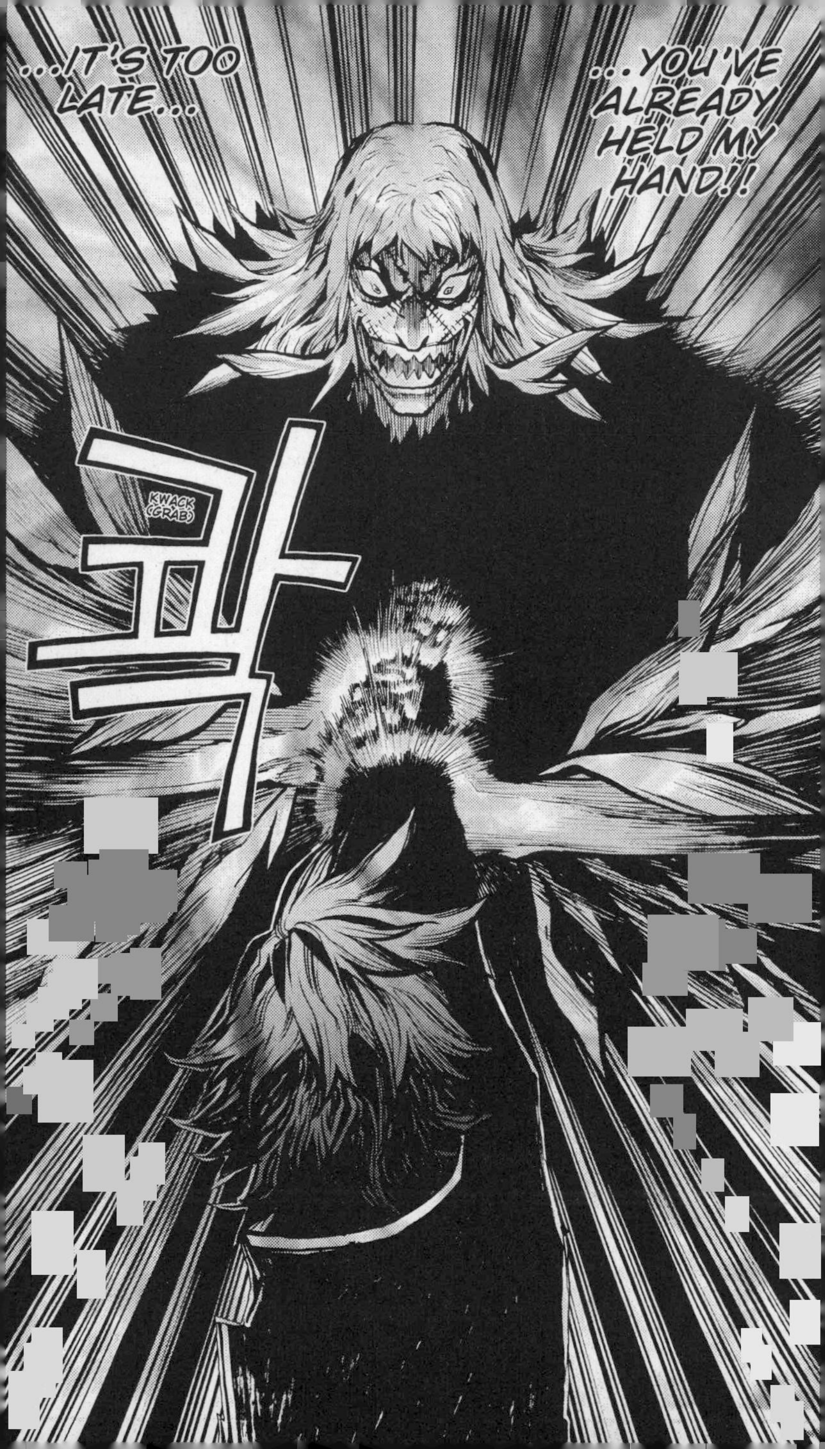
...IT'S TOO LATE...
...YOU'VE ALREADY HELD MY HAND!!
콱
KWACK (GRAB)

키이이이...
KIIIIII
(CREAK)

DEDEDE
(CRACK)

AND
NOW
...

...YOU'LL
BE RE-
BORN
WITH
THE
CLOAK
!!

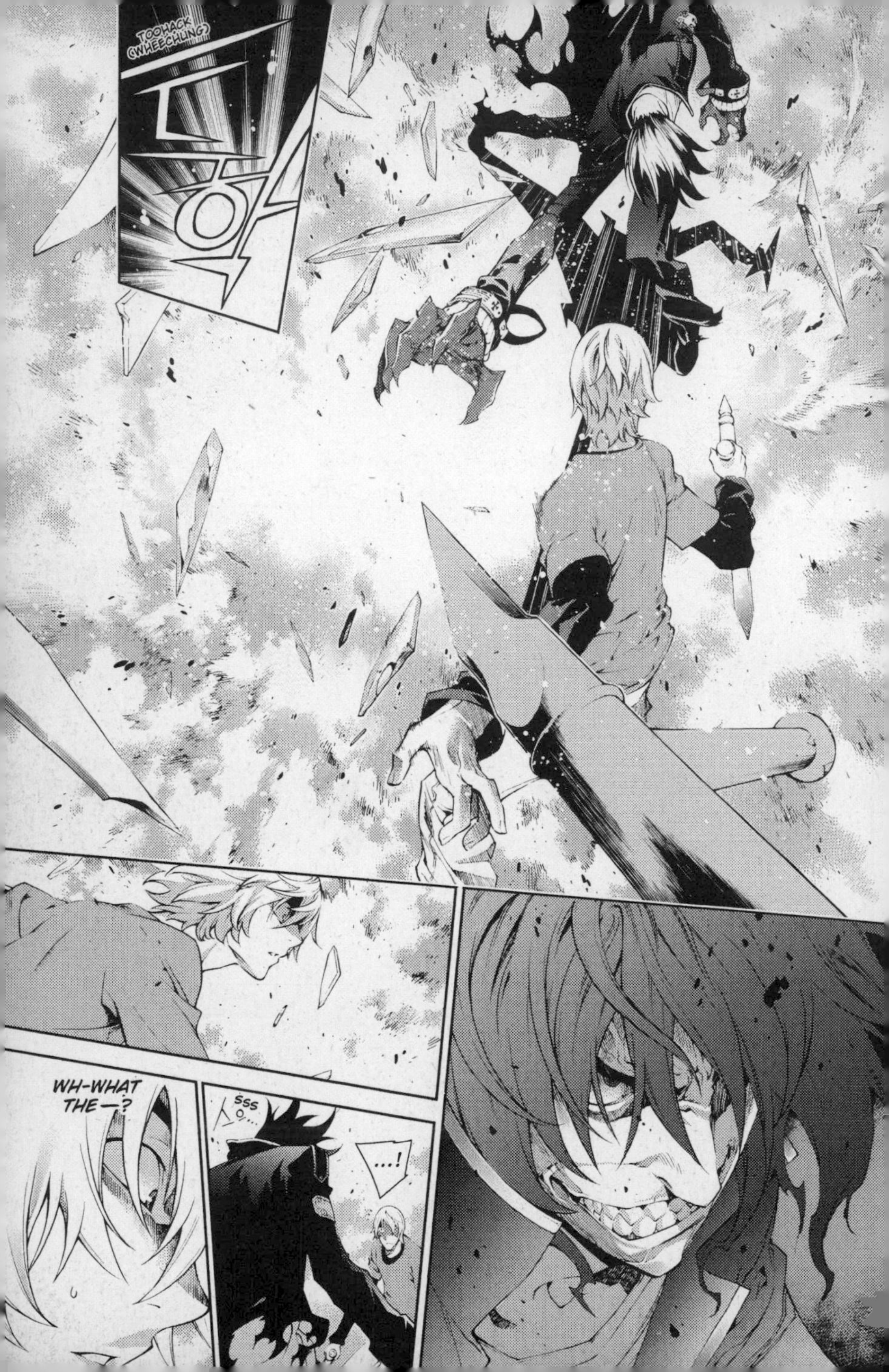
TOOHACK (WHEECHLING)
WH-WHAT THE—?
SSS...
...!

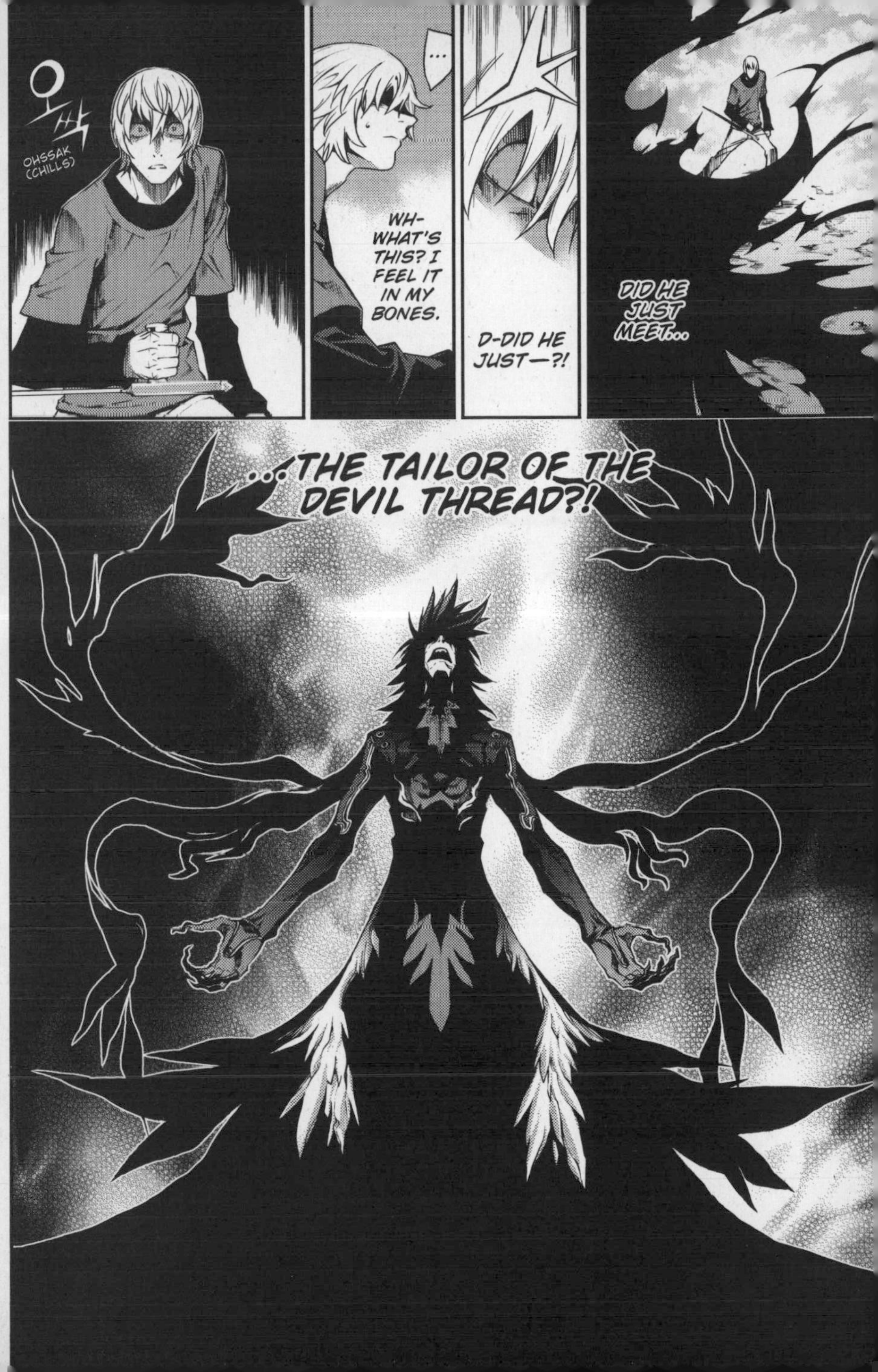

오싹
OHSSAK (CHILLS)
...
WH- WHAT'S THIS? I FEEL IT IN MY BONES.
D-DID HE JUST—?!
DID HE JUST MEET...
...THE TAILOR OF THE DEVIL THREAD?!

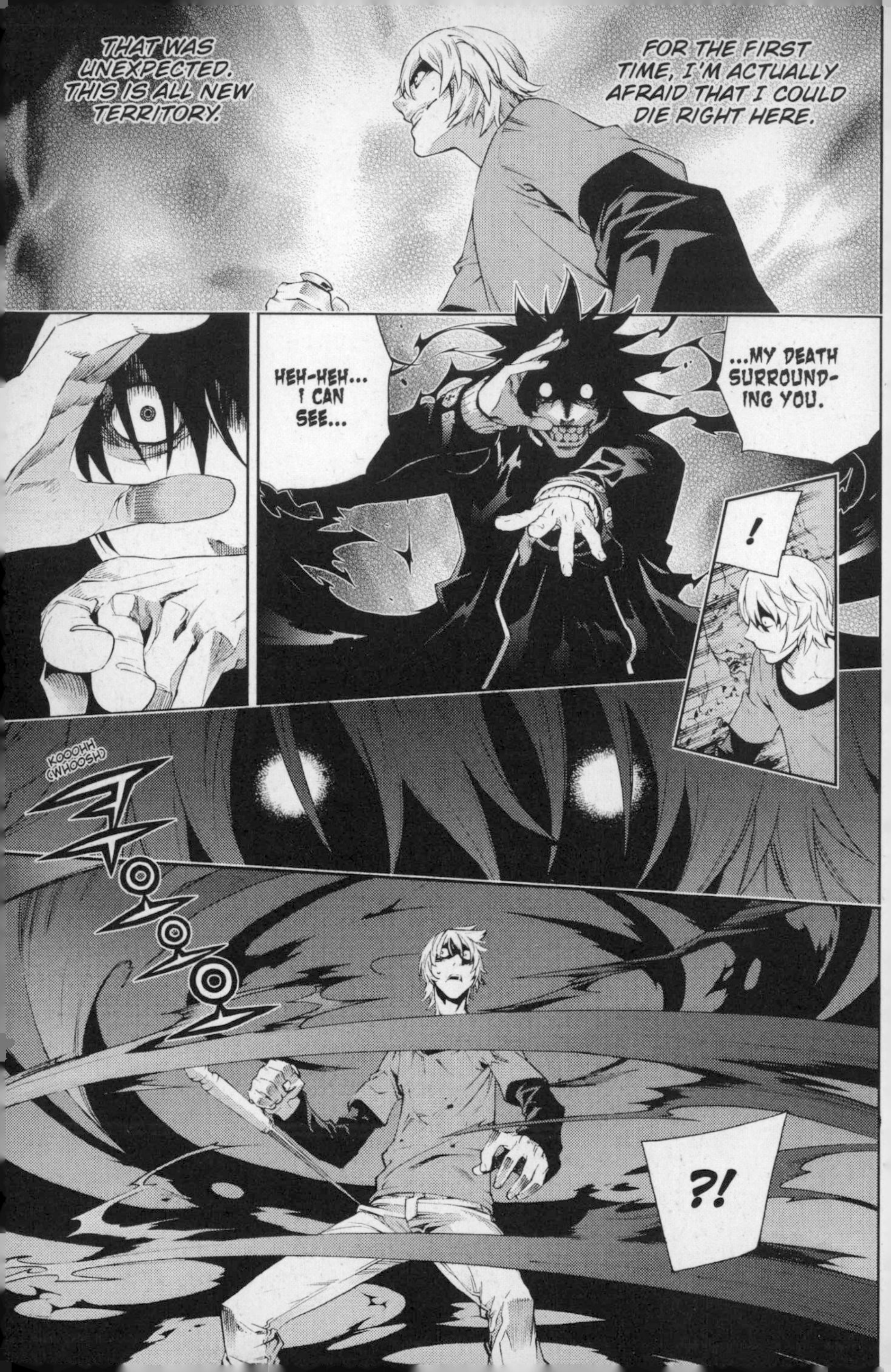
THAT WAS UNEXPECTED. THIS IS ALL NEW TERRITORY.
FOR THE FIRST TIME, I'M ACTUALLY AFRAID THAT I COULD DIE RIGHT HERE.
HEH-HEH... I CAN SEE...
...MY DEATH SURROUNDING YOU.
!
KOOOHH (WHOOSH)
?!

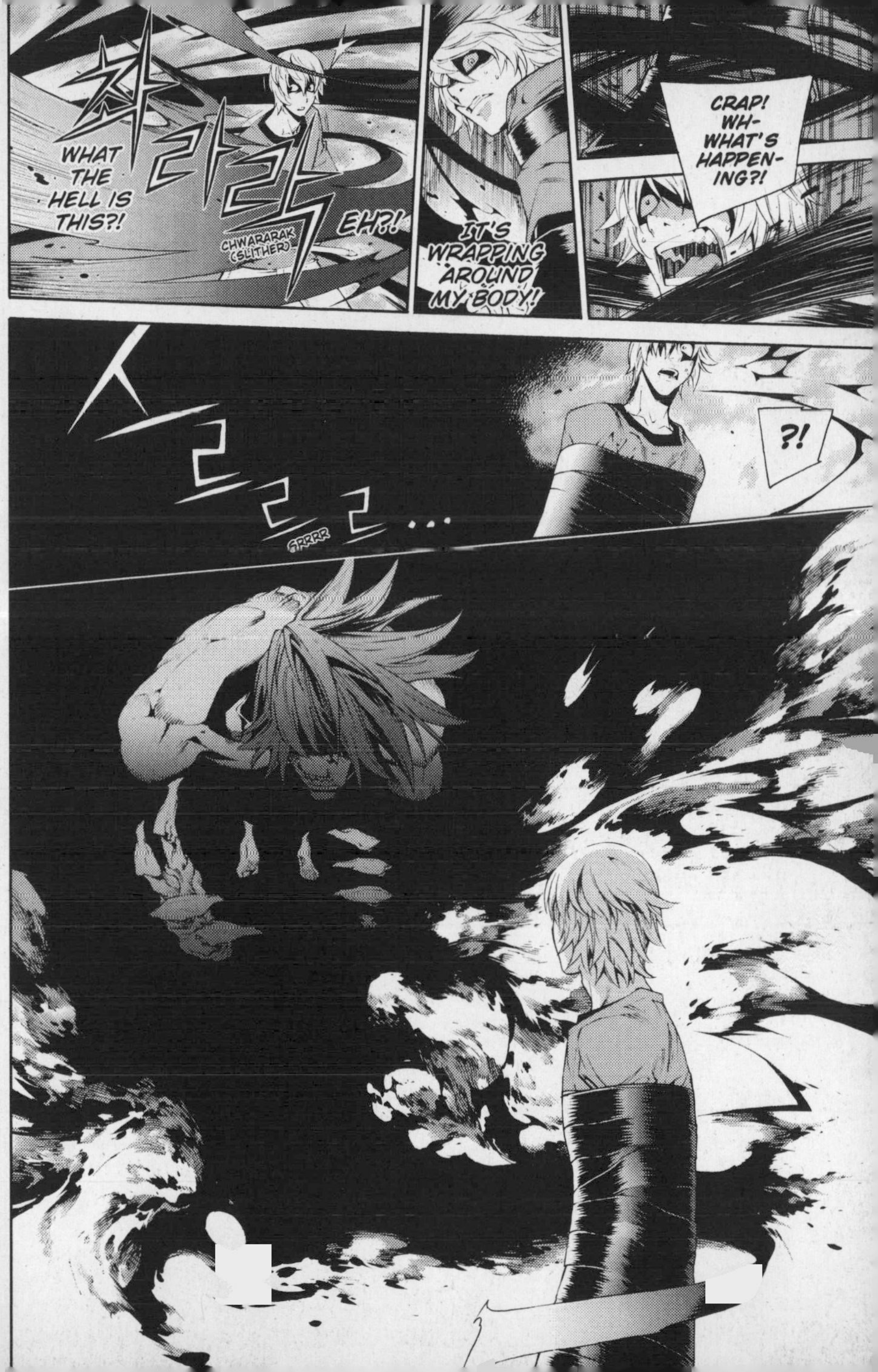
WHAT THE HELL IS THIS?!
CHWARARAK (SLITHER)
EH?!
IT'S WRAPPING AROUND MY BODY!
CRAP! WH-WHAT'S HAPPENING?!
GRRRR
?!

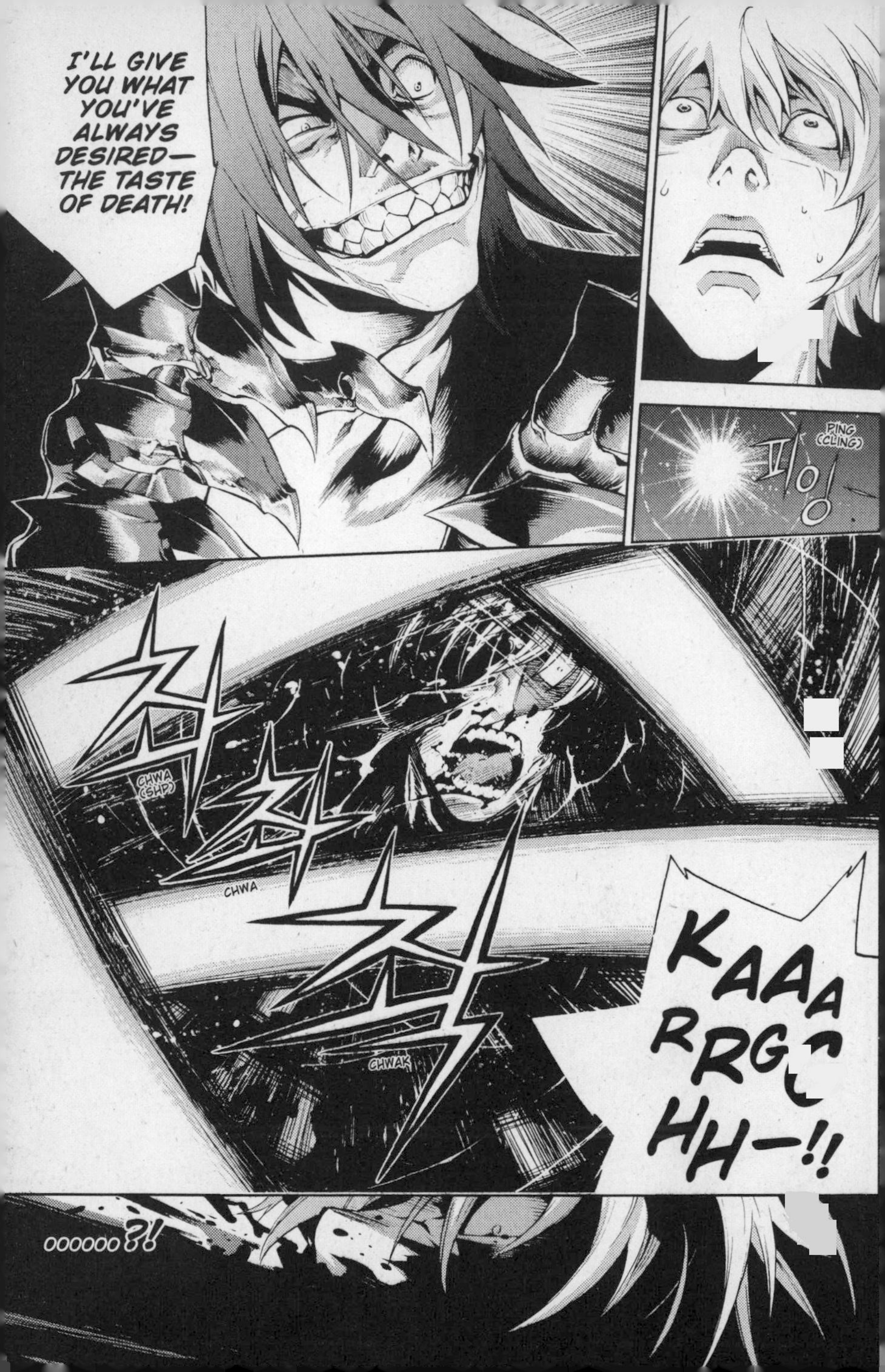
I'LL GIVE YOU WHAT YOU'VE ALWAYS DESIRED—THE TASTE OF DEATH!
PING (CLING)
CHWA (SHP)
CHWA
CHWAK
KAAARRRGHHH—!!
OOOOOO?!

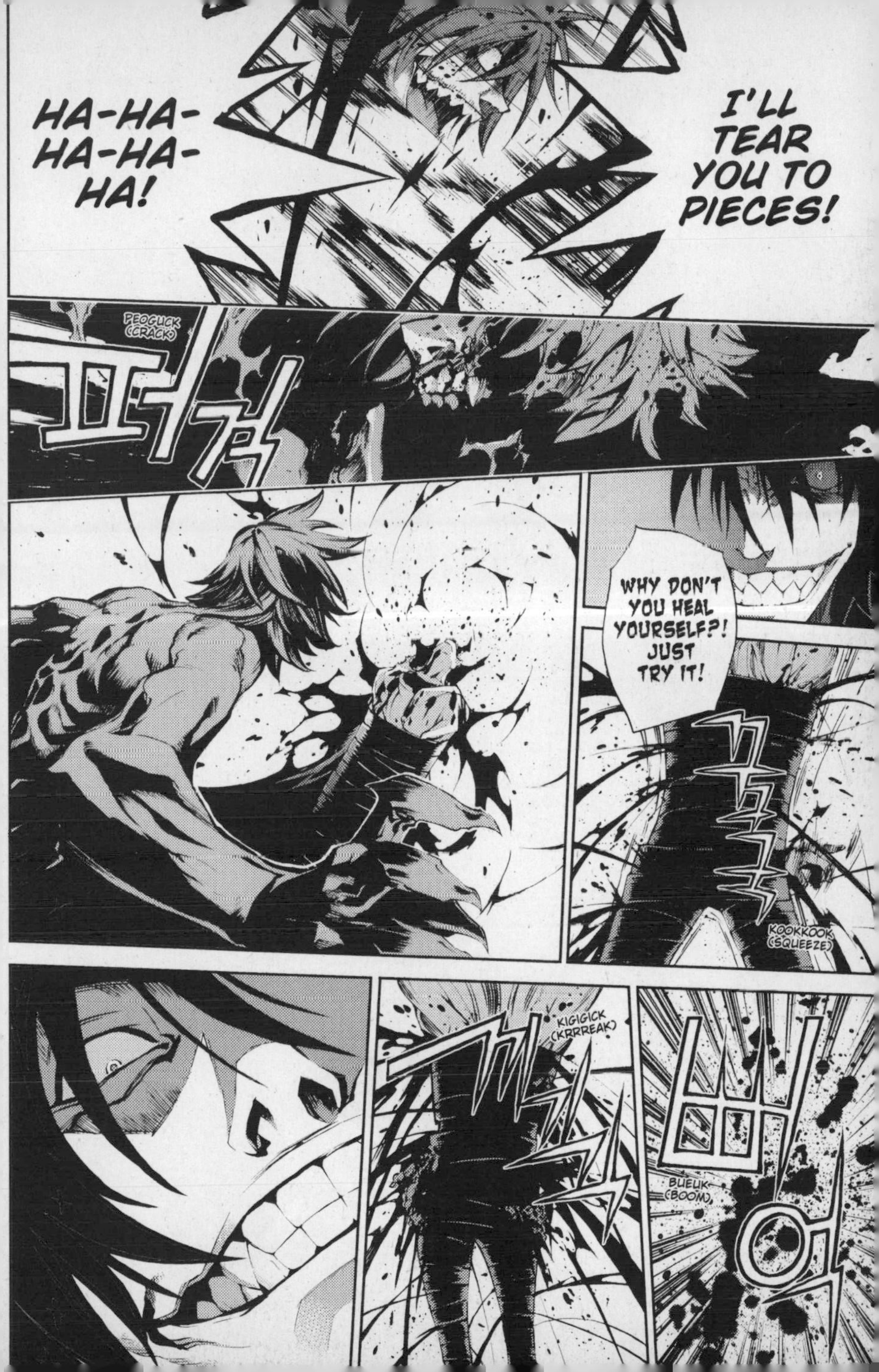
HA-HA-HA-HA-HA!
I'LL TEAR YOU TO PIECES!
PEOGUCK (CRACK)
WHY DON'T YOU HEAL YOURSELF?! JUST TRY IT!
KOOKKOOK (SQUEEZE)
KIGIGICK (KRRREAK)
BUEUK (BOOM)

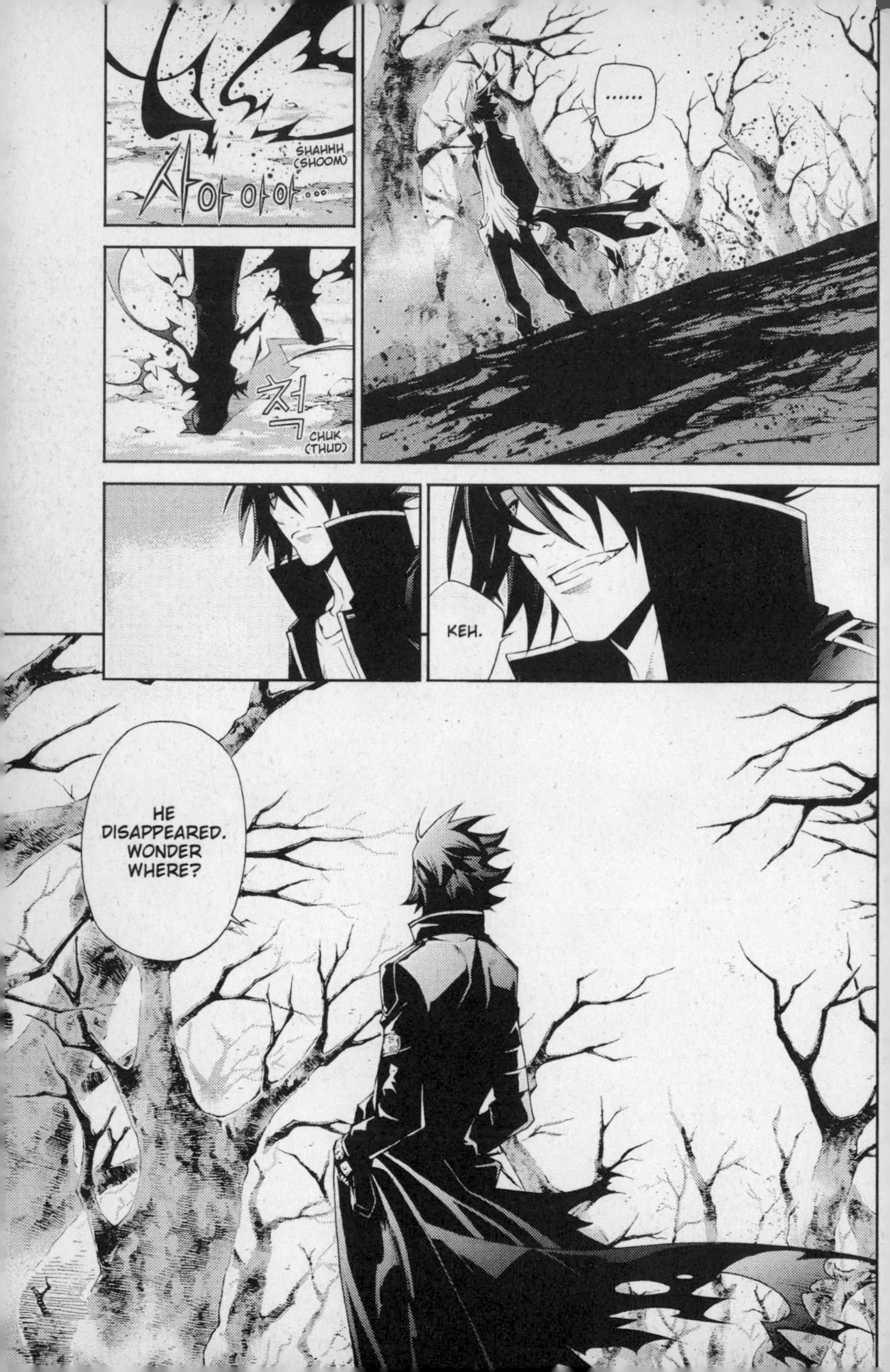
SHAHHH (SHOOM)
샤아아 아아...
척
CHUK (THUD)
......
KEH.
HE DISAPPEARED. WONDER WHERE?

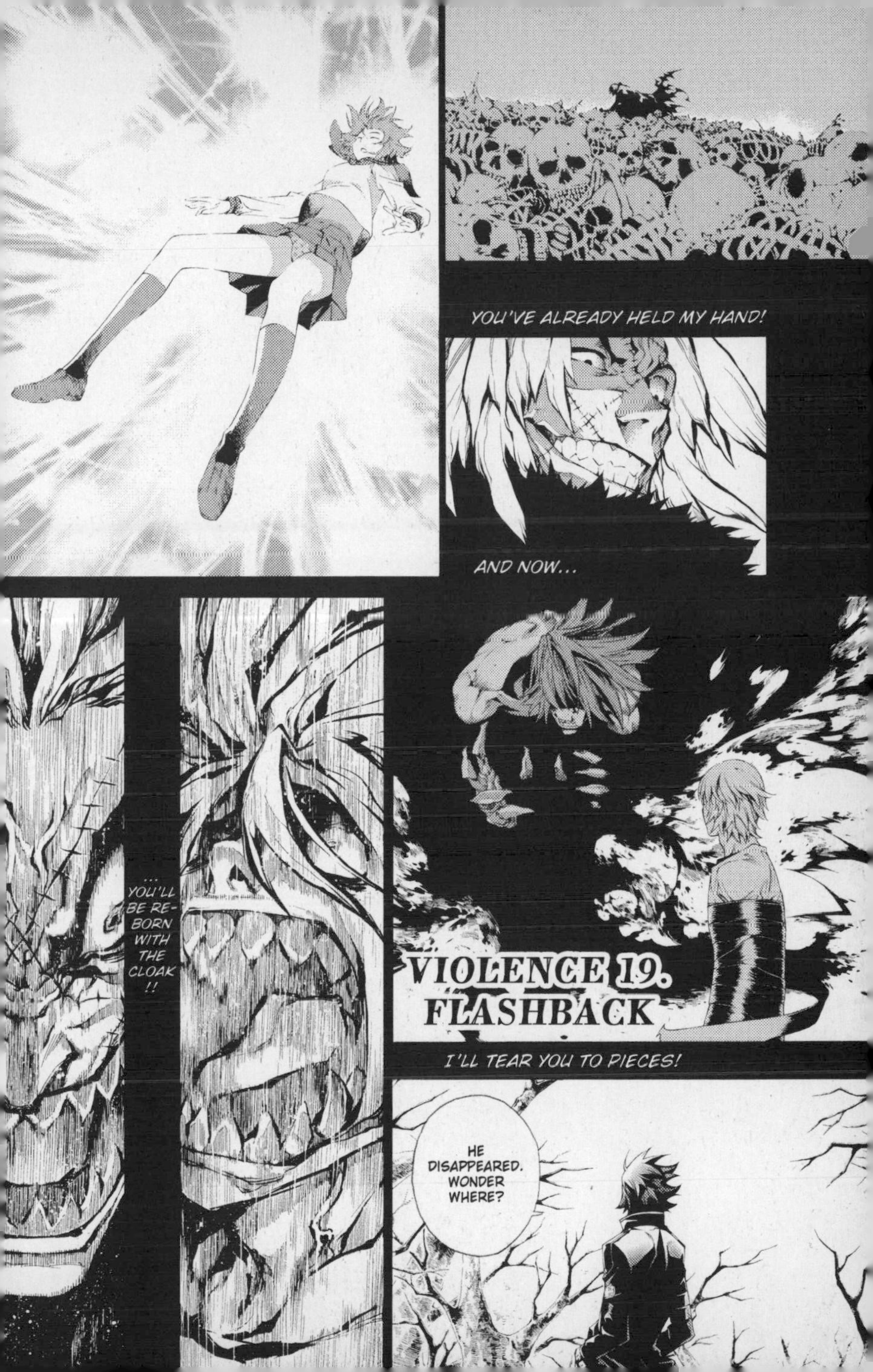
YOU'VE ALREADY HELD MY HAND!
AND NOW...
...YOU'LL BE RE-BORN WITH THE CLOAK!!
VIOLENCE 19. FLASHBACK
I'LL TEAR YOU TO PIECES!
HE DISAPPEARED. WONDER WHERE?

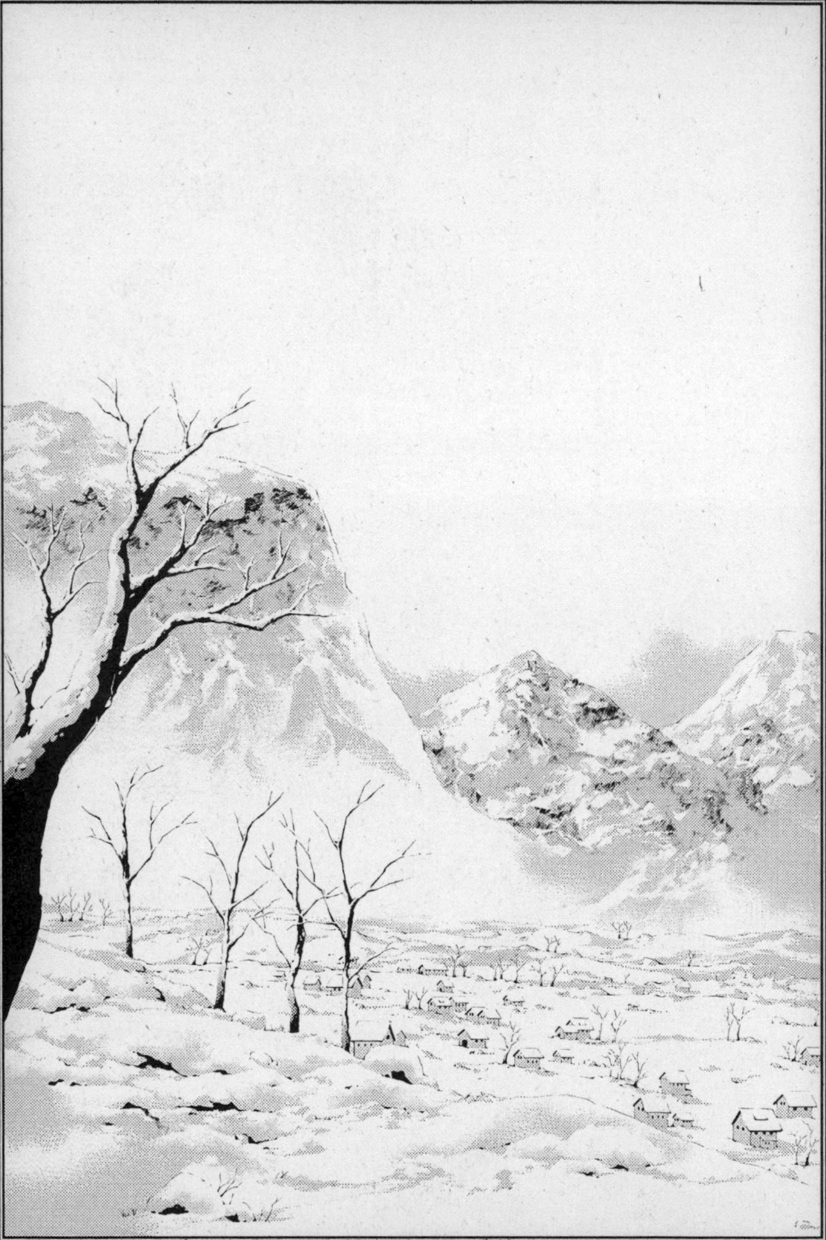

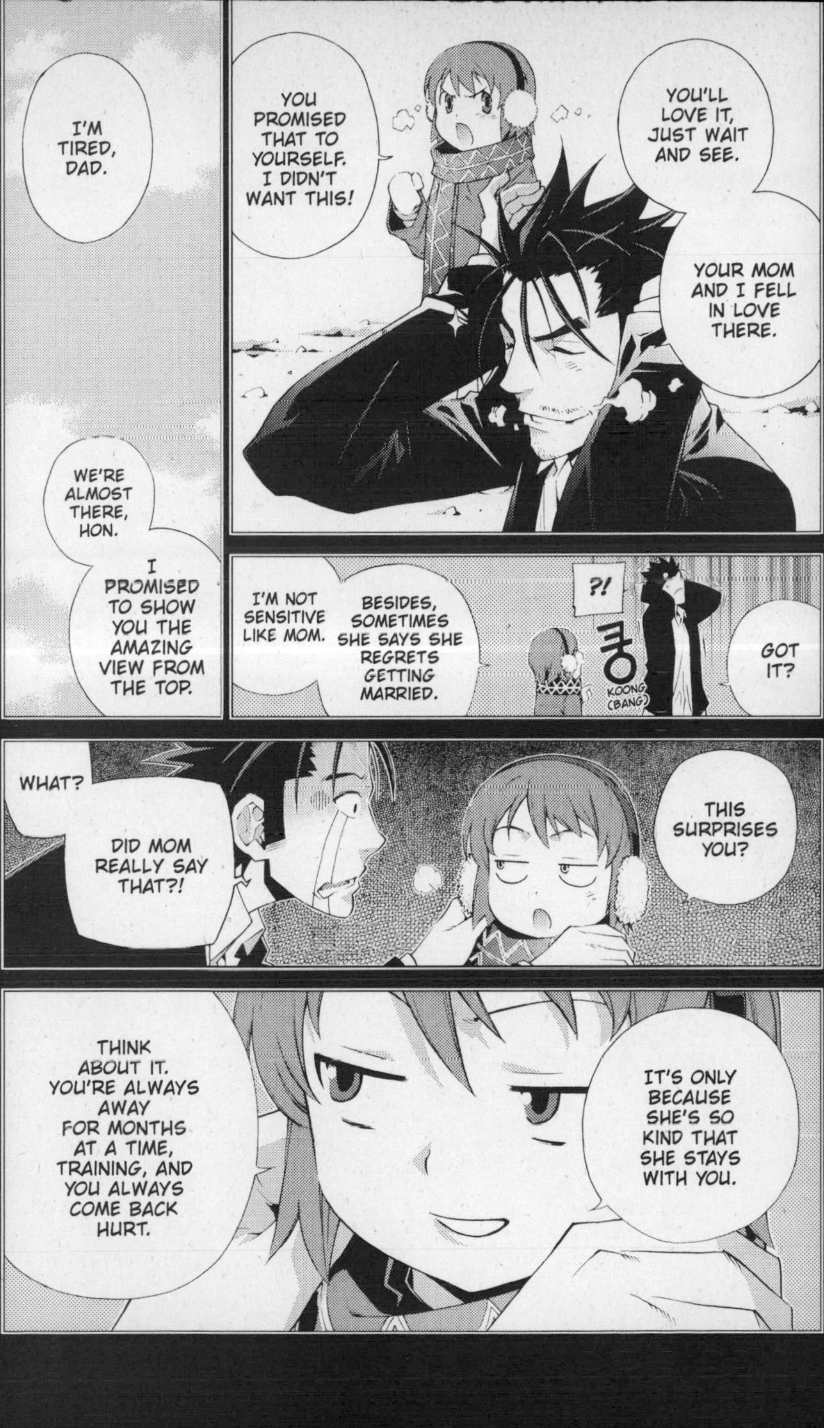
I'M TIRED, DAD.
WE'RE ALMOST THERE, HON.
I PROMISED TO SHOW YOU THE AMAZING VIEW FROM THE TOP.
YOU PROMISED THAT TO YOURSELF. I DIDN'T WANT THIS!
YOU'LL LOVE IT, JUST WAIT AND SEE.
YOUR MOM AND I FELL IN LOVE THERE.
I'M NOT SENSITIVE LIKE MOM.
BESIDES, SOMETIMES SHE SAYS SHE REGRETS GETTING MARRIED.
?!
쿵
KOONG (BANG)
GOT IT?
WHAT?
DID MOM REALLY SAY THAT?!
THIS SURPRISES YOU?
THINK ABOUT IT. YOU'RE ALWAYS AWAY FOR MONTHS AT A TIME, TRAINING, AND YOU ALWAYS COME BACK HURT.
IT'S ONLY BECAUSE SHE'S SO KIND THAT SHE STAYS WITH YOU.

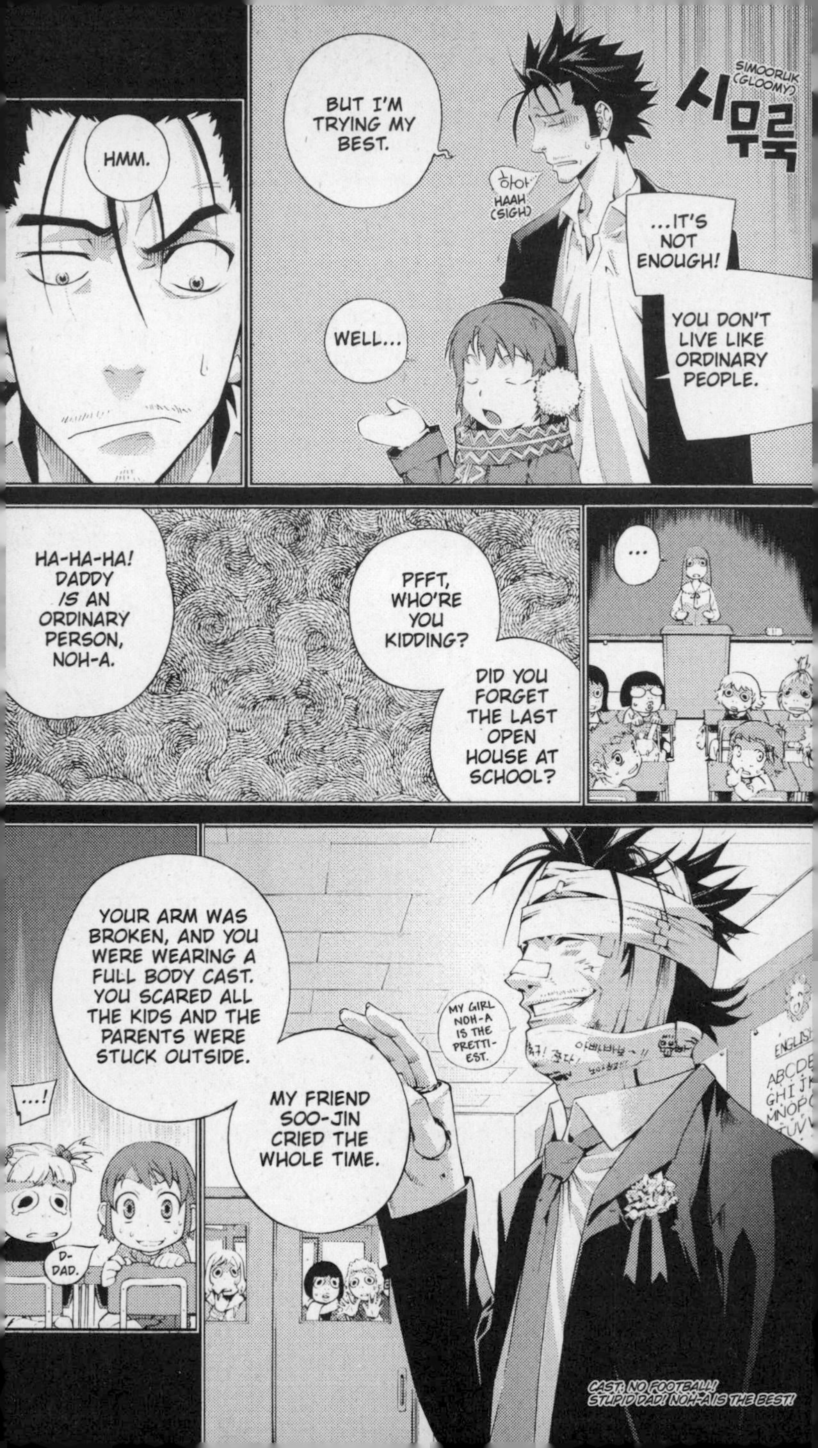
HMM.
BUT I'M TRYING MY BEST.
시무룩
SIMOORUK (GLOOMY)
하아
HAAH (SIGH)
...IT'S NOT ENOUGH!
WELL...
YOU DON'T LIVE LIKE ORDINARY PEOPLE.
HA-HA-HA! DADDY IS AN ORDINARY PERSON, NOH-A.
PFFT, WHO'RE YOU KIDDING?
DID YOU FORGET THE LAST OPEN HOUSE AT SCHOOL?
...
YOUR ARM WAS BROKEN, AND YOU WERE WEARING A FULL BODY CAST. YOU SCARED ALL THE KIDS AND THE PARENTS WERE STUCK OUTSIDE.
MY FRIEND SOO-JIN CRIED THE WHOLE TIME.
...!
D-DAD.
MY GIRL NOH-A IS THE PRETTI-EST.
CAST: NO FOOTBALL!
STUPID DAD! NOH-A IS THE BEST!

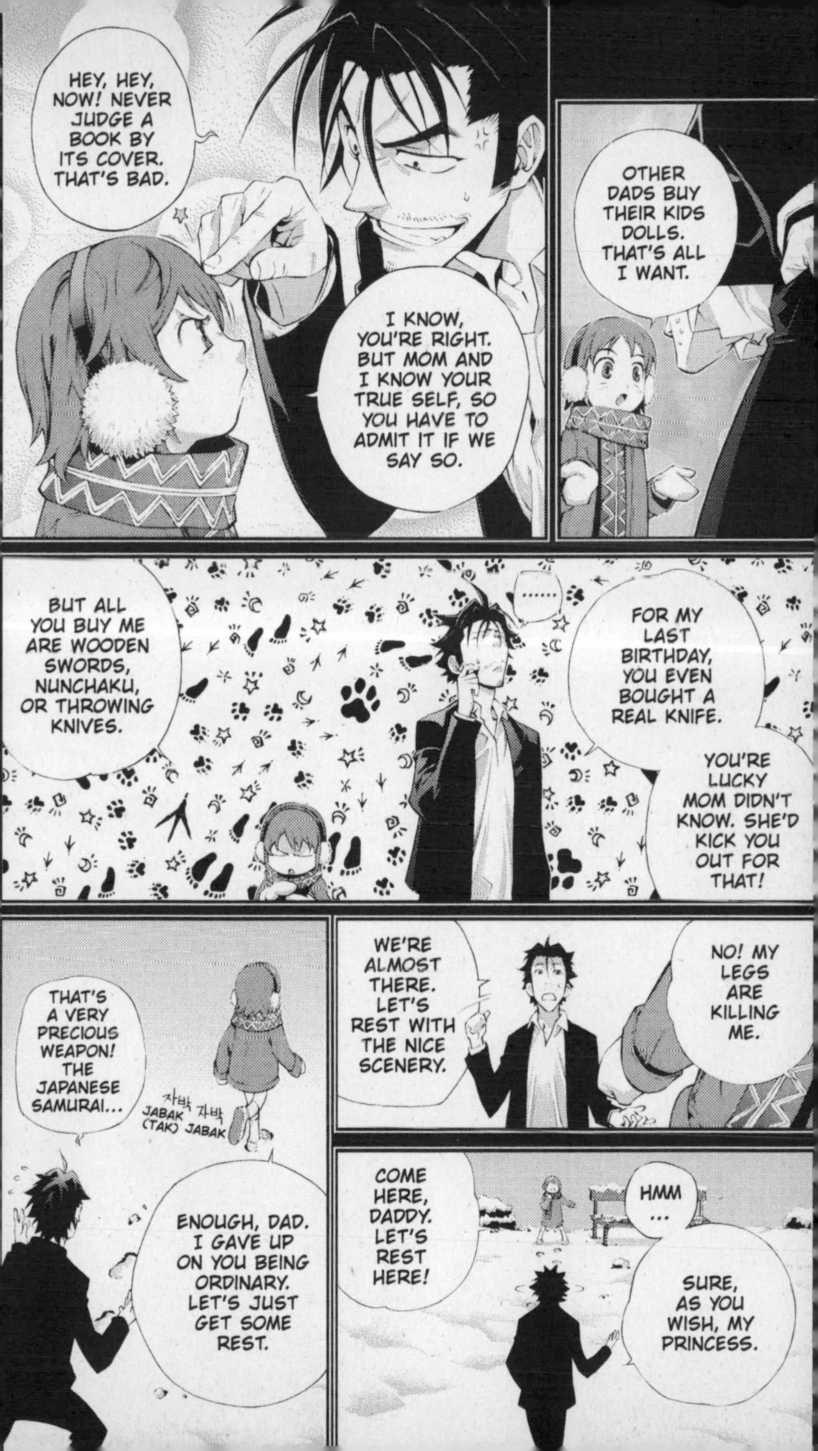

HEY, HEY, NOW! NEVER JUDGE A BOOK BY ITS COVER. THAT'S BAD.
I KNOW, YOU'RE RIGHT. BUT MOM AND I KNOW YOUR TRUE SELF, SO YOU HAVE TO ADMIT IT IF WE SAY SO.
OTHER DADS BUY THEIR KIDS DOLLS. THAT'S ALL I WANT.
BUT ALL YOU BUY ME ARE WOODEN SWORDS, NUNCHAKU, OR THROWING KNIVES.
....
FOR MY LAST BIRTHDAY, YOU EVEN BOUGHT A REAL KNIFE.
YOU'RE LUCKY MOM DIDN'T KNOW. SHE'D KICK YOU OUT FOR THAT!
THAT'S A VERY PRECIOUS WEAPON! THE JAPANESE SAMURAI...
자박 자박
JABAK (TAK) JABAK
ENOUGH, DAD. I GAVE UP ON YOU BEING ORDINARY. LET'S JUST GET SOME REST.
WE'RE ALMOST THERE. LET'S REST WITH THE NICE SCENERY.
NO! MY LEGS ARE KILLING ME.
COME HERE, DADDY. LET'S REST HERE!
HMM ...
SURE, AS YOU WISH, MY PRINCESS.

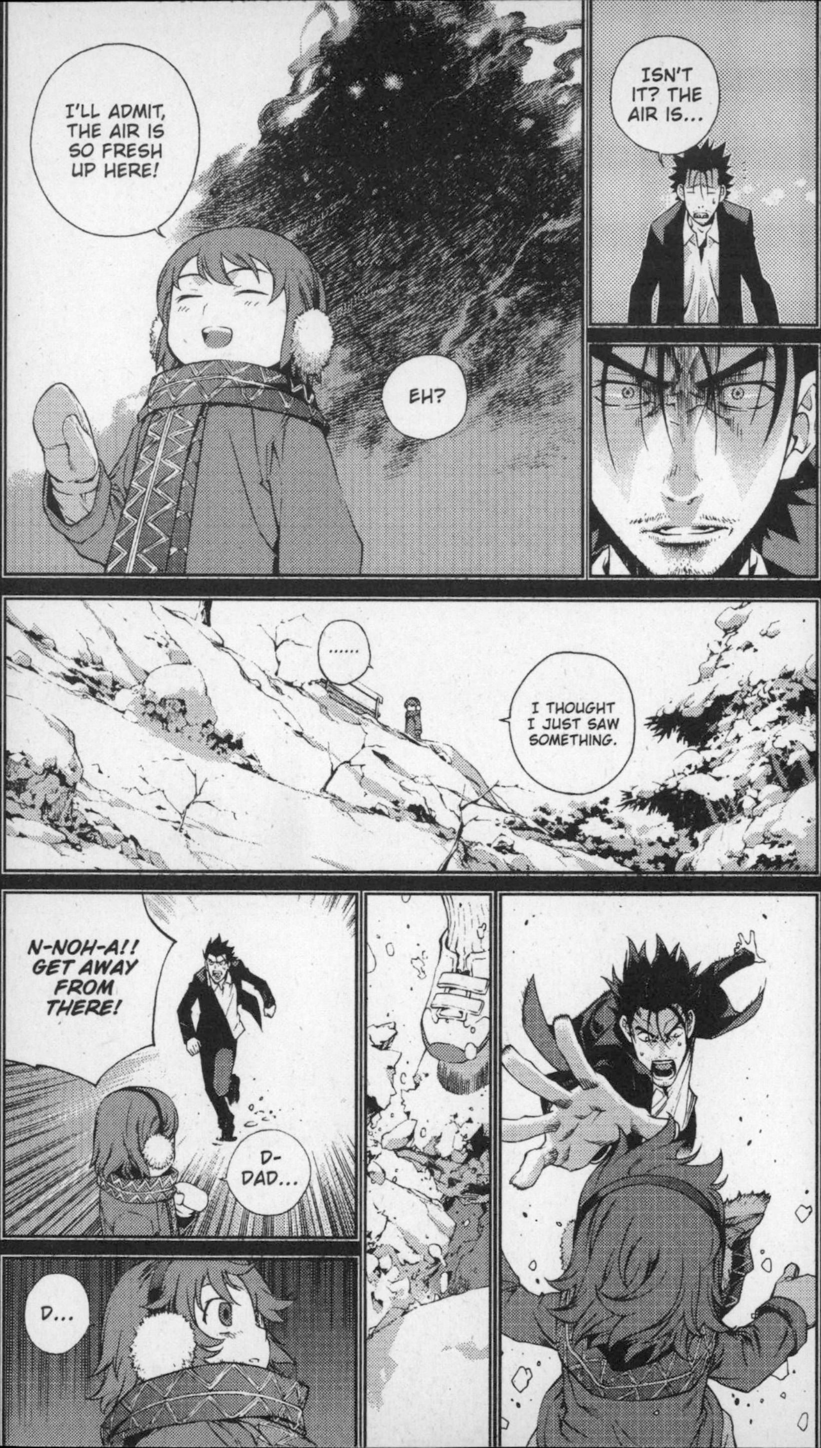
I'LL ADMIT, THE AIR IS SO FRESH UP HERE!
EH?
ISN'T IT? THE AIR IS...
......
I THOUGHT I JUST SAW SOMETHING.
N-NOH-A!! GET AWAY FROM THERE!
D-DAD...
D...

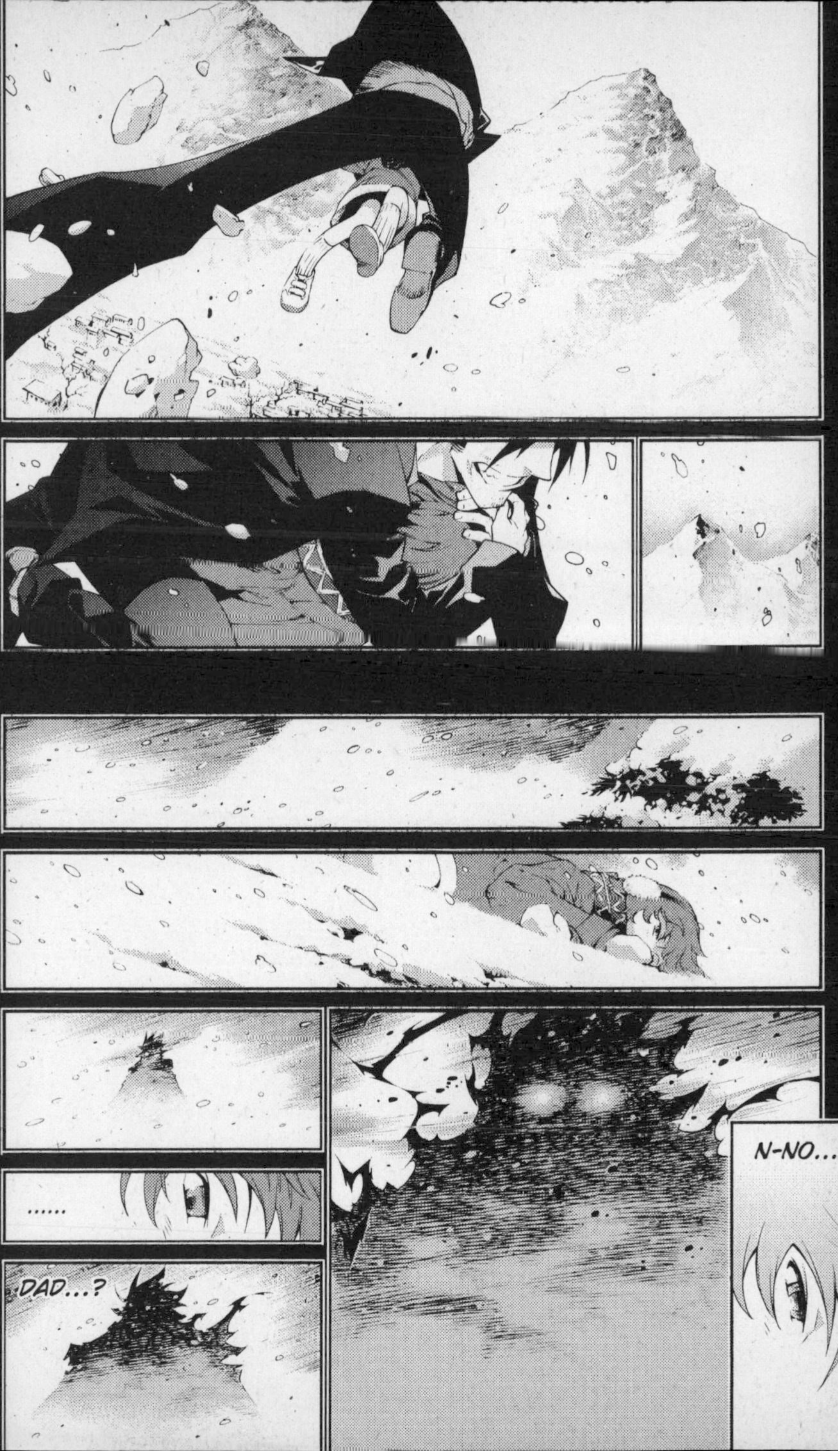
......
DAD...?
N-NO...

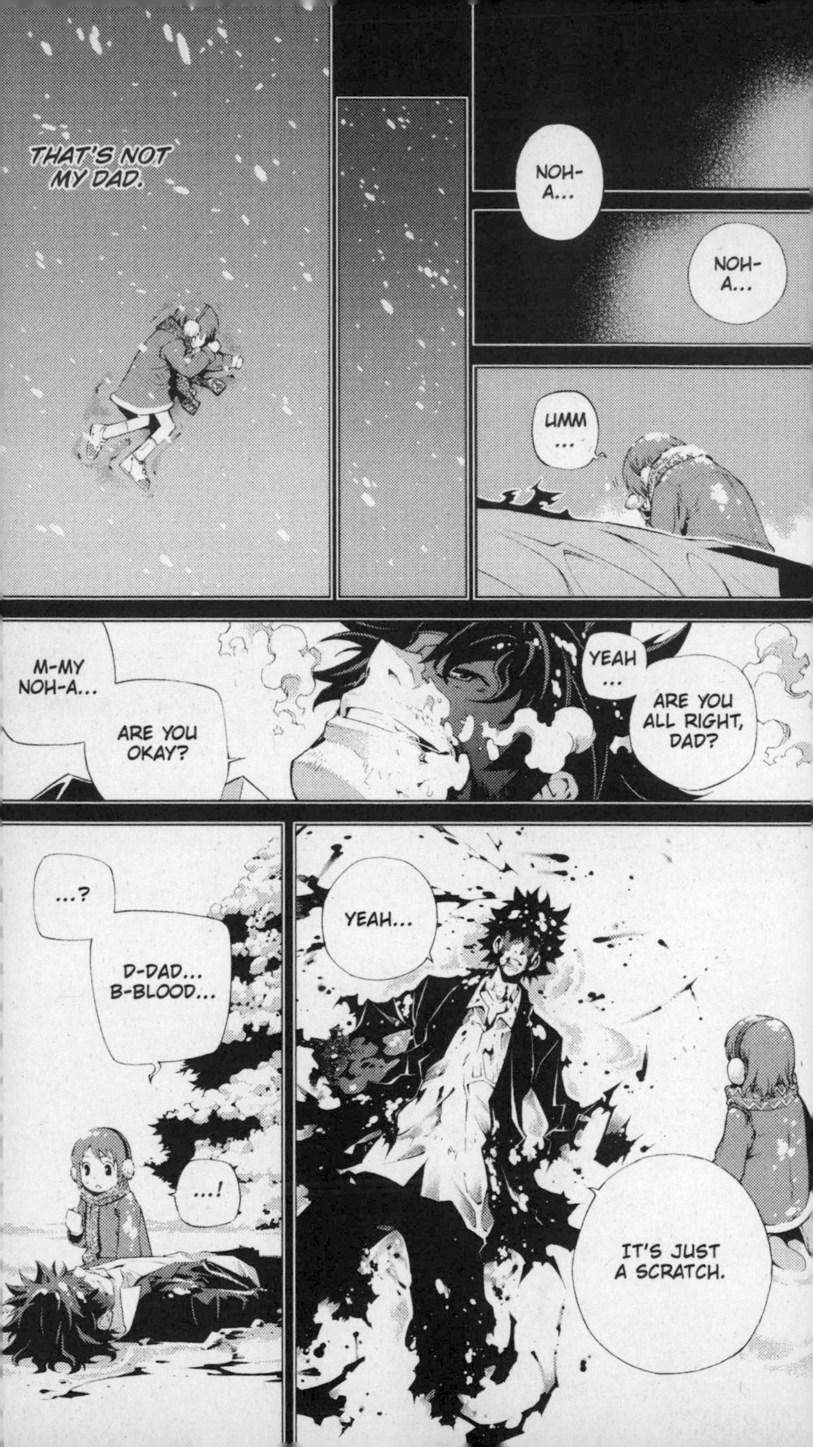
THAT'S NOT MY DAD.
NOH-A...
NOH-A...
UMM...
M-MY NOH-A...
ARE YOU OKAY?
YEAH...
ARE YOU ALL RIGHT, DAD?
...?
D-DAD... B-BLOOD...
...!
YEAH...
IT'S JUST A SCRATCH.

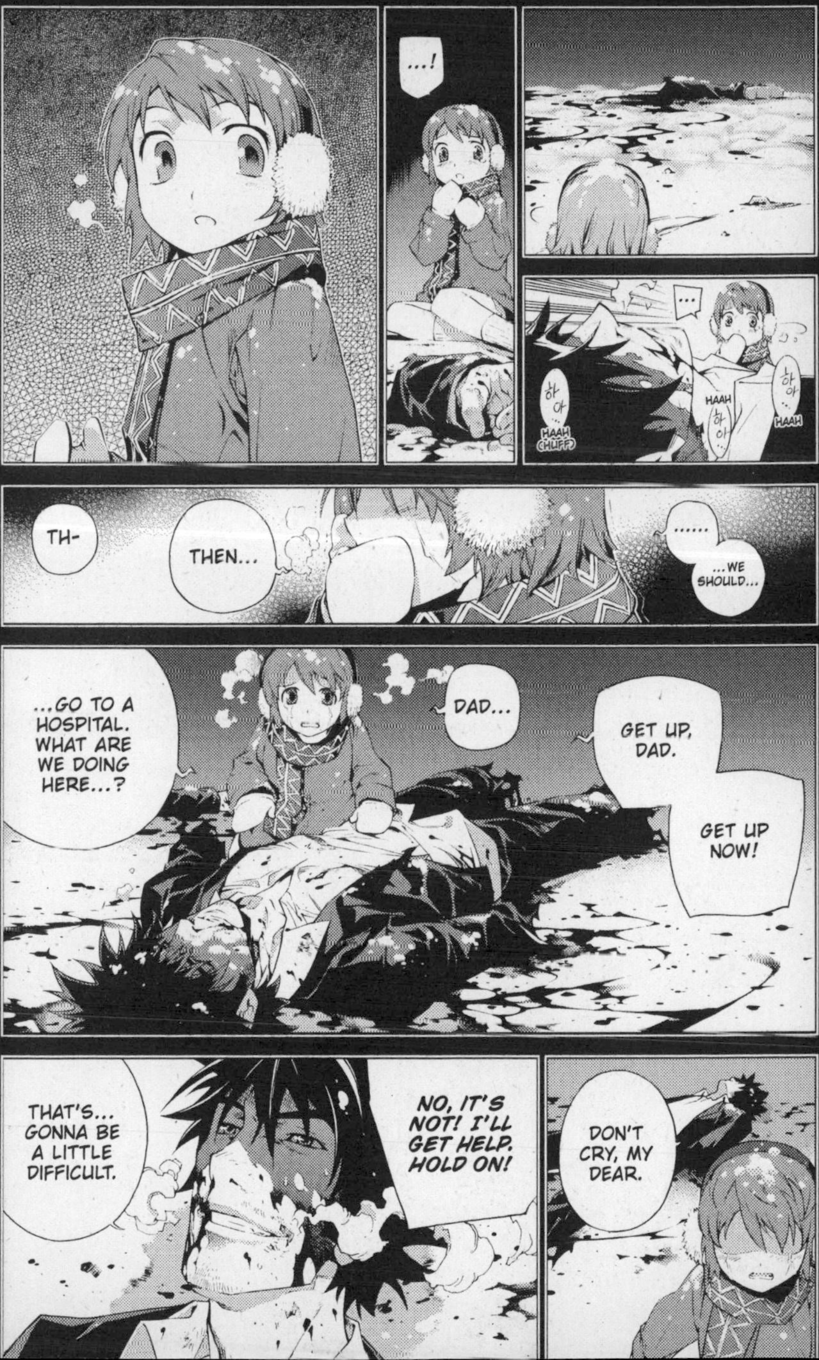
...!
...
하아...
HAAH (HUFF)
HAAH
하아...
하아...
HAAH
TH-
THEN...
......
...WE SHOULD...
...GO TO A HOSPITAL. WHAT ARE WE DOING HERE...?
DAD...
GET UP, DAD.
GET UP NOW!
THAT'S... GONNA BE A LITTLE DIFFICULT.
NO, IT'S NOT! I'LL GET HELP. HOLD ON!
DON'T CRY, MY DEAR.

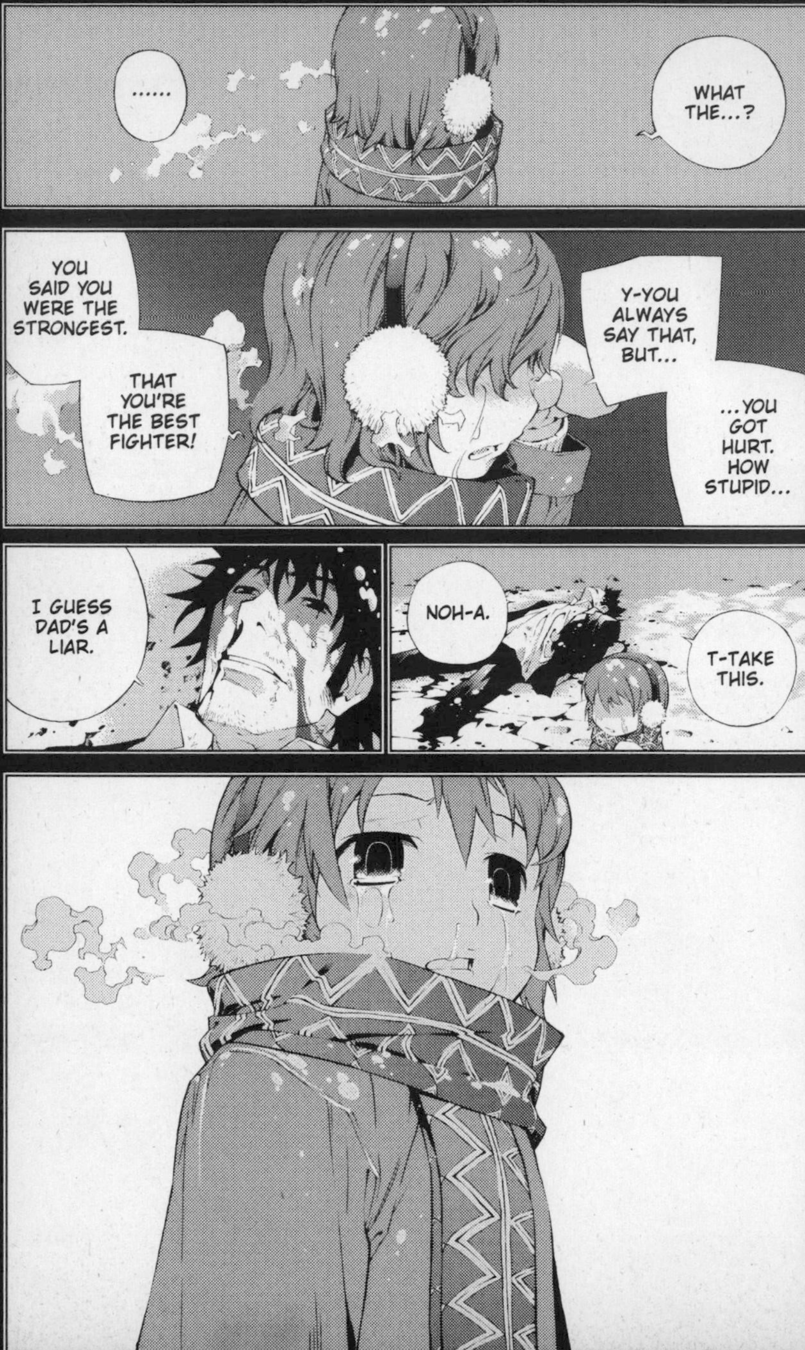
......
WHAT THE...?
YOU SAID YOU WERE THE STRONGEST.
THAT YOU'RE THE BEST FIGHTER!
Y-YOU ALWAYS SAY THAT, BUT...
...YOU GOT HURT. HOW STUPID...
I GUESS DAD'S A LIAR.
NOH-A.
T-TAKE THIS.

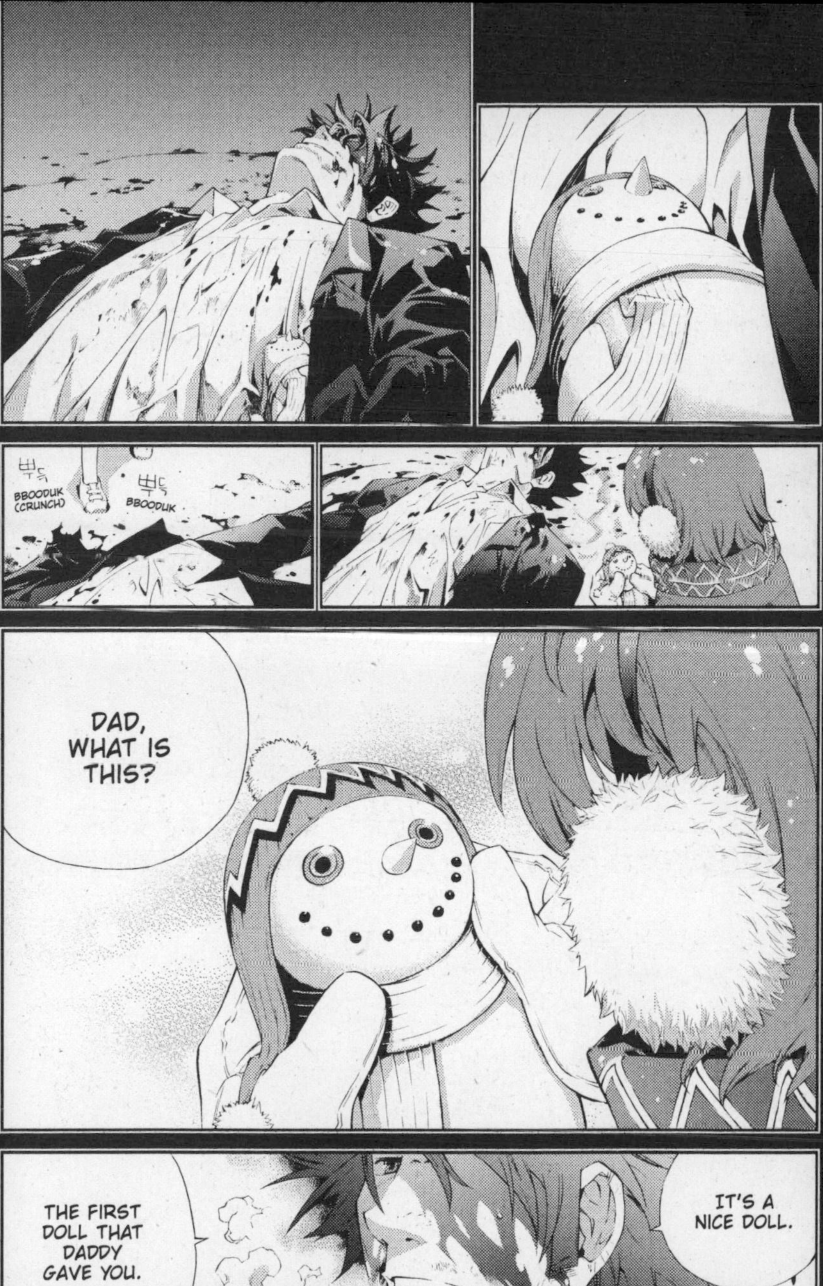
뿌득
BBOODUK (CRUNCH)
뿌득
BBOODUK
DAD, WHAT IS THIS?
THE FIRST DOLL THAT DADDY GAVE YOU.
IT'S A NICE DOLL.

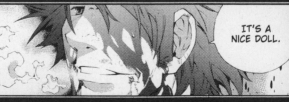

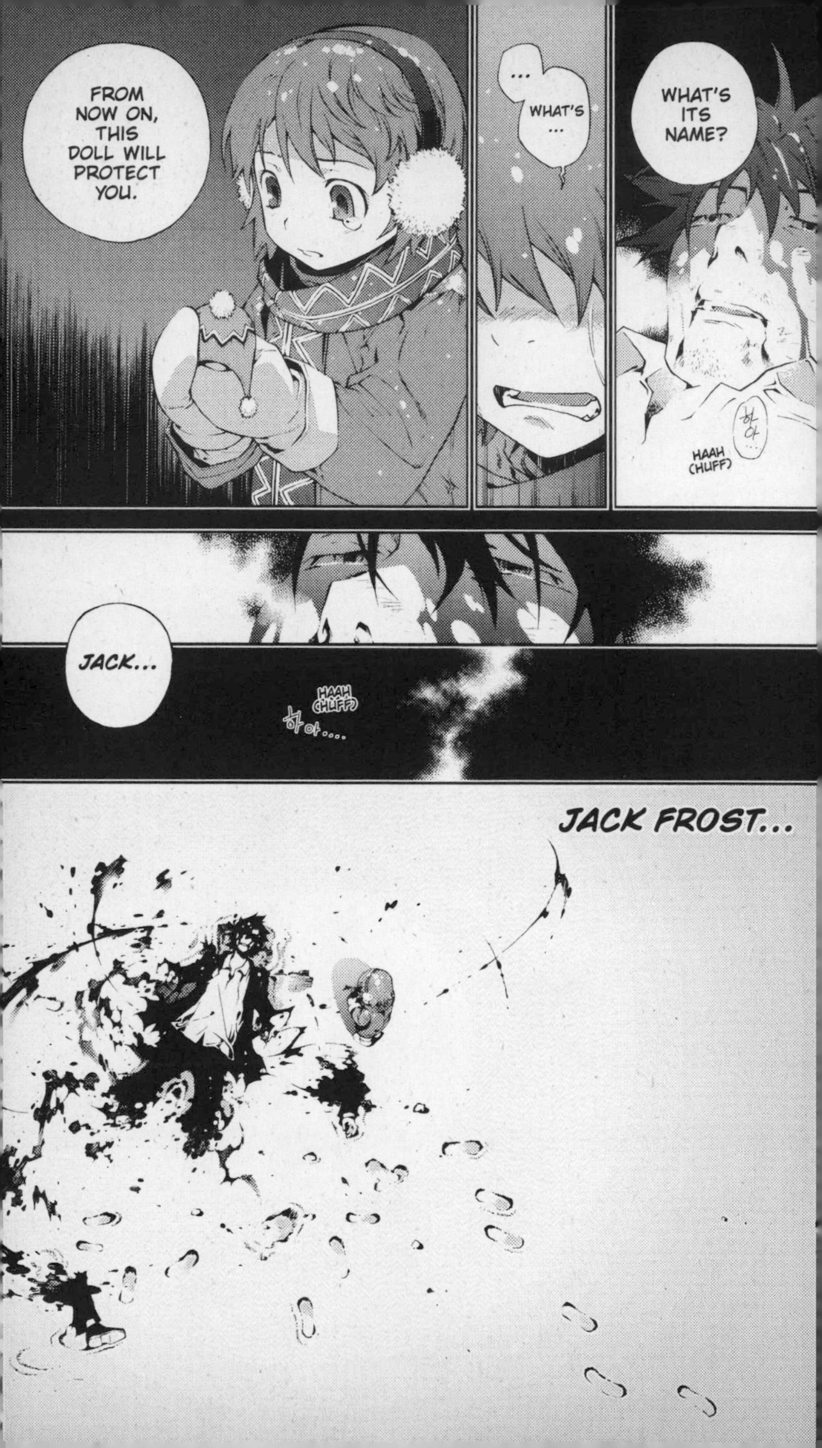
FROM NOW ON, THIS DOLL WILL PROTECT YOU.
... WHAT'S ...
WHAT'S ITS NAME?
하아...
HAAH (HUFF)
JACK...
HAAH (HUFF)
하아....
JACK FROST...

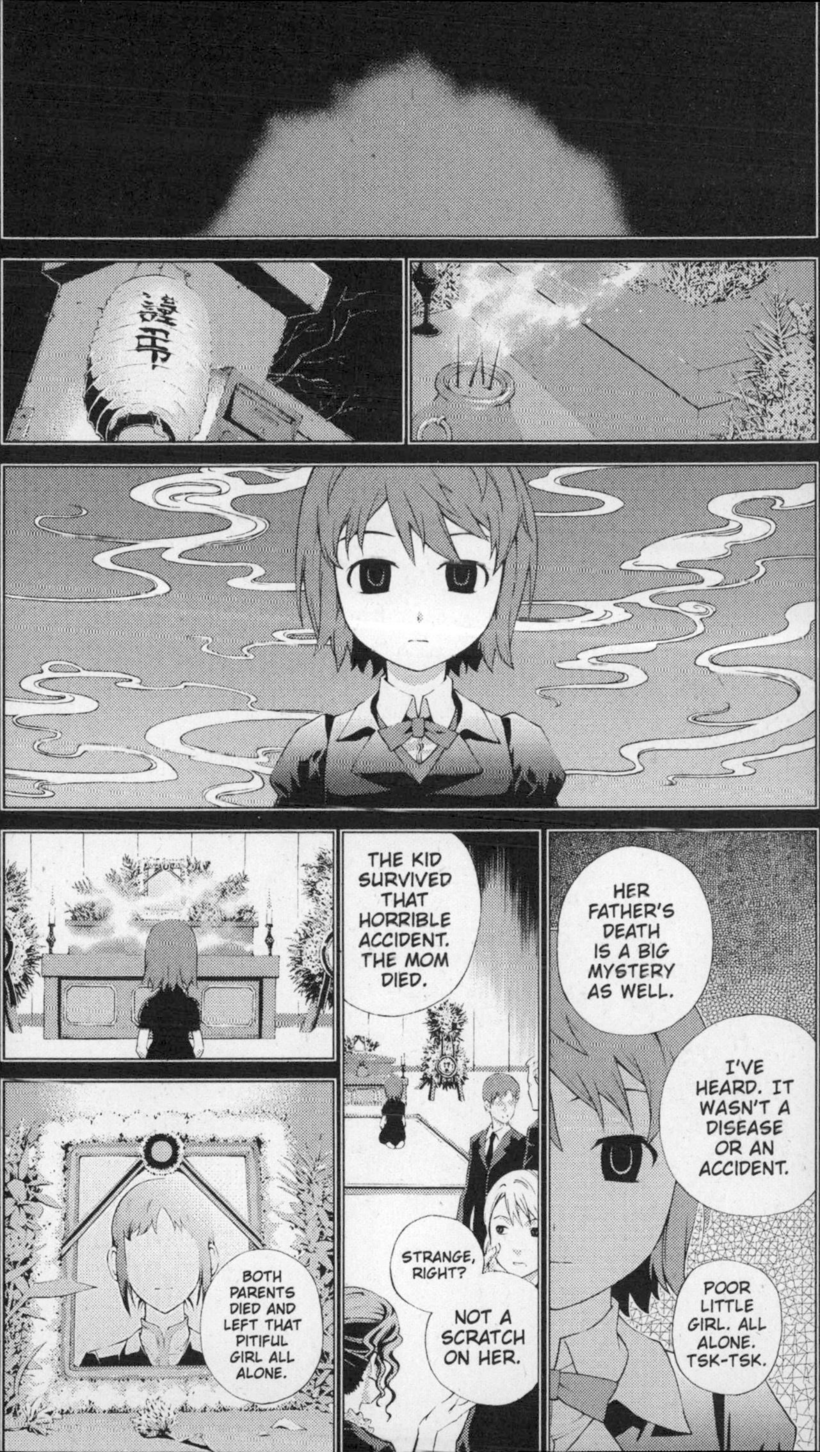
BOTH PARENTS DIED AND LEFT THAT PITIFUL GIRL ALL ALONE.
THE KID SURVIVED THAT HORRIBLE ACCIDENT. THE MOM DIED.
STRANGE, RIGHT?
NOT A SCRATCH ON HER.
HER FATHER'S DEATH IS A BIG MYSTERY AS WELL.
I'VE HEARD. IT WASN'T A DISEASE OR AN ACCIDENT.
POOR LITTLE GIRL. ALL ALONE. TSK-TSK.

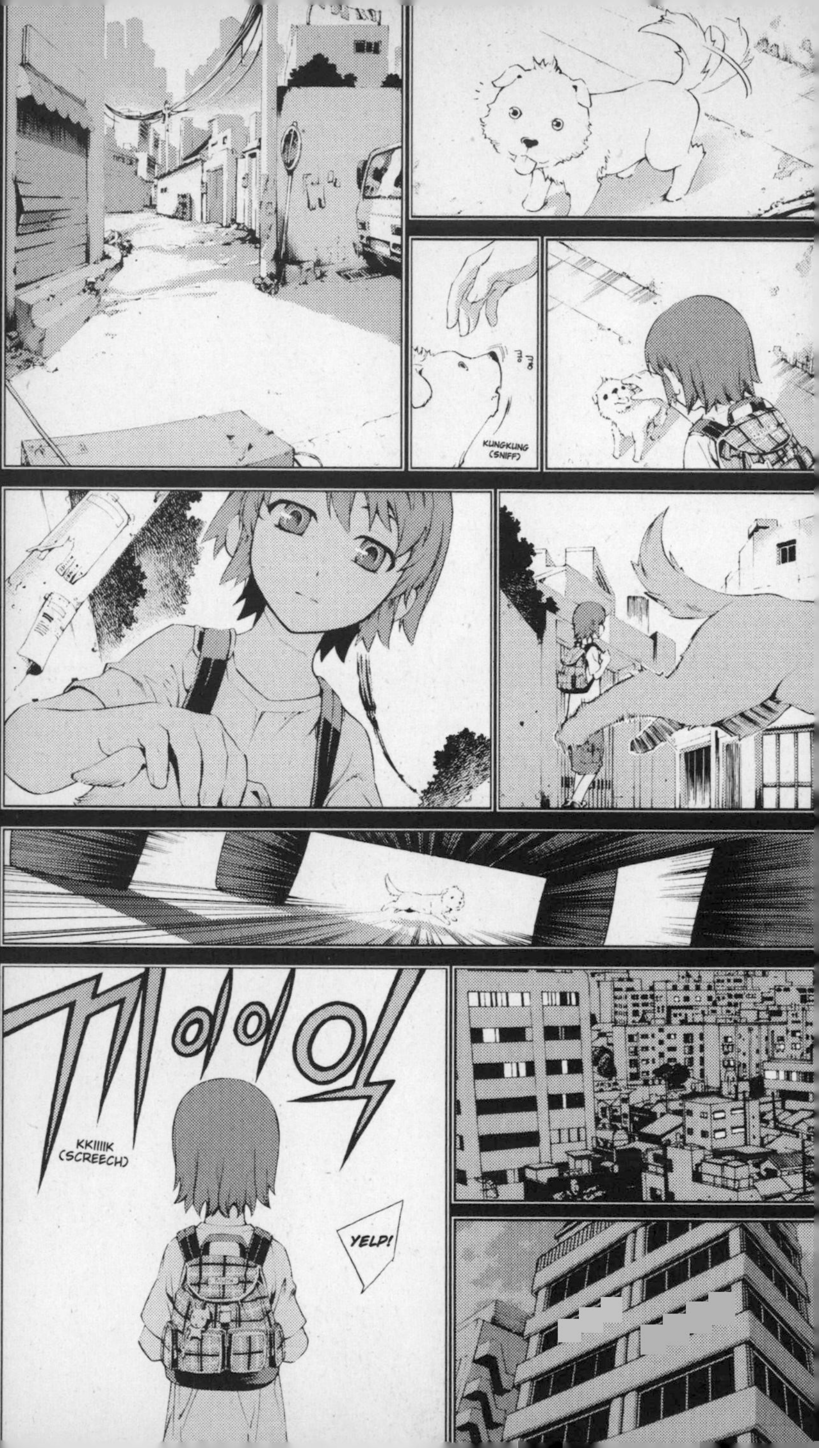
KUNGKUNG
(SNIFF)
끼이이익
KKIIIIK
(SCREECH)
YELP!

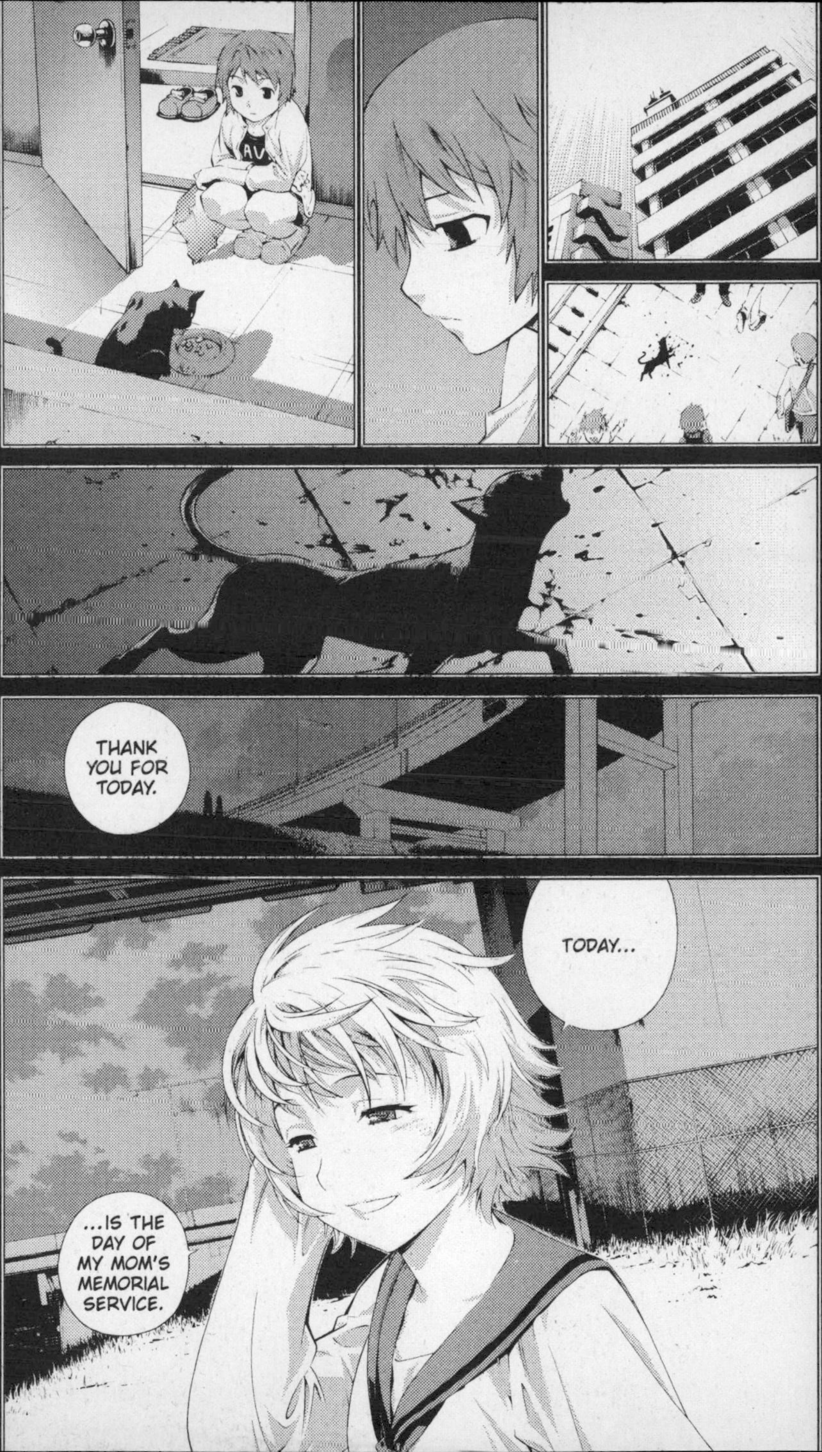
THANK YOU FOR TODAY.
TODAY...
...IS THE DAY OF MY MOM'S MEMORIAL SERVICE.

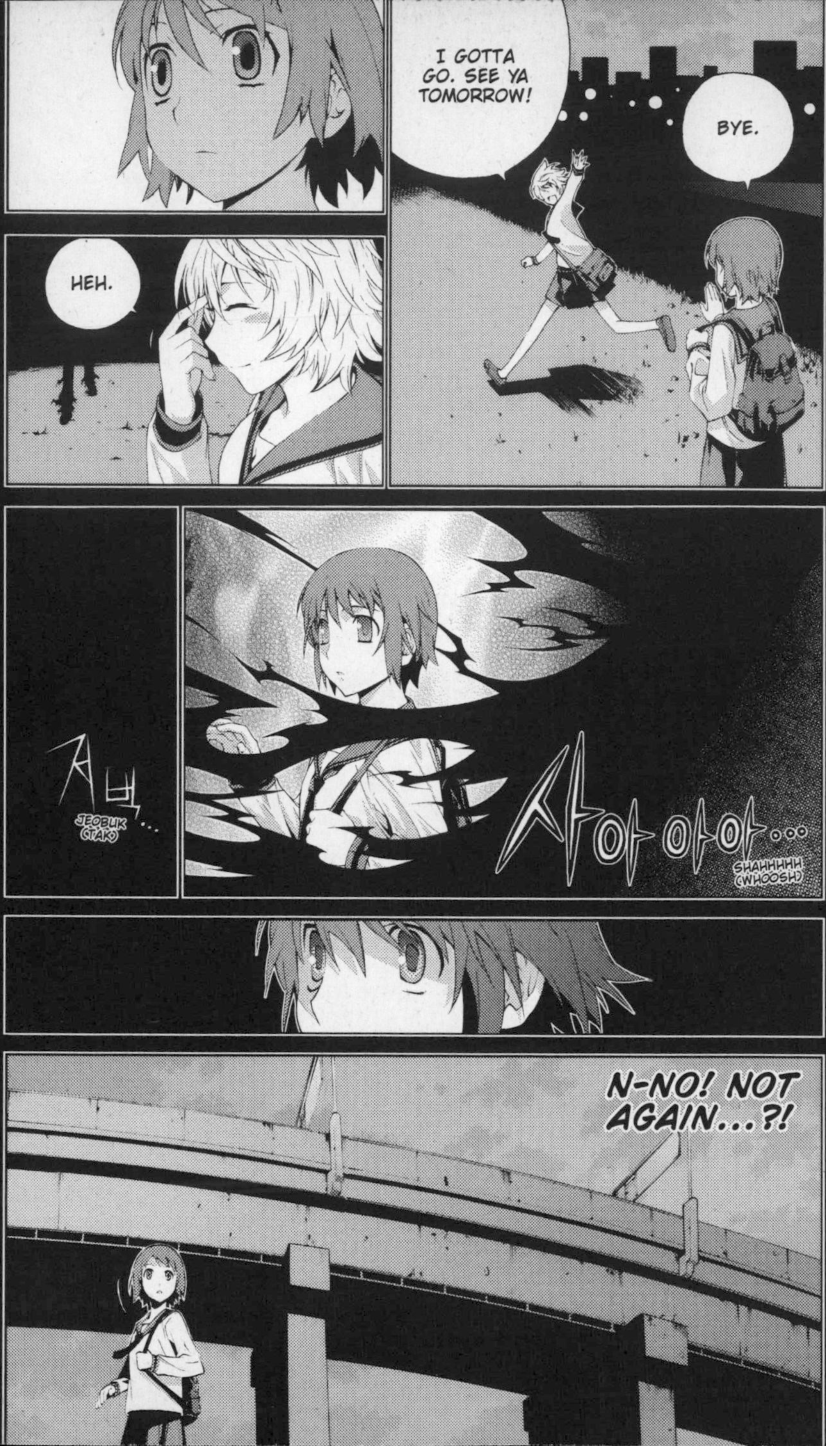
HEH.
I GOTTA GO. SEE YA TOMORROW!
BYE.
저벅...
JEOBUK (TAK)
샤아아아아...
SHAHHHHH (WHOOSH)
N-NO! NOT AGAIN...?!

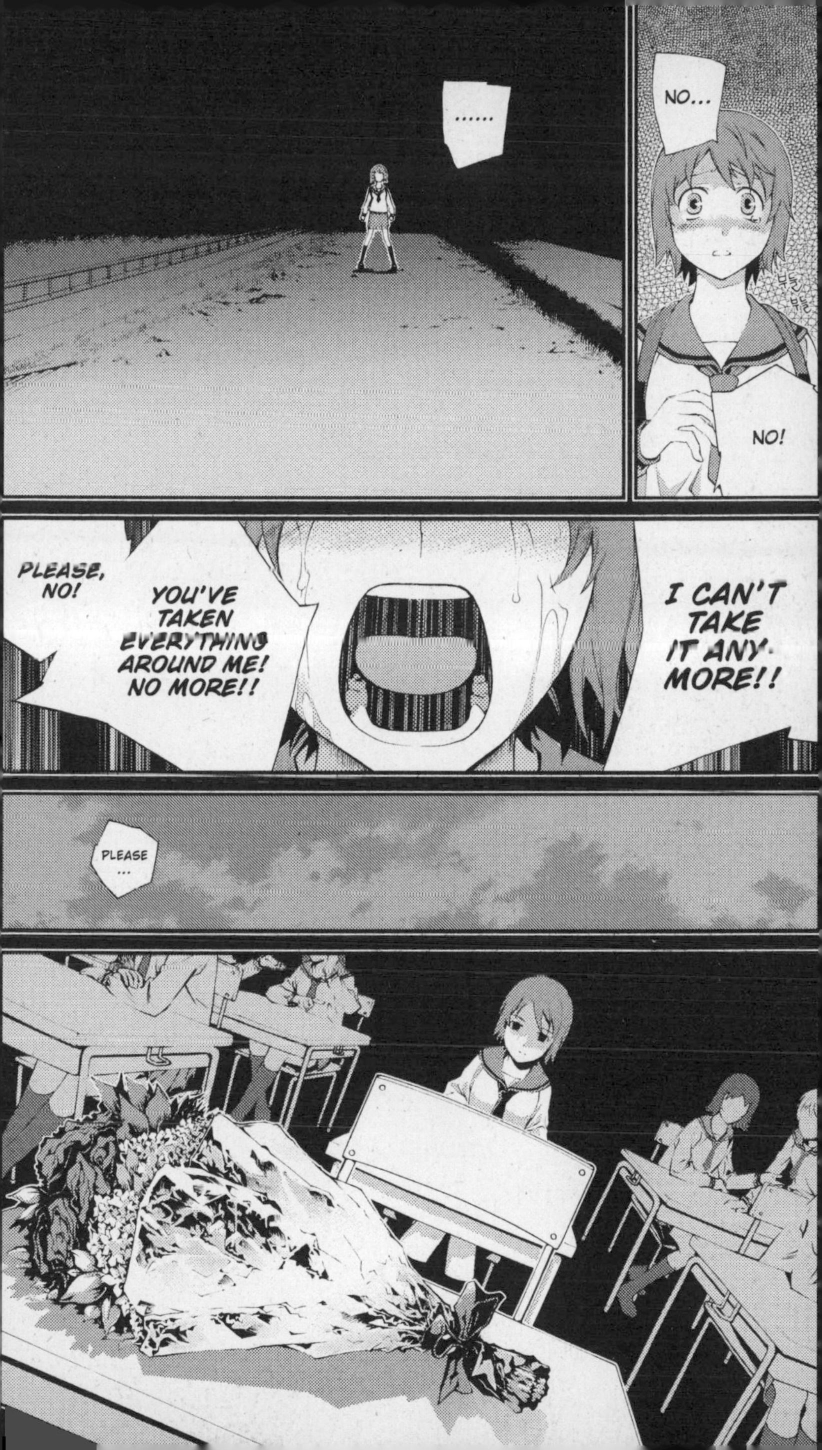
......
NO...
NO!
PLEASE, NO!
YOU'VE TAKEN EVERYTHING AROUND ME! NO MORE!!
I CAN'T TAKE IT ANY MORE!!
PLEASE ...

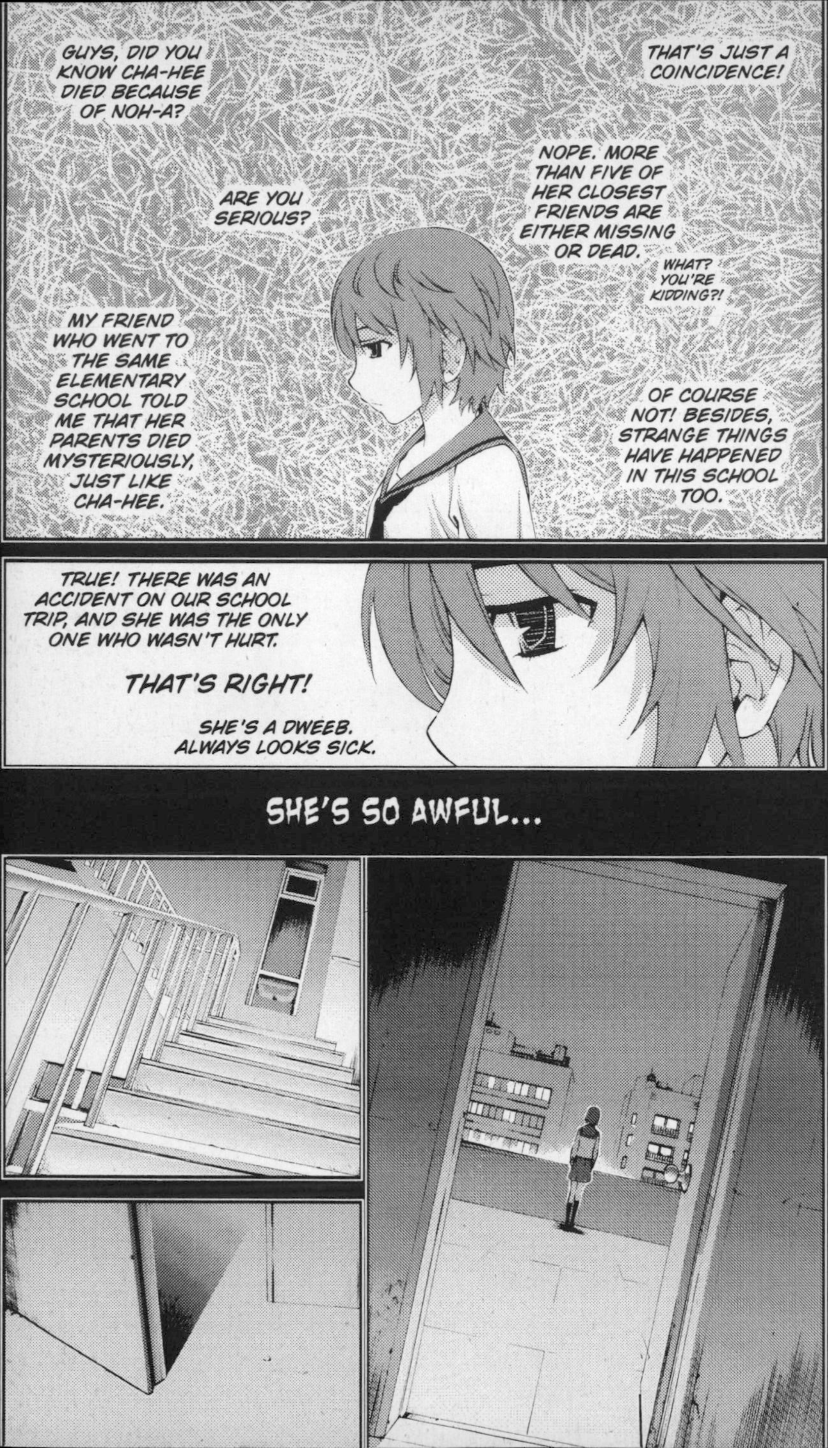
GUYS, DID YOU KNOW CHA-HEE DIED BECAUSE OF NOH-A?
THAT'S JUST A COINCIDENCE!
NOPE. MORE THAN FIVE OF HER CLOSEST FRIENDS ARE EITHER MISSING OR DEAD.
ARE YOU SERIOUS?
WHAT? YOU'RE KIDDING?!
MY FRIEND WHO WENT TO THE SAME ELEMENTARY SCHOOL TOLD ME THAT HER PARENTS DIED MYSTERIOUSLY, JUST LIKE CHA-HEE.
OF COURSE NOT! BESIDES, STRANGE THINGS HAVE HAPPENED IN THIS SCHOOL TOO.
TRUE! THERE WAS AN ACCIDENT ON OUR SCHOOL TRIP, AND SHE WAS THE ONLY ONE WHO WASN'T HURT.
THAT'S RIGHT!
SHE'S A DWEEB. ALWAYS LOOKS SICK.
SHE'S SO AWFUL...

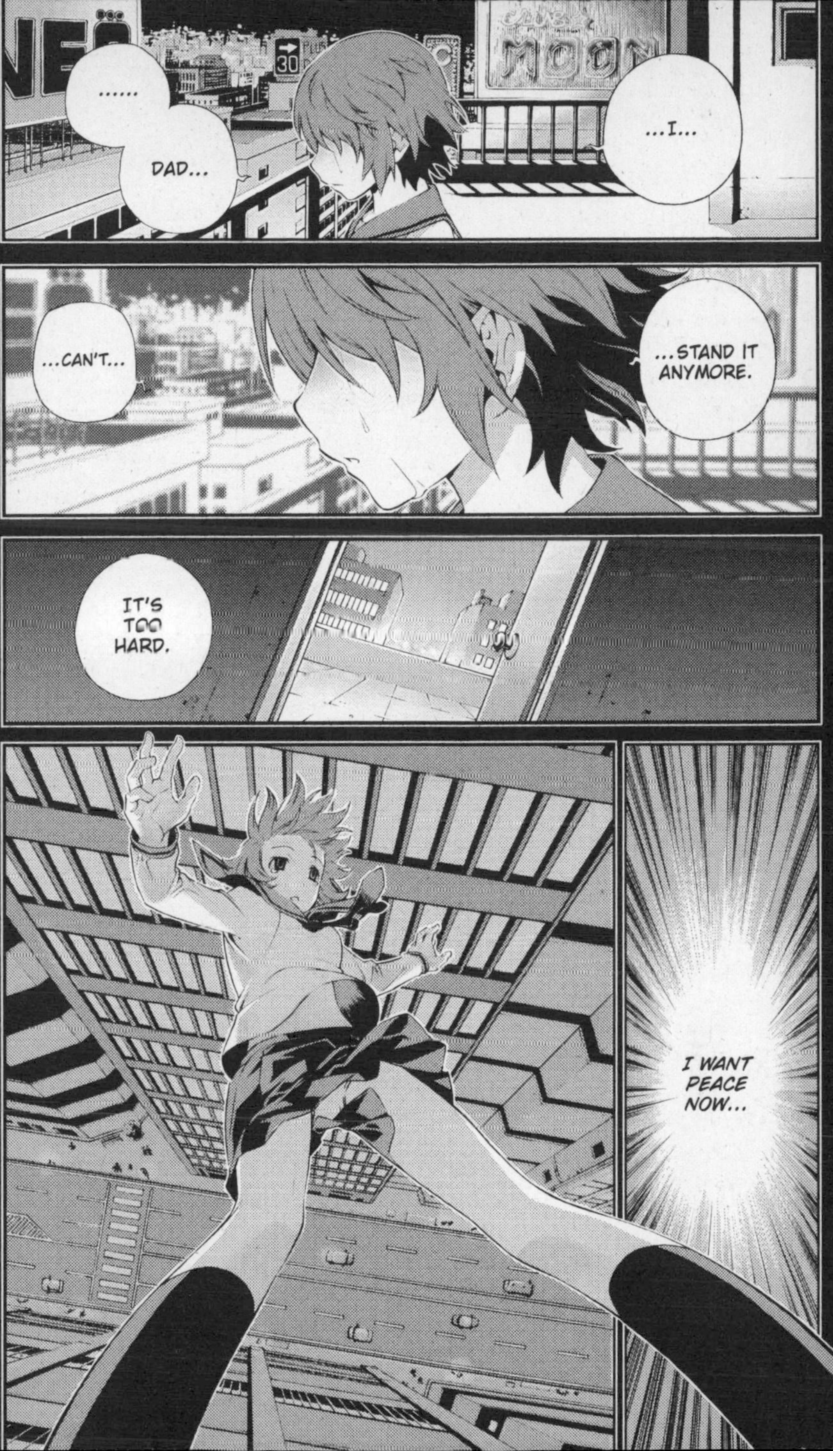
......
DAD...
...I...
...CAN'T...
...STAND IT ANYMORE.
IT'S TOO HARD.
I WANT PEACE NOW...

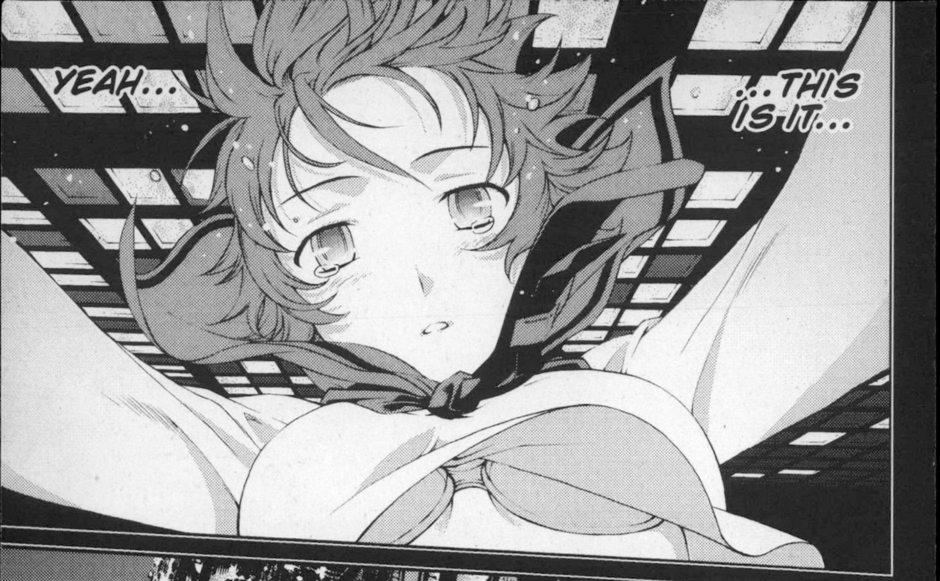
YEAH...
...THIS IS IT...
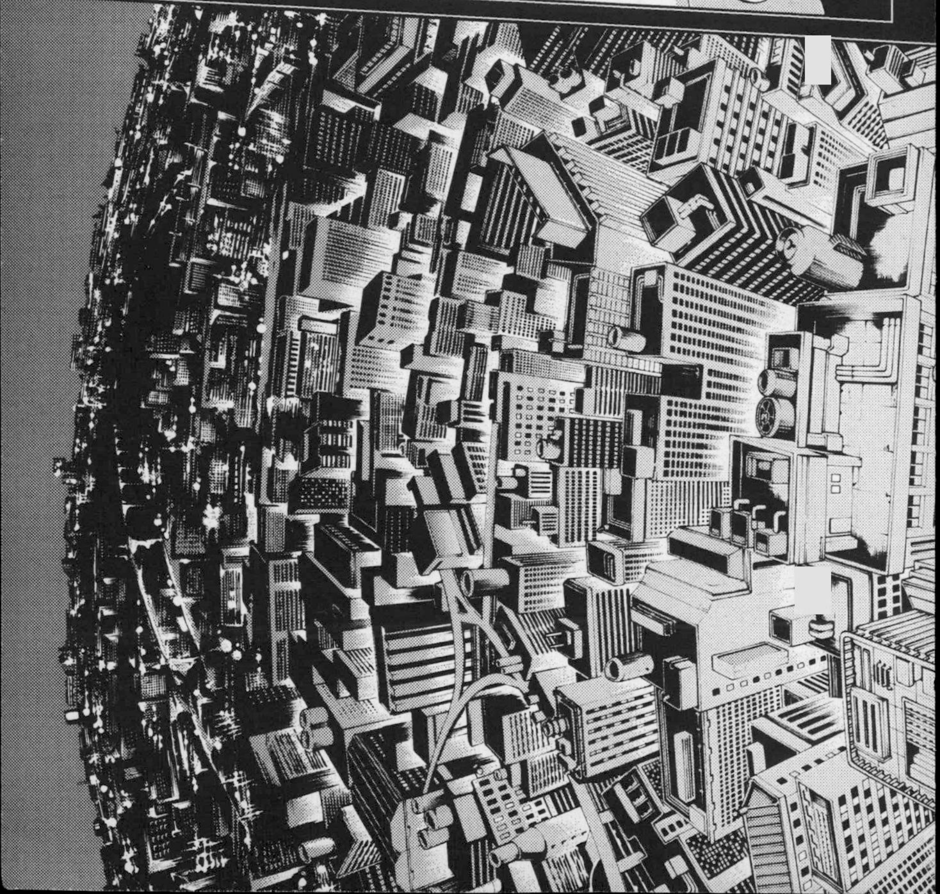

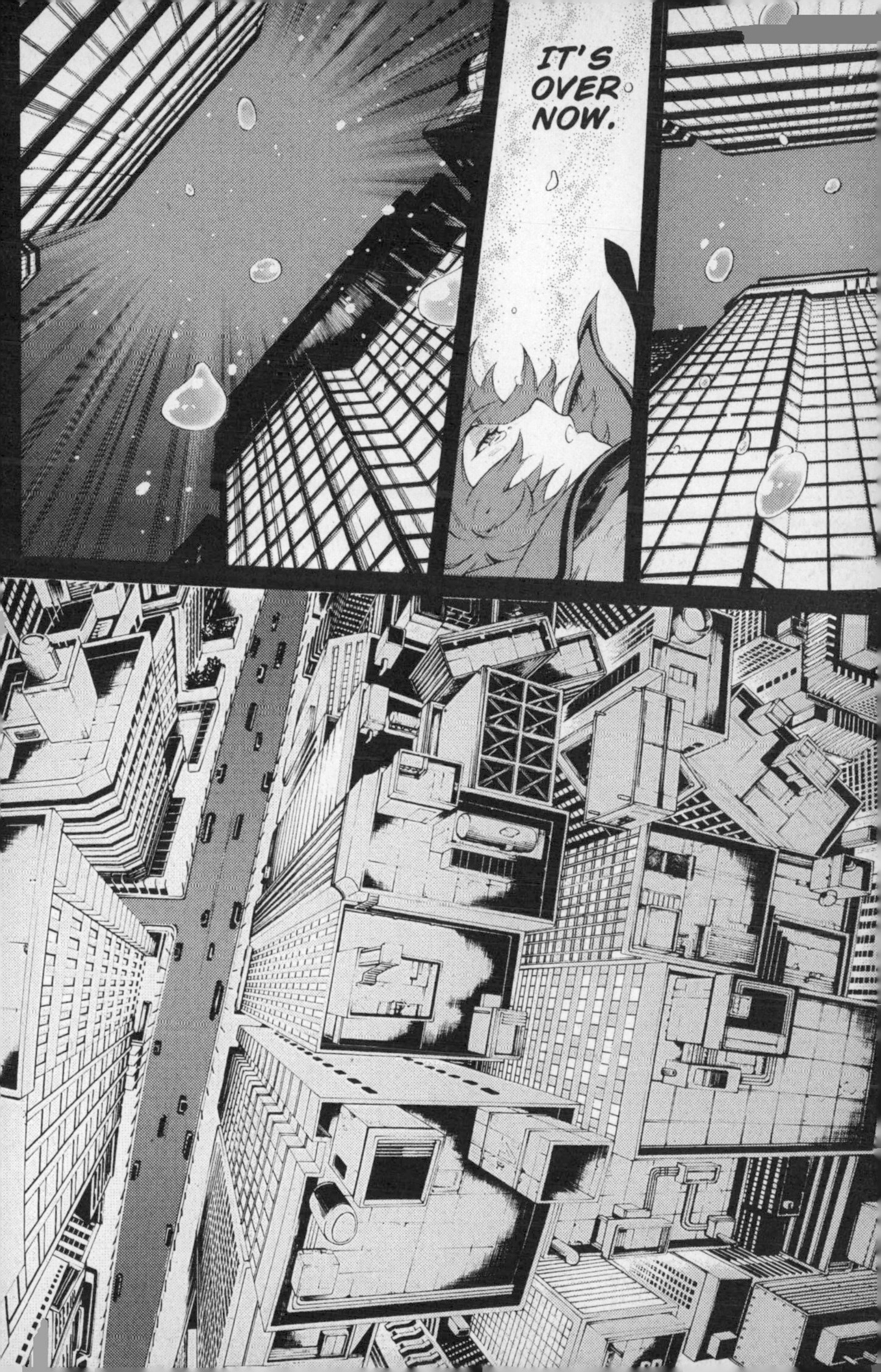
IT'S OVER NOW.

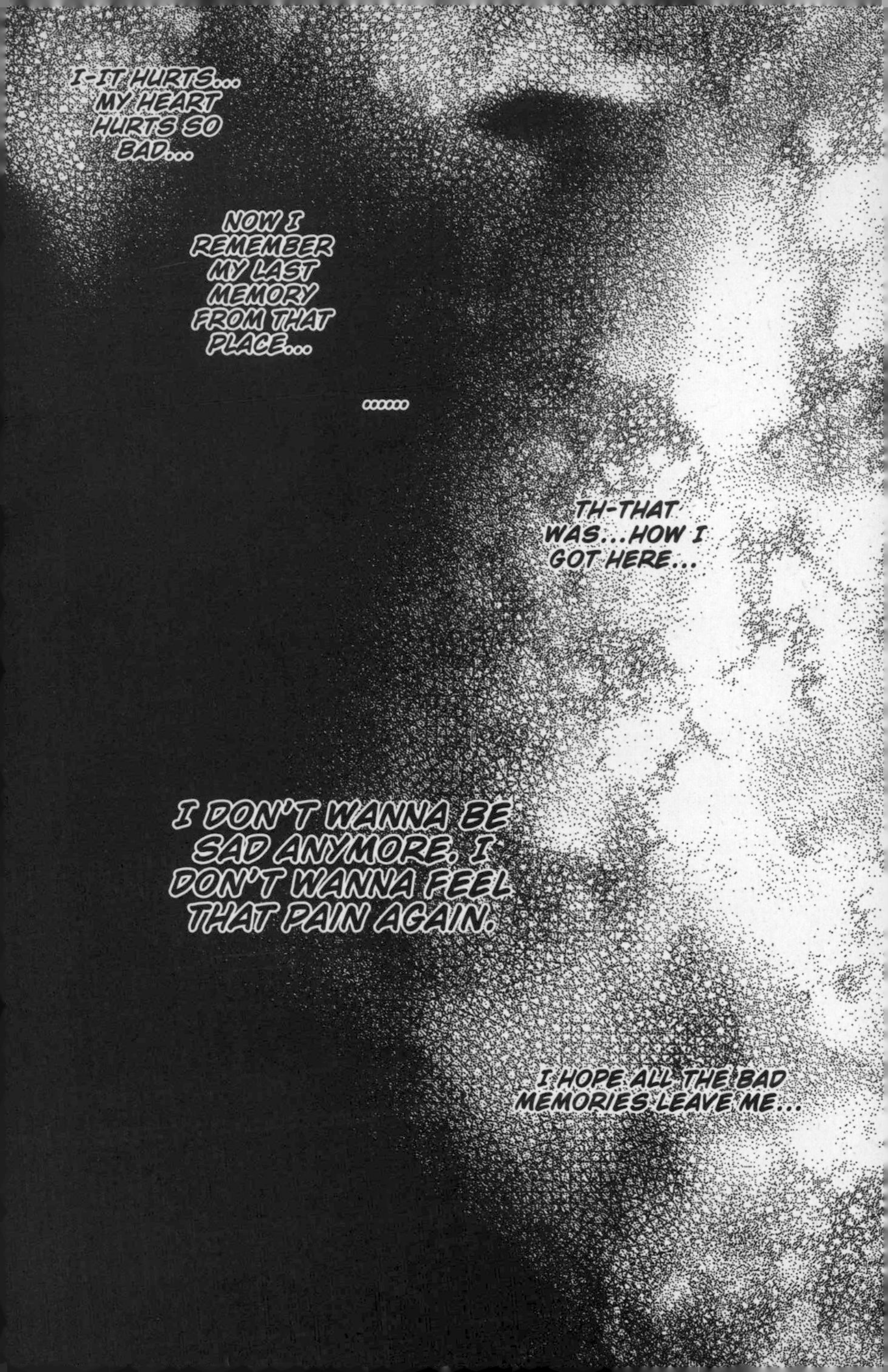
I-IT HURTS... MY HEART HURTS SO BAD...
NOW I REMEMBER MY LAST MEMORY FROM THAT PLACE...
......
TH-THAT WAS...HOW I GOT HERE...
I DON'T WANNA BE SAD ANYMORE. I DON'T WANNA FEEL THAT PAIN AGAIN.
I HOPE ALL THE BAD MEMORIES LEAVE ME...

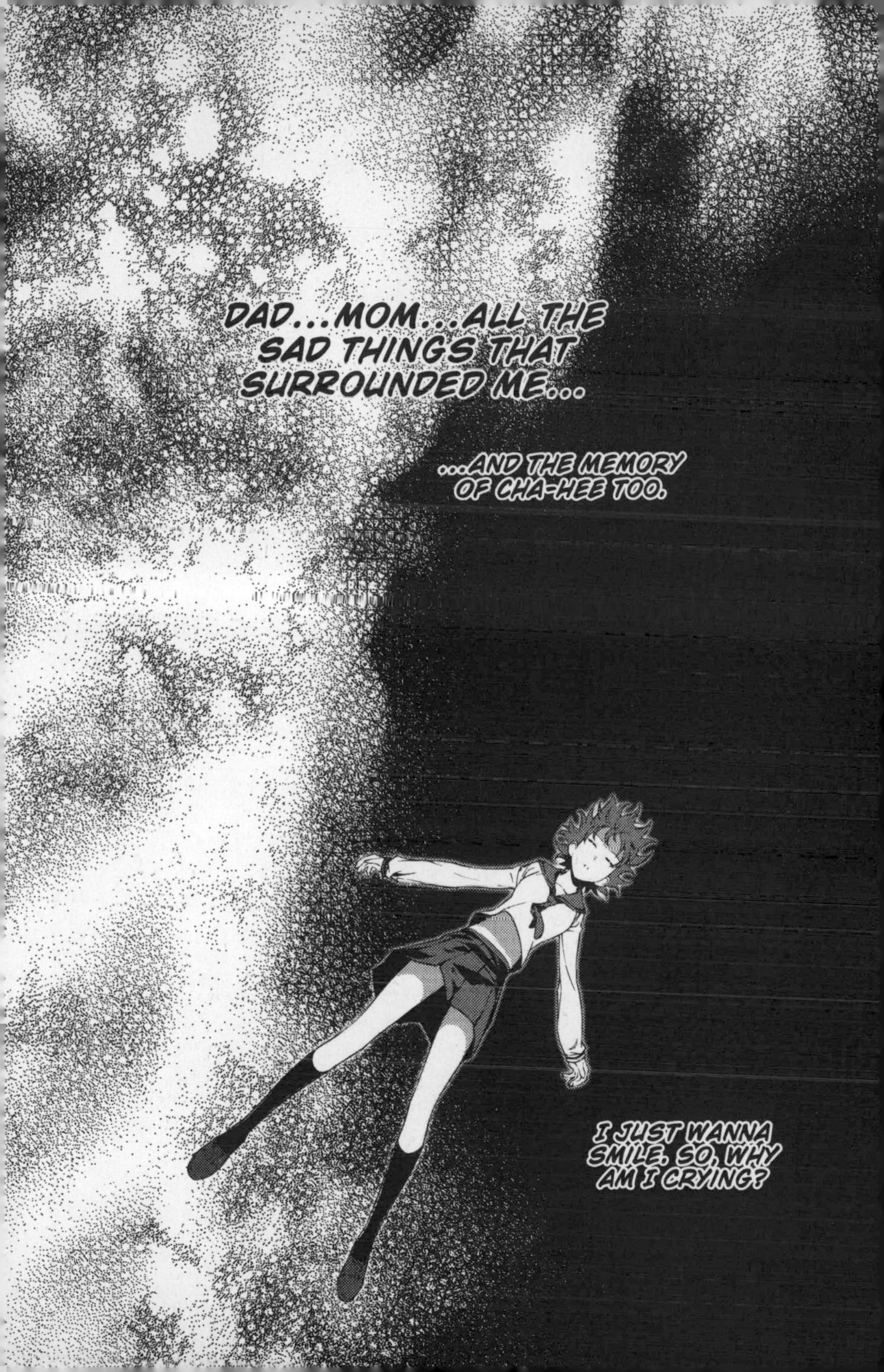
DAD...MOM...ALL THE SAD THINGS THAT SURROUNDED ME...
...AND THE MEMORY OF CHA-HEE TOO.
I JUST WANNA SMILE. SO, WHY AM I CRYING?

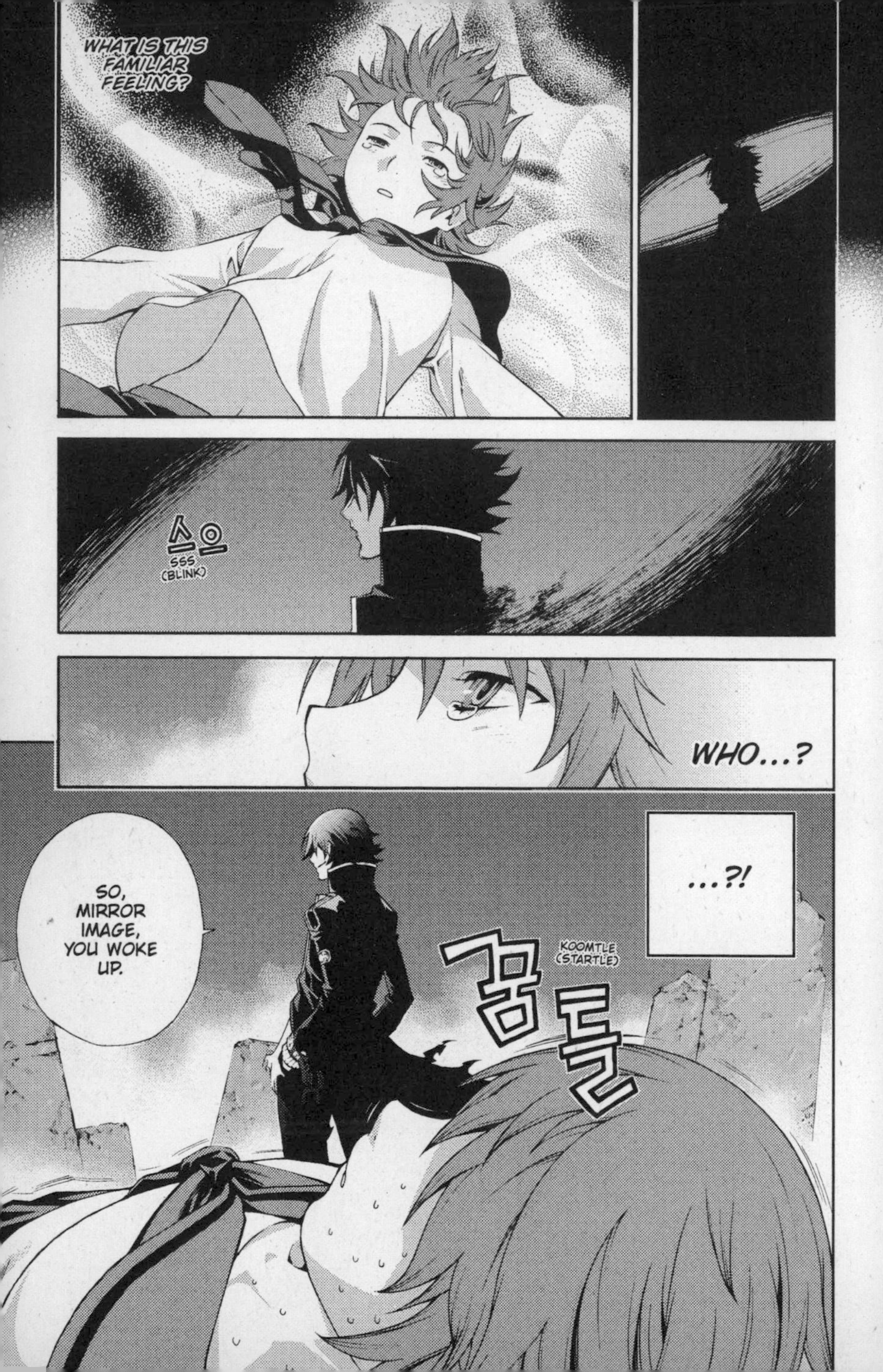
WHAT IS THIS FAMILIAR FEELING?
스으
SSS (BLINK)
WHO...?
SO, MIRROR IMAGE, YOU WOKE UP.
...?!
꿈틀
KOOMTLE (STARTLE)

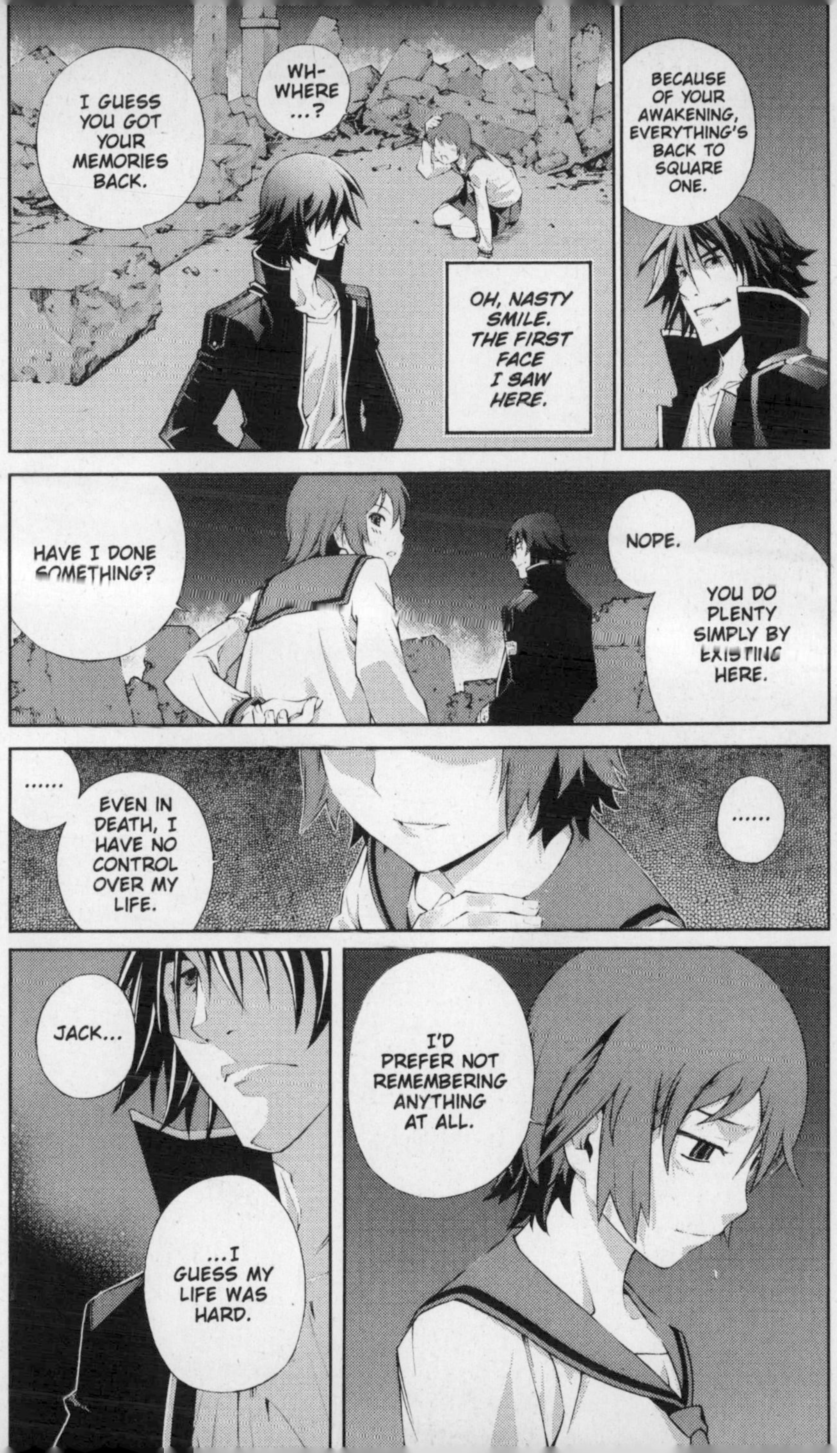
BECAUSE OF YOUR AWAKENING, EVERYTHING'S BACK TO SQUARE ONE.
WH- WHERE ...?
I GUESS YOU GOT YOUR MEMORIES BACK.
OH, NASTY SMILE. THE FIRST FACE I SAW HERE.
HAVE I DONE SOMETHING?
NOPE.
YOU DO PLENTY SIMPLY BY EXISTING HERE.
......
......
EVEN IN DEATH, I HAVE NO CONTROL OVER MY LIFE.
I'D PREFER NOT REMEMBERING ANYTHING AT ALL.
JACK...
...I GUESS MY LIFE WAS HARD.

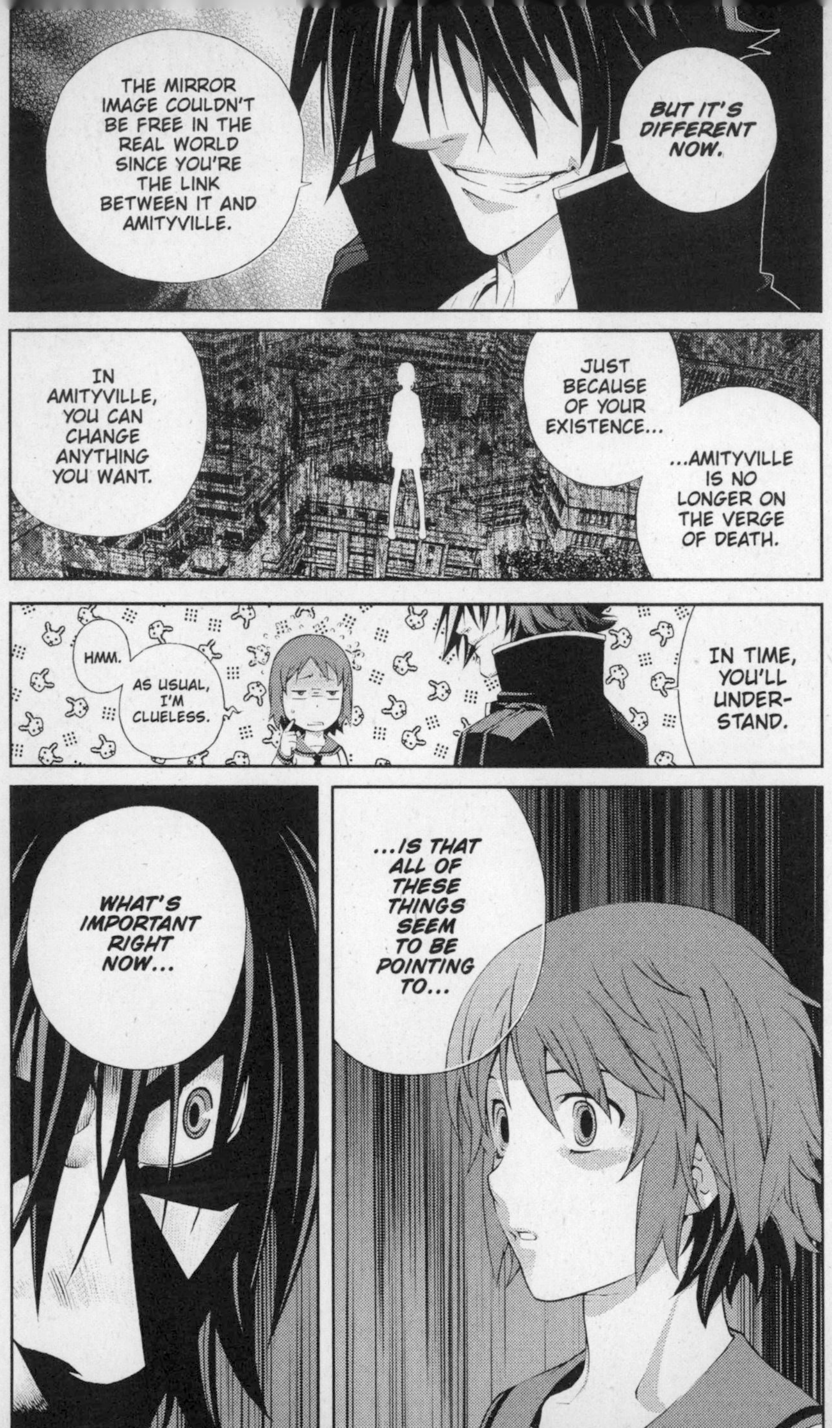
THE MIRROR IMAGE COULDN'T BE FREE IN THE REAL WORLD SINCE YOU'RE THE LINK BETWEEN IT AND AMITYVILLE.
BUT IT'S DIFFERENT NOW.
IN AMITYVILLE, YOU CAN CHANGE ANYTHING YOU WANT.
JUST BECAUSE OF YOUR EXISTENCE...
...AMITYVILLE IS NO LONGER ON THE VERGE OF DEATH.
HMM.
AS USUAL, I'M CLUELESS.
IN TIME, YOU'LL UNDER-STAND.
WHAT'S IMPORTANT RIGHT NOW...
...IS THAT ALL OF THESE THINGS SEEM TO BE POINTING TO...

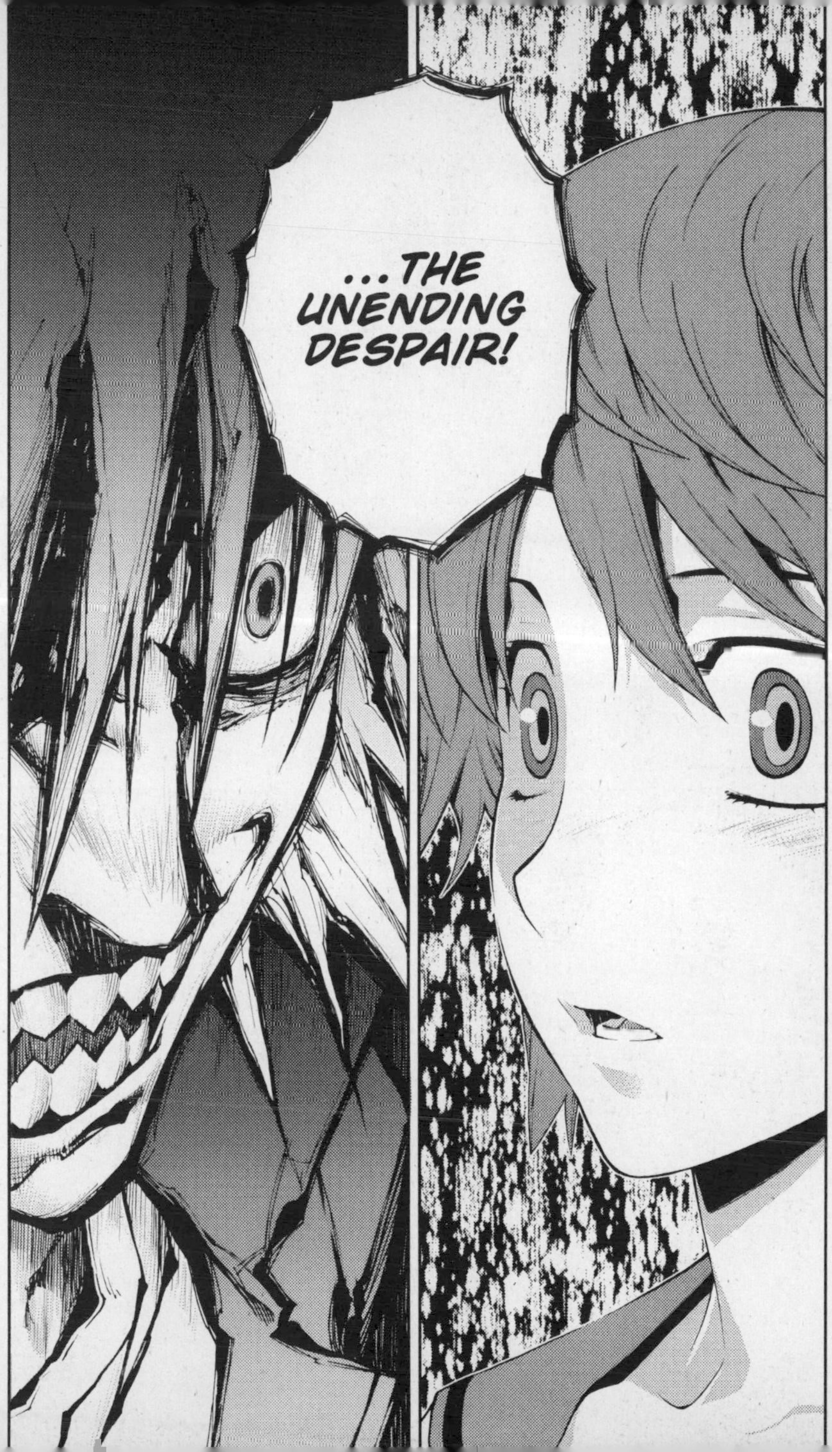
...THE UNENDING DESPAIR!

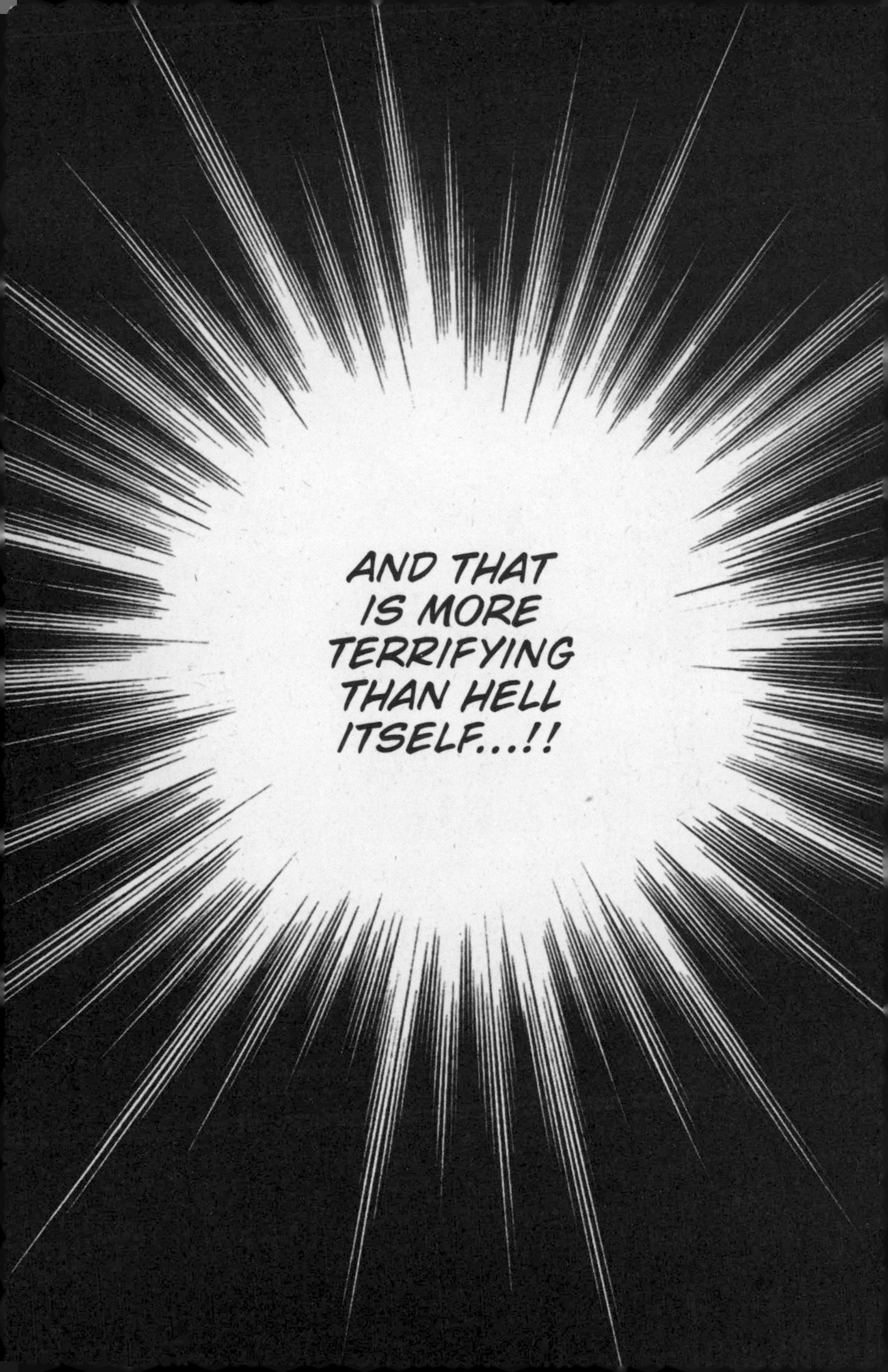
AND THAT IS MORE TERRIFYING THAN HELL ITSELF...!!

VIOLENCE 20. PAUSE

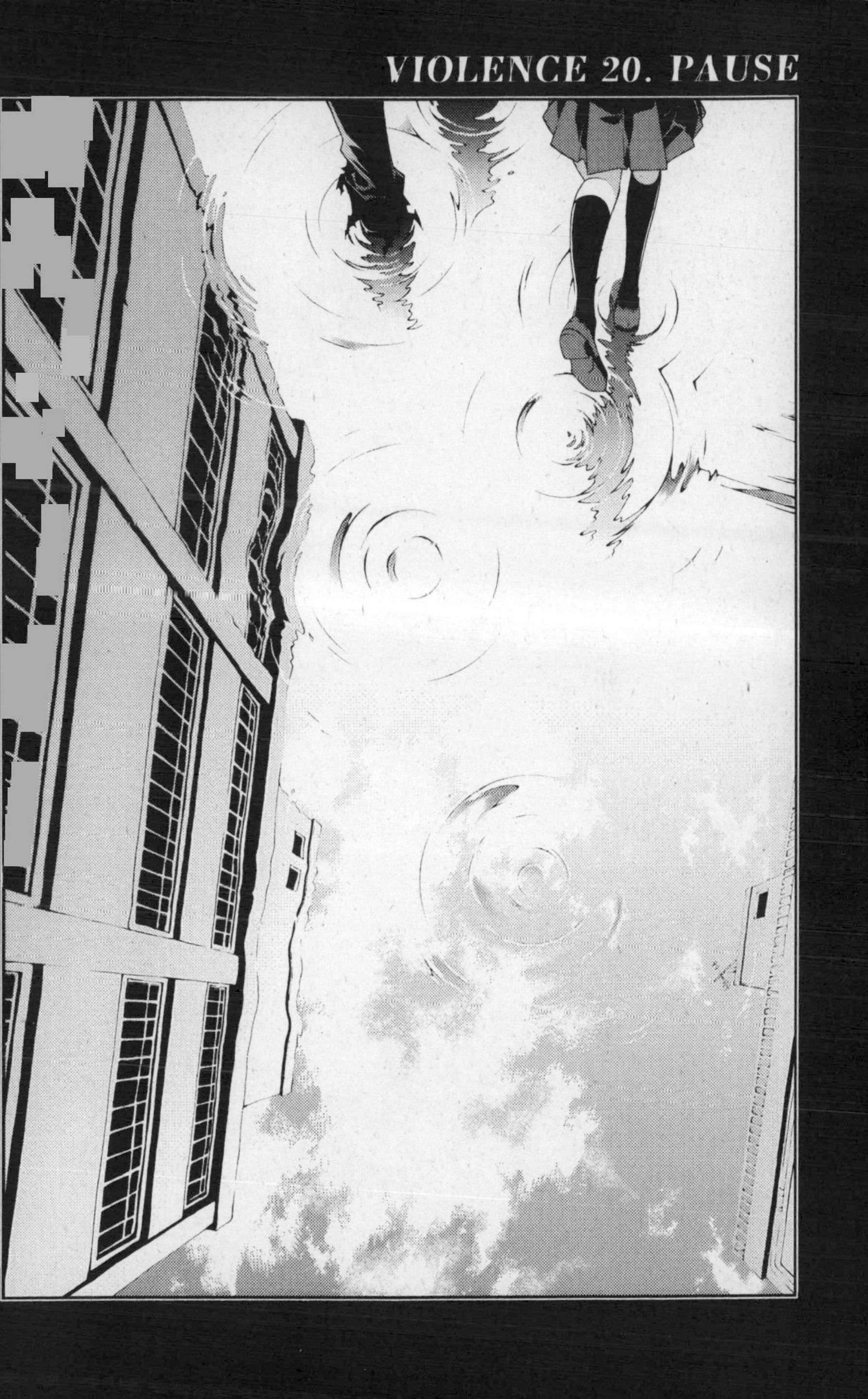

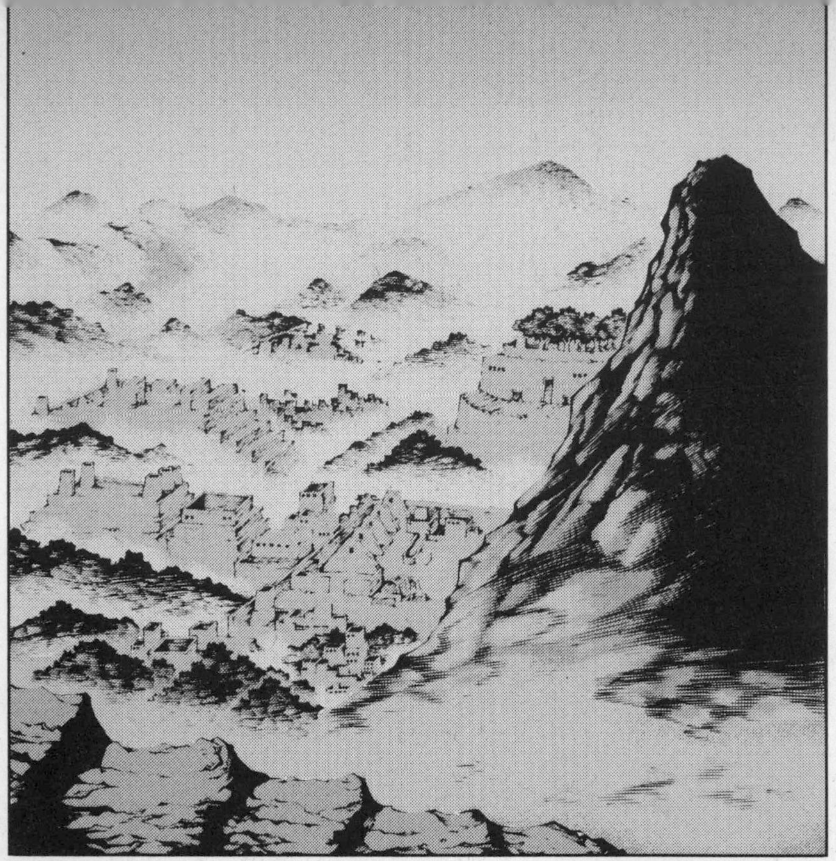

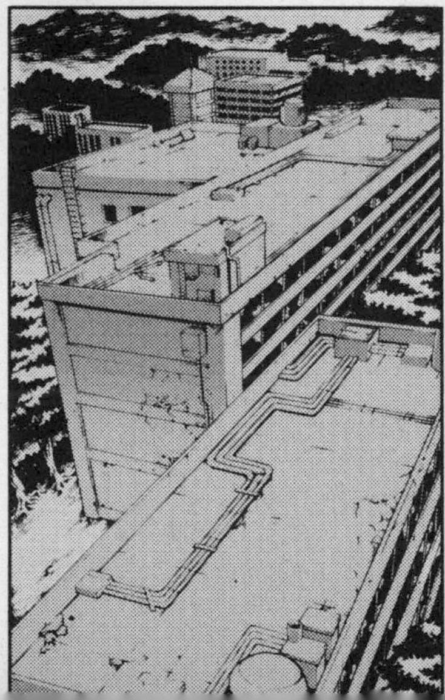

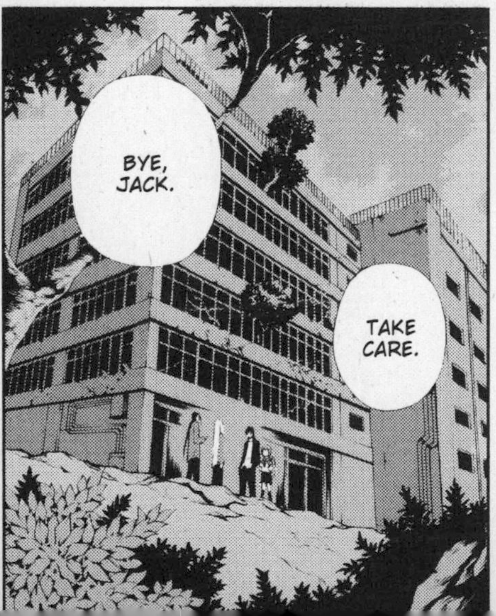
BYE, JACK.
TAKE CARE.

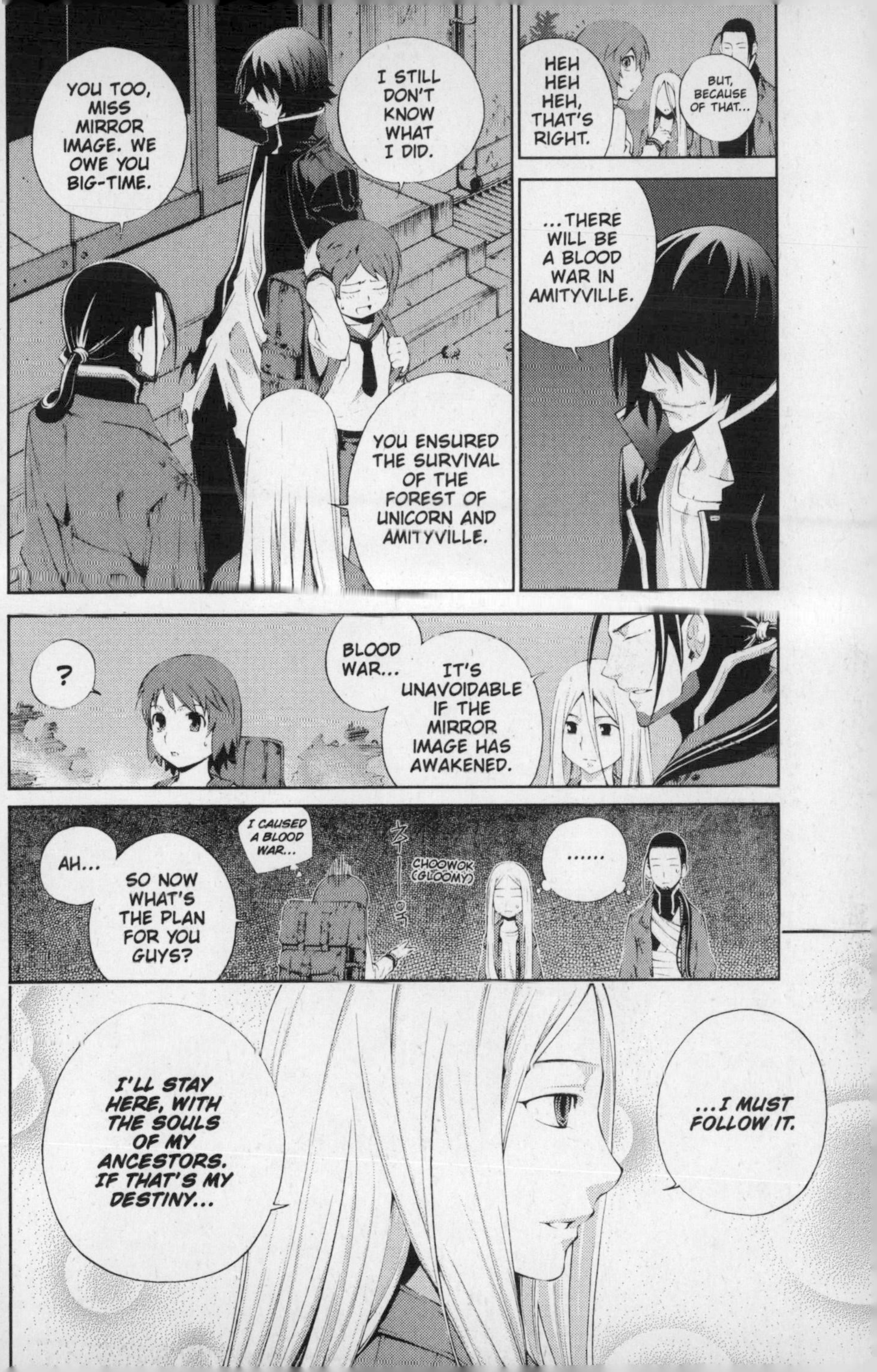
YOU TOO, MISS MIRROR IMAGE. WE OWE YOU BIG-TIME.
I STILL DON'T KNOW WHAT I DID.
YOU ENSURED THE SURVIVAL OF THE FOREST OF UNICORN AND AMITYVILLE.
HEH HEH HEH, THAT'S RIGHT.
BUT, BECAUSE OF THAT...
...THERE WILL BE A BLOOD WAR IN AMITYVILLE.
?
BLOOD WAR...
IT'S UNAVOIDABLE IF THE MIRROR IMAGE HAS AWAKENED.
AH...
SO NOW WHAT'S THE PLAN FOR YOU GUYS?
I CAUSED A BLOOD WAR...
CHOOWOK (GLOOMY)
......
I'LL STAY HERE, WITH THE SOULS OF MY ANCESTORS. IF THAT'S MY DESTINY...
...I MUST FOLLOW IT.

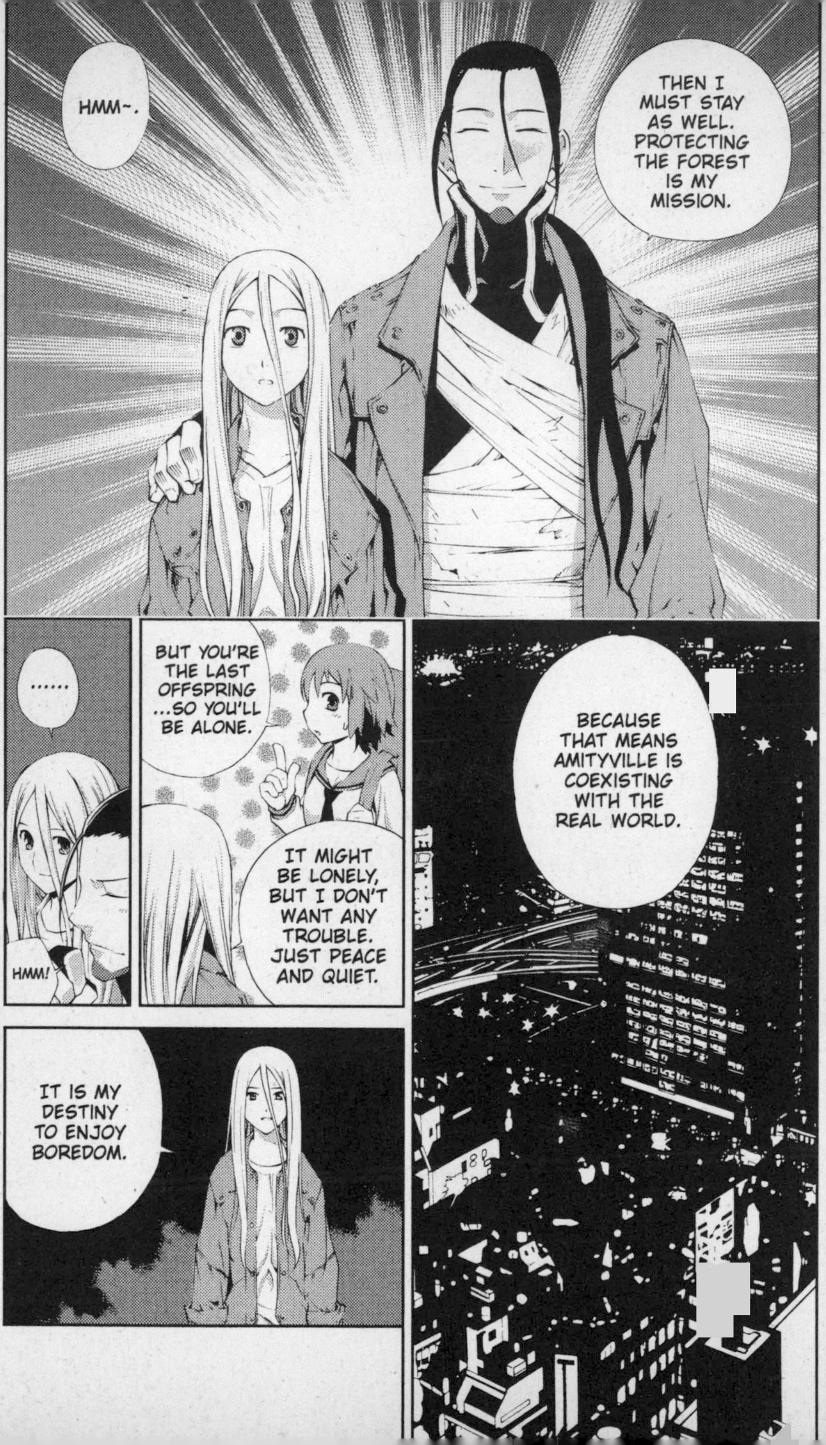
HMM~.
THEN I MUST STAY AS WELL. PROTECTING THE FOREST IS MY MISSION.
......
HMM!
BUT YOU'RE THE LAST OFFSPRING ...SO YOU'LL BE ALONE.
IT MIGHT BE LONELY, BUT I DON'T WANT ANY TROUBLE. JUST PEACE AND QUIET.
IT IS MY DESTINY TO ENJOY BOREDOM.
BECAUSE THAT MEANS AMITYVILLE IS COEXISTING WITH THE REAL WORLD.

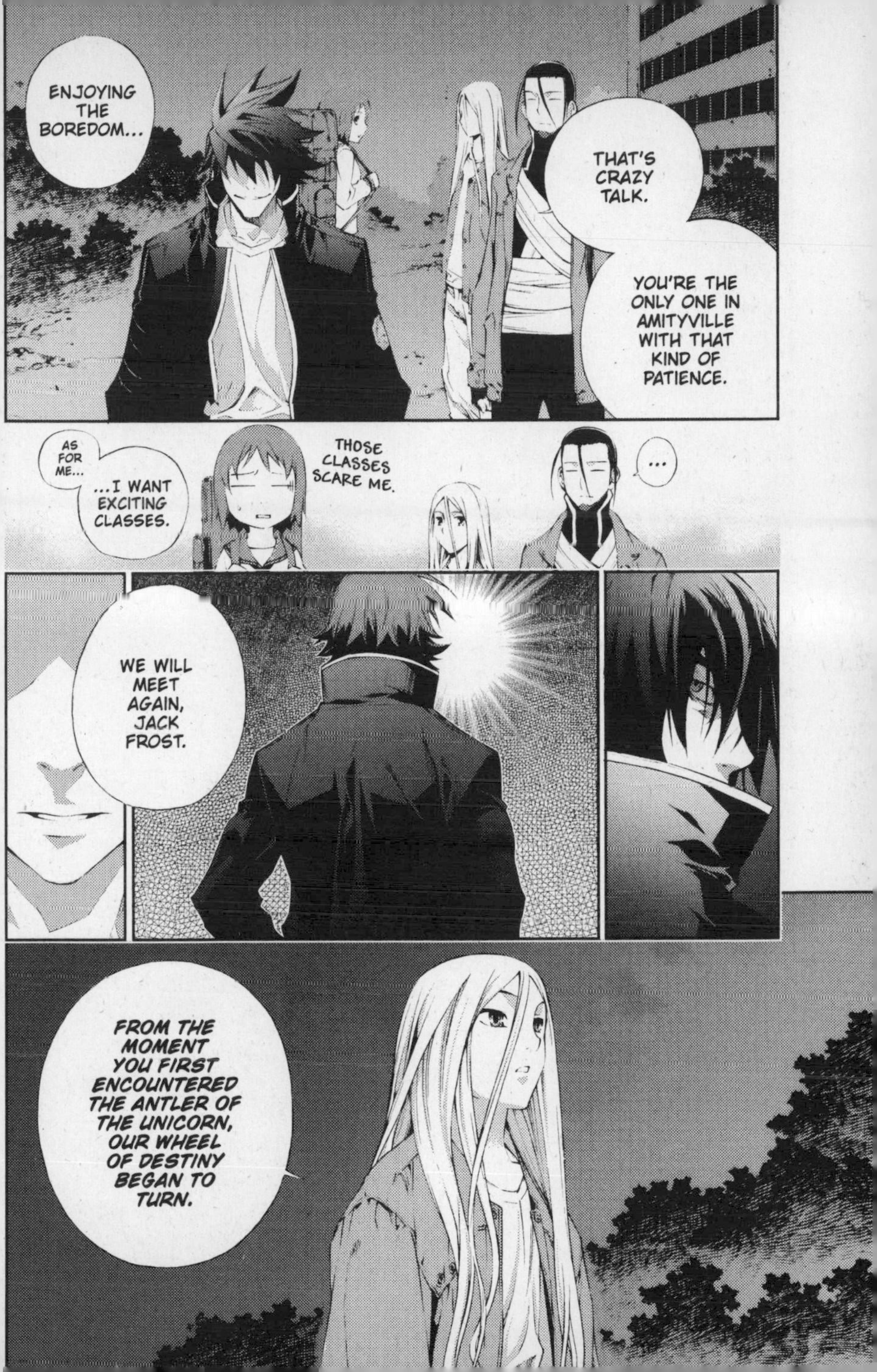
ENJOYING THE BOREDOM...
THAT'S CRAZY TALK.
YOU'RE THE ONLY ONE IN AMITYVILLE WITH THAT KIND OF PATIENCE.
AS FOR ME...
...I WANT EXCITING CLASSES.
THOSE CLASSES SCARE ME.
...
WE WILL MEET AGAIN, JACK FROST.
FROM THE MOMENT YOU FIRST ENCOUNTERED THE ANTLER OF THE UNICORN, OUR WHEEL OF DESTINY BEGAN TO TURN.

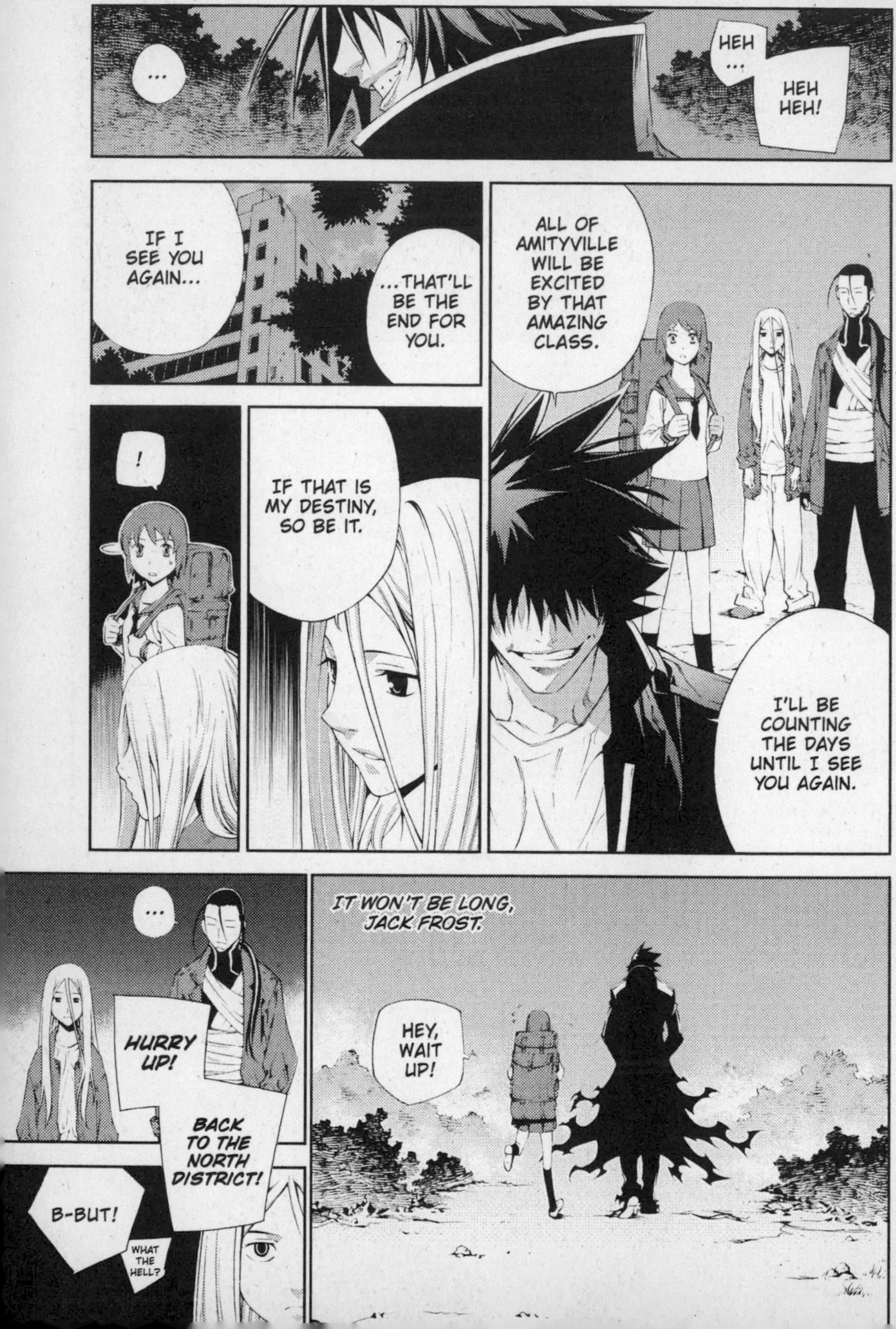
...
HEH ...
HEH HEH!
IF I SEE YOU AGAIN...
...THAT'LL BE THE END FOR YOU.
!
IF THAT IS MY DESTINY, SO BE IT.
ALL OF AMITYVILLE WILL BE EXCITED BY THAT AMAZING CLASS.
I'LL BE COUNTING THE DAYS UNTIL I SEE YOU AGAIN.
...
HURRY UP!
BACK TO THE NORTH DISTRICT!
B-BUT!
WHAT THE HELL?
IT WON'T BE LONG, JACK FROST.
HEY, WAIT UP!

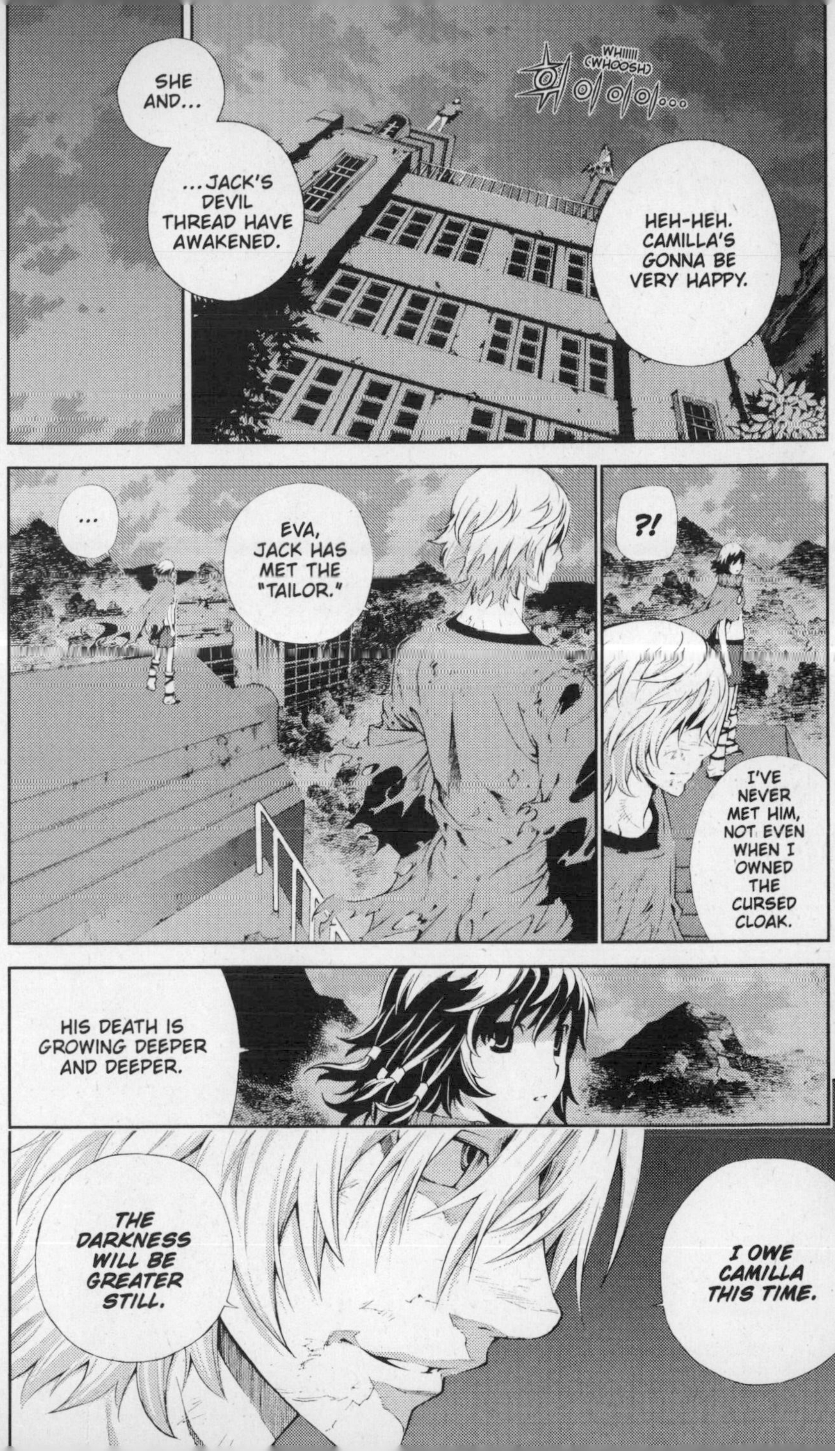
SHE AND...
...JACK'S DEVIL THREAD HAVE AWAKENED.
WHIIIII (WHOOSH)
화이이이...
HEH-HEH. CAMILLA'S GONNA BE VERY HAPPY.
...
EVA, JACK HAS MET THE "TAILOR."
?!
I'VE NEVER MET HIM, NOT EVEN WHEN I OWNED THE CURSED CLOAK.
HIS DEATH IS GROWING DEEPER AND DEEPER.
THE DARKNESS WILL BE GREATER STILL.
I OWE CAMILLA THIS TIME.

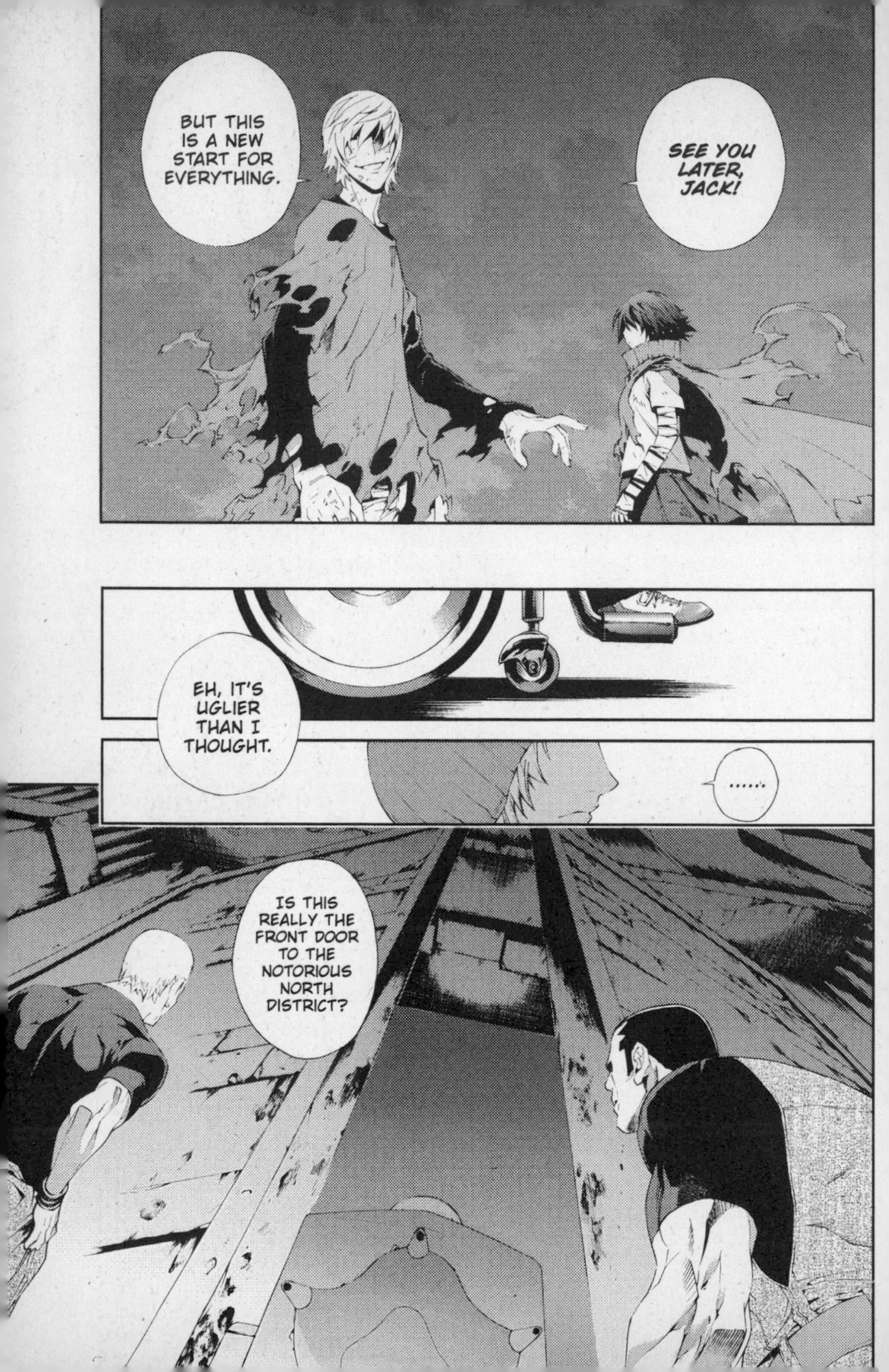
BUT THIS IS A NEW START FOR EVERYTHING.
SEE YOU LATER, JACK!
EH, IT'S UGLIER THAN I THOUGHT.
......
IS THIS REALLY THE FRONT DOOR TO THE NOTORIOUS NORTH DISTRICT?

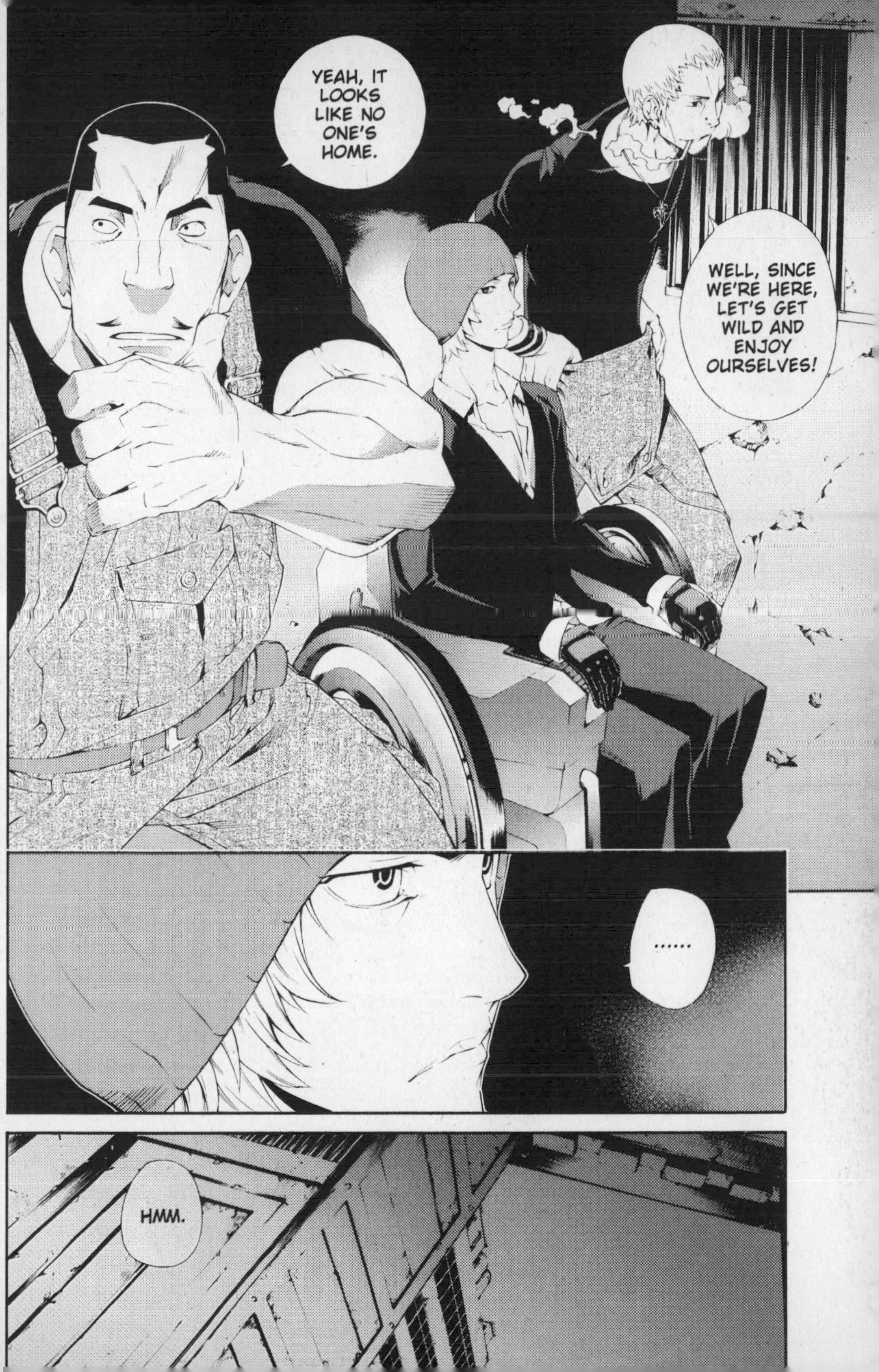
YEAH, IT LOOKS LIKE NO ONE'S HOME.
WELL, SINCE WE'RE HERE, LET'S GET WILD AND ENJOY OURSELVES!
......
HMM.

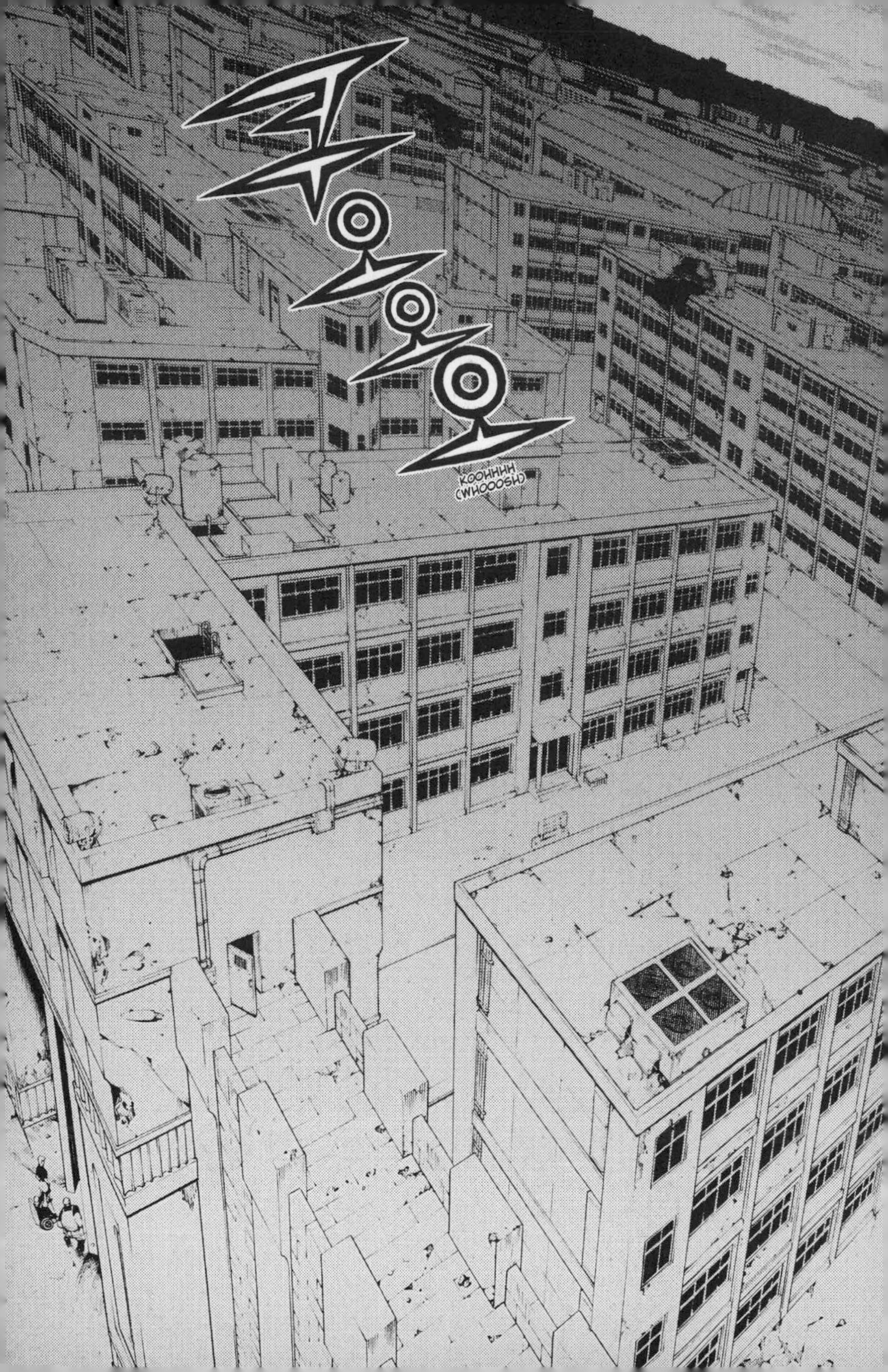
KOOHHHH
(WHOOOSH)

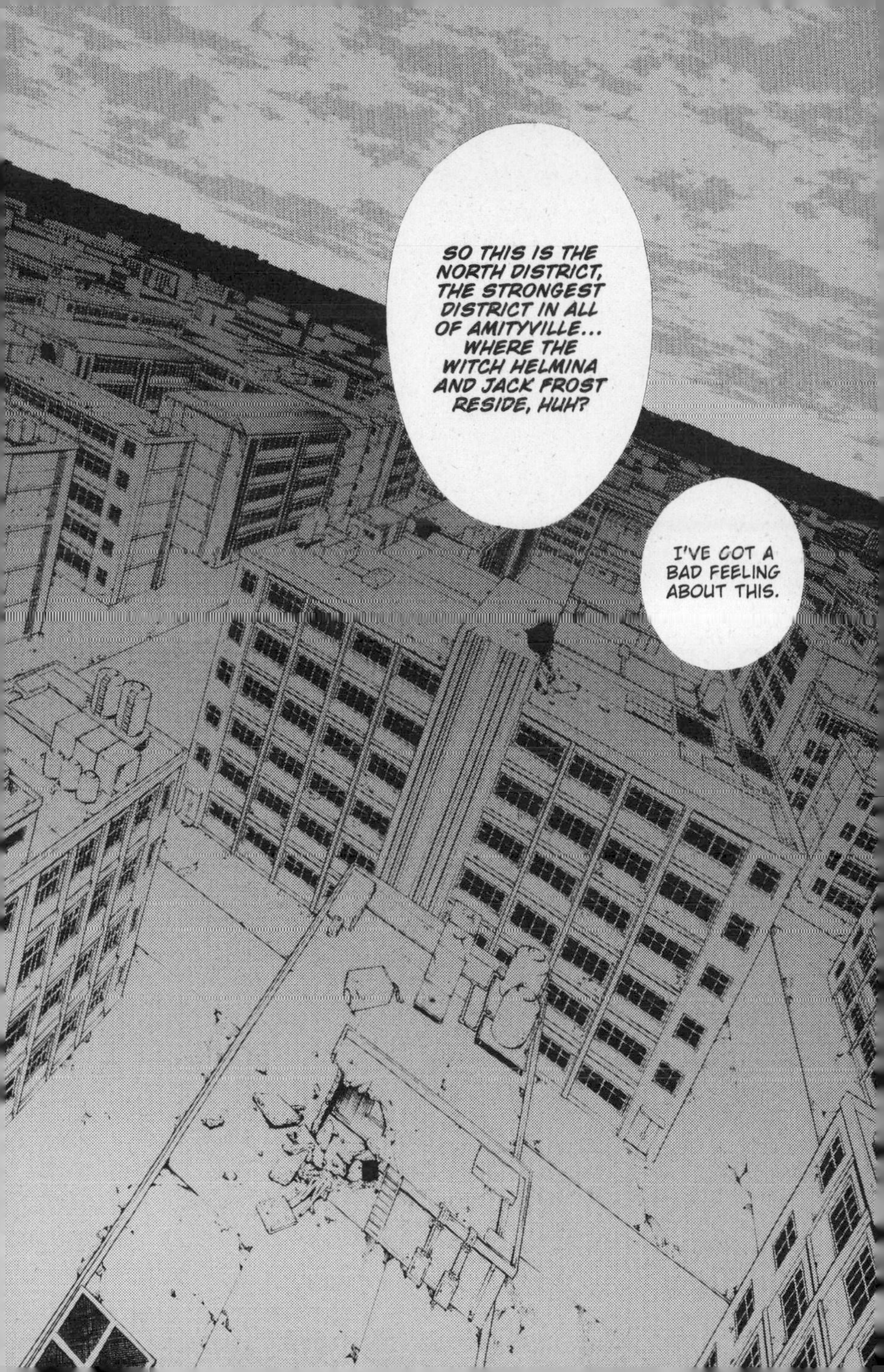
SO THIS IS THE NORTH DISTRICT, THE STRONGEST DISTRICT IN ALL OF AMITYVILLE... WHERE THE WITCH HELMINA AND JACK FROST RESIDE, HUH?
I'VE GOT A BAD FEELING ABOUT THIS.

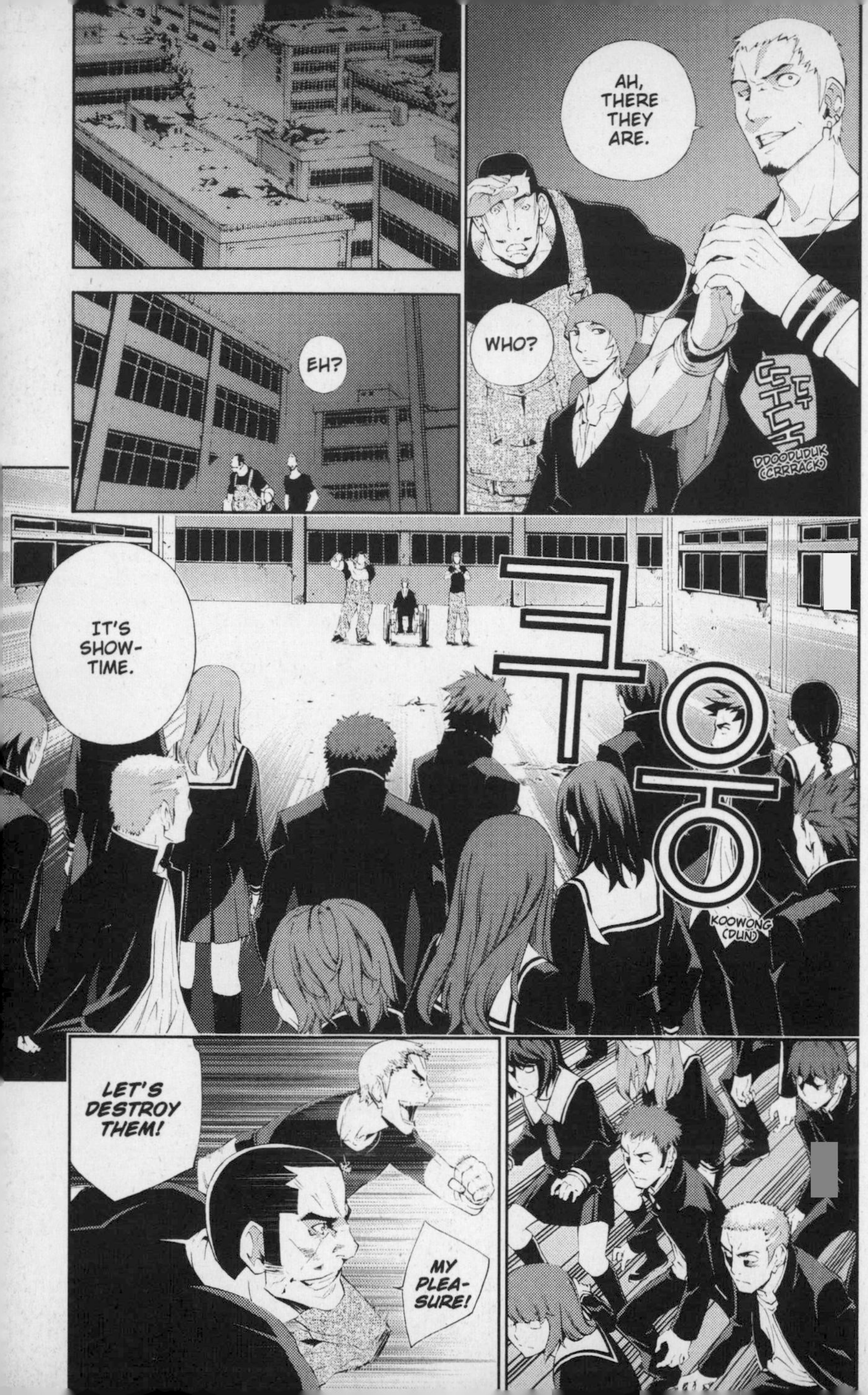
EH?
AH, THERE THEY ARE.
WHO?
DDOODUDUK (CRRRACK)
IT'S SHOW-TIME.
쿠웅
KOOWONG (DUN)
LET'S DESTROY THEM!
MY PLEA-SURE!

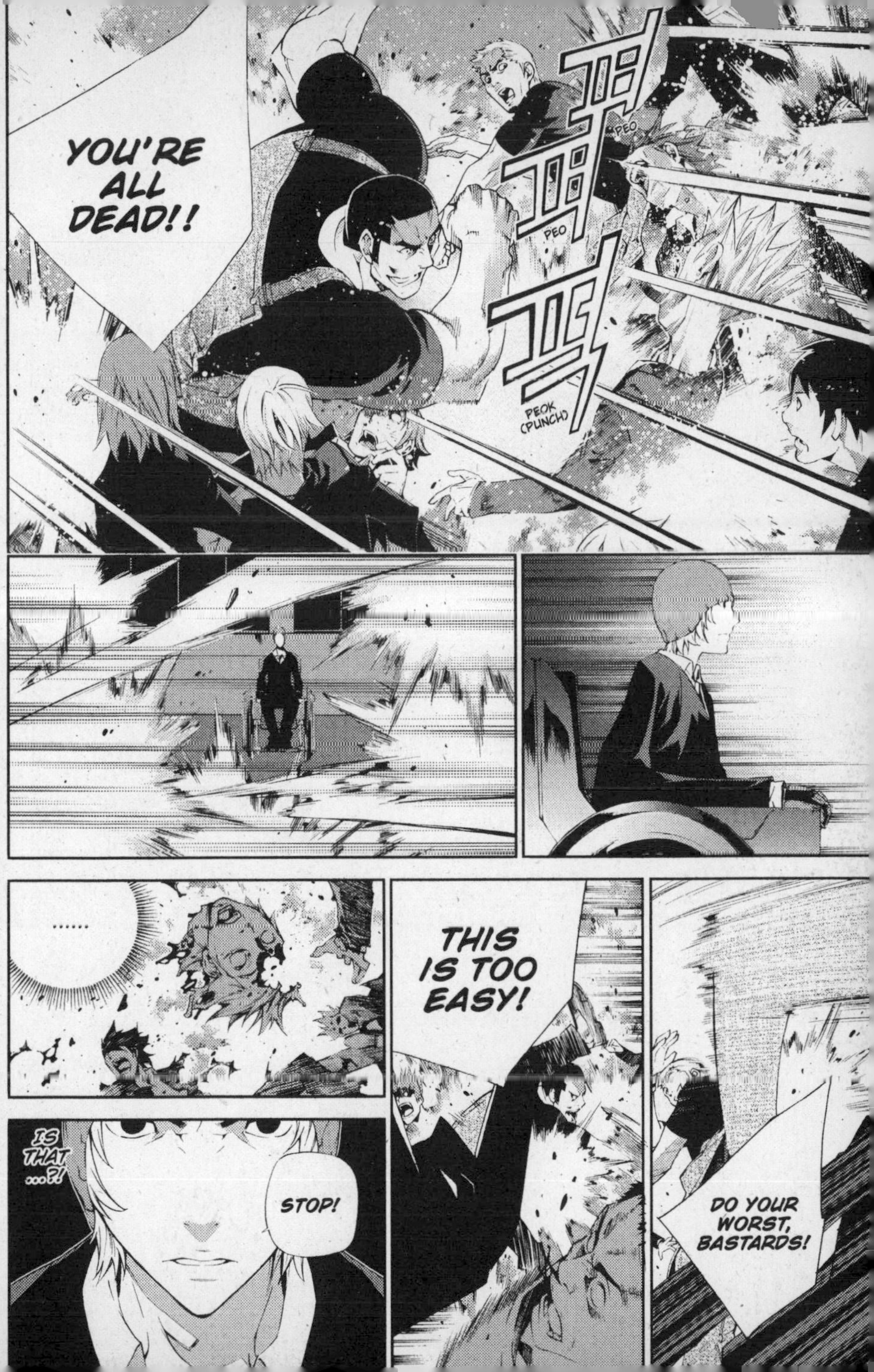
YOU'RE ALL DEAD!!
PEO
PEO
PEOK (PUNCH)
......
IS THAT ...?!
STOP!
THIS IS TOO EASY!
DO YOUR WORST, BASTARDS!

I SAID STOP!!

WOOMJIL (STARTLE)

?!

?

THEY'RE SHIELDS.

THOSE WEAKLINGS BEFORE YOU ARE ALL MERE SHIELDS.

GET BACK.

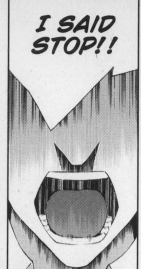

WHAT A WEAK SPELL.

TADACK (TAK)

TADACK

TADACK

TADACK

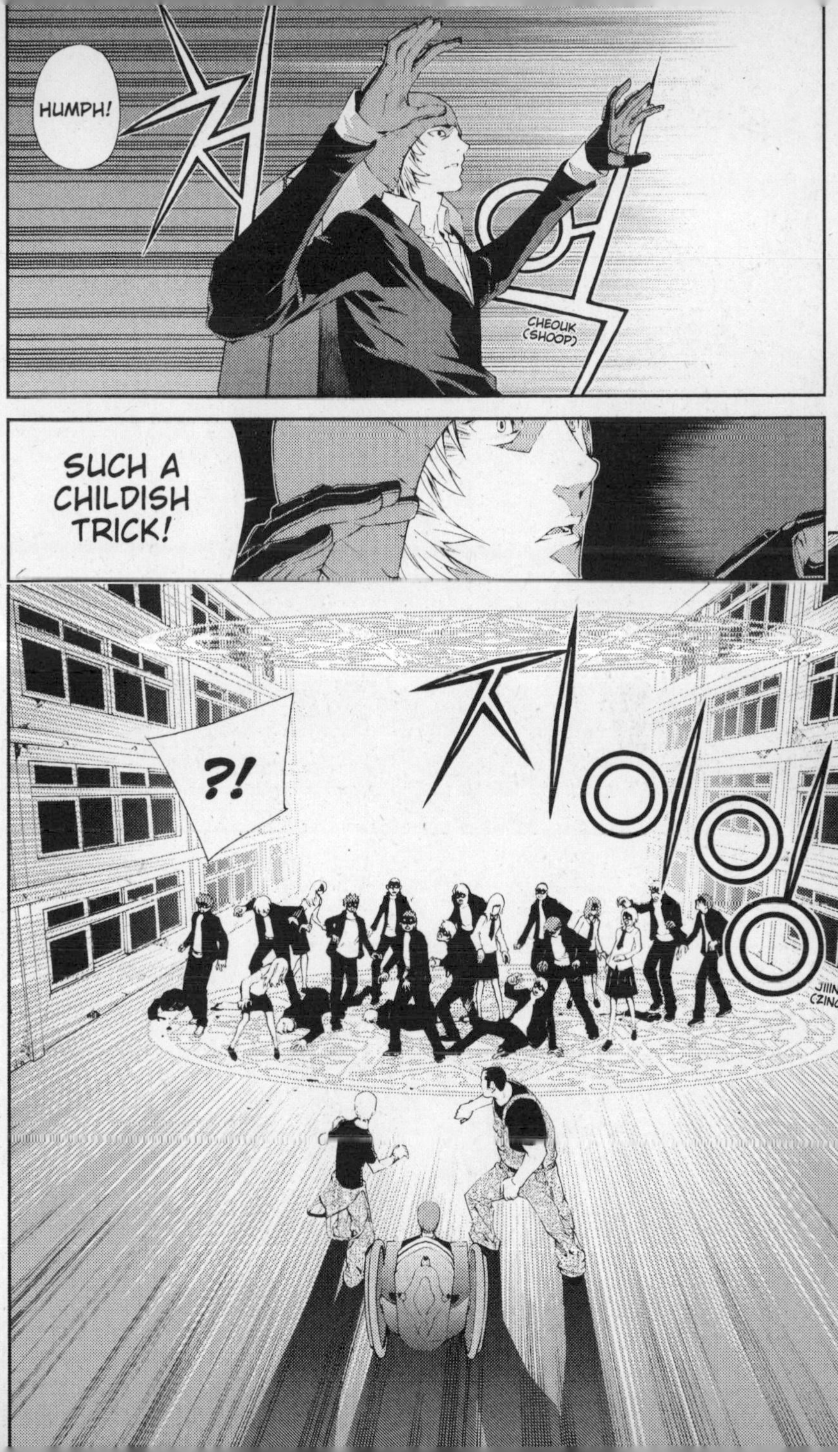
HUMPH!
CHEOUK (SHOOP)
SUCH A CHILDISH TRICK!
?!
JIIING (ZING)

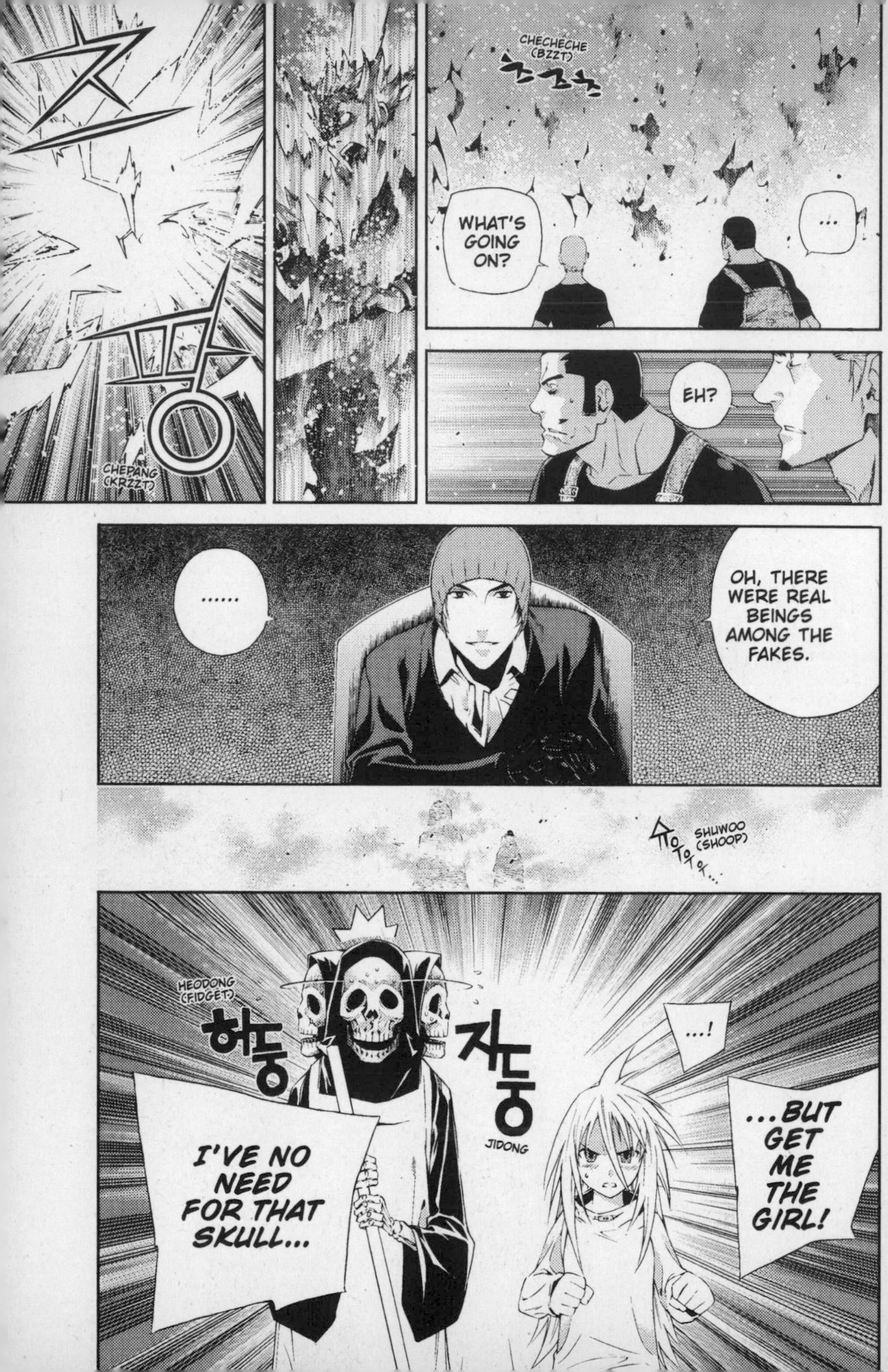
CHEPANG (KRZZT)
CHECHECHE (BZZT)
WHAT'S GOING ON?
...
EH?
......
OH, THERE WERE REAL BEINGS AMONG THE FAKES.
SHUWOO (SHOOP)
HEODONG (FIDGET)
허둥
지둥
JIDONG
I'VE NO NEED FOR THAT SKULL...
...!
...BUT GET ME THE GIRL!

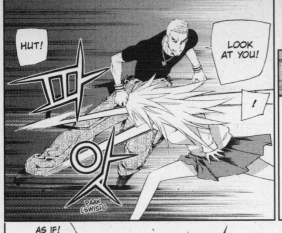

HUT!

LOOK AT YOU!

!

PAAK (SWISH)

BINGGLE (SPIN)

?!

AS IF! YOU'RE SUPPOSED TO BELONG TO THE NORTH DISTRICT, HUH?

TUNG (PUNCH)

HEE HEE.

....!

COME ON!

AR- GH!

....!

TAK (SHP)

-!!

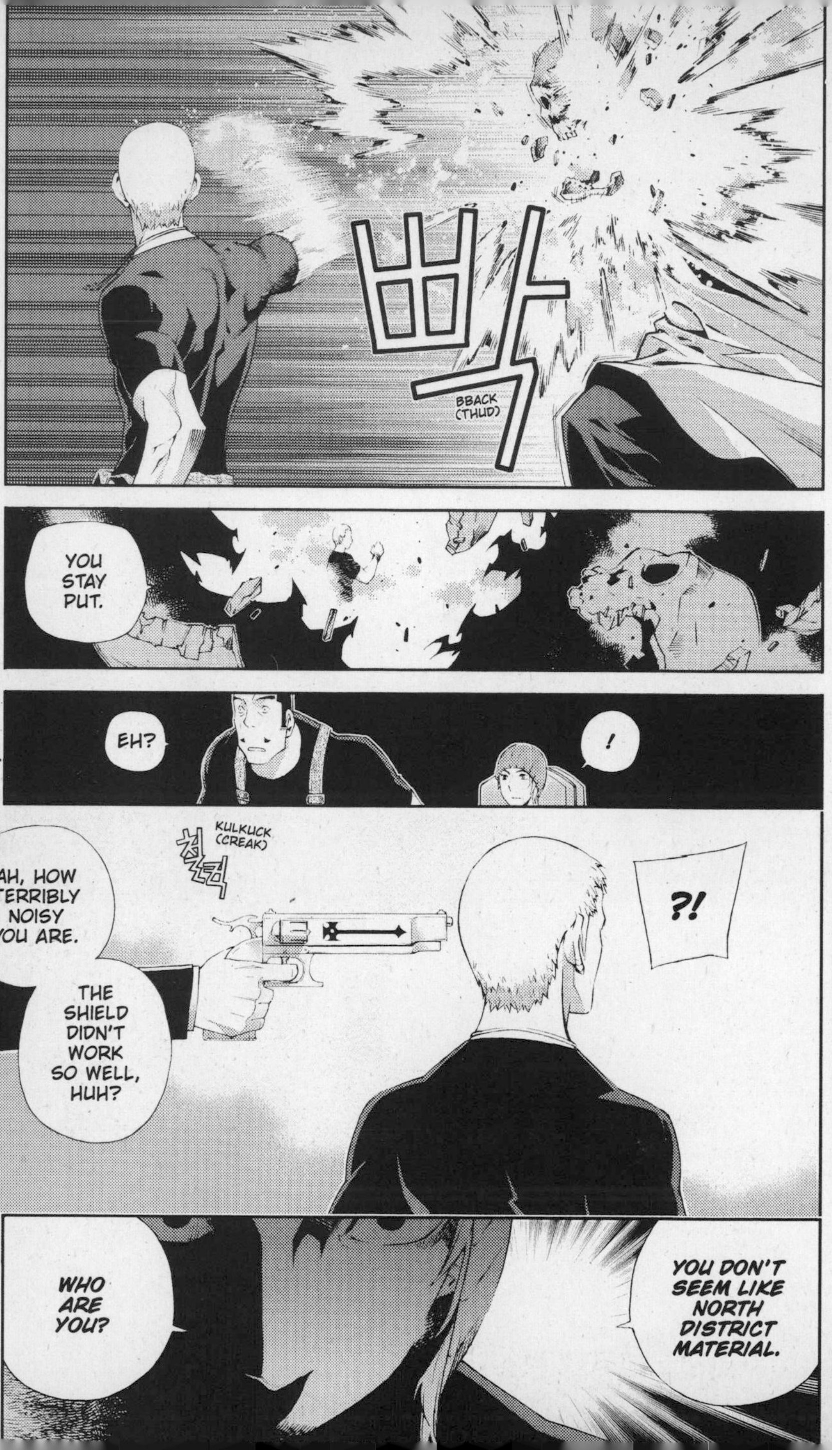

빡
BBACK (THUD)
YOU STAY PUT.
!
EH?
?!
철컥
KULKUCK (CREAK)
AH, HOW TERRIBLY NOISY YOU ARE.
THE SHIELD DIDN'T WORK SO WELL, HUH?
YOU DON'T SEEM LIKE NORTH DISTRICT MATERIAL.
WHO ARE YOU?

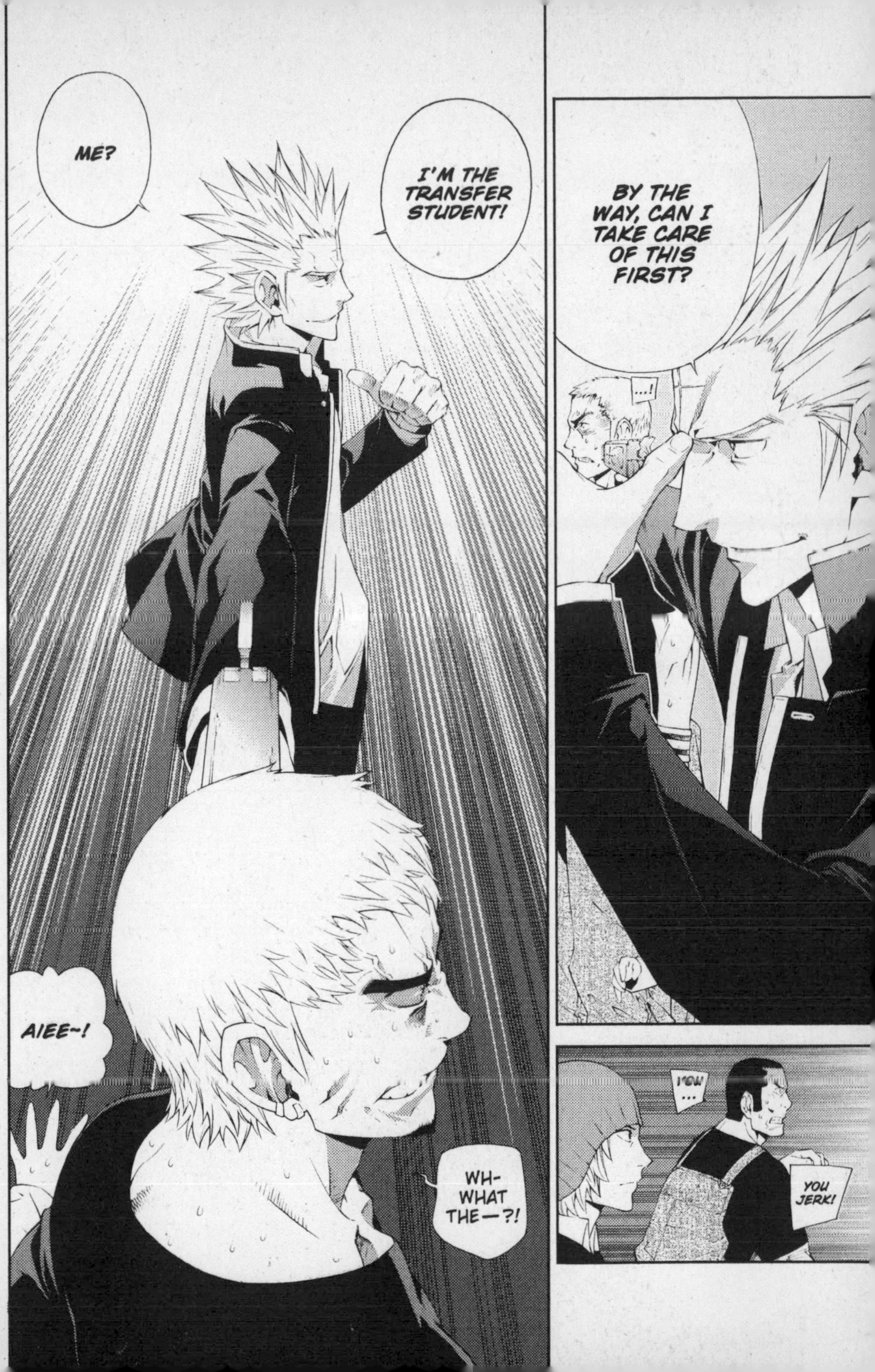
ME?
I'M THE TRANSFER STUDENT!
AIEE~!
WH- WHAT THE—?!
BY THE WAY, CAN I TAKE CARE OF THIS FIRST?
...!
YOU JERK!

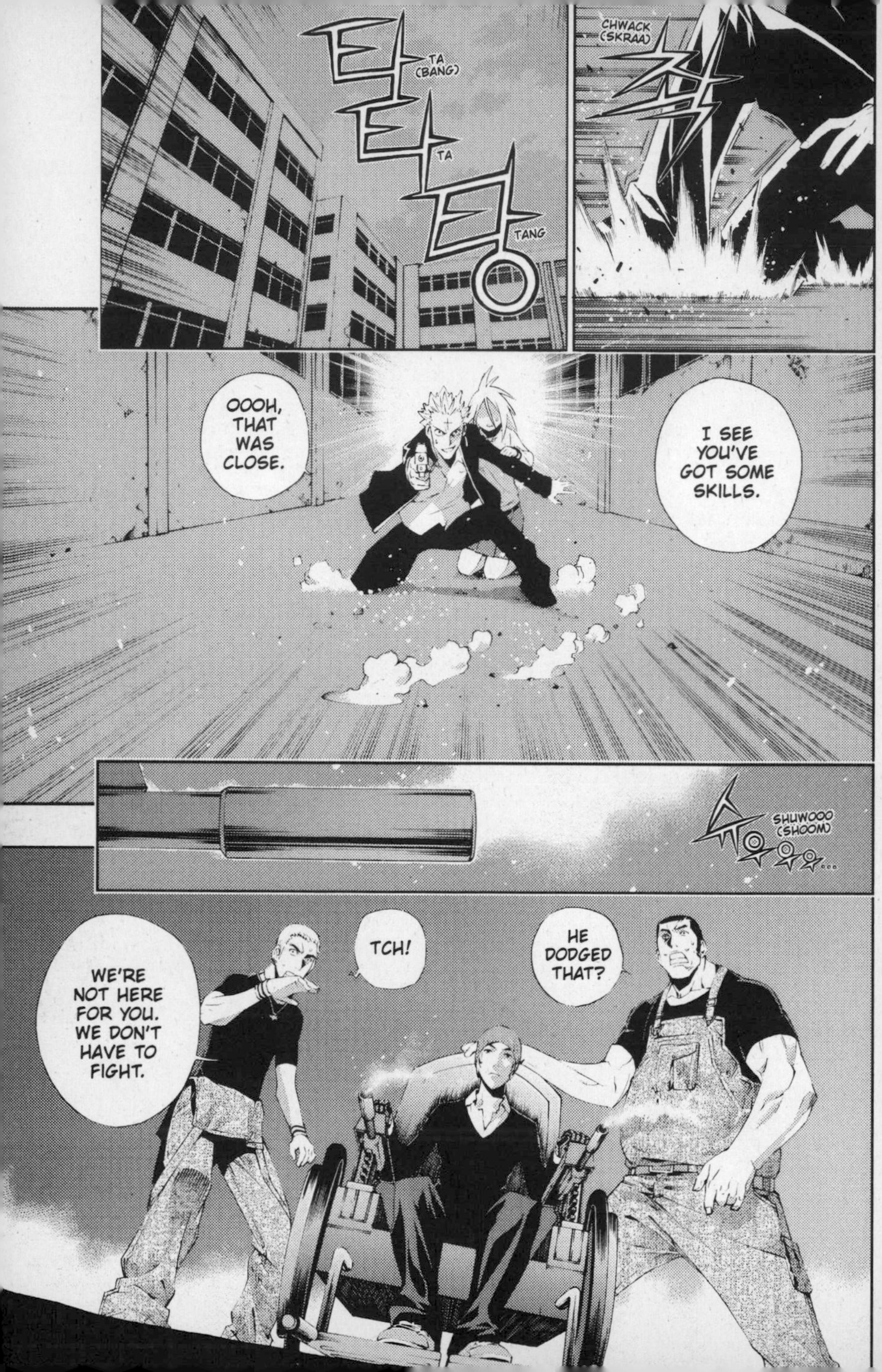
TA (BANG)
TA
TANG
CHWACK (SKRAA)
OOOH, THAT WAS CLOSE.
I SEE YOU'VE GOT SOME SKILLS.
SHUWOOO (SHOOM)
WE'RE NOT HERE FOR YOU. WE DON'T HAVE TO FIGHT.
TCH!
HE DODGED THAT?

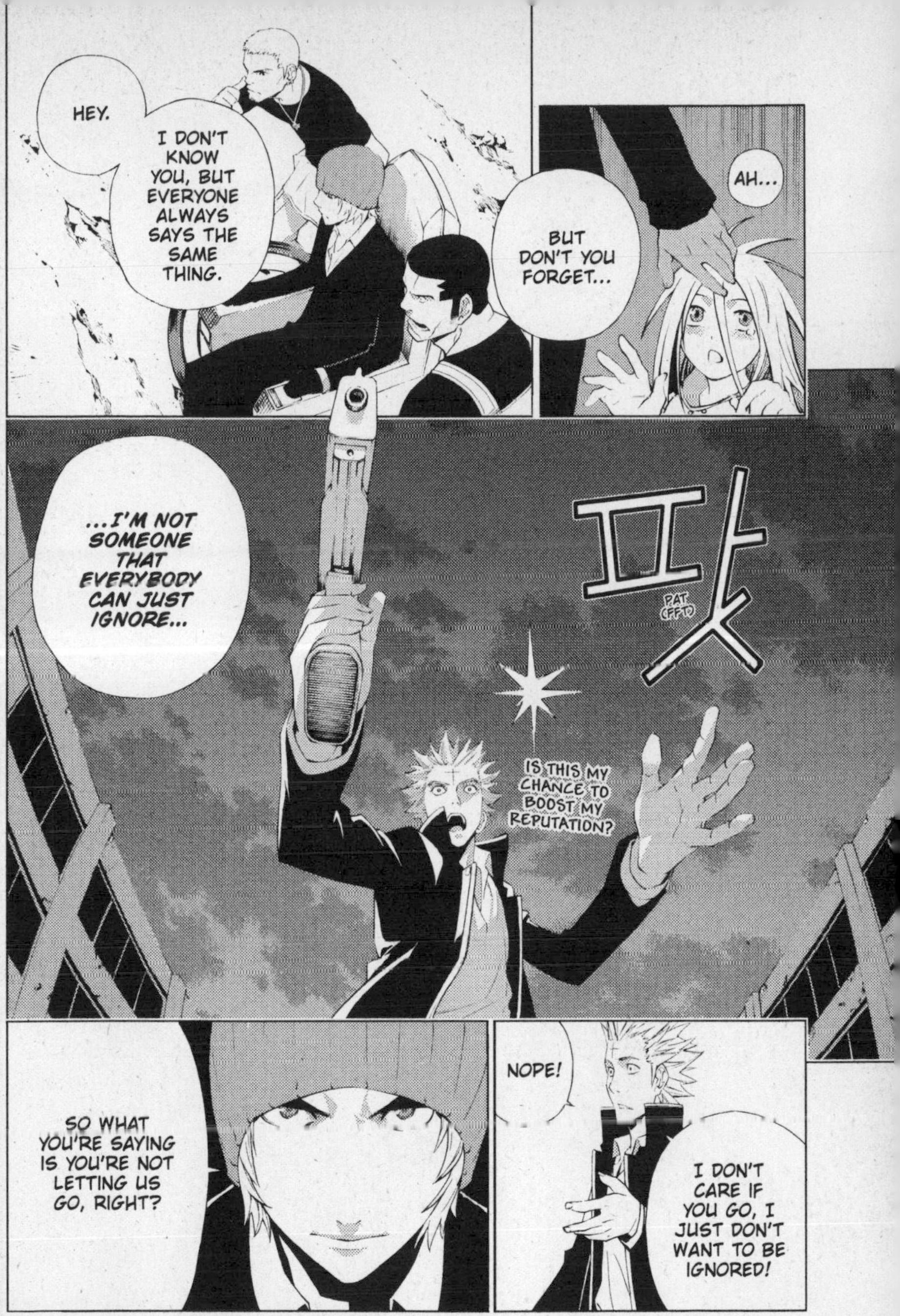
HEY.
I DON'T KNOW YOU, BUT EVERYONE ALWAYS SAYS THE SAME THING.
BUT DON'T YOU FORGET...
AH...
...I'M NOT SOMEONE THAT EVERYBODY CAN JUST IGNORE...
PAT (FFT)
IS THIS MY CHANCE TO BOOST MY REPUTATION?
SO WHAT YOU'RE SAYING IS YOU'RE NOT LETTING US GO, RIGHT?
NOPE!
I DON'T CARE IF YOU GO, I JUST DON'T WANT TO BE IGNORED!

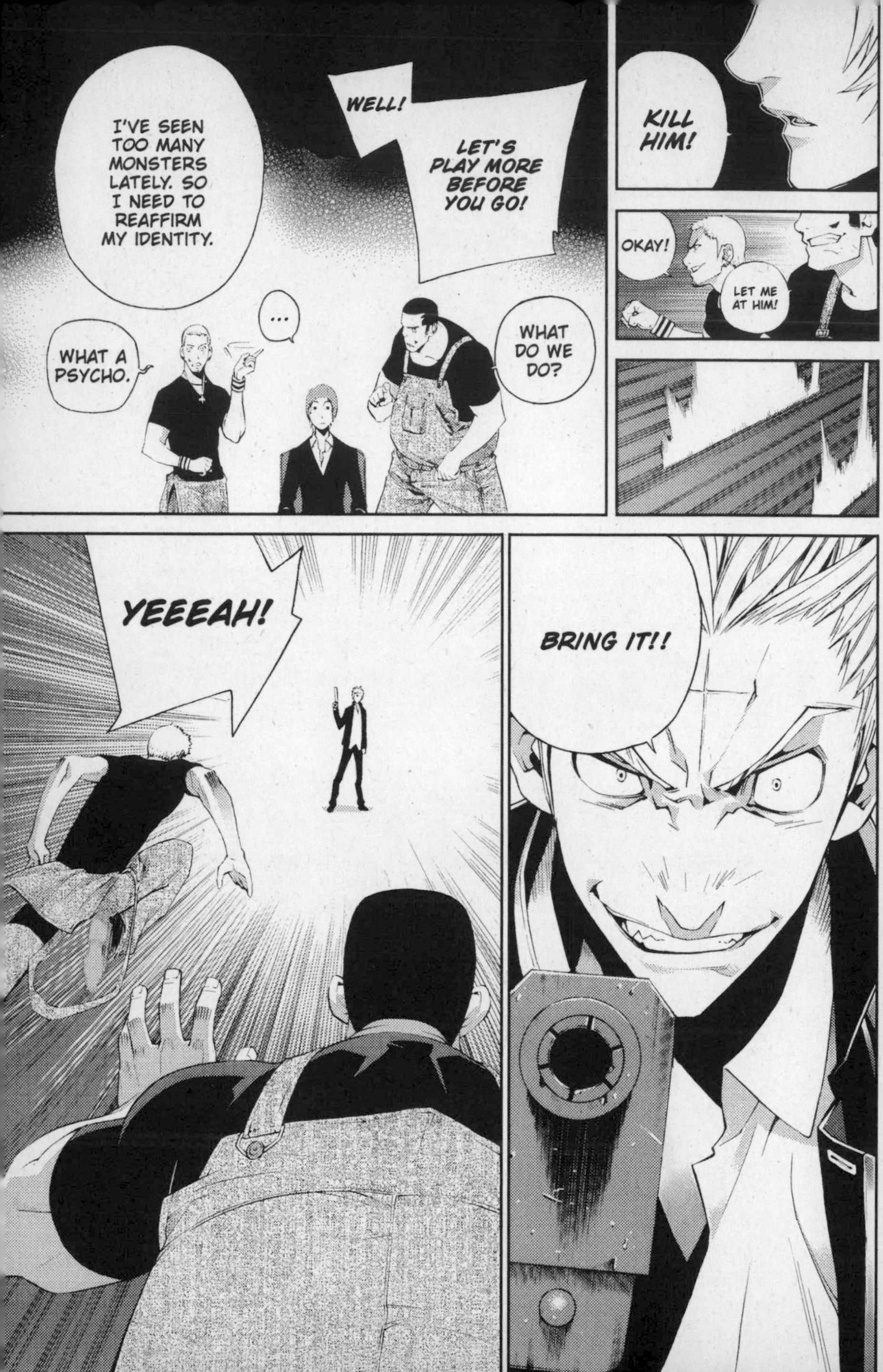
I'VE SEEN TOO MANY MONSTERS LATELY. SO I NEED TO REAFFIRM MY IDENTITY.
WELL!
LET'S PLAY MORE BEFORE YOU GO!
WHAT A PSYCHO.
...
WHAT DO WE DO?
KILL HIM!
OKAY!
LET ME AT HIM!
YEEEAH!
BRING IT!!

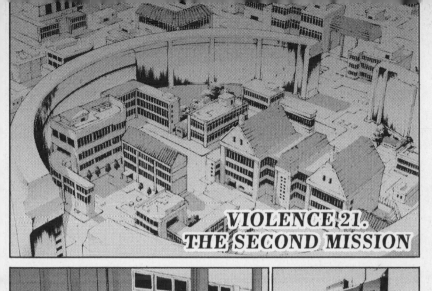

VIOLENCE 21.
THE SECOND MISSION

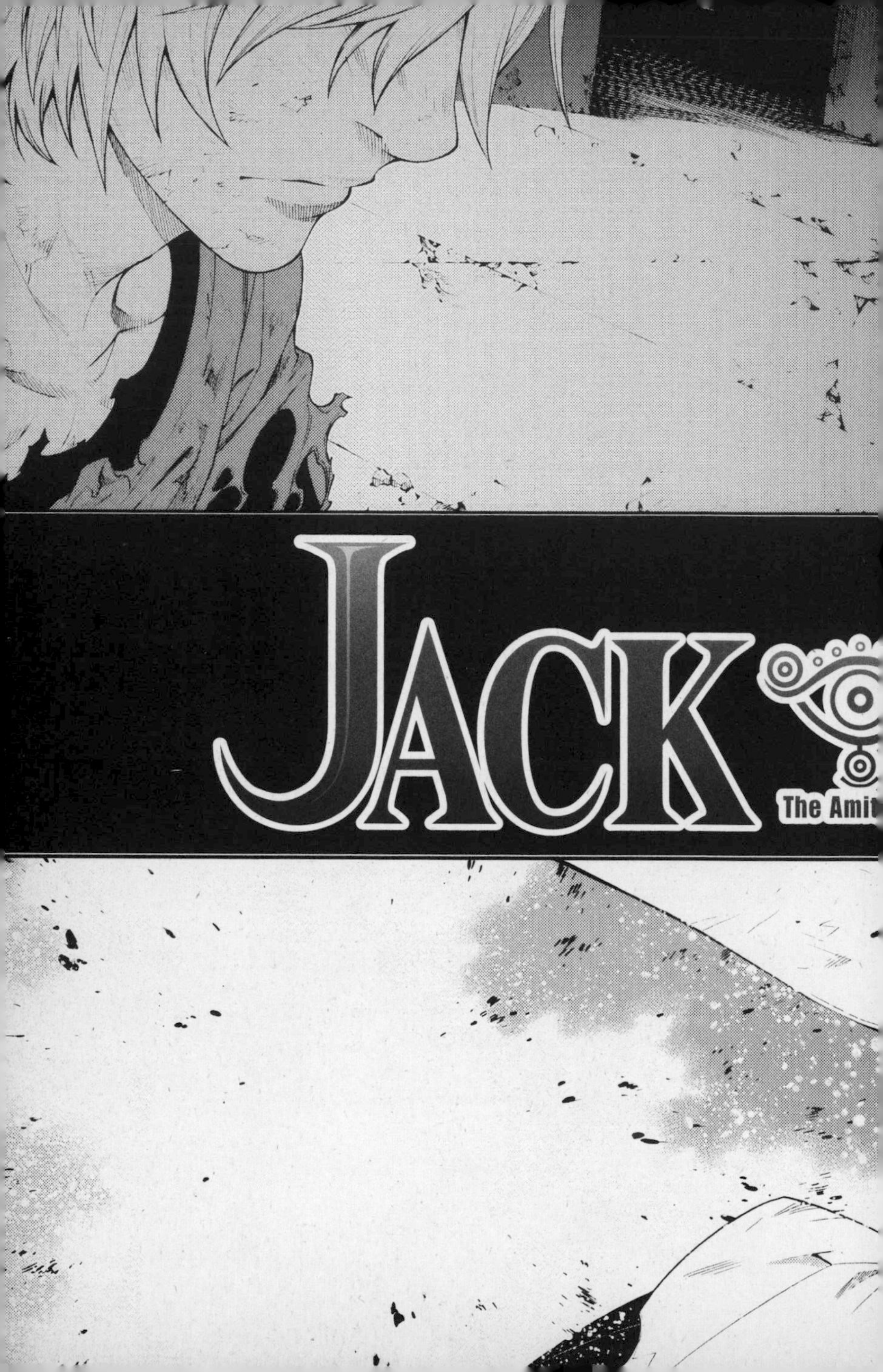
JACK
The Amit

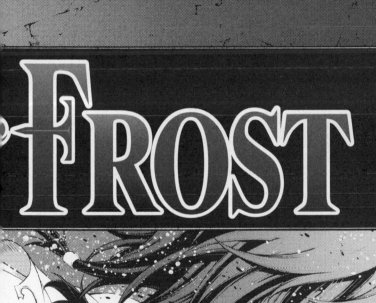

FROST

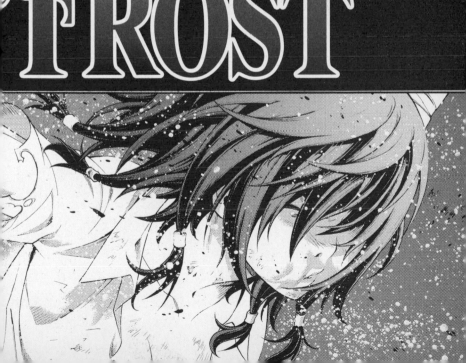

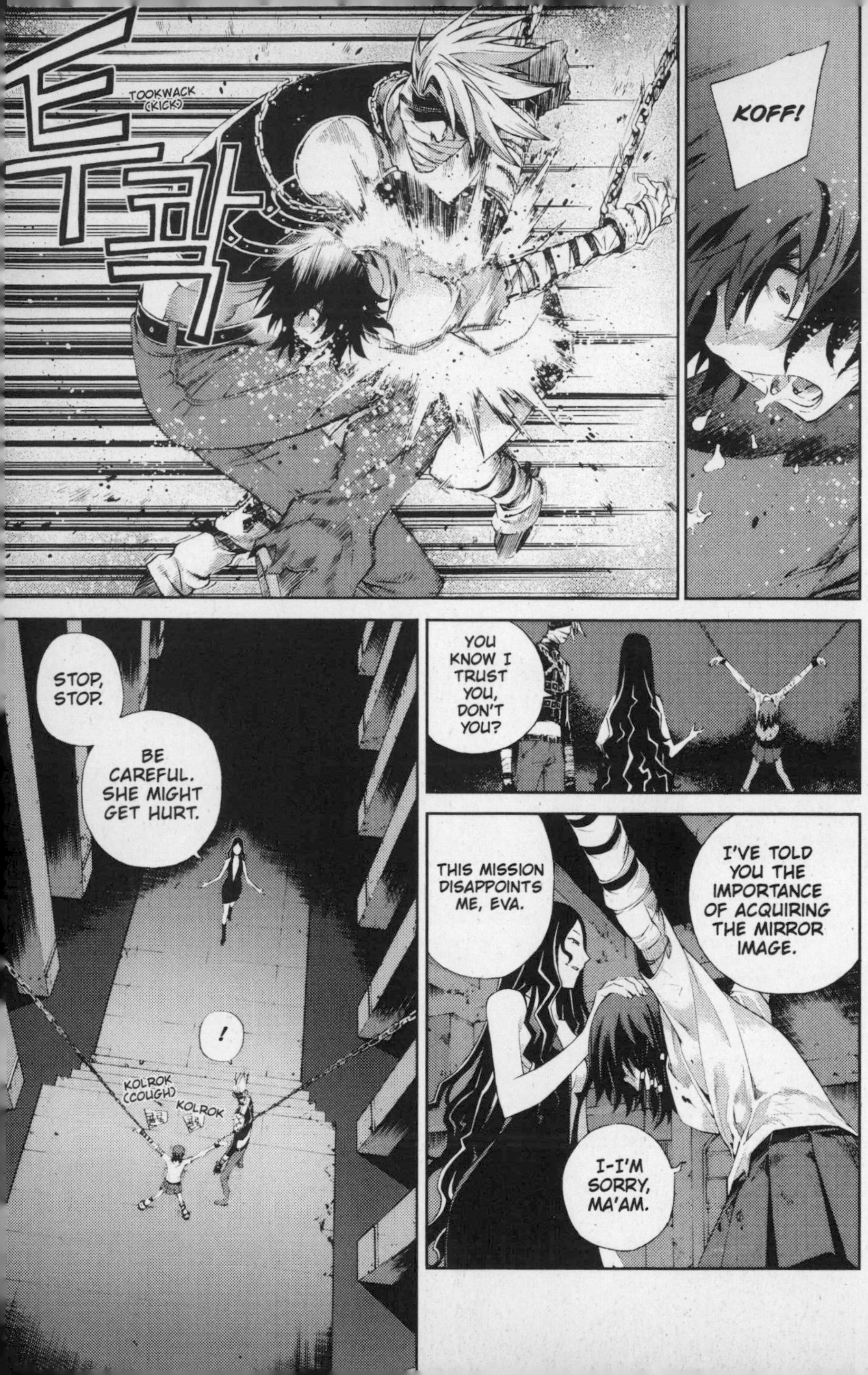
TOOKWACK (KICK)
KOFF!
STOP, STOP.
BE CAREFUL. SHE MIGHT GET HURT.
!
KOLROK (COUGH)
KOLROK
YOU KNOW I TRUST YOU, DON'T YOU?
THIS MISSION DISAPPOINTS ME, EVA.
I'VE TOLD YOU THE IMPORTANCE OF ACQUIRING THE MIRROR IMAGE.
I-I'M SORRY, MA'AM.

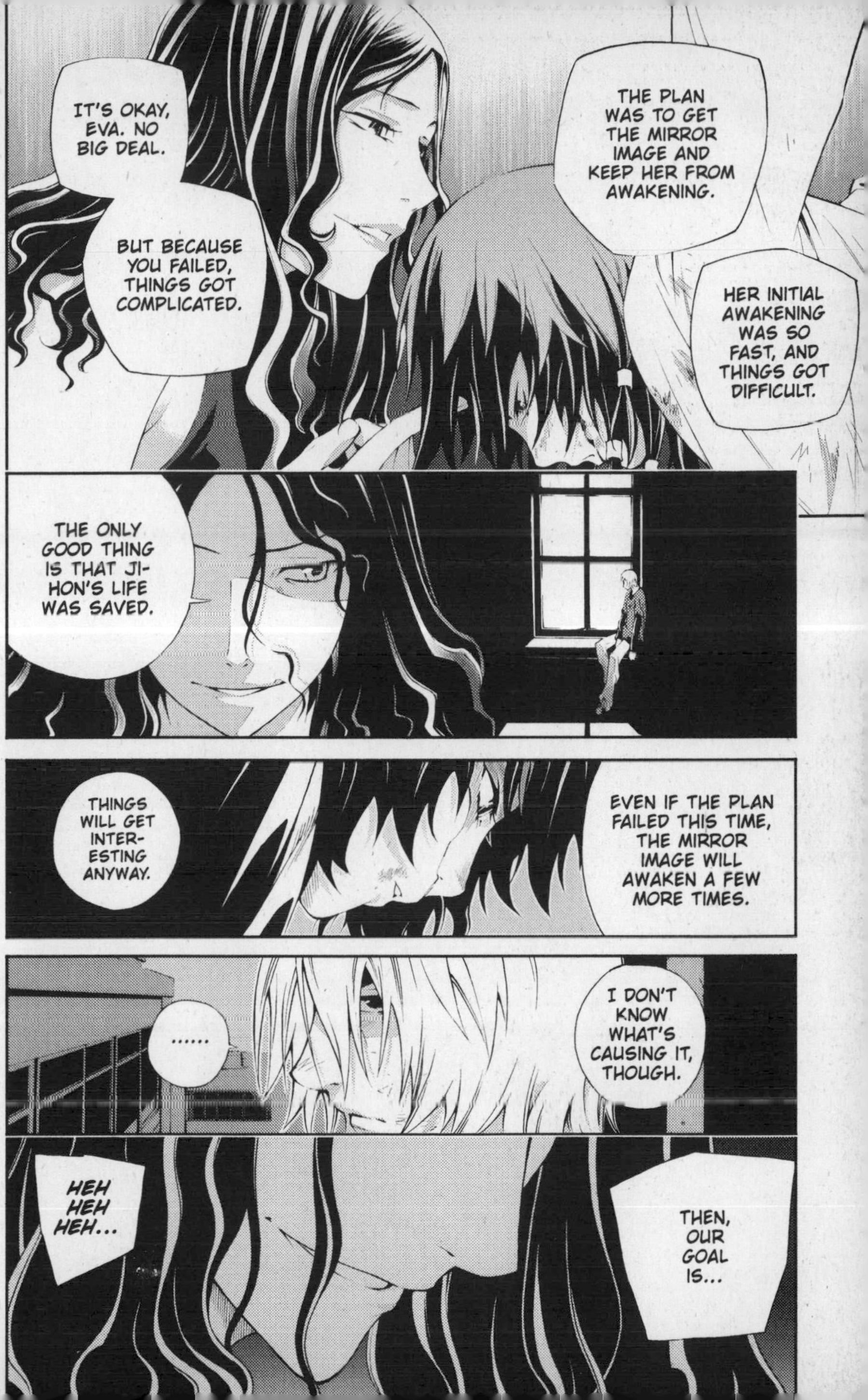

IT'S OKAY, EVA. NO BIG DEAL.
BUT BECAUSE YOU FAILED, THINGS GOT COMPLICATED.
THE PLAN WAS TO GET THE MIRROR IMAGE AND KEEP HER FROM AWAKENING.
HER INITIAL AWAKENING WAS SO FAST, AND THINGS GOT DIFFICULT.
THE ONLY GOOD THING IS THAT JI-HON'S LIFE WAS SAVED.
THINGS WILL GET INTER-ESTING ANYWAY.
EVEN IF THE PLAN FAILED THIS TIME, THE MIRROR IMAGE WILL AWAKEN A FEW MORE TIMES.
......
I DON'T KNOW WHAT'S CAUSING IT, THOUGH.
HEH HEH HEH...
THEN, OUR GOAL IS...

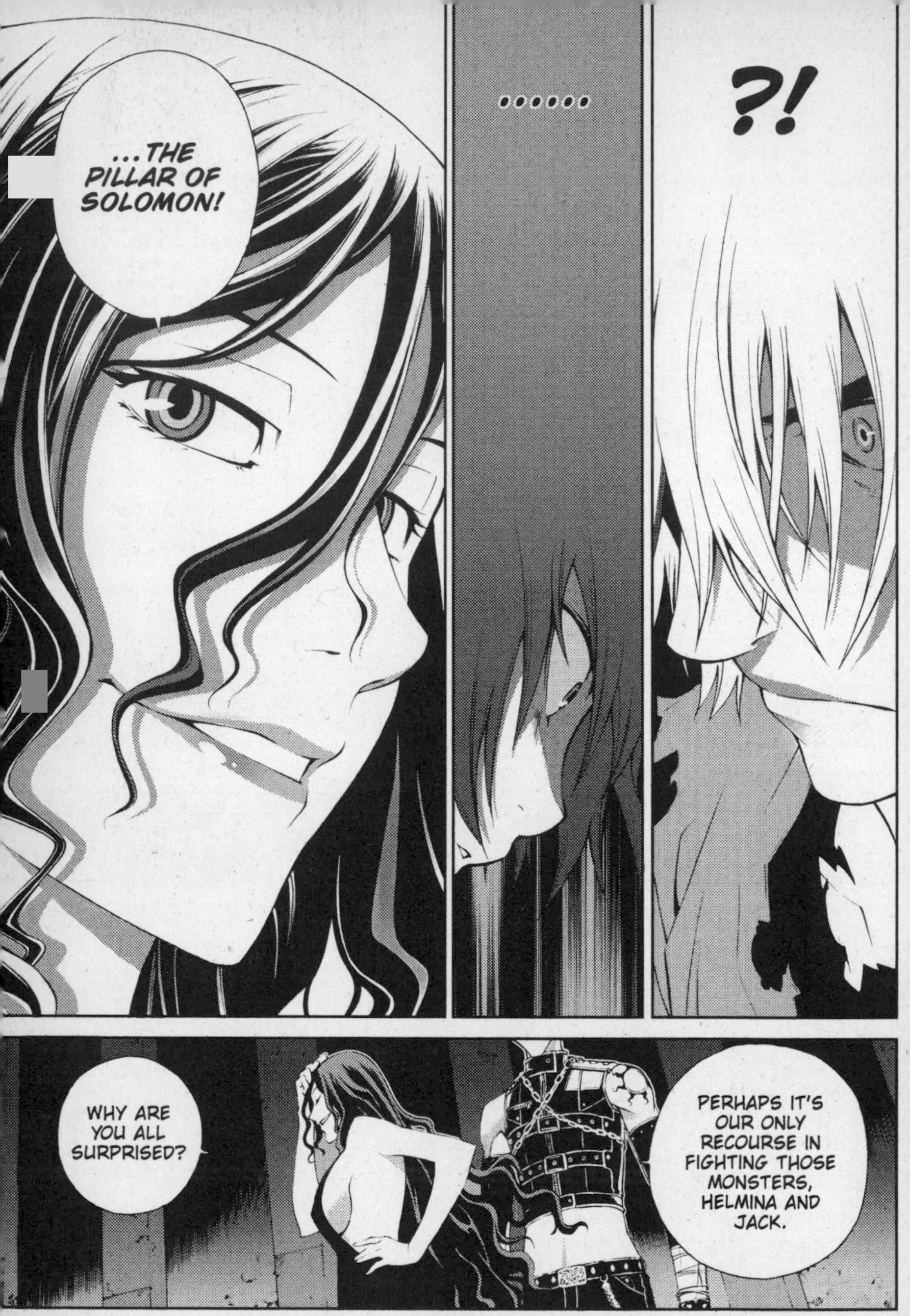
...THE PILLAR OF SOLOMON!
......
?!
WHY ARE YOU ALL SURPRISED?
PERHAPS IT'S OUR ONLY RECOURSE IN FIGHTING THOSE MONSTERS, HELMINA AND JACK.

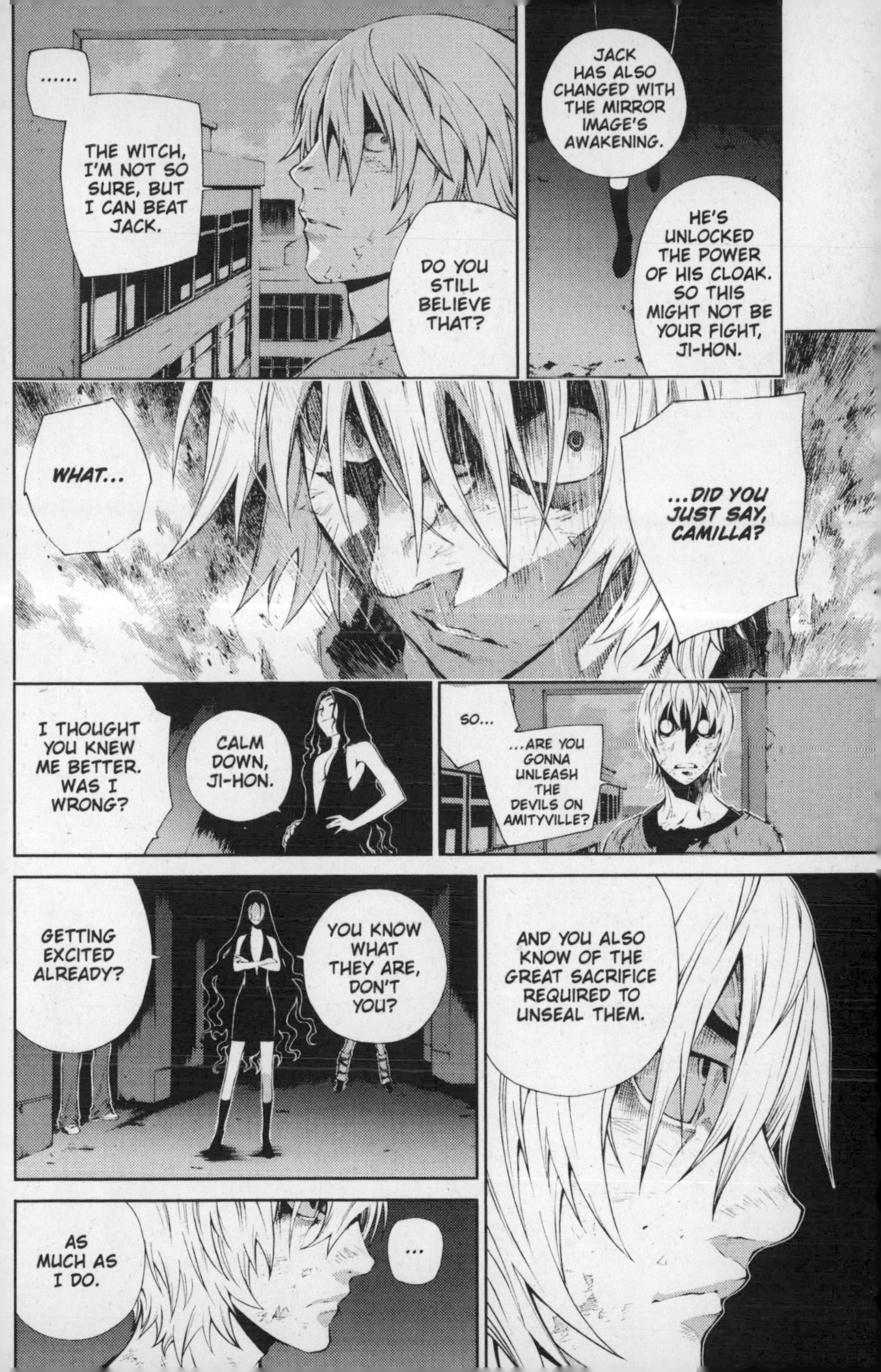
......
THE WITCH, I'M NOT SO SURE, BUT I CAN BEAT JACK.
DO YOU STILL BELIEVE THAT?
JACK HAS ALSO CHANGED WITH THE MIRROR IMAGE'S AWAKENING.
HE'S UNLOCKED THE POWER OF HIS CLOAK. SO THIS MIGHT NOT BE YOUR FIGHT, JI-HON.
WHAT...
...DID YOU JUST SAY, CAMILLA?
I THOUGHT YOU KNEW ME BETTER. WAS I WRONG?
CALM DOWN, JI-HON.
SO...
...ARE YOU GONNA UNLEASH THE DEVILS ON AMITYVILLE?
GETTING EXCITED ALREADY?
YOU KNOW WHAT THEY ARE, DON'T YOU?
AS MUCH AS I DO.
...
AND YOU ALSO KNOW OF THE GREAT SACRIFICE REQUIRED TO UNSEAL THEM.

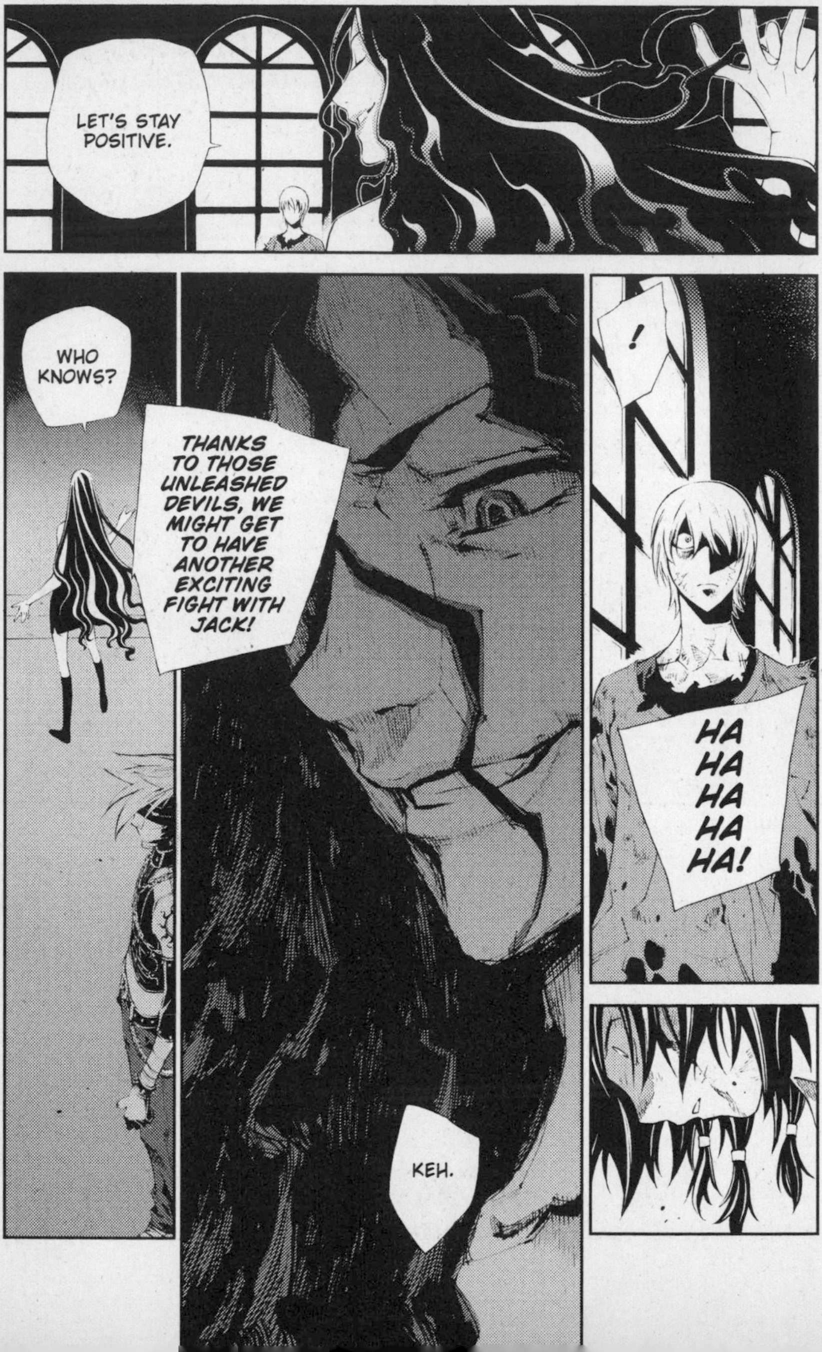
LET'S STAY POSITIVE.
WHO KNOWS?
THANKS TO THOSE UNLEASHED DEVILS, WE MIGHT GET TO HAVE ANOTHER EXCITING FIGHT WITH JACK!
KEH.
!
HA HA HA HA HA!

HMPH
...

HEH.

STAY
POSITIVE...?

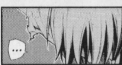

...

THE PILLAR
OF SOLOMON
IS SEALED IN
THE "LOST
LAKE."

HAVE YOU
FORGOTTEN
THAT ONLY
TWO PEOPLE
KNOW ITS
LOCATION?

HOW
COULD I
FORGET
SUCH
PERTINENT
INFORMA-
TION?

......

SO THEN,
DO YOU HAVE
A PLAN?

DON'T
WORRY.

SOONER OR
LATER, THE
LOST LAKE'S
LOCATION
WILL BE...

...REVEALED
BY HELMINA.

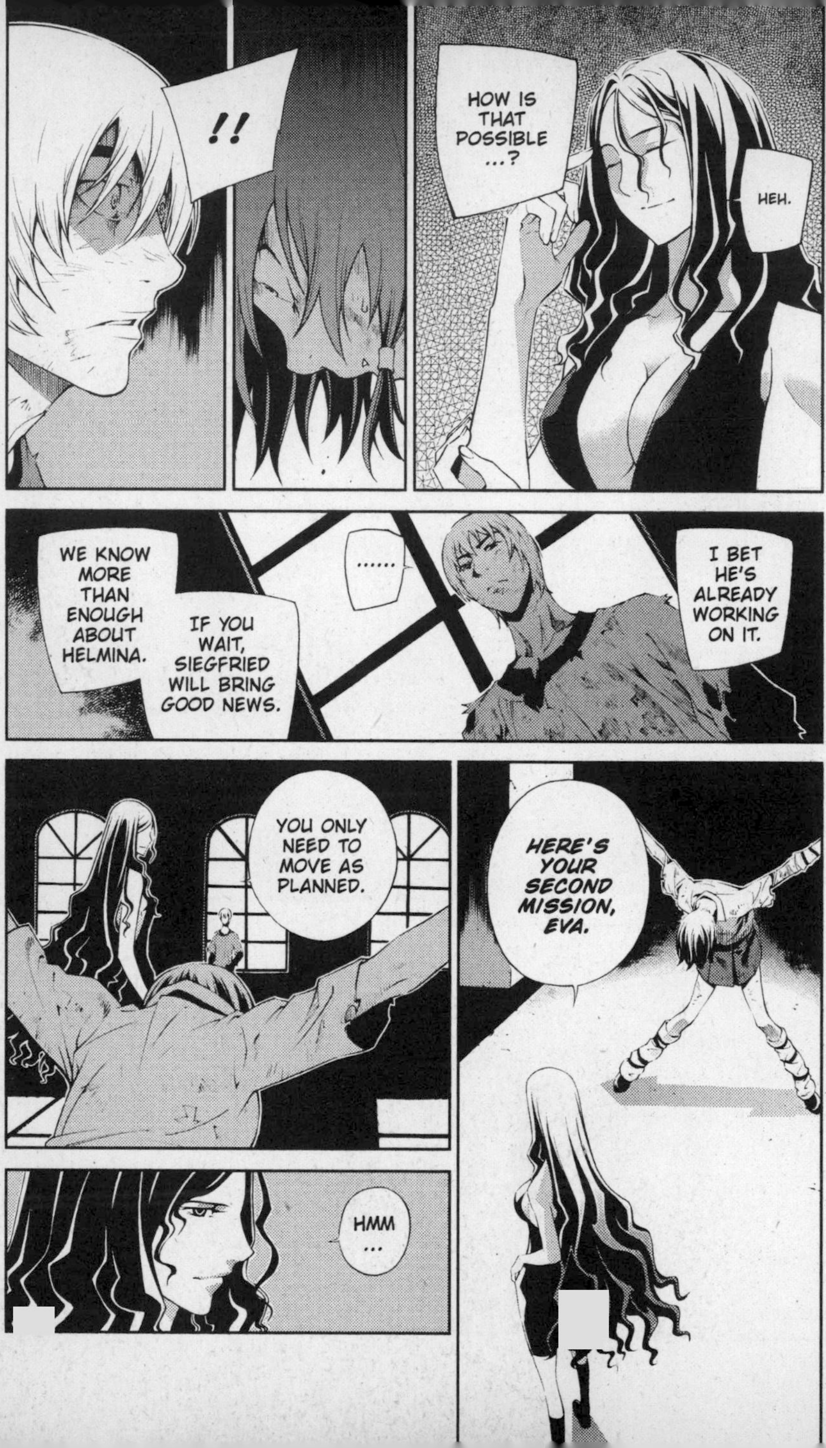
!!
HOW IS THAT POSSIBLE ...?
HEH.
WE KNOW MORE THAN ENOUGH ABOUT HELMINA.
IF YOU WAIT, SIEGFRIED WILL BRING GOOD NEWS.
......
I BET HE'S ALREADY WORKING ON IT.
YOU ONLY NEED TO MOVE AS PLANNED.
HMM ...
HERE'S YOUR SECOND MISSION, EVA.

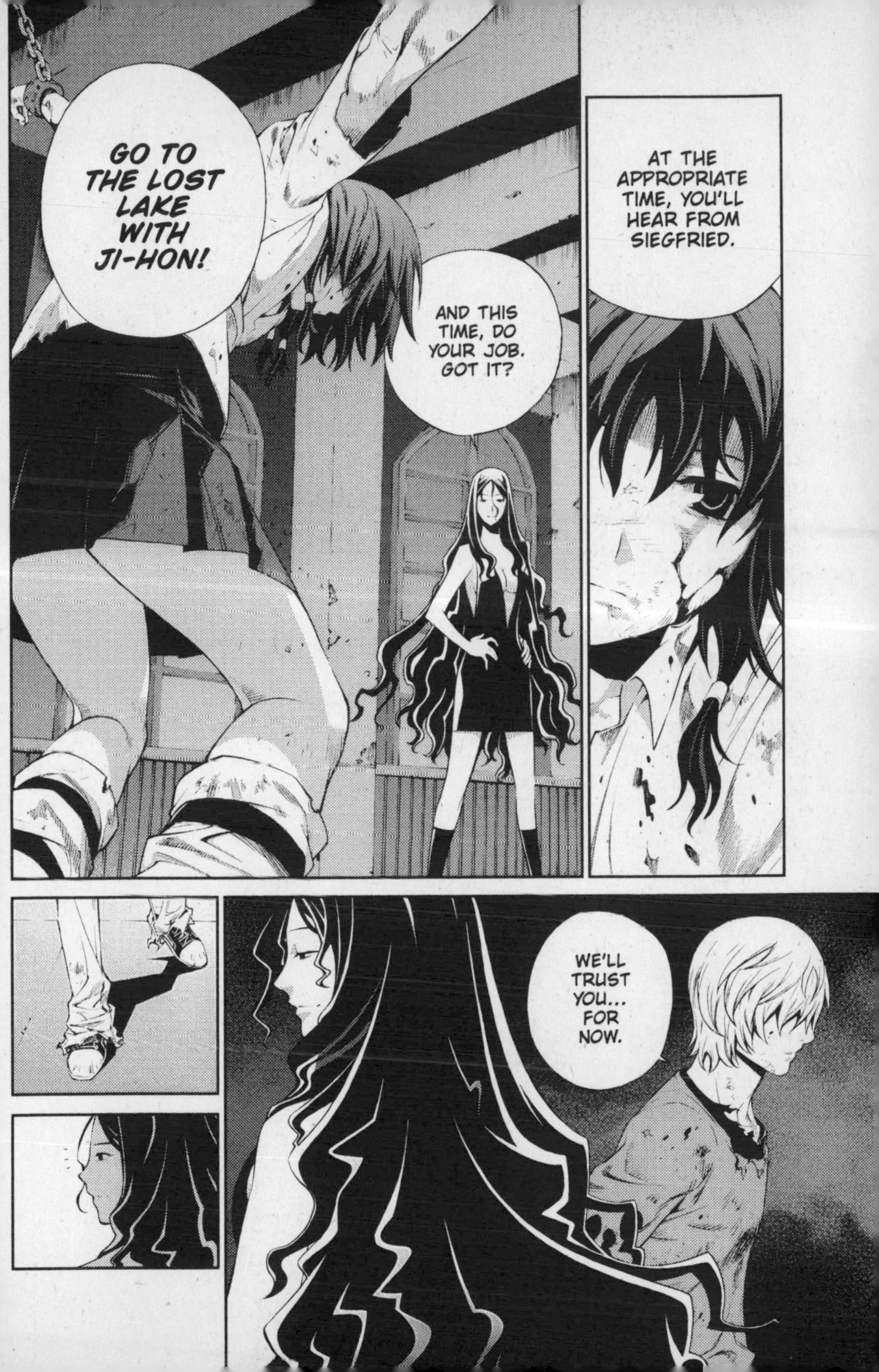
GO TO THE LOST LAKE WITH JI-HON!
AND THIS TIME, DO YOUR JOB. GOT IT?
AT THE APPROPRIATE TIME, YOU'LL HEAR FROM SIEGFRIED.
WE'LL TRUST YOU... FOR NOW.

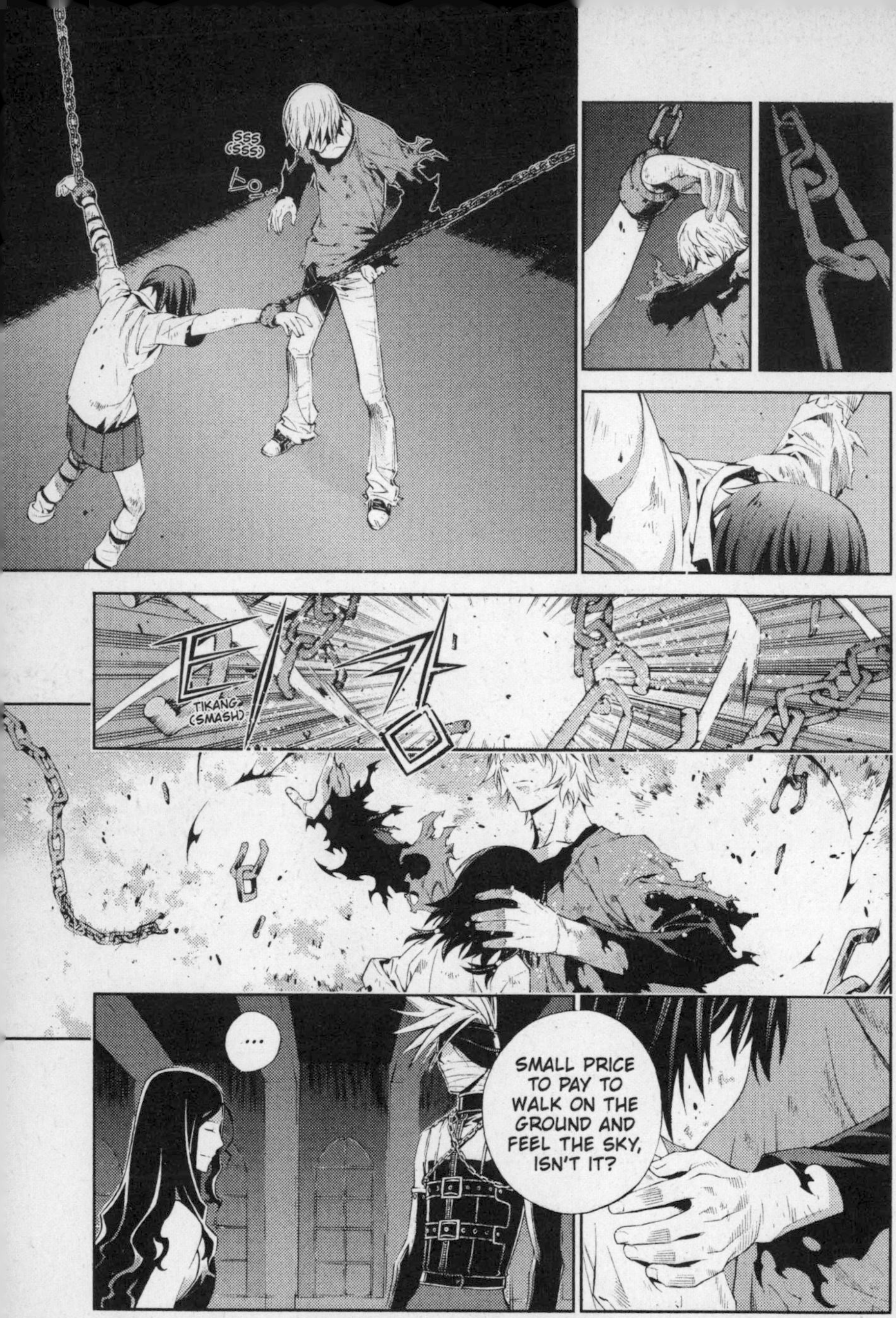

SSS (SSS)
스으...
티캉
TIKANG (SMASH)
....
SMALL PRICE TO PAY TO WALK ON THE GROUND AND FEEL THE SKY, ISN'T IT?

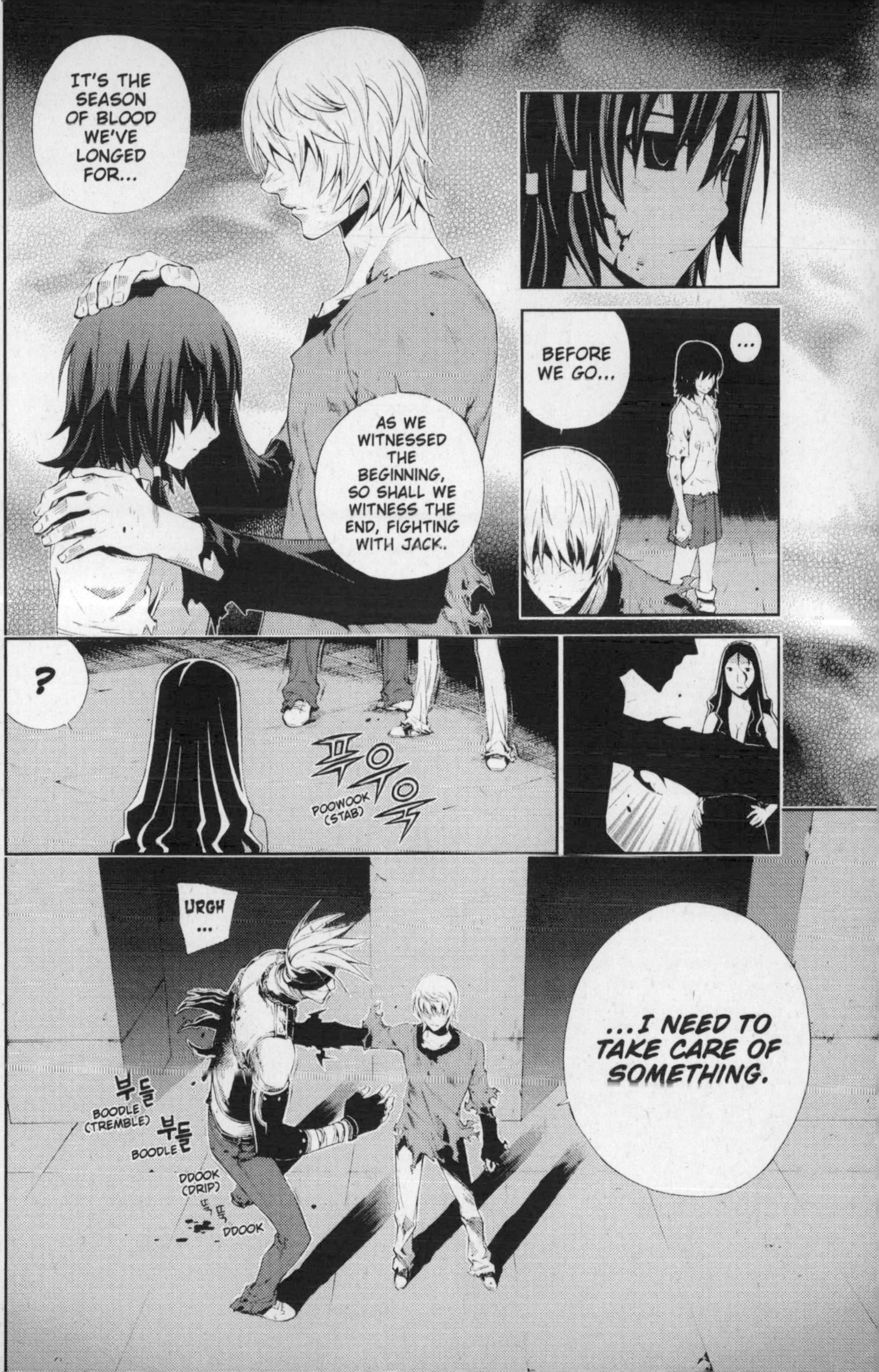
IT'S THE SEASON OF BLOOD WE'VE LONGED FOR...
AS WE WITNESSED THE BEGINNING, SO SHALL WE WITNESS THE END, FIGHTING WITH JACK.
BEFORE WE GO...
...
?
푸우욱
POOWOOK (STAB)
URGH ...
부들
BOODLE (TREMBLE)
부들
BOODLE
DDOOK (DRIP)
뚝 뚝
DDOOK
...I NEED TO TAKE CARE OF SOMETHING.

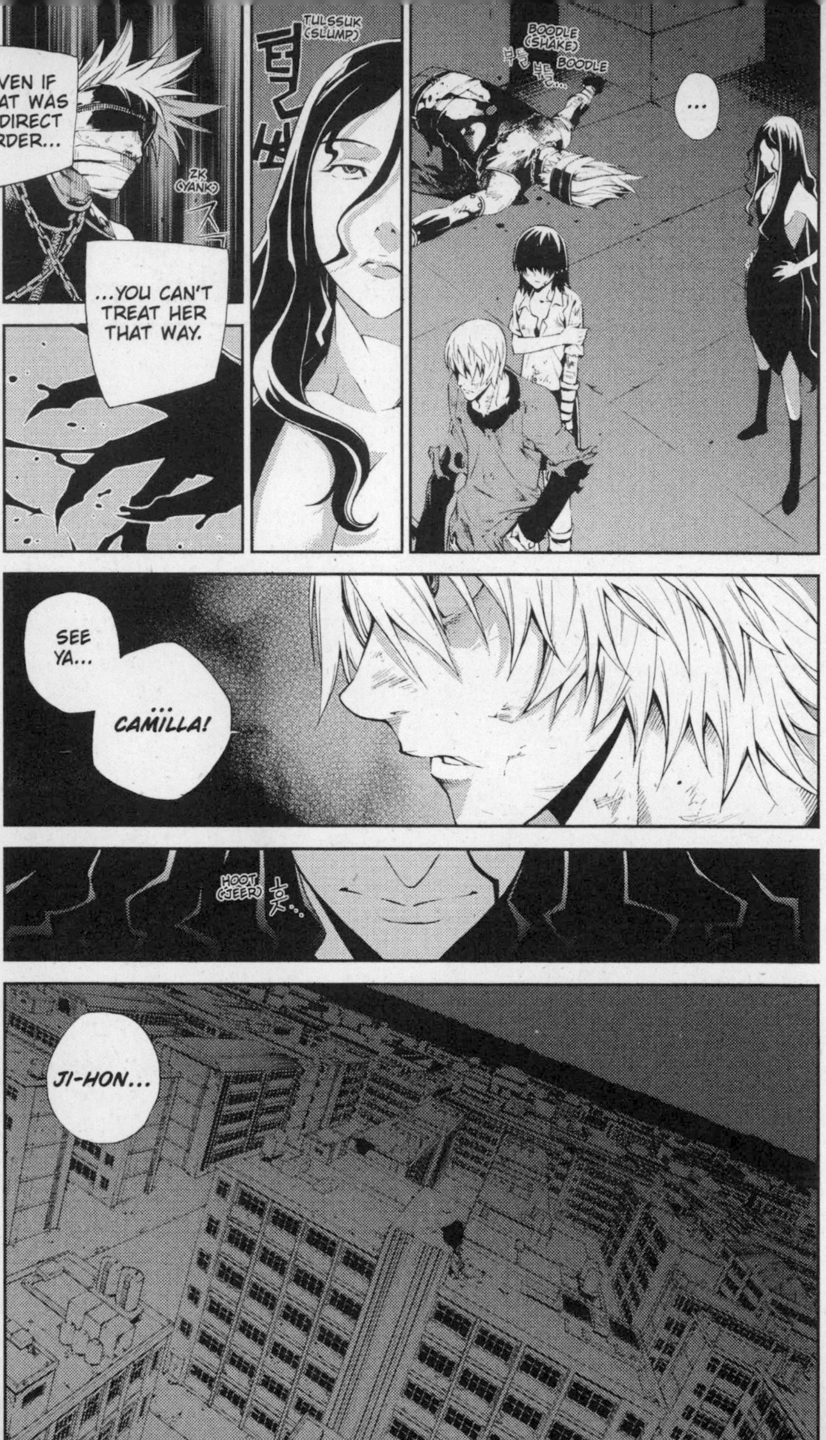
EVEN IF THAT WAS A DIRECT ORDER...
ZK (YANK)
...YOU CAN'T TREAT HER THAT WAY.
TULSSUK (SLUMP)
털썩
BOODLE (SHAKE)
부들 부들...
BOODLE
...
SEE YA...
...CAMILLA!
HOOT (JEER)
훗...
JI-HON...

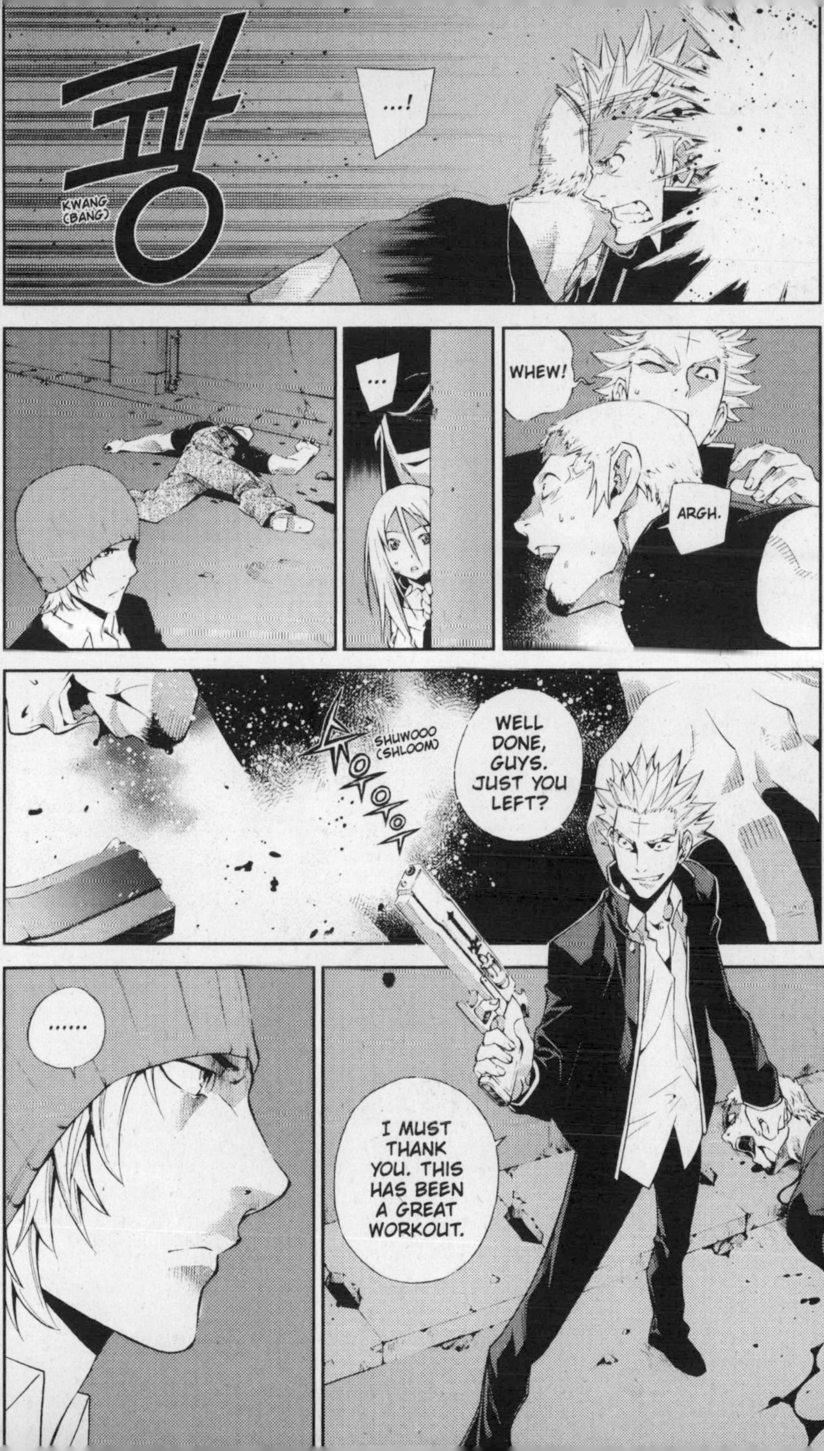
광
KWANG (BANG)
...!
...
WHEW!
ARGH.
SHUWOOO (SHLOOM)
WELL DONE, GUYS. JUST YOU LEFT?
......
I MUST THANK YOU. THIS HAS BEEN A GREAT WORKOUT.

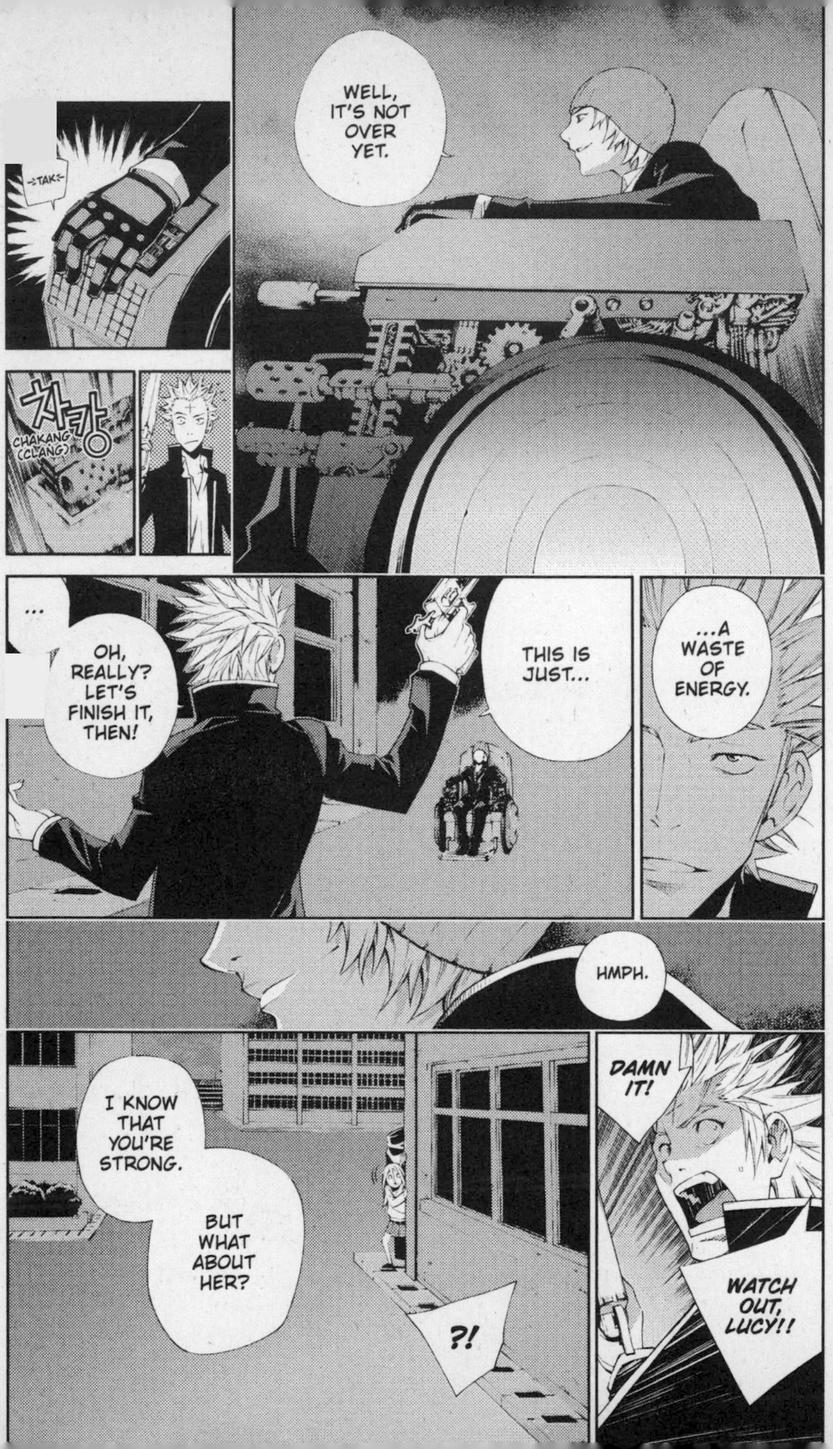
TAK
차캉
CHAKANG (CLANG)
WELL, IT'S NOT OVER YET.
...
OH, REALLY? LET'S FINISH IT, THEN!
THIS IS JUST...
...A WASTE OF ENERGY.
HMPH.
I KNOW THAT YOU'RE STRONG.
BUT WHAT ABOUT HER?
?!
DAMN IT!
WATCH OUT, LUCY!!

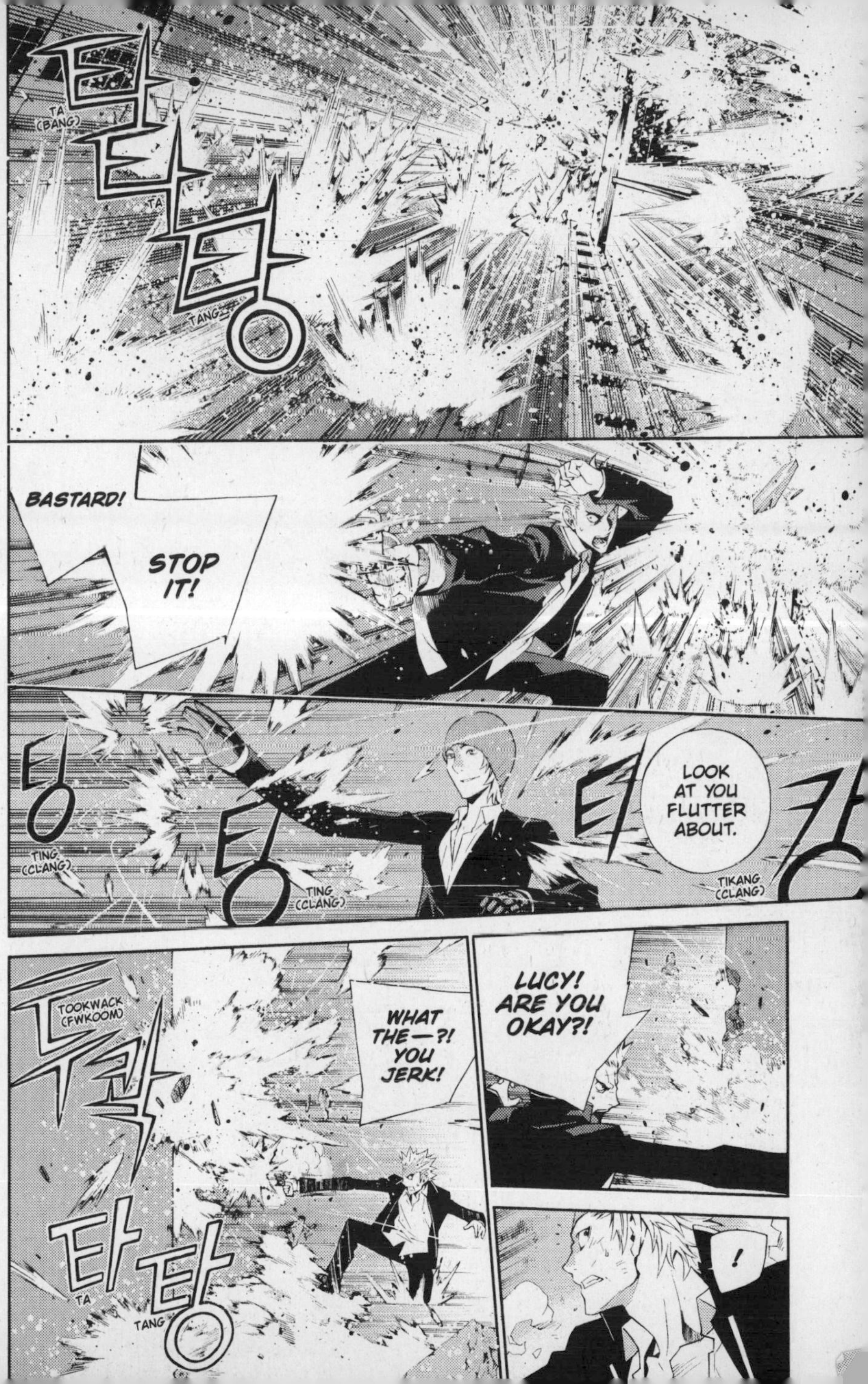
TA (BANG)
TA
TANG
BASTARD!
STOP IT!
TING (CLANG)
TING (CLANG)
LOOK AT YOU FLUTTER ABOUT.
TIKANG (CLANG)
TOOKWACK (FWKOOM)
WHAT THE—?! YOU JERK!
TA
TANG
LUCY! ARE YOU OKAY?!
!

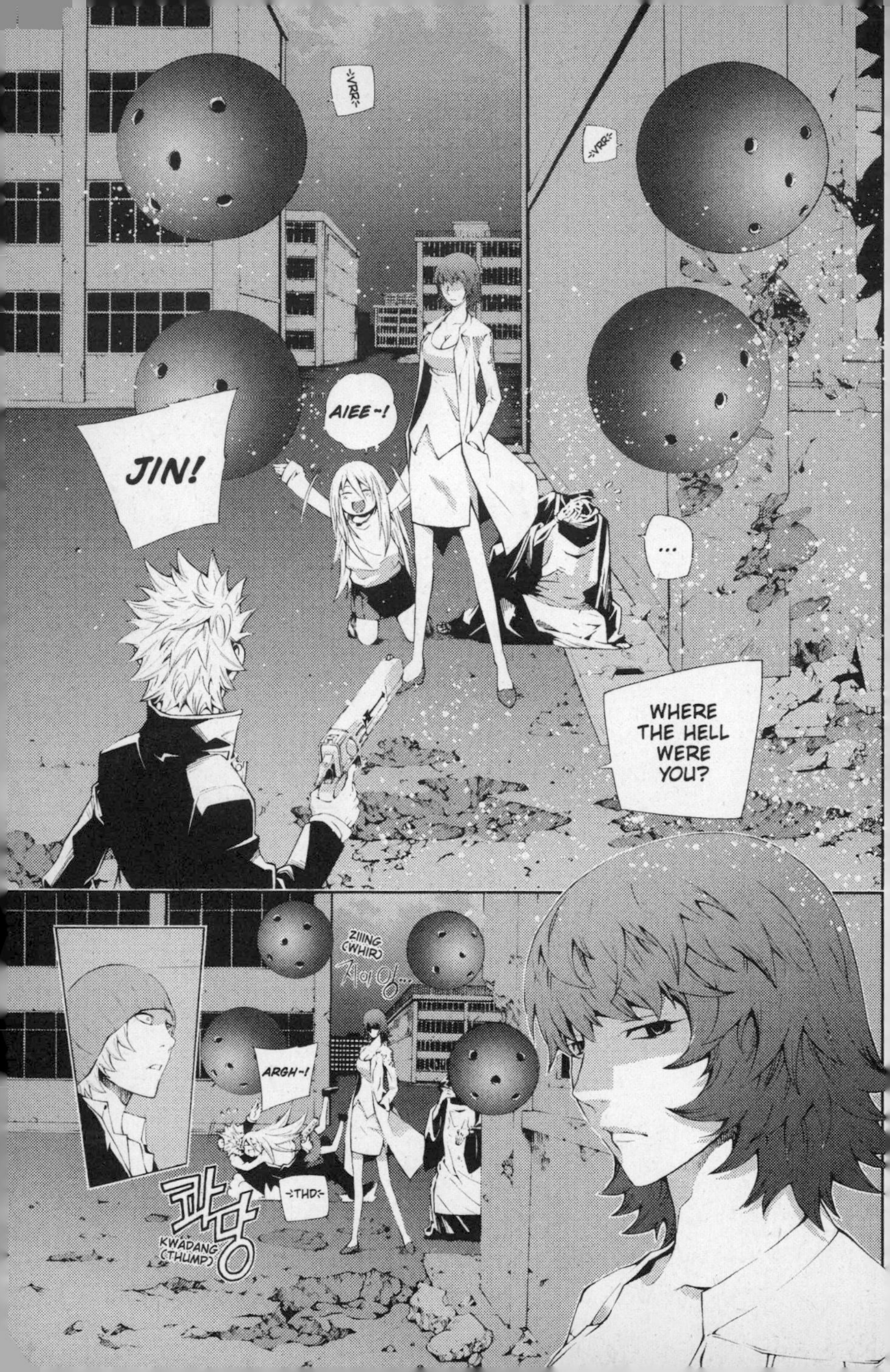
~VRR~
~VRR~
AIEE~!
JIN!
...
WHERE THE HELL WERE YOU?
ZIIING (WHIR)
지이잉...
ARGH~!
~THD~
콰당
KWADANG (THUMP)

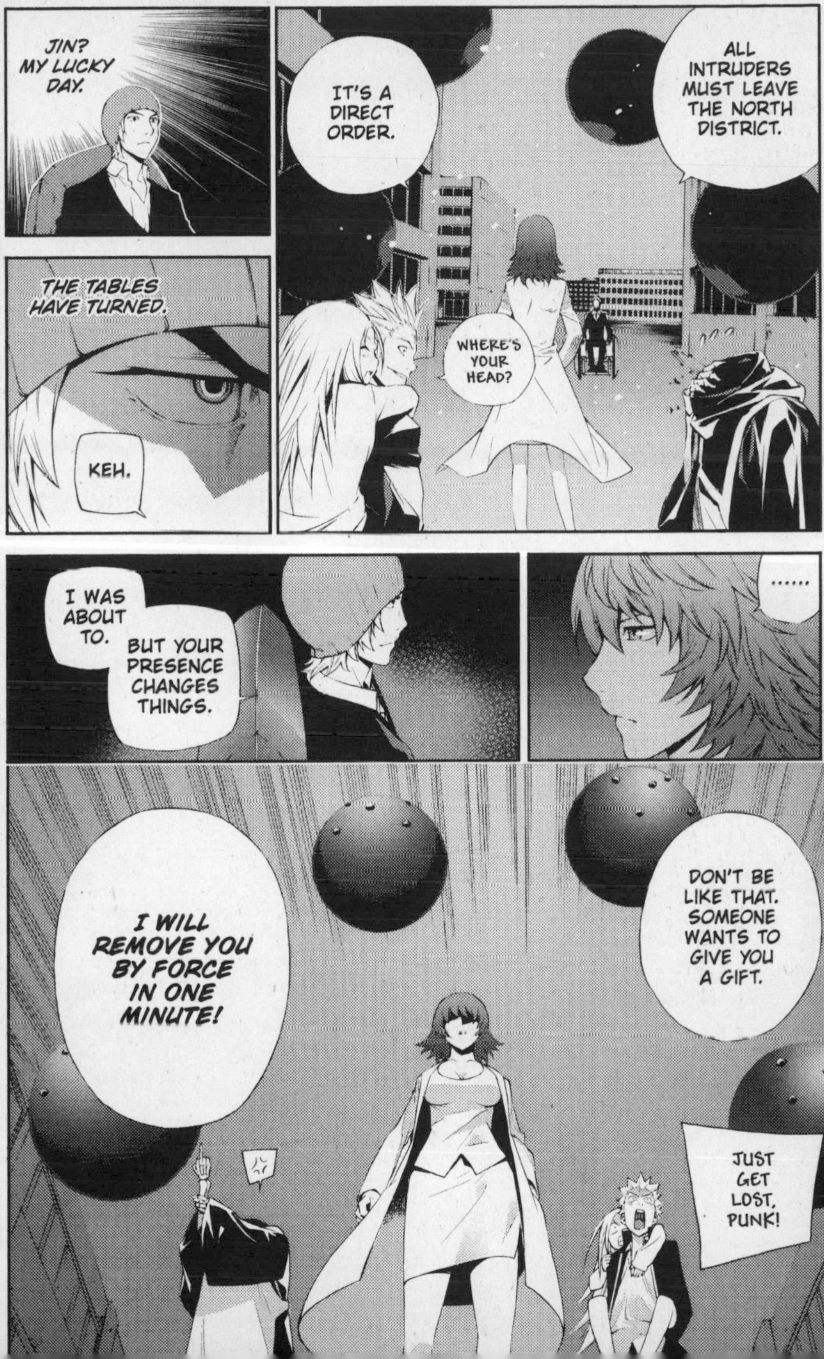

JIN? MY LUCKY DAY.
THE TABLES HAVE TURNED.
KEH.
IT'S A DIRECT ORDER.
ALL INTRUDERS MUST LEAVE THE NORTH DISTRICT.
WHERE'S YOUR HEAD?
I WAS ABOUT TO.
BUT YOUR PRESENCE CHANGES THINGS.
......
I WILL REMOVE YOU BY FORCE IN ONE MINUTE!
DON'T BE LIKE THAT. SOMEONE WANTS TO GIVE YOU A GIFT.
JUST GET LOST, PUNK!

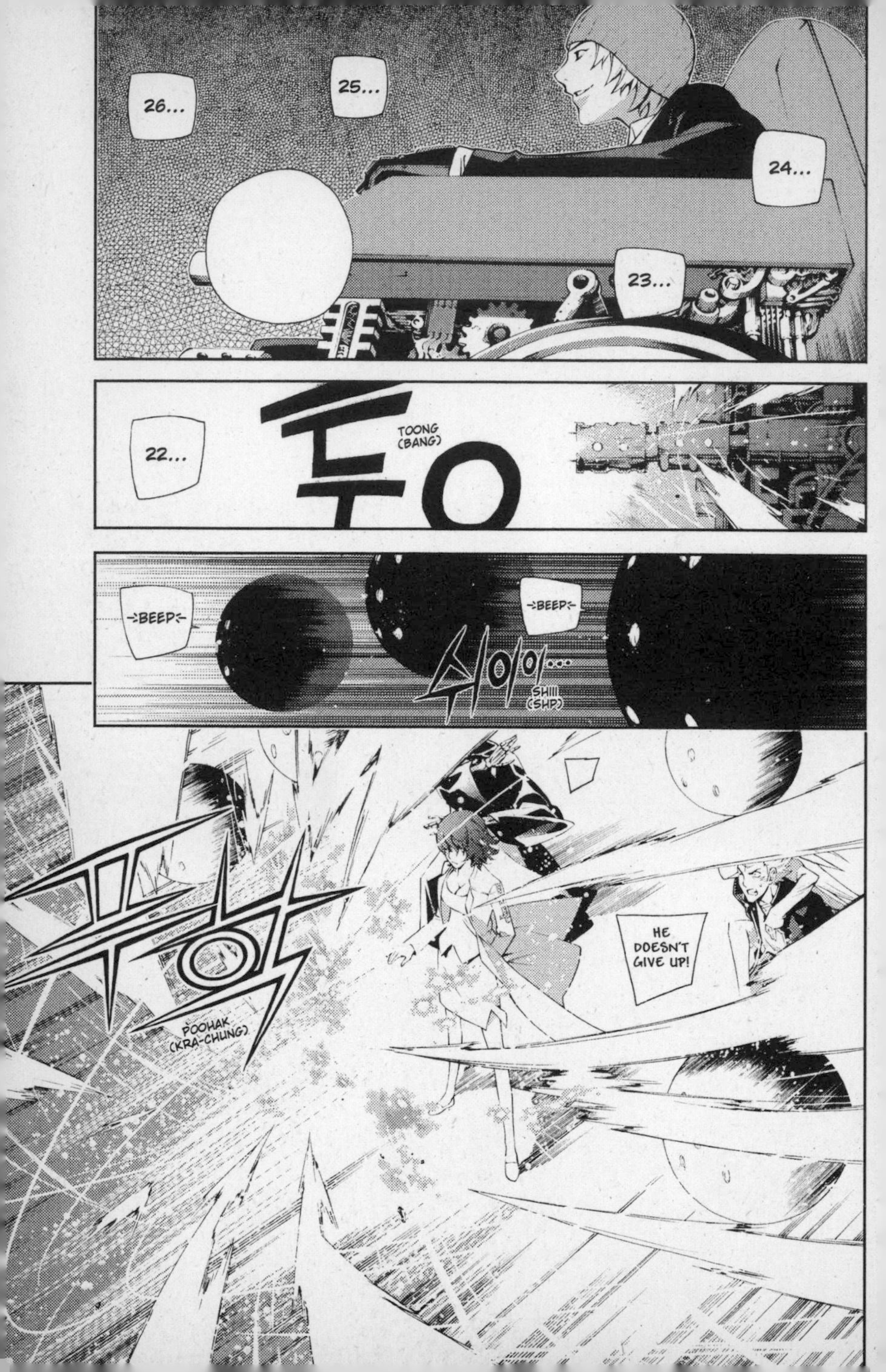
26...
25...
24...
23...
22...
TOONG (BANG)
-BEEP-
-BEEP-
SHIII (SHP)
POOHAK (KRA-CHUNG)
HE DOESN'T GIVE UP!

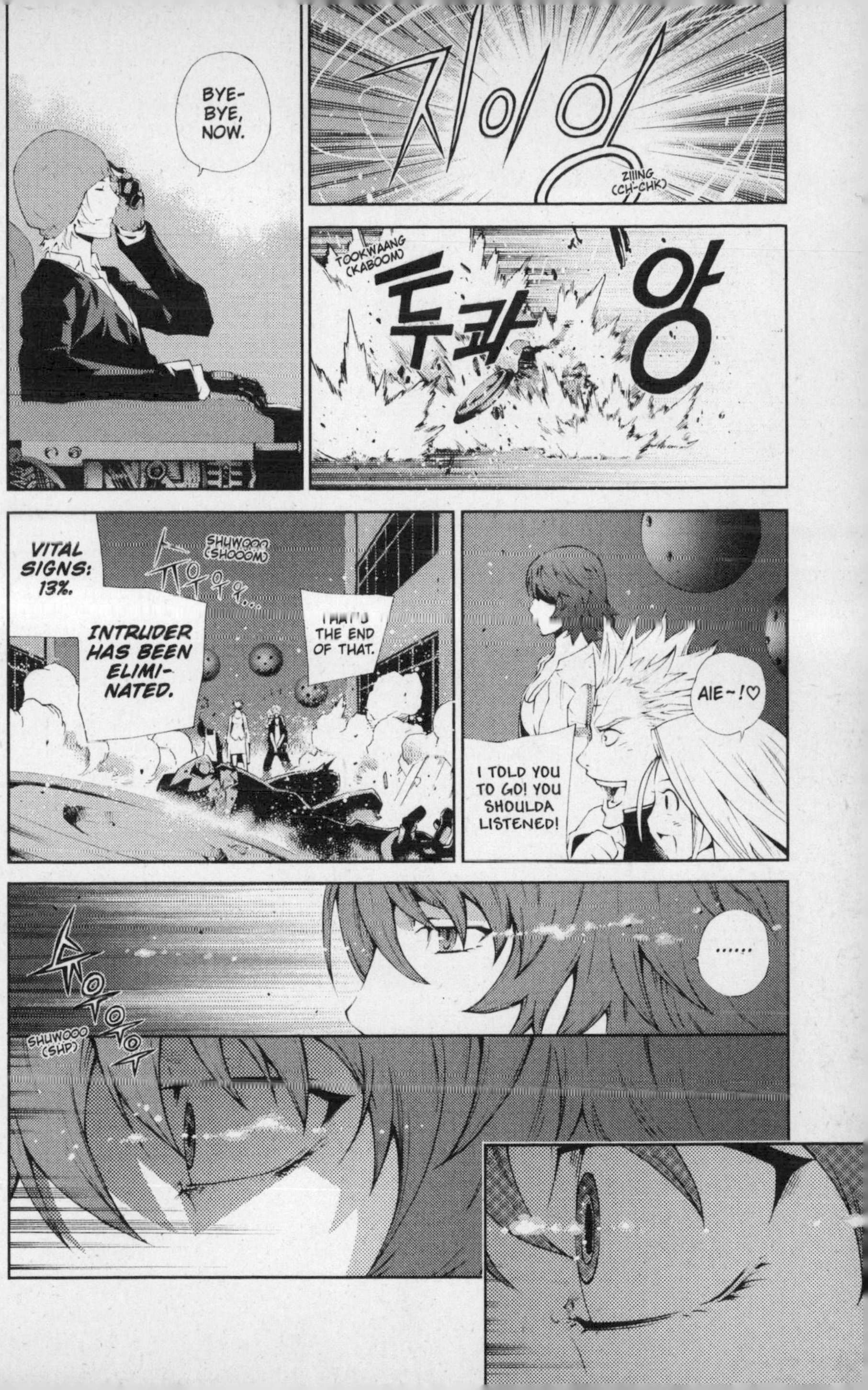
BYE-BYE, NOW.
지이잉
ZIIING (CH-CHK)
두콰앙
TOOKWAANG (KABOOM)
VITAL SIGNS: 13%.
SHUWOOO (SHOOOM)
INTRUDER HAS BEEN ELIMINATED.
THAT'S THE END OF THAT.
AIE~!♡
I TOLD YOU TO GO! YOU SHOULDA LISTENED!
......
SHUWOOO (SHP)

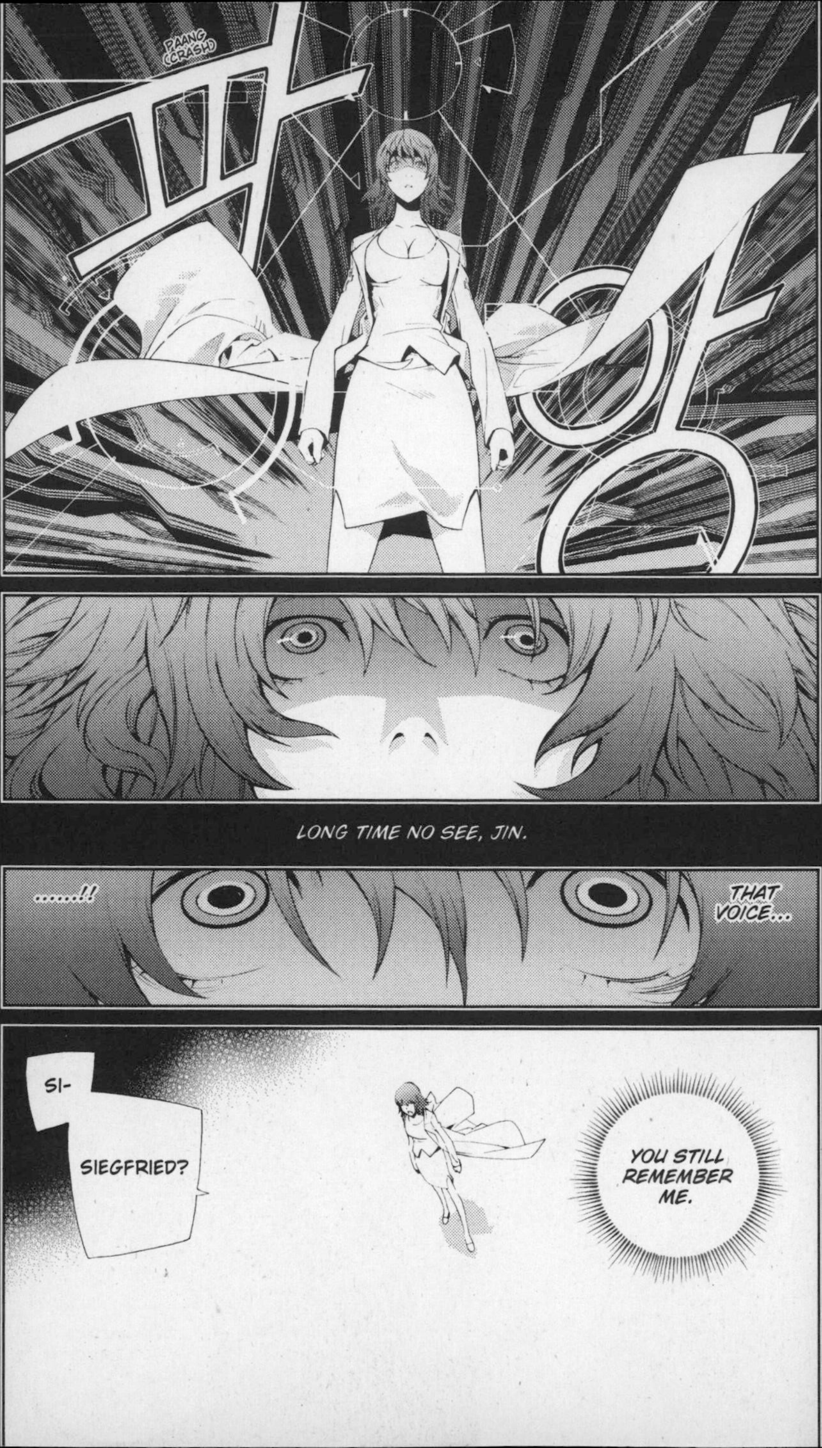
PAANG (CRASH)
LONG TIME NO SEE, JIN.
......!!
THAT VOICE...
SI-
SIEGFRIED?
YOU STILL REMEMBER ME.

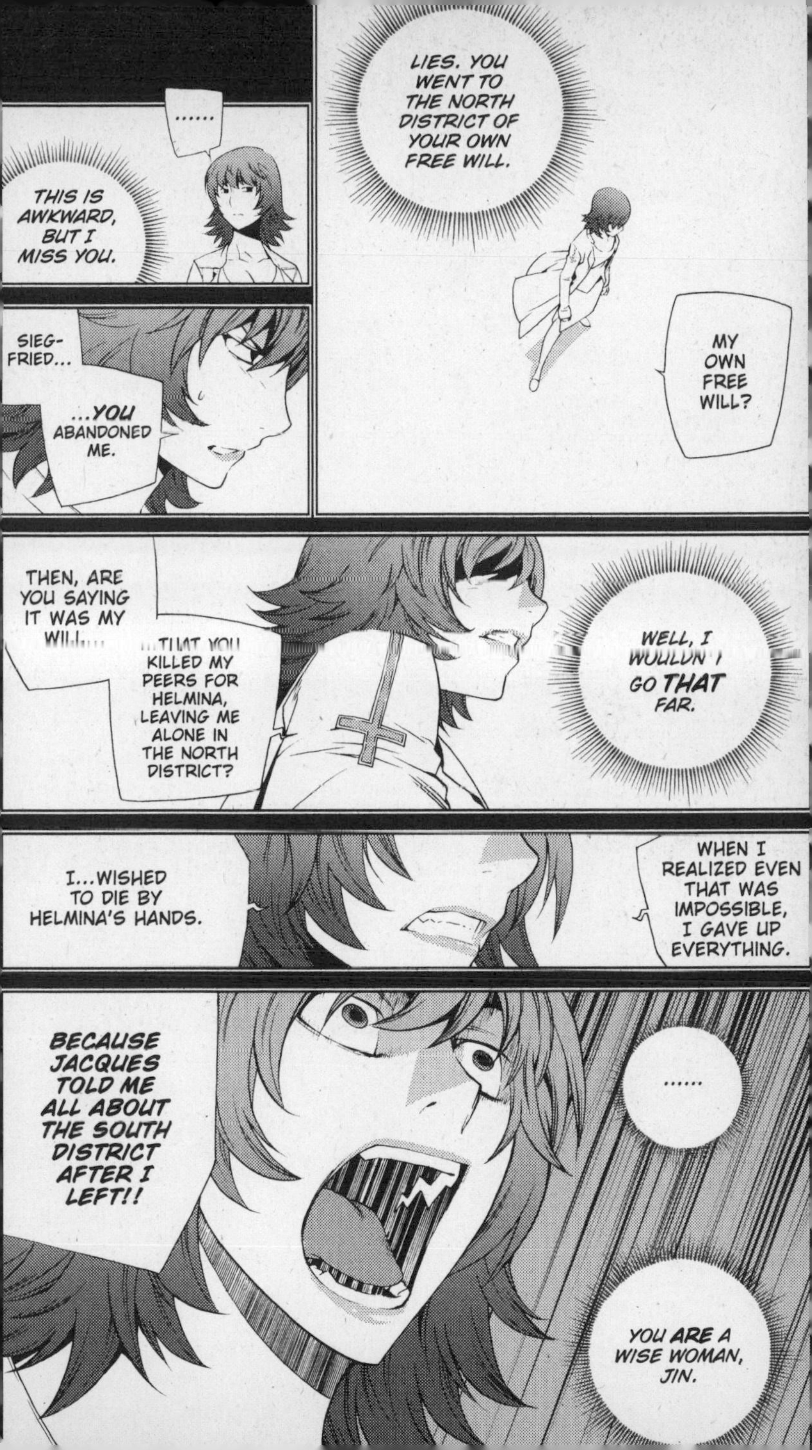
……
THIS IS AWKWARD, BUT I MISS YOU.
SIEG-FRIED...
...YOU ABANDONED ME.
LIES. YOU WENT TO THE NORTH DISTRICT OF YOUR OWN FREE WILL.
MY OWN FREE WILL?
THEN, ARE YOU SAYING IT WAS MY WILL...
...THAT YOU KILLED MY PEERS FOR HELMINA, LEAVING ME ALONE IN THE NORTH DISTRICT?
WELL, I WOULDN'T GO THAT FAR.
I...WISHED TO DIE BY HELMINA'S HANDS.
WHEN I REALIZED EVEN THAT WAS IMPOSSIBLE, I GAVE UP EVERYTHING.
BECAUSE JACQUES TOLD ME ALL ABOUT THE SOUTH DISTRICT AFTER I LEFT!!
……
YOU ARE A WISE WOMAN, JIN.

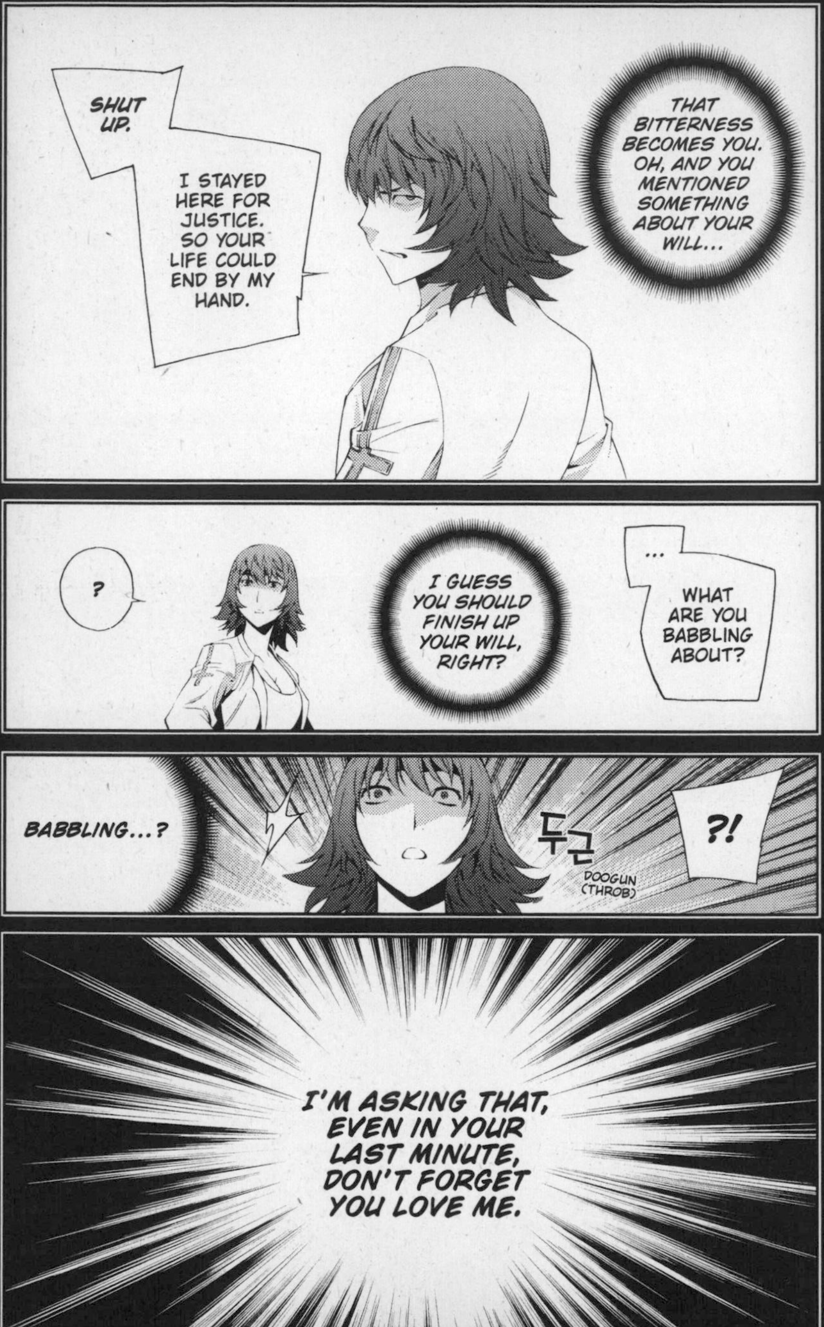
SHUT UP.
I STAYED HERE FOR JUSTICE. SO YOUR LIFE COULD END BY MY HAND.
THAT BITTERNESS BECOMES YOU. OH, AND YOU MENTIONED SOMETHING ABOUT YOUR WILL...
?
I GUESS YOU SHOULD FINISH UP YOUR WILL, RIGHT?
...
WHAT ARE YOU BABBLING ABOUT?
BABBLING...?
두근
DOOGUN (THROB)
?!
I'M ASKING THAT, EVEN IN YOUR LAST MINUTE, DON'T FORGET YOU LOVE ME.

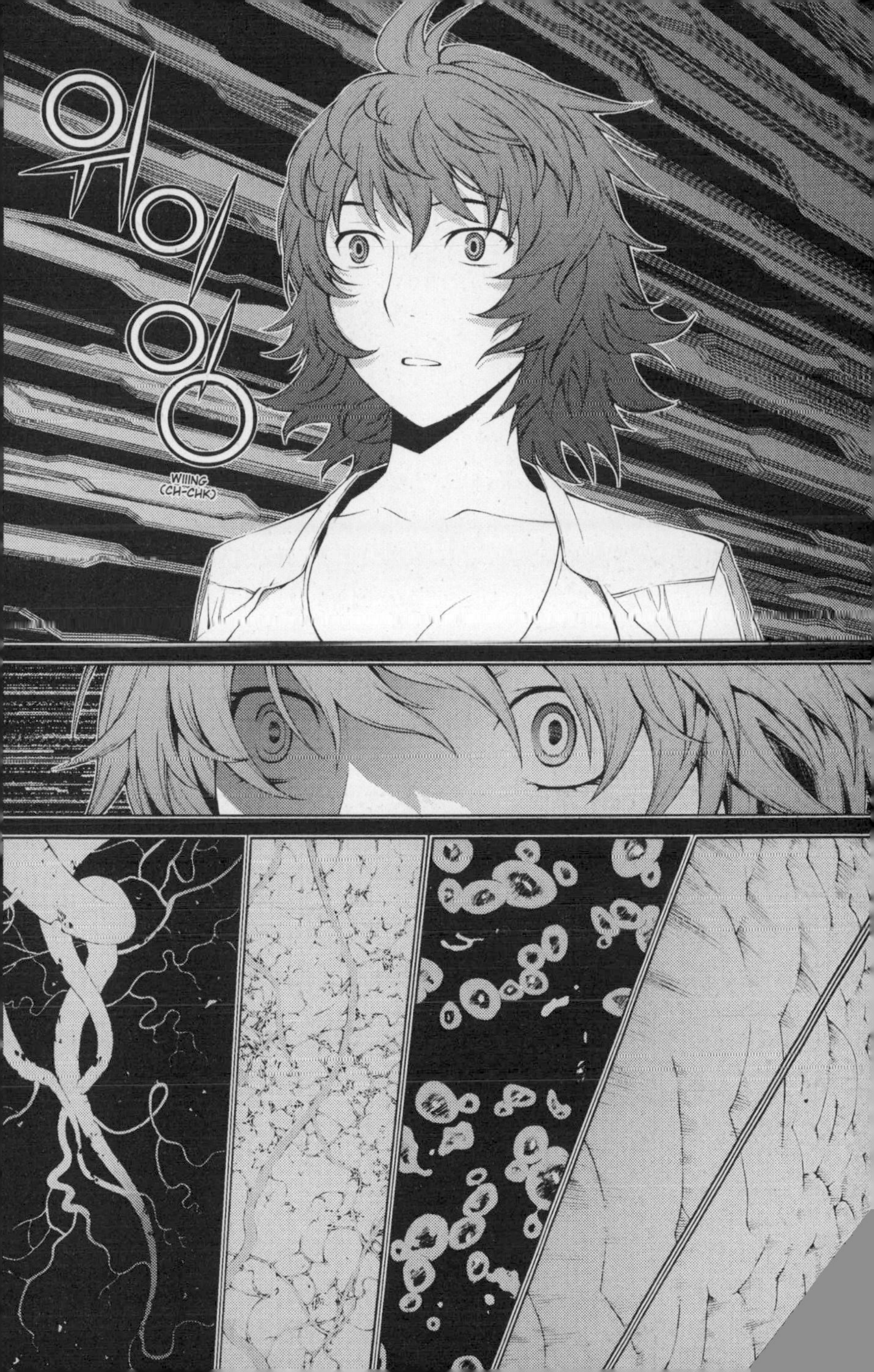
WIIING
(CH-CHK)

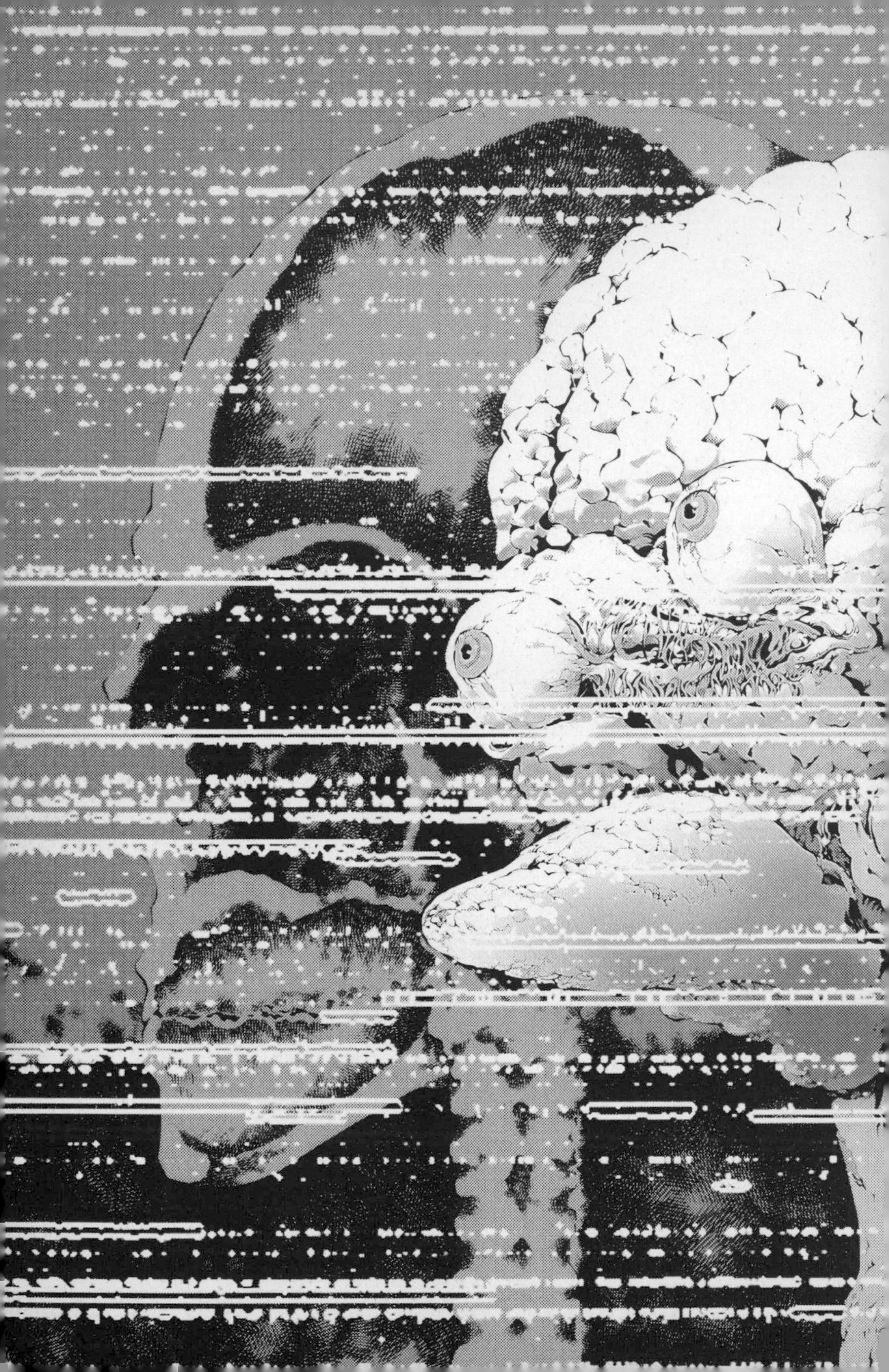

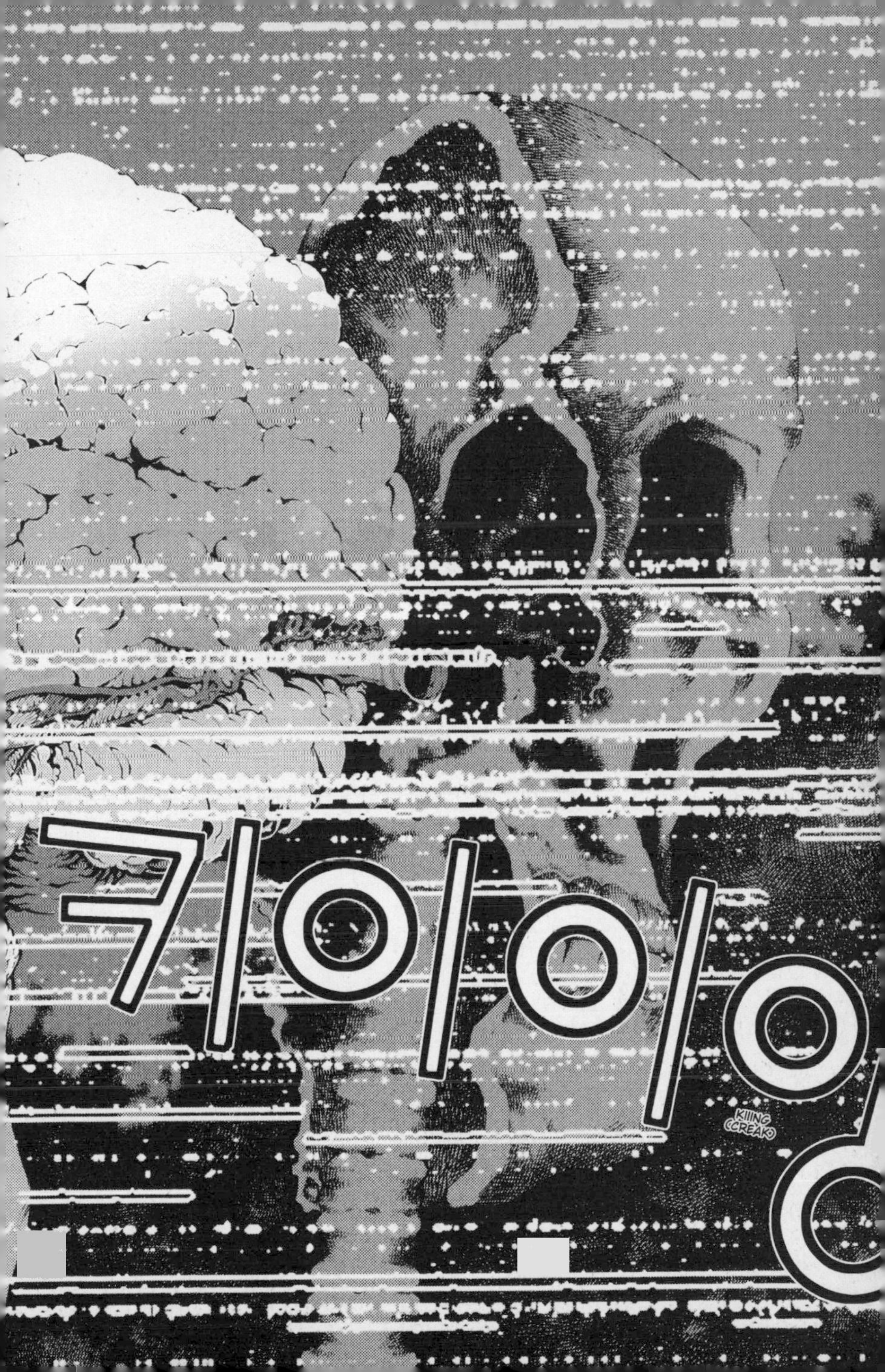
KIIING
(CREAK)

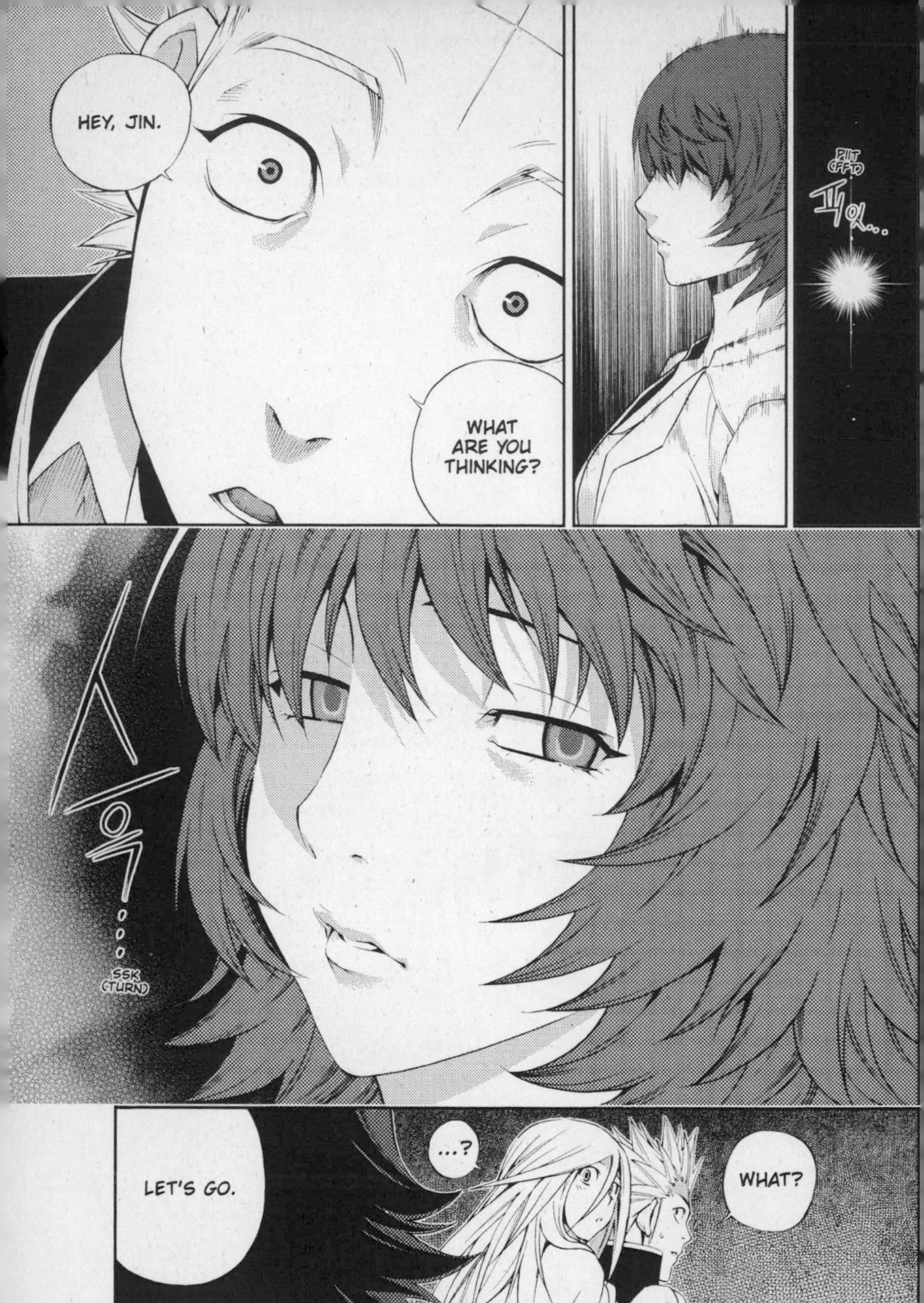
HEY, JIN.
WHAT ARE YOU THINKING?
PIIT (FFT)
피잇...
스윽...
SSK (TURN)
LET'S GO.
...?
WHAT?

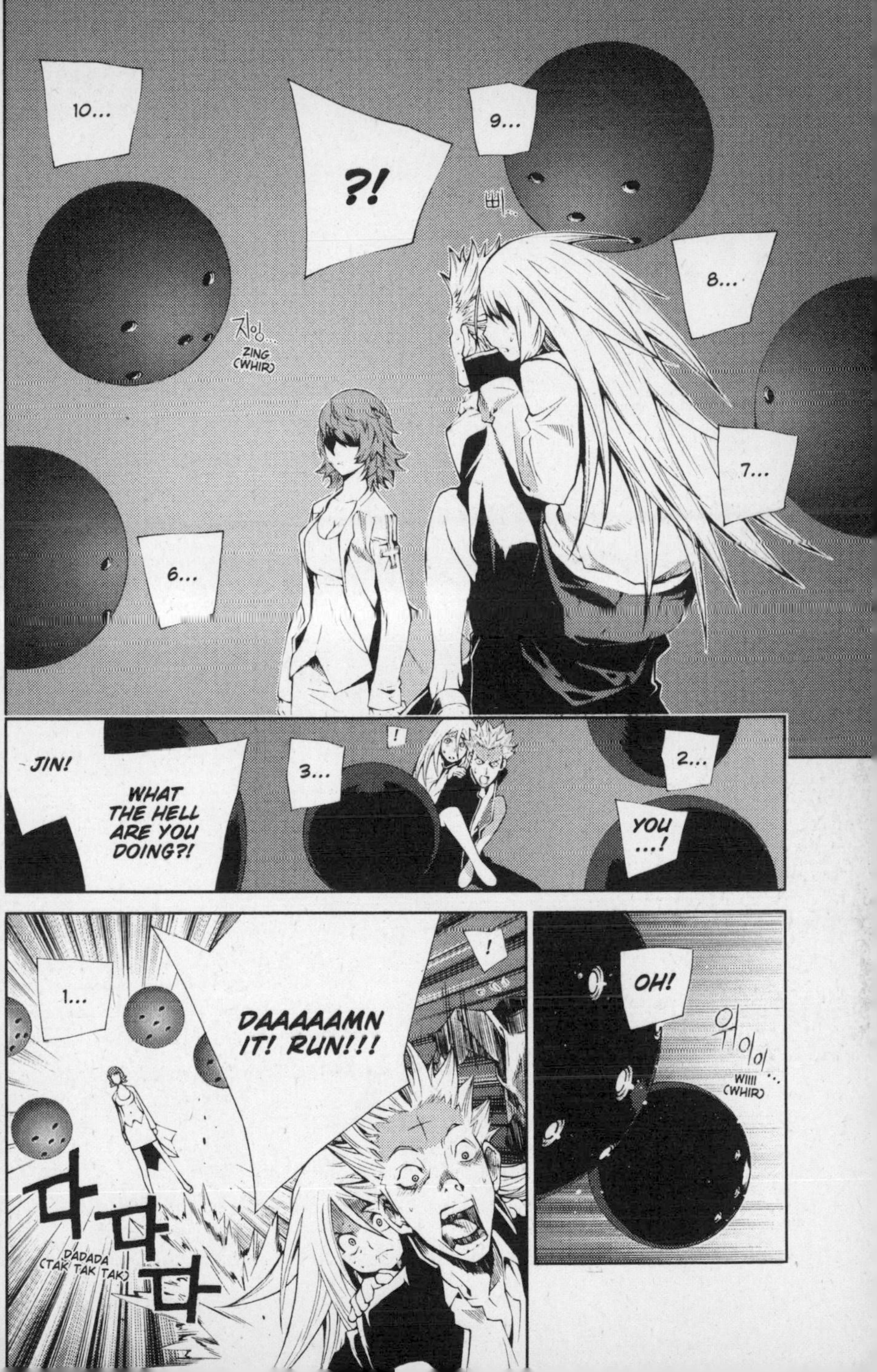
10...
?!
9...
삐...
8...
지잉...
ZING (WHIR)
7...
6...
JIN!
WHAT THE HELL ARE YOU DOING?!
3...
!
2...
YOU ...!
1...
DAAAAAMN IT! RUN!!!
!
따따따
DADADA (TAK TAK TAK)
OH!
위이이...
WIIII (WHIR)

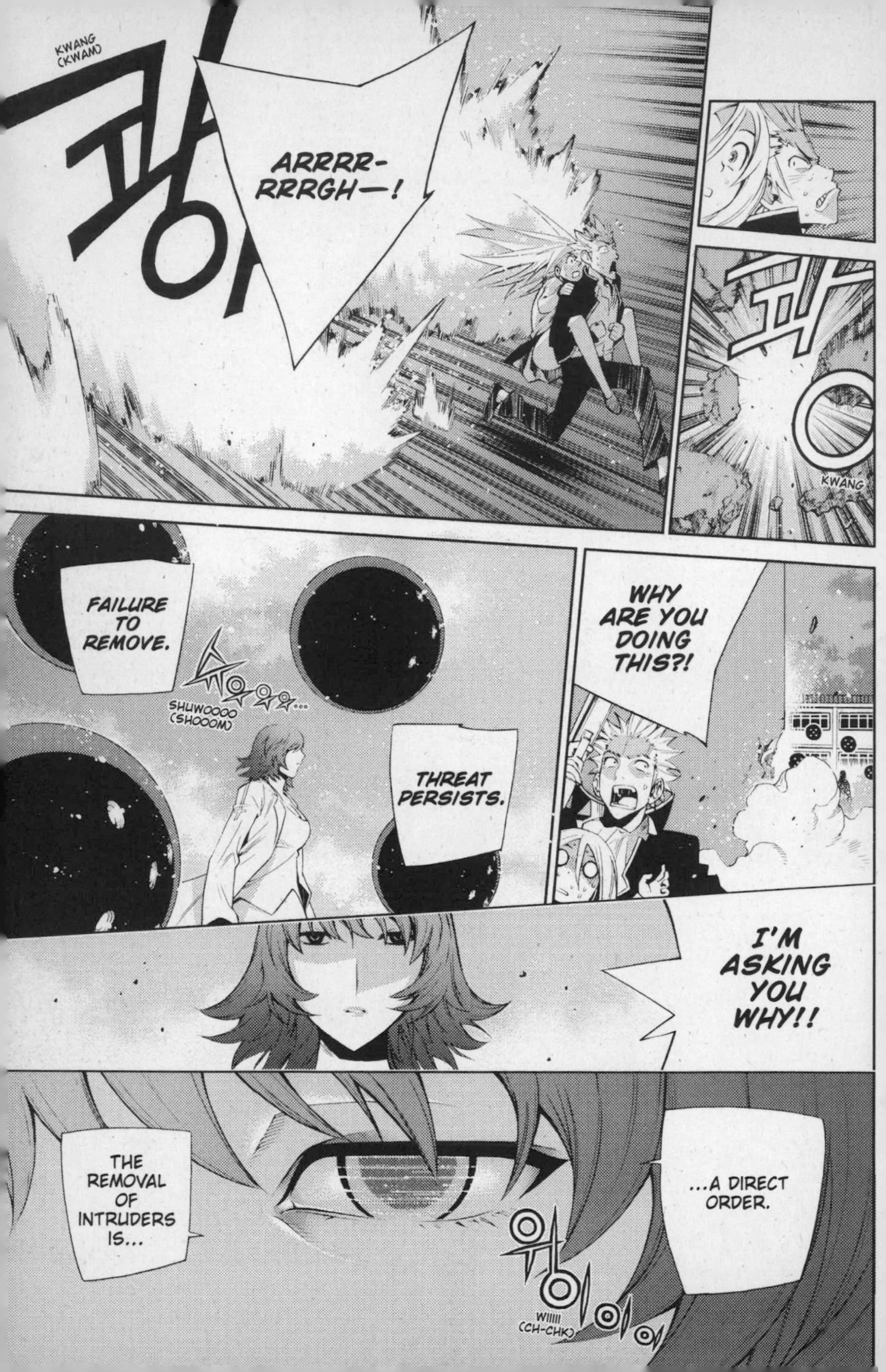
KWANG (KWAM)
ARRRR-RRRGH—!
KWANG
FAILURE TO REMOVE.
SHUWOOOO (SHOOOM)
THREAT PERSISTS.
WHY ARE YOU DOING THIS?!
I'M ASKING YOU WHY!!
THE REMOVAL OF INTRUDERS IS...
WIIIII (CH-CHK)
...A DIRECT ORDER.

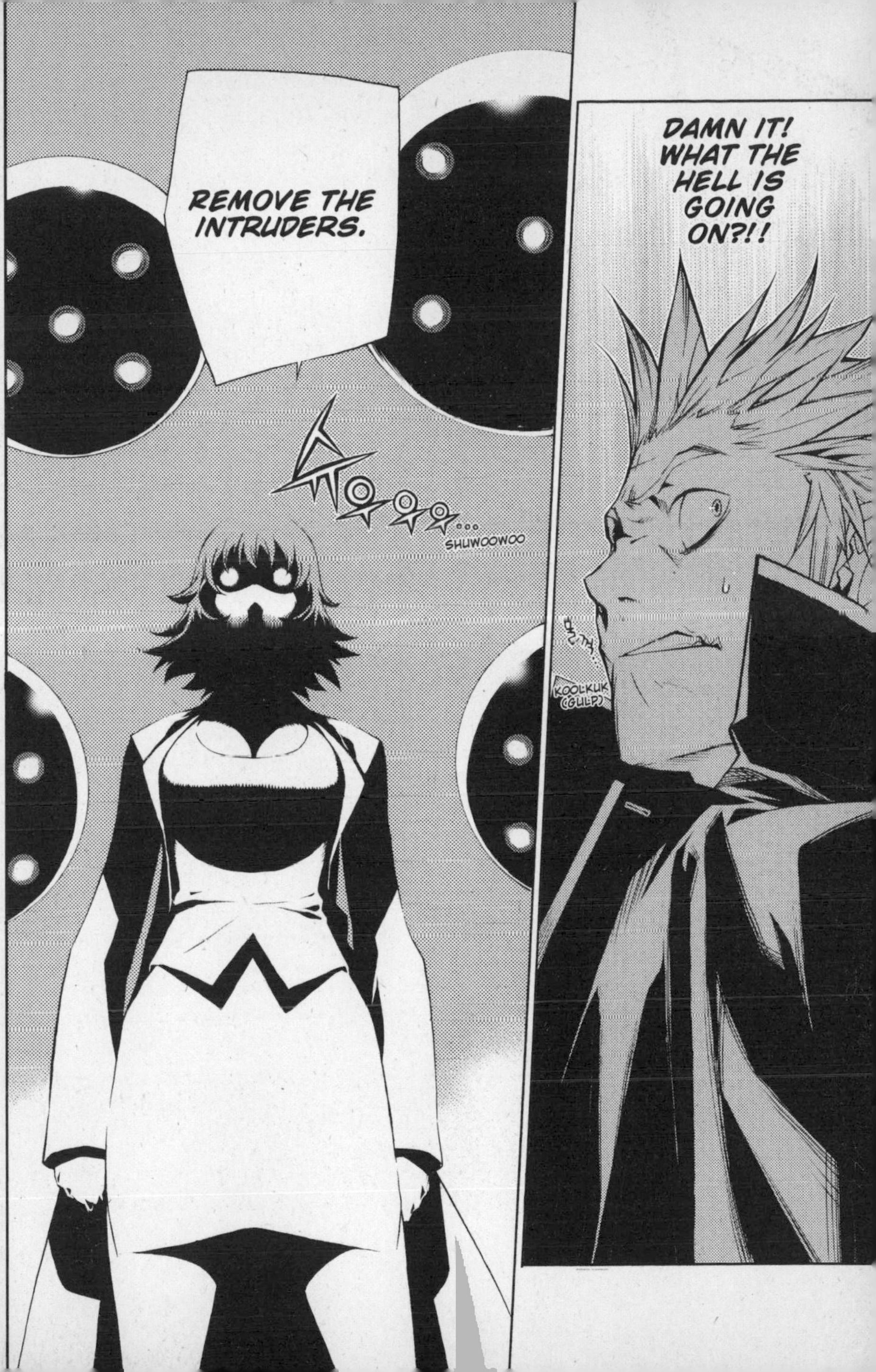
REMOVE THE INTRUDERS.
SHUWOOWOO
DAMN IT! WHAT THE HELL IS GOING ON?!!
KOOLKUK (GULP)

JACK FROST

The Amityville

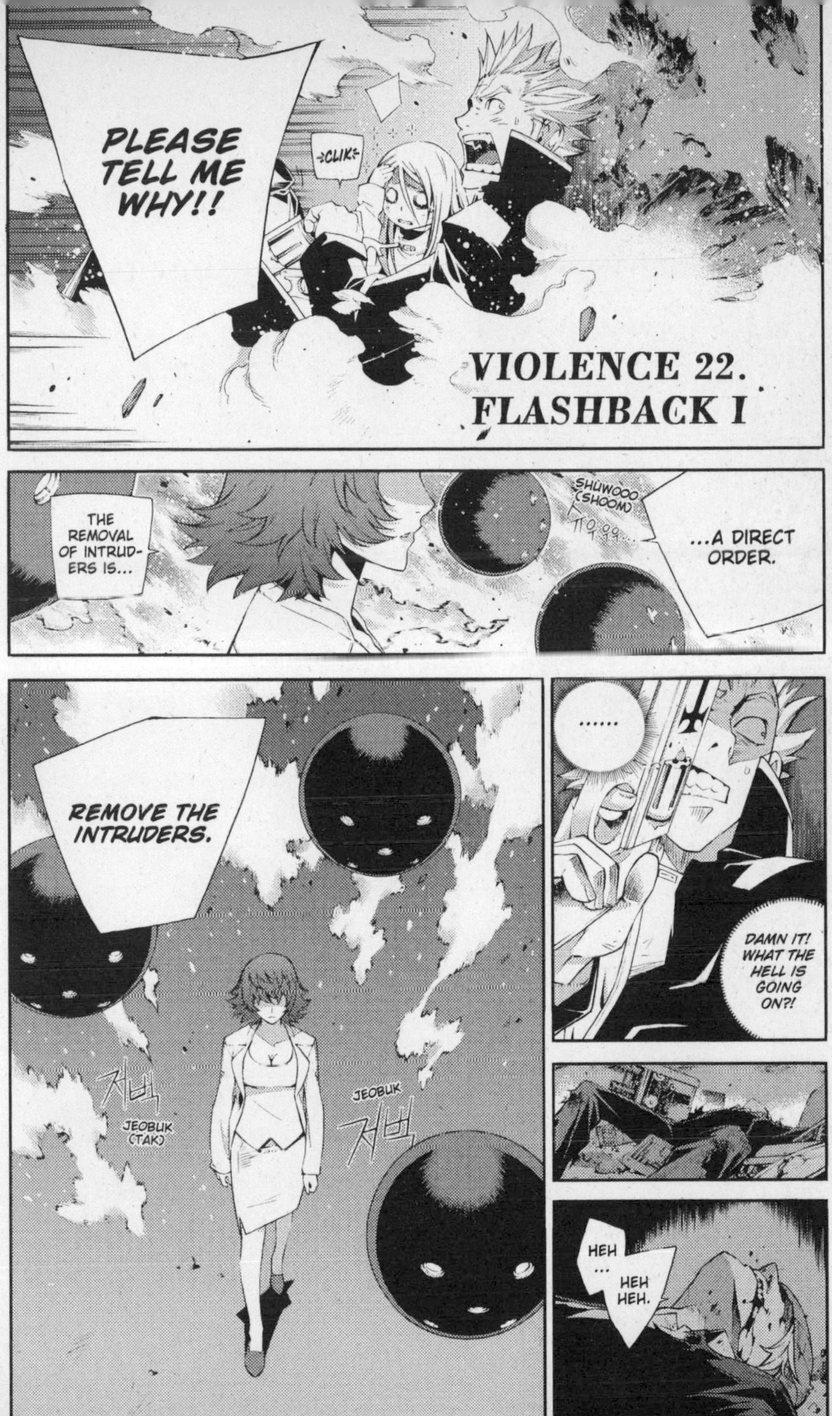
PLEASE TELL ME WHY!!
CLIK
VIOLENCE 22. FLASHBACK I
THE REMOVAL OF INTRUD-ERS IS...
SHUWOOO (SHOOM)
...A DIRECT ORDER.
REMOVE THE INTRUDERS.
저벅
JEOBUK (TAK)
JEOBUK
저벅
......
DAMN IT! WHAT THE HELL IS GOING ON?!
HEH ... HEH HEH.

I TOLD YOU...
...IT'S NOT OVER YET. HEH-HEH...
WOULDN'T YOU AGREE...
...JIN?
I EXPECT A STIRRING FINALE!

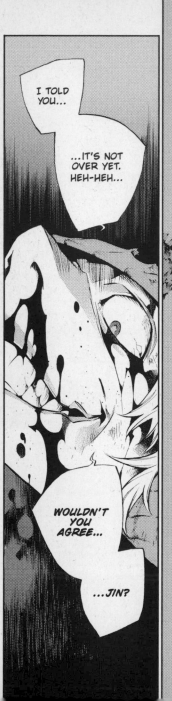

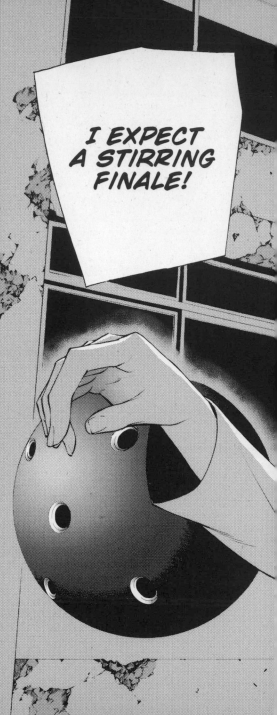

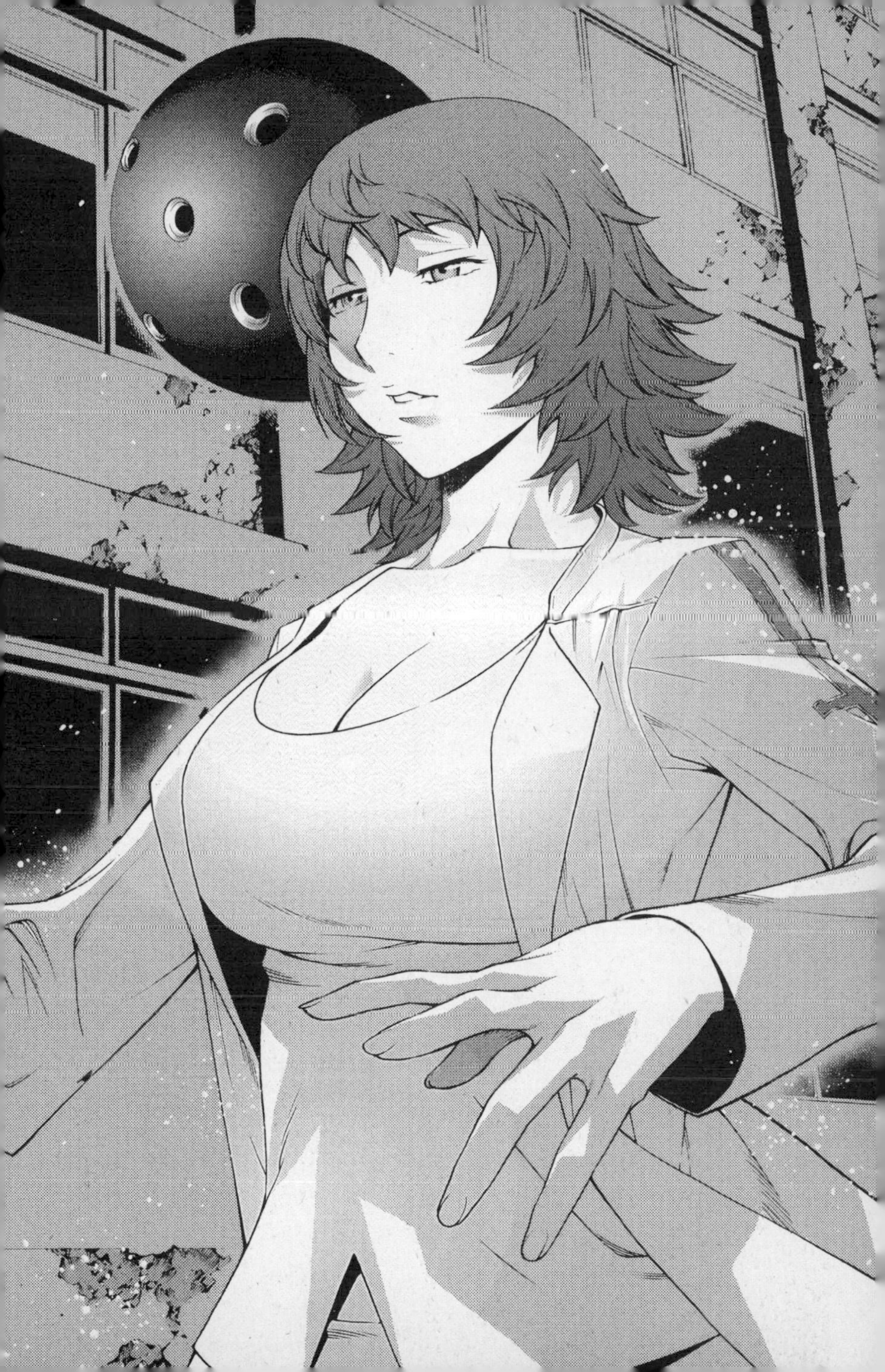

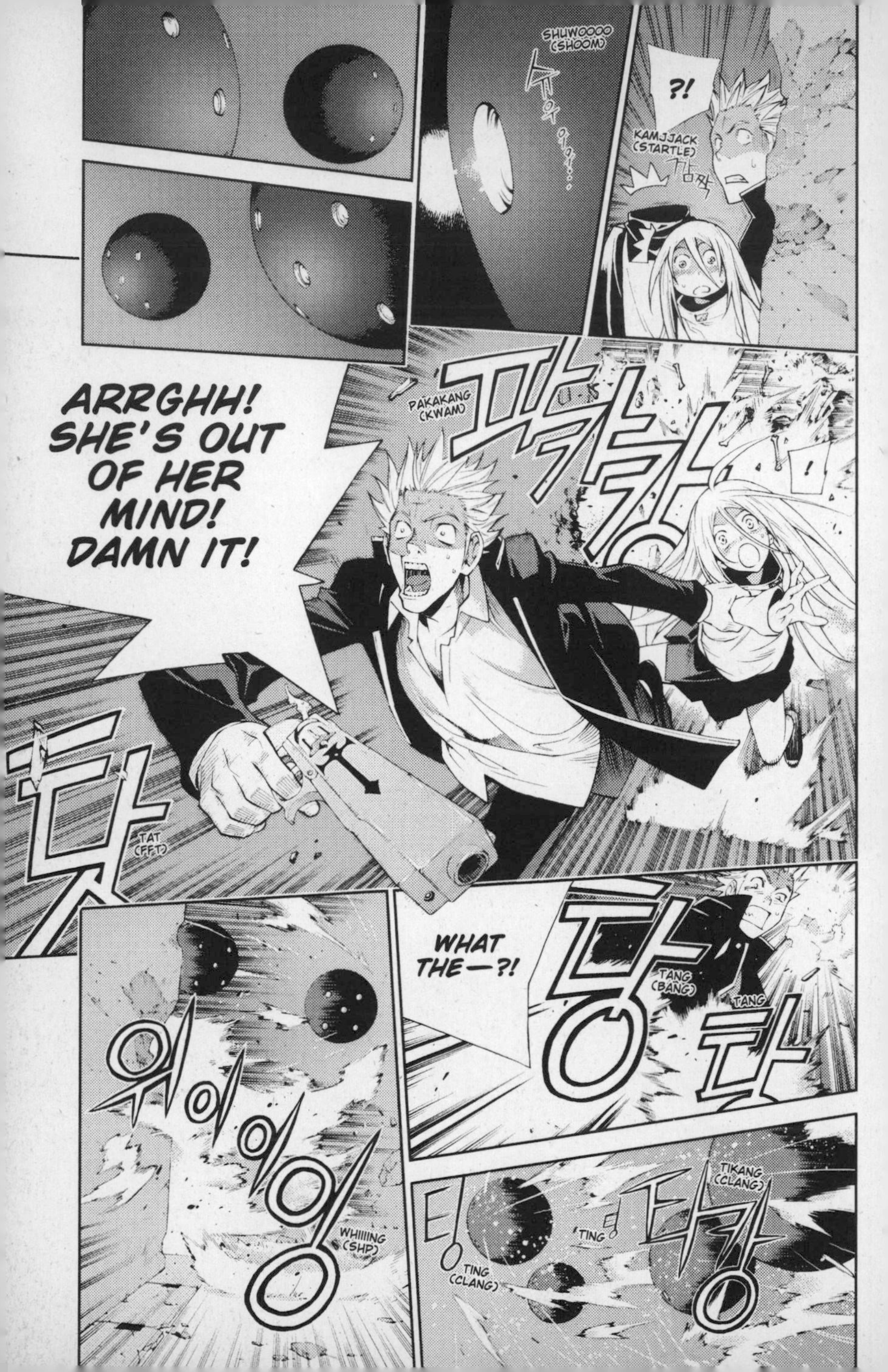

SHUWOOOO (SHOOM)
?!
KAMJJACK (STARTLE)
ARRGHH! SHE'S OUT OF HER MIND! DAMN IT!
PAKAKANG (KWAM)
!
TAT (FFT)
WHIIIING (SHP)
WHAT THE—?!
TANG (BANG)
TANG
TIKANG (CLANG)
TING
TING (CLANG)

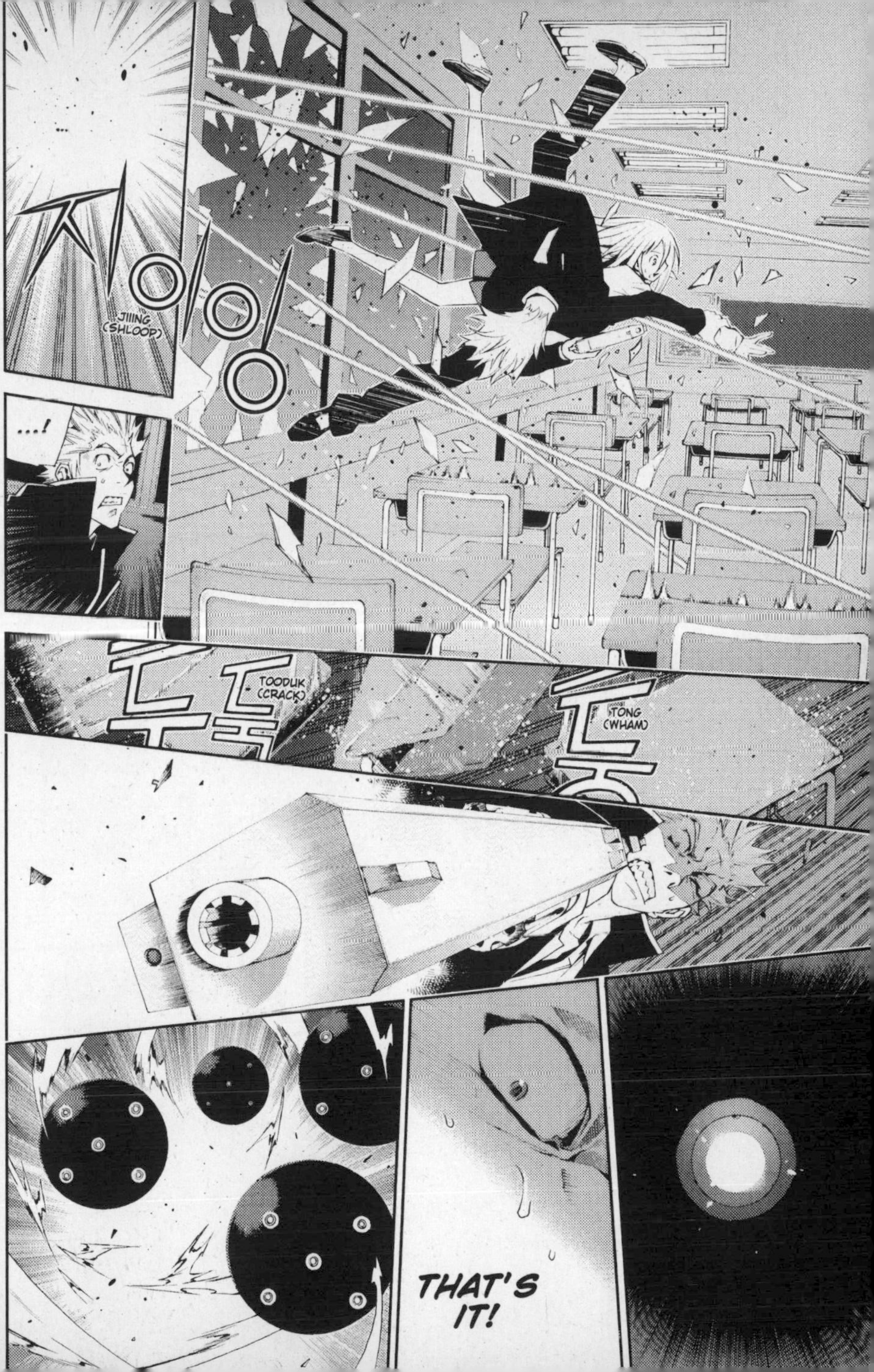
...
JIIING (SHLOOP)
...!
TOODUK (CRACK)
TONG (WHAM)
THAT'S IT!

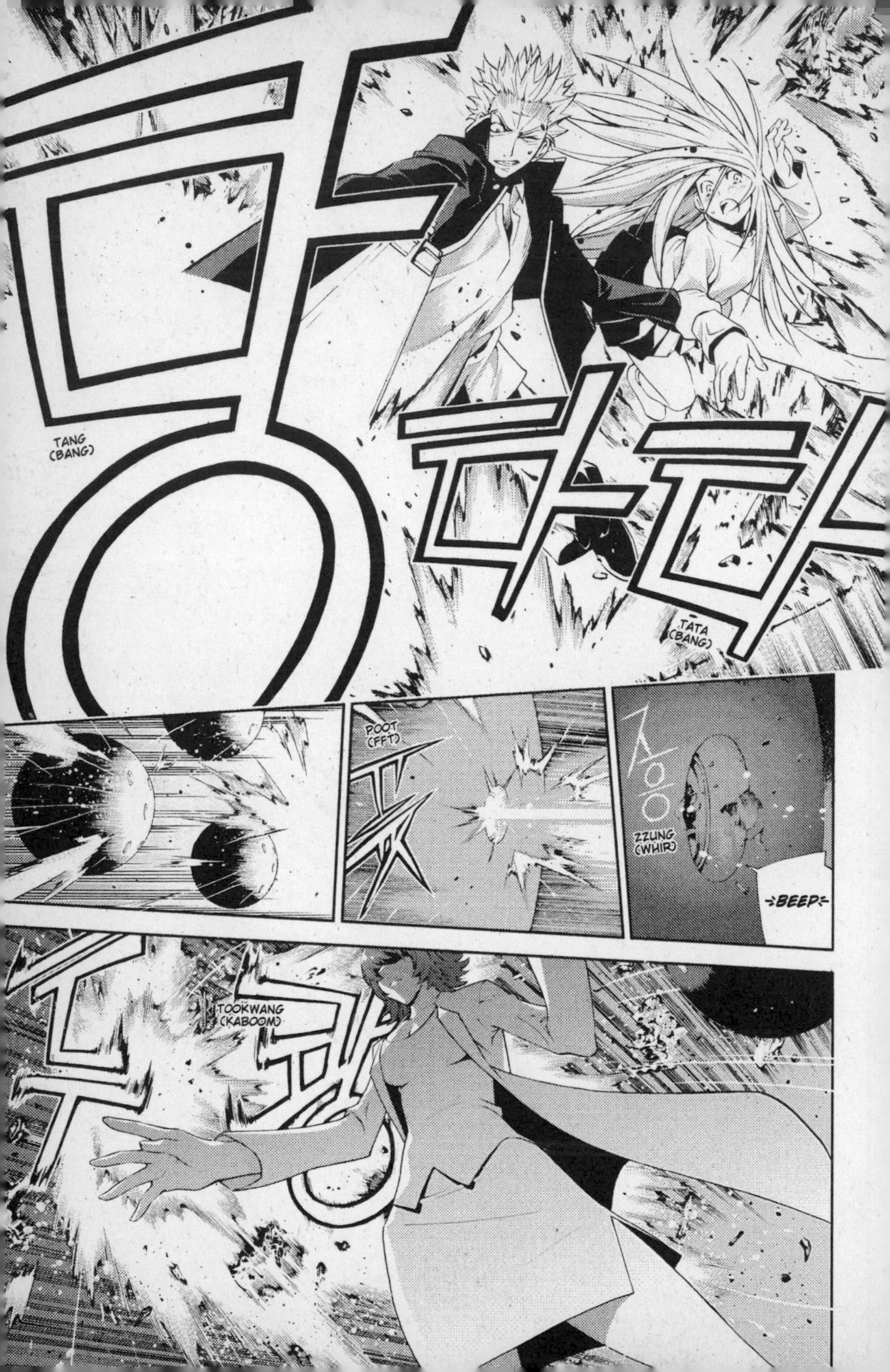
TANG (BANG)
TATA (BANG)
POOT (FFT)
ZZUNG (WHIR)
BEEP
TOOKWANG (KABOOM)

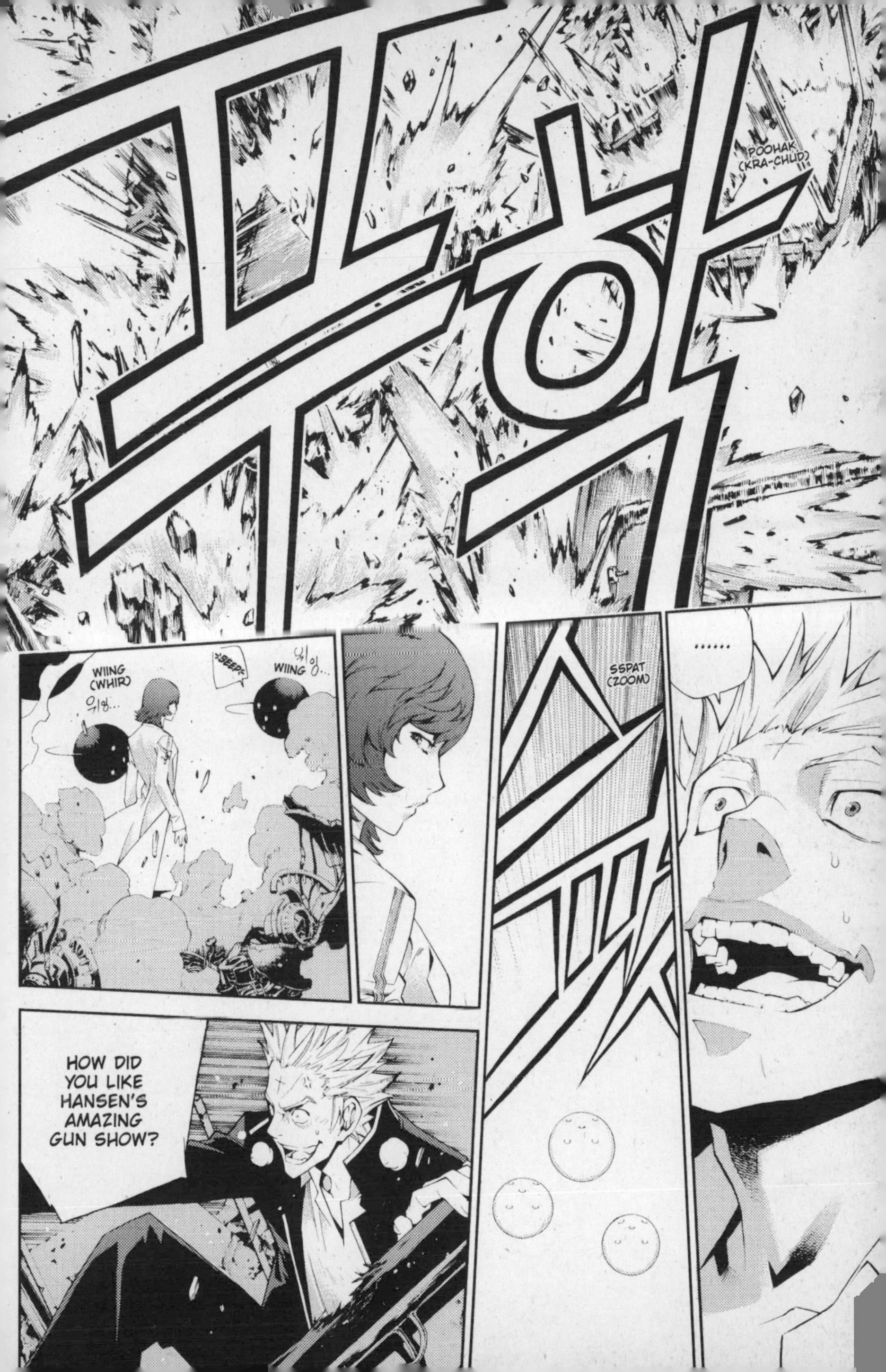
POOHAK
(KRA-CHUD)
WIING
(WHIR)
BEEP
WIING
SSPAT
(ZOOM)
......
HOW DID YOU LIKE HANSEN'S AMAZING GUN SHOW?

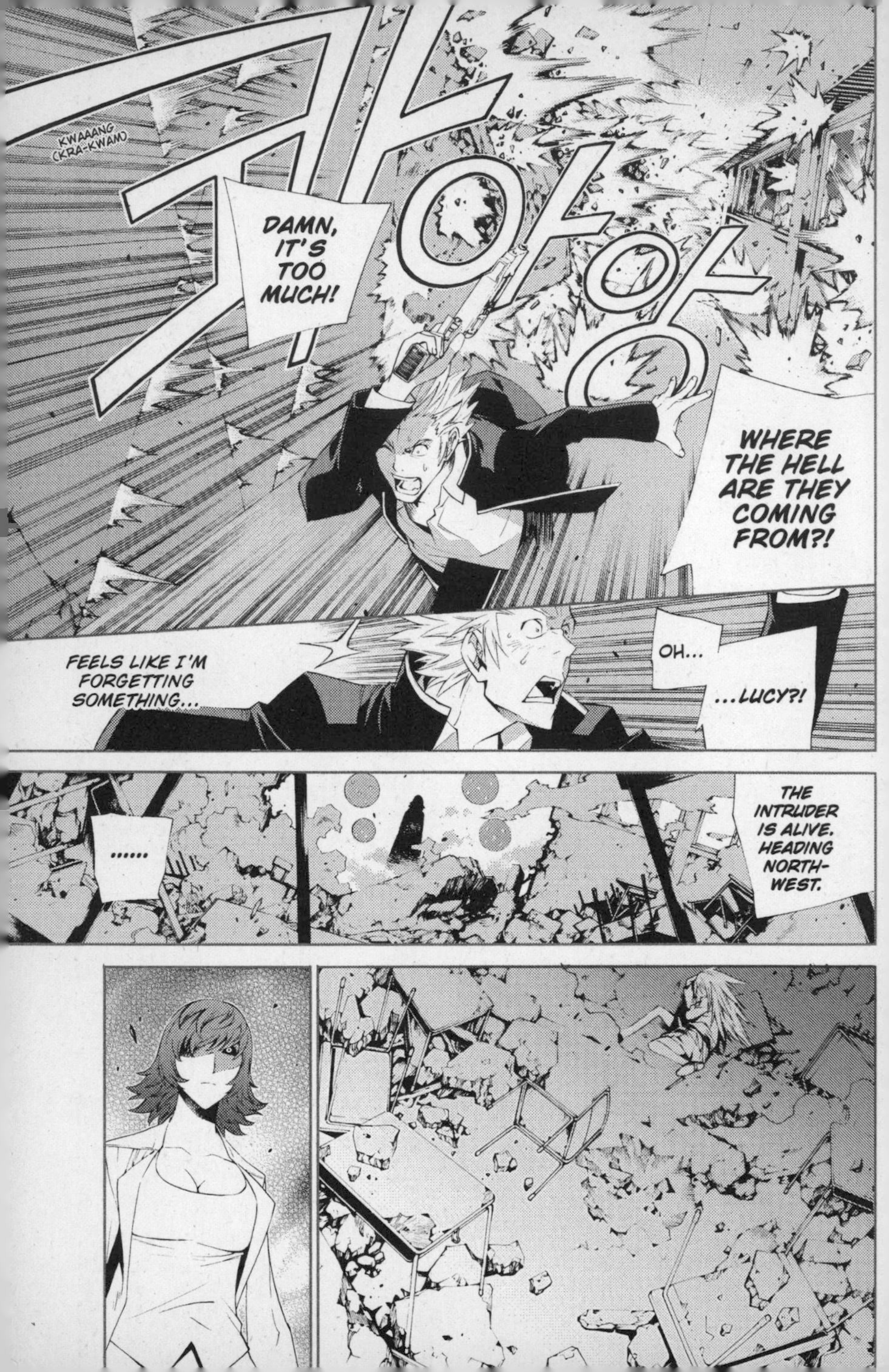
KWAAANG (KRA-KWAM)
DAMN, IT'S TOO MUCH!
WHERE THE HELL ARE THEY COMING FROM?!
FEELS LIKE I'M FORGETTING SOMETHING...
OH...
...LUCY?!
......
THE INTRUDER IS ALIVE. HEADING NORTH-WEST.

REMOVAL OF INTRUDERS IS A DIRECT ORDER.

...

INTRUDER. INTRUDER.

...... AH...

DAMN! JUST ONE BULLET LEFT.

HANSEN

AND LUCY'S NO HELP AT ALL!

AH, WHAT DO I DO?!

I CAN'T JUST LEAVE HER BEHIND!

......

AH ...

DAMN IT!

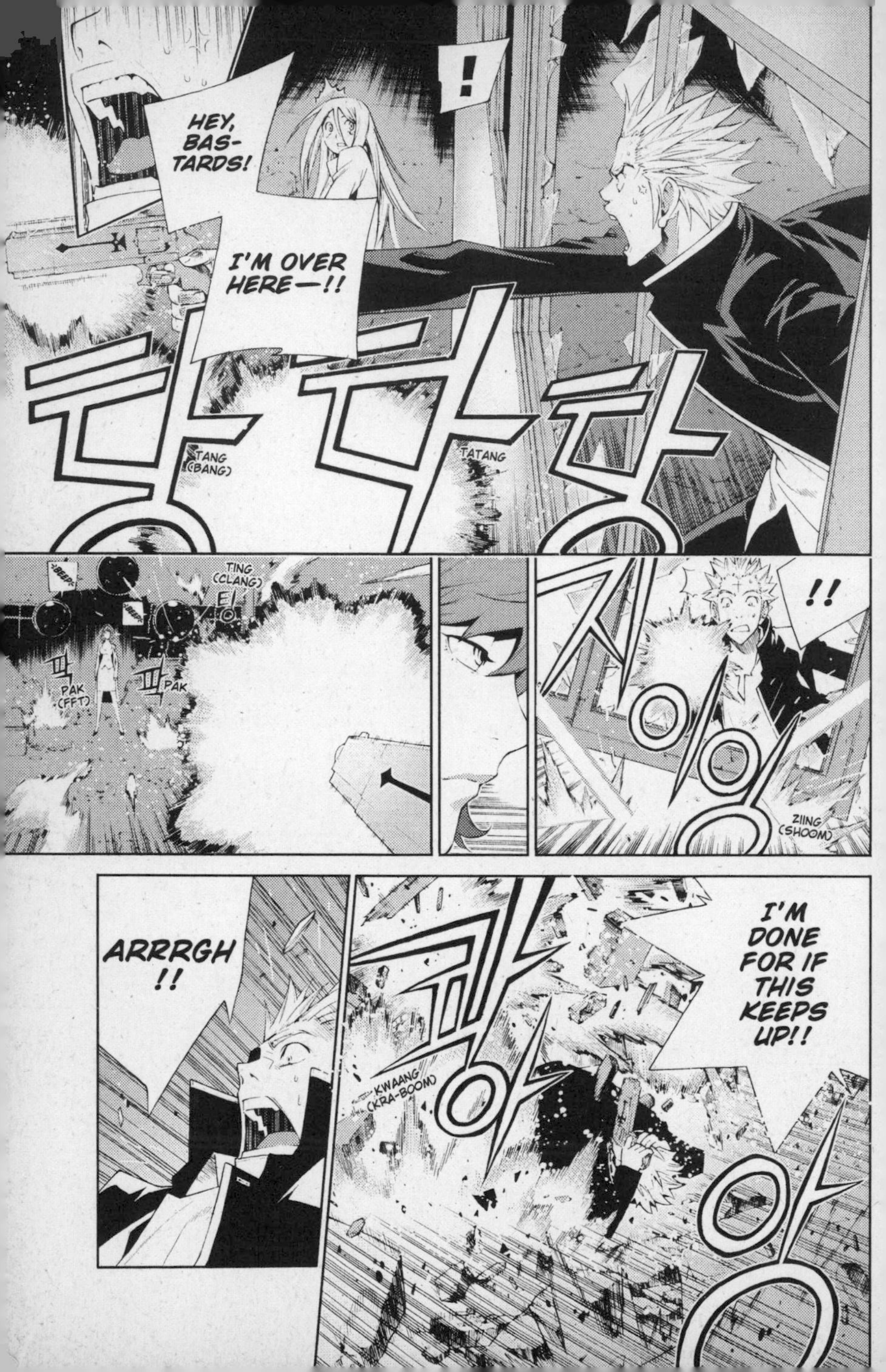

HEY, BAS-TARDS!
!
I'M OVER HERE—!!
TANG (BANG)
TATANG
BEEP
TING (CLANG)
BEEP
PAK (FFT)
PAK
!!
ZIING (SHOOM)
ARRRGH!!
KWAANG (KRA-BOOM)
I'M DONE FOR IF THIS KEEPS UP!!

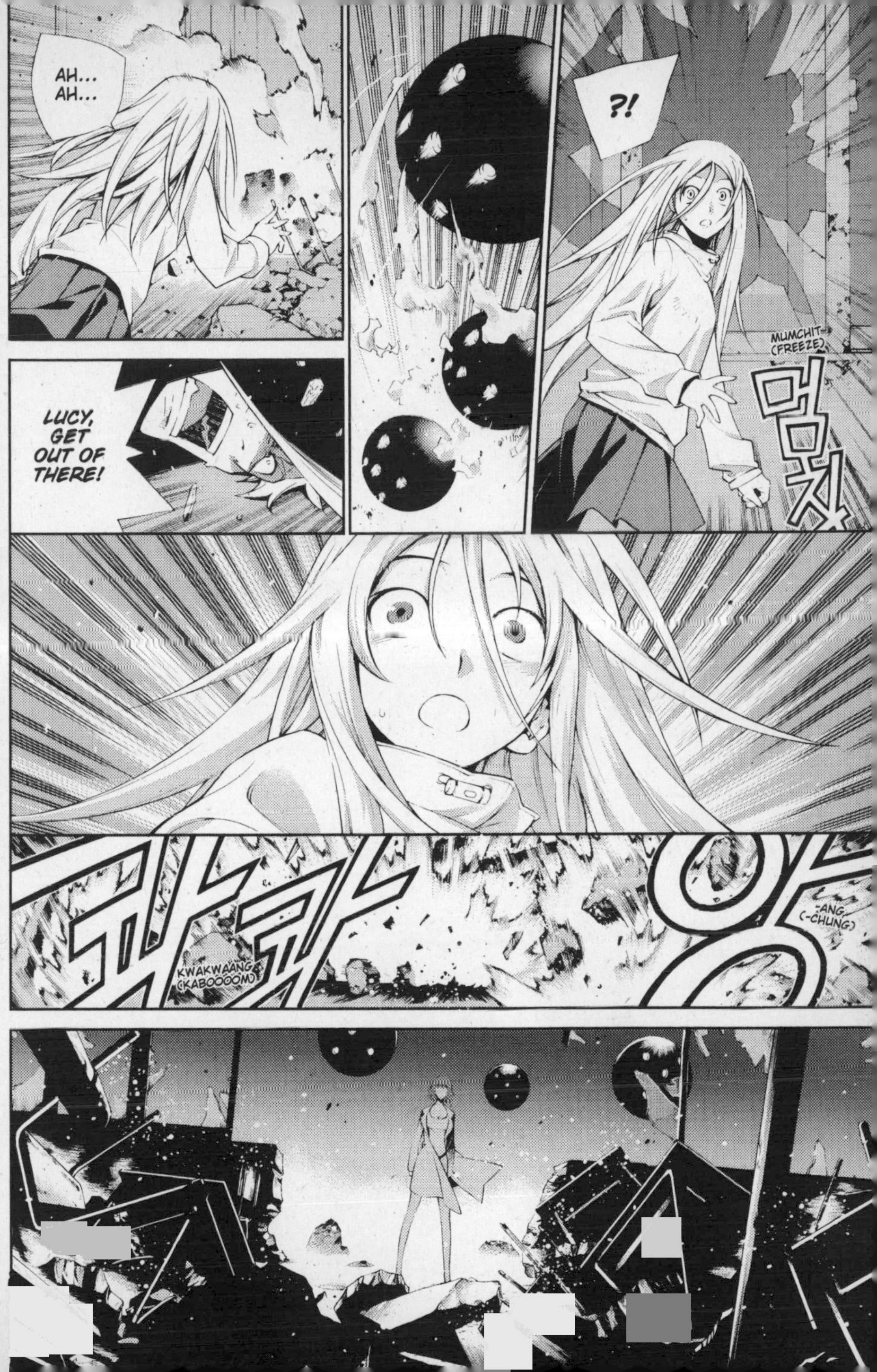
AH... AH...
LUCY, GET OUT OF THERE!
?!
MUMCHIT (FREEZE)
멈칫
KWAKWAANG (KABOOOOM)
-ANG (-CHUNG)

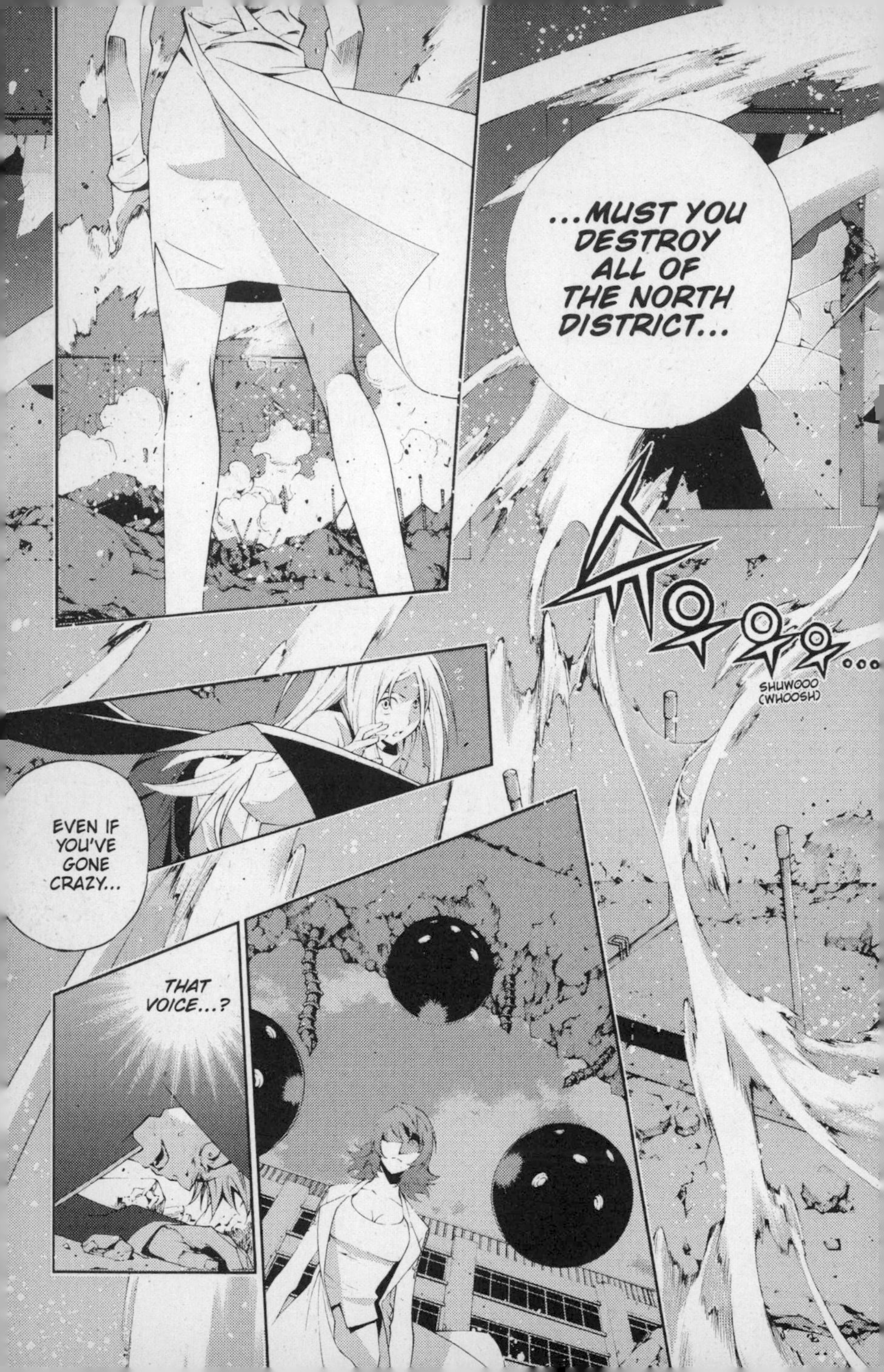
...MUST YOU DESTROY ALL OF THE NORTH DISTRICT...
SHUWOOO (WHOOSH)
EVEN IF YOU'VE GONE CRAZY...
THAT VOICE...?

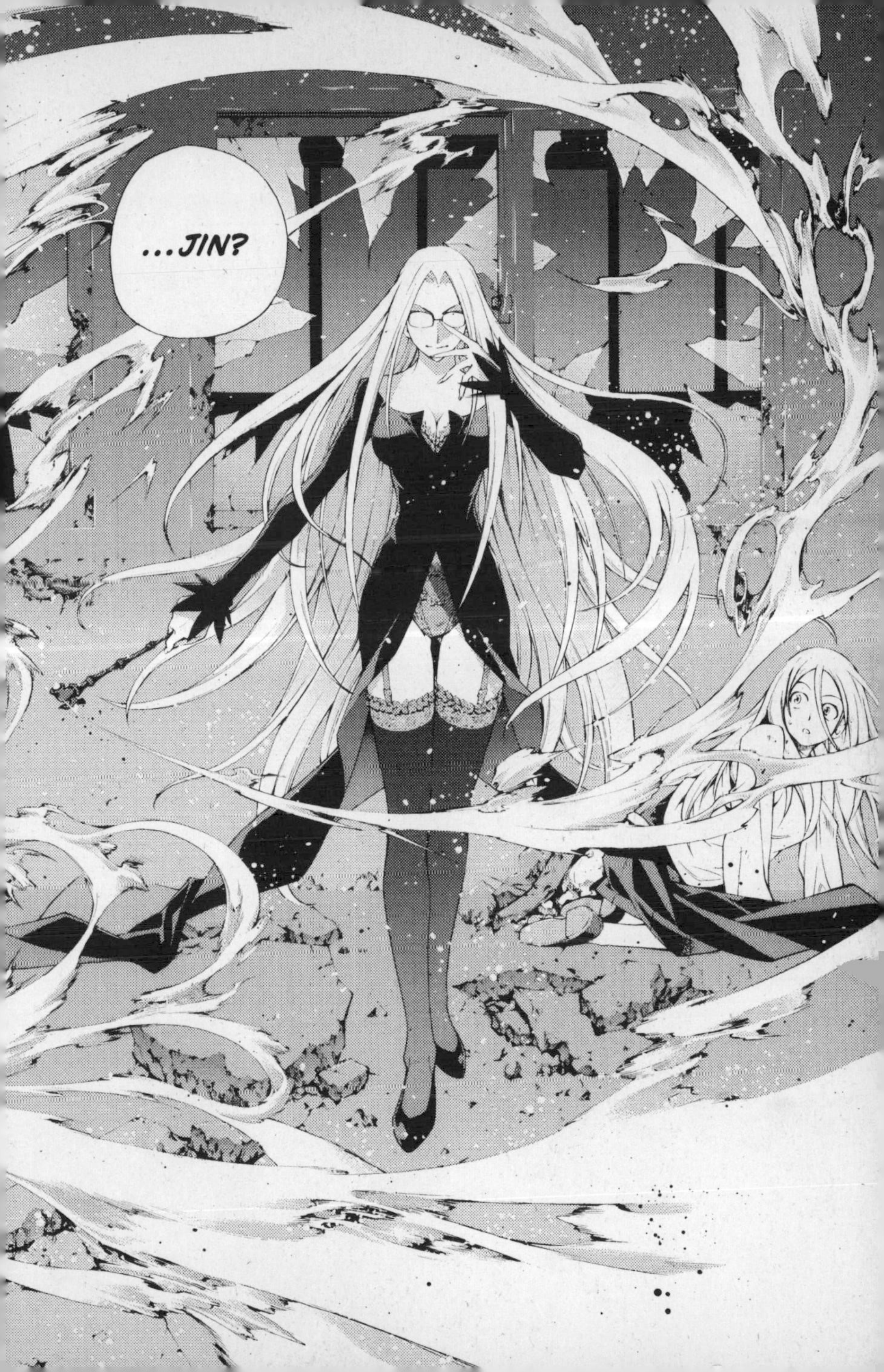
...JIN?

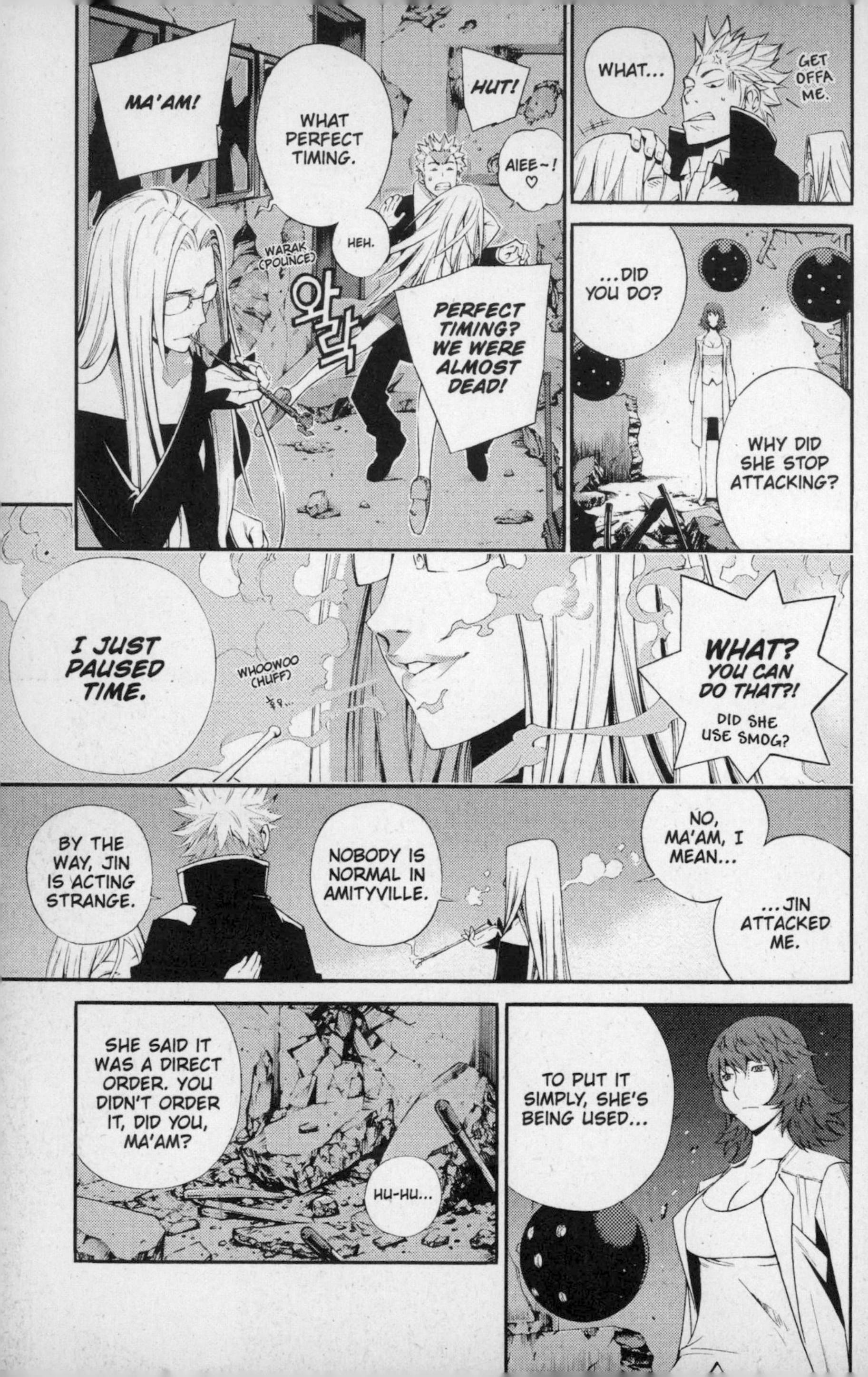
MA'AM!
WHAT PERFECT TIMING.
HUT!
AIEE~! ♡
HEH.
WARAK (POUNCE)
와락
PERFECT TIMING? WE WERE ALMOST DEAD!
WHAT...
GET OFFA ME.
...DID YOU DO?
WHY DID SHE STOP ATTACKING?
I JUST PAUSED TIME.
WHOOWOO (HUFF)
후우...
WHAT? YOU CAN DO THAT?!
DID SHE USE SMOG?
BY THE WAY, JIN IS ACTING STRANGE.
NOBODY IS NORMAL IN AMITYVILLE.
NO, MA'AM, I MEAN...
...JIN ATTACKED ME.
SHE SAID IT WAS A DIRECT ORDER. YOU DIDN'T ORDER IT, DID YOU, MA'AM?
HU-HU...
TO PUT IT SIMPLY, SHE'S BEING USED...

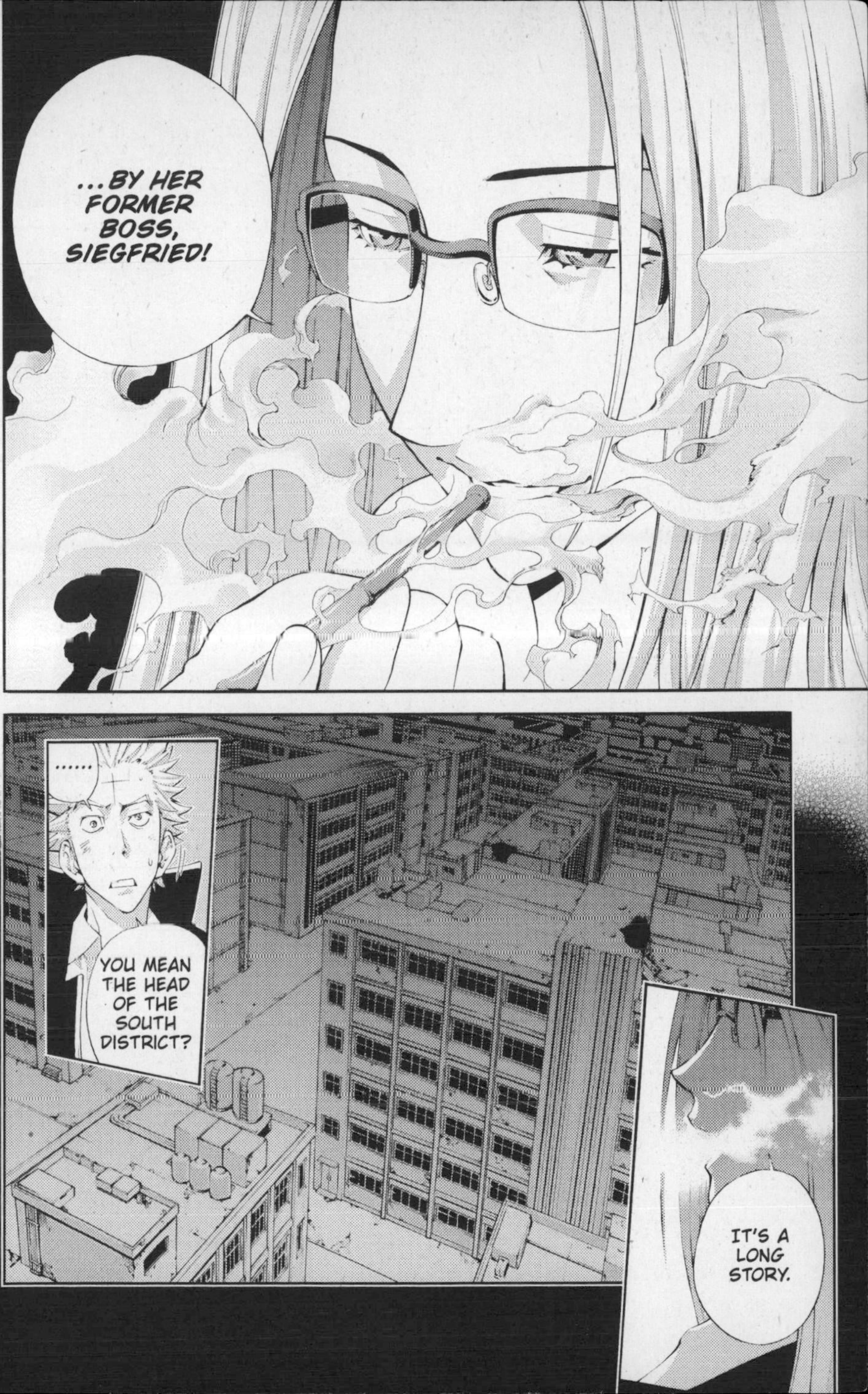
...BY HER FORMER BOSS, SIEGFRIED!
......
YOU MEAN THE HEAD OF THE SOUTH DISTRICT?
IT'S A LONG STORY.

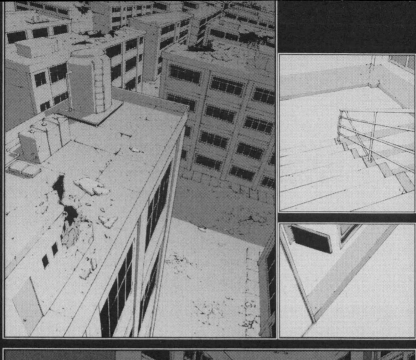

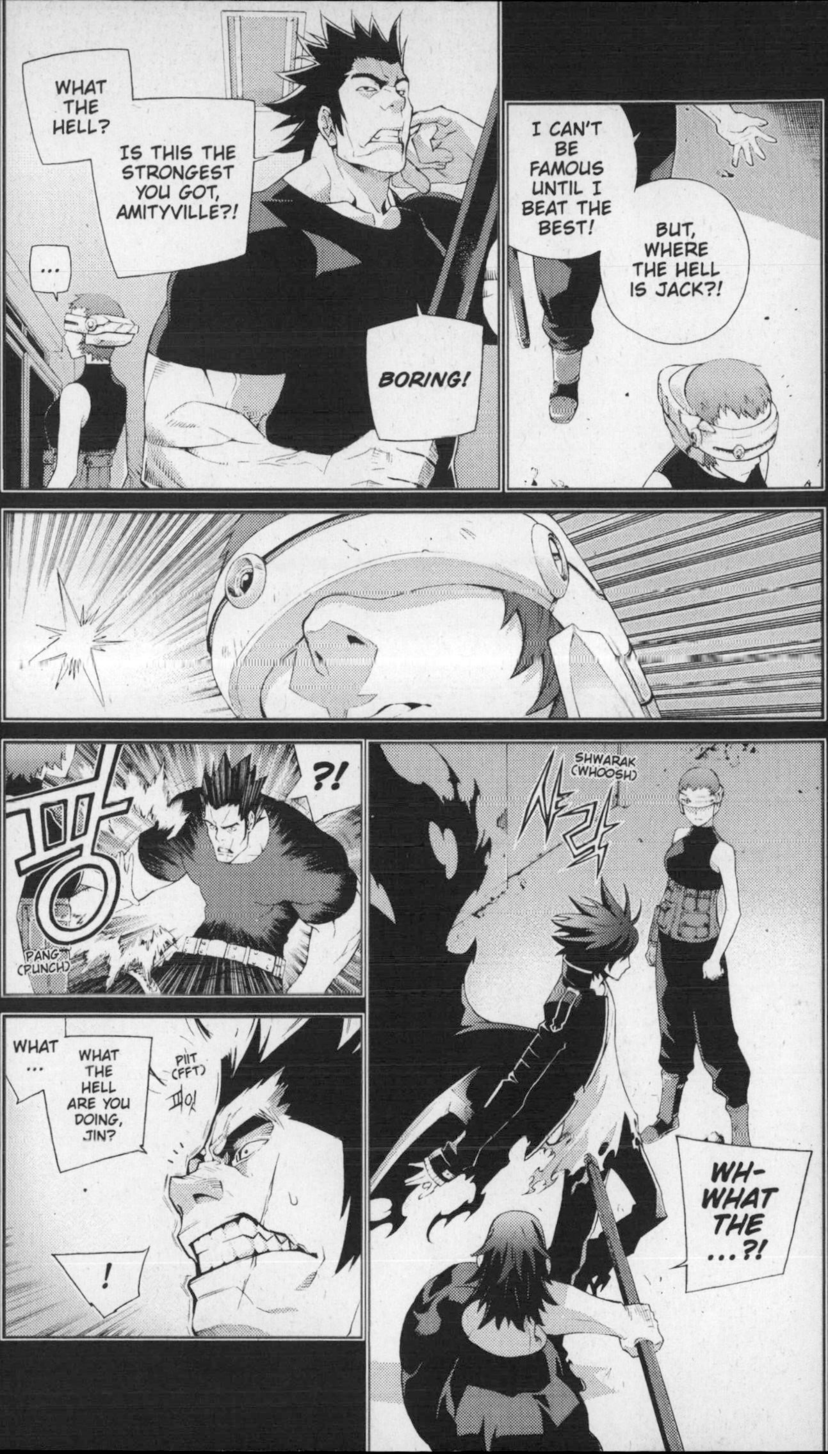
WHAT THE HELL?
IS THIS THE STRONGEST YOU GOT, AMITYVILLE?!
...
BORING!
I CAN'T BE FAMOUS UNTIL I BEAT THE BEST!
BUT, WHERE THE HELL IS JACK?!
?!
PANG (PUNCH)
WHAT...
WHAT THE HELL ARE YOU DOING, JIN?
PIIT (FFT)
!
SHWARAK (WHOOSH)
WH-WHAT THE...?!

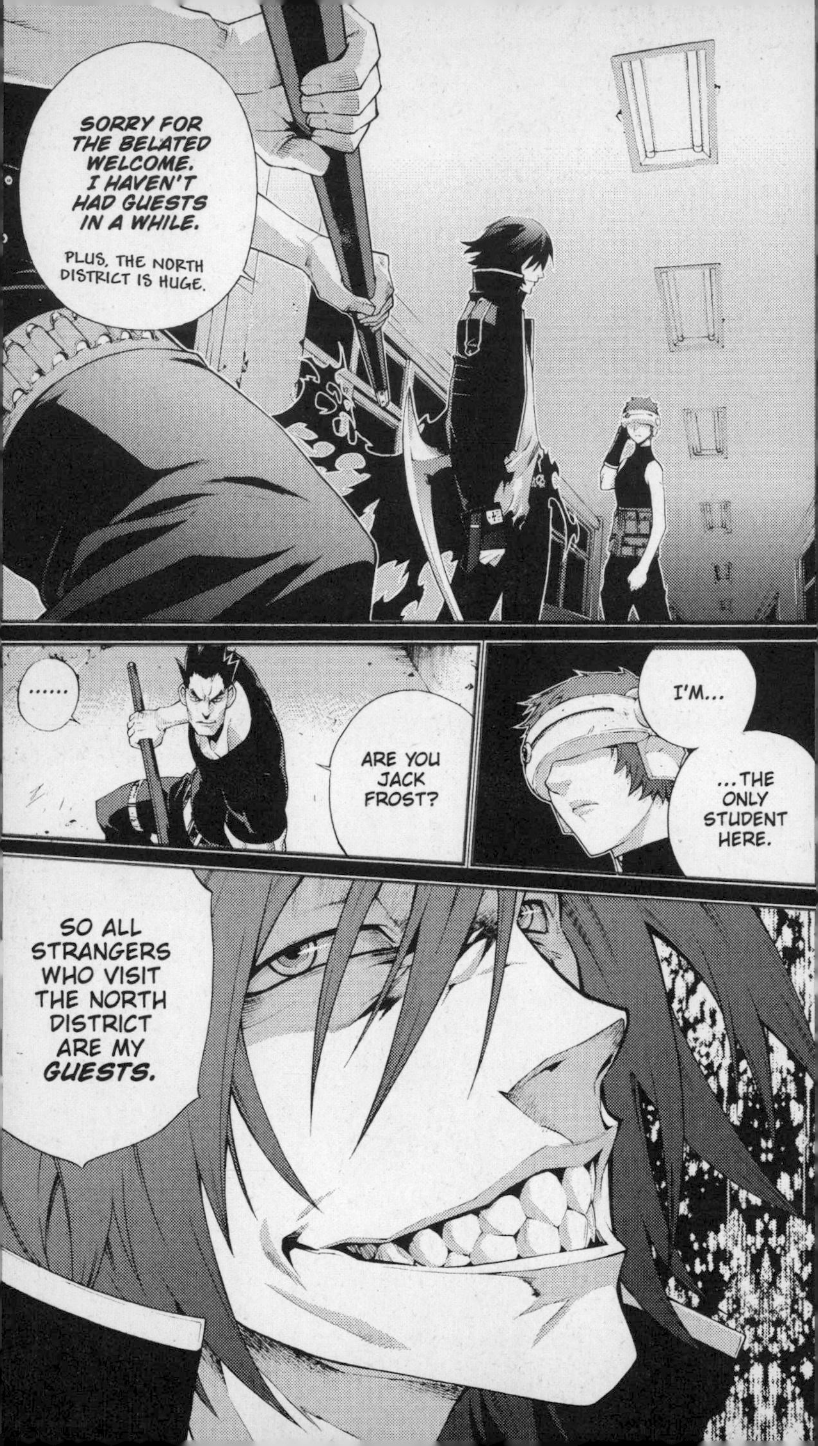
SORRY FOR THE BELATED WELCOME. I HAVEN'T HAD GUESTS IN A WHILE.
PLUS, THE NORTH DISTRICT IS HUGE.
I'M...
...THE ONLY STUDENT HERE.
......
ARE YOU JACK FROST?
SO ALL STRANGERS WHO VISIT THE NORTH DISTRICT ARE MY GUESTS.

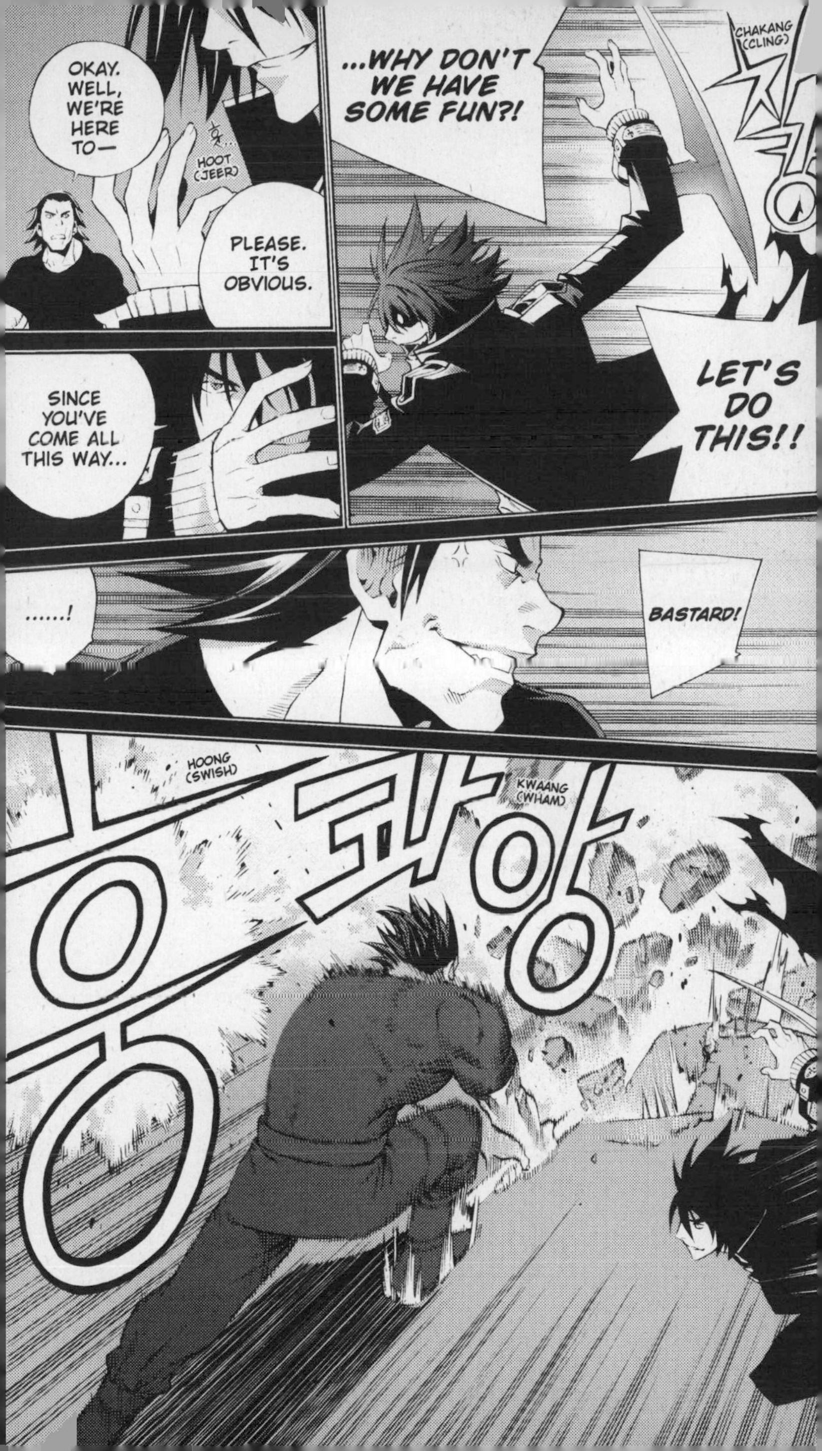
OKAY. WELL, WE'RE HERE TO—
HOOT (JEER)
PLEASE. IT'S OBVIOUS.
...WHY DON'T WE HAVE SOME FUN?!
CHAKANG (CLING)
SINCE YOU'VE COME ALL THIS WAY...
LET'S DO THIS!!
......!
BASTARD!
HOONG (SWISH)
KWAANG (WHAM)

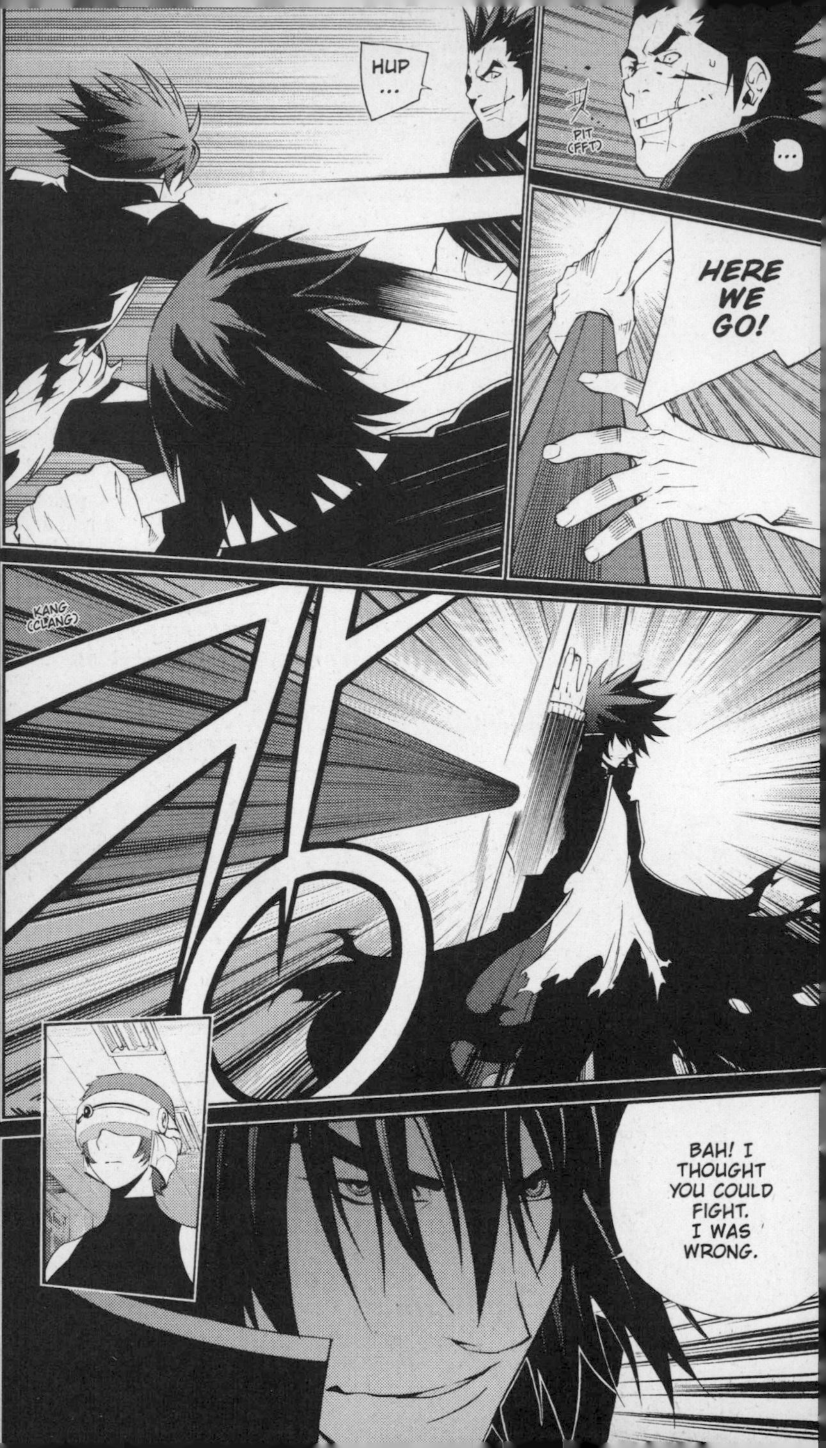

PIT (FFT)
...
HUP ...
HERE WE GO!
KANG (CLANG)
BAH! I THOUGHT YOU COULD FIGHT. I WAS WRONG.

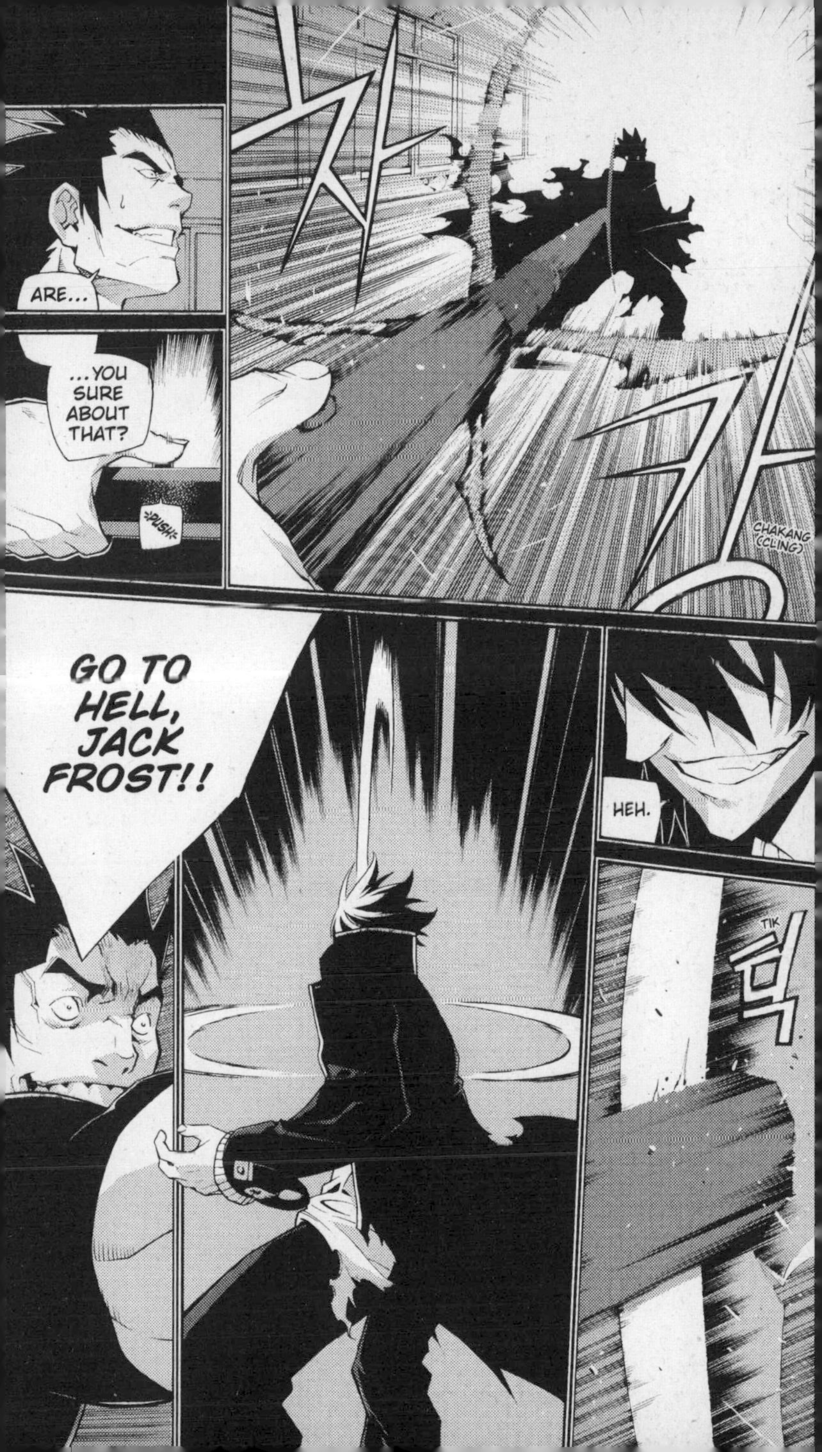
ARE...
...YOU SURE ABOUT THAT?
PUSH
CHAKANG (CLING)
GO TO HELL, JACK FROST!!
HEH.
TIK

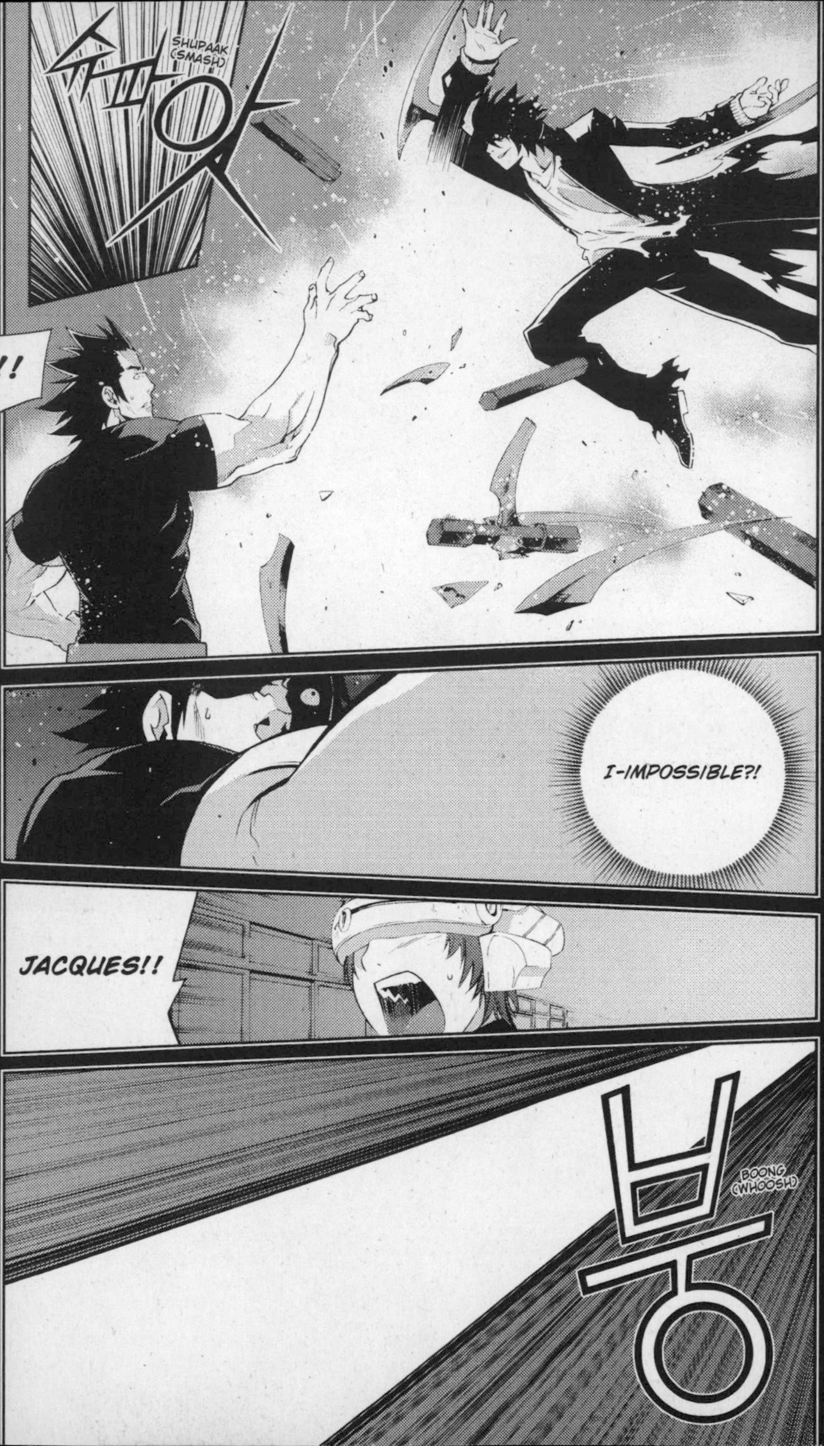
SHUPAAK (SMASH)
!!
I-IMPOSSIBLE?!
JACQUES!!
BOONG (WHOOSH)

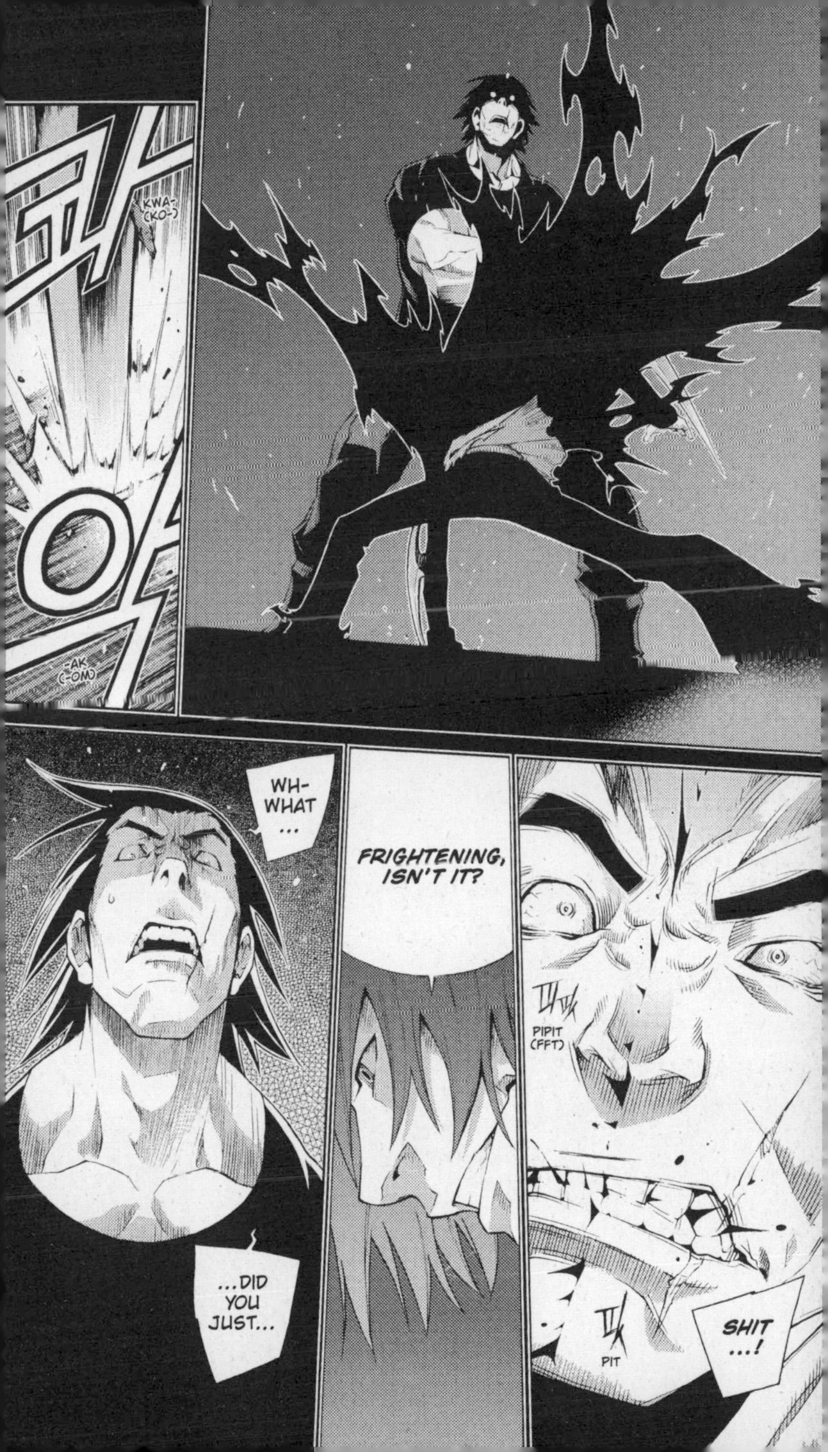

KWA-
(KO-)
-AK
(-OM)
WH-
WHAT
...
...DID
YOU
JUST...
FRIGHTENING,
ISN'T IT?
PIPIT
(FFT)
PIT
SHIT
...!

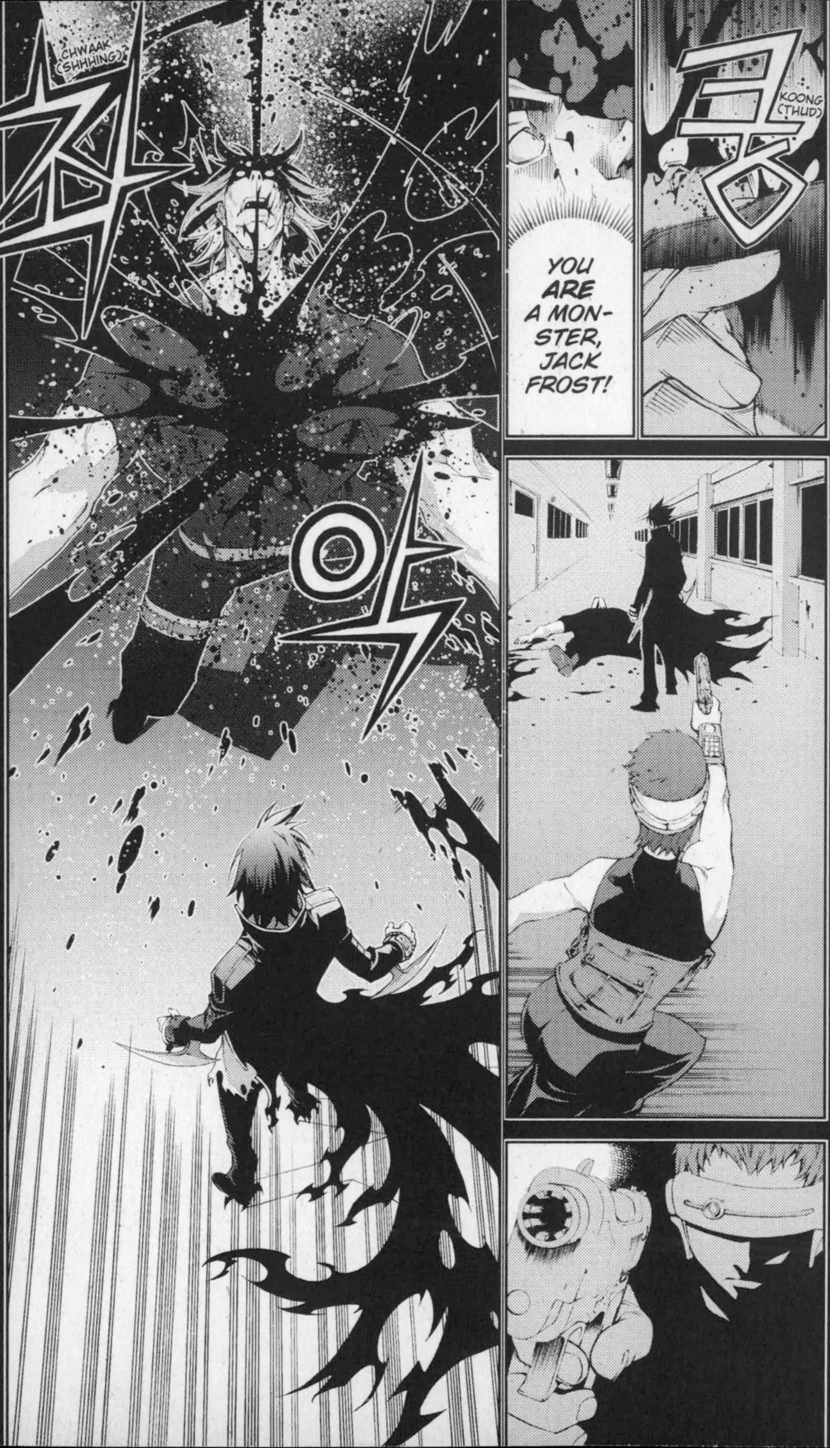
CHWAAK (SHHHING)
YOU ARE A MON-STER, JACK FROST!
KOONG (THUD)

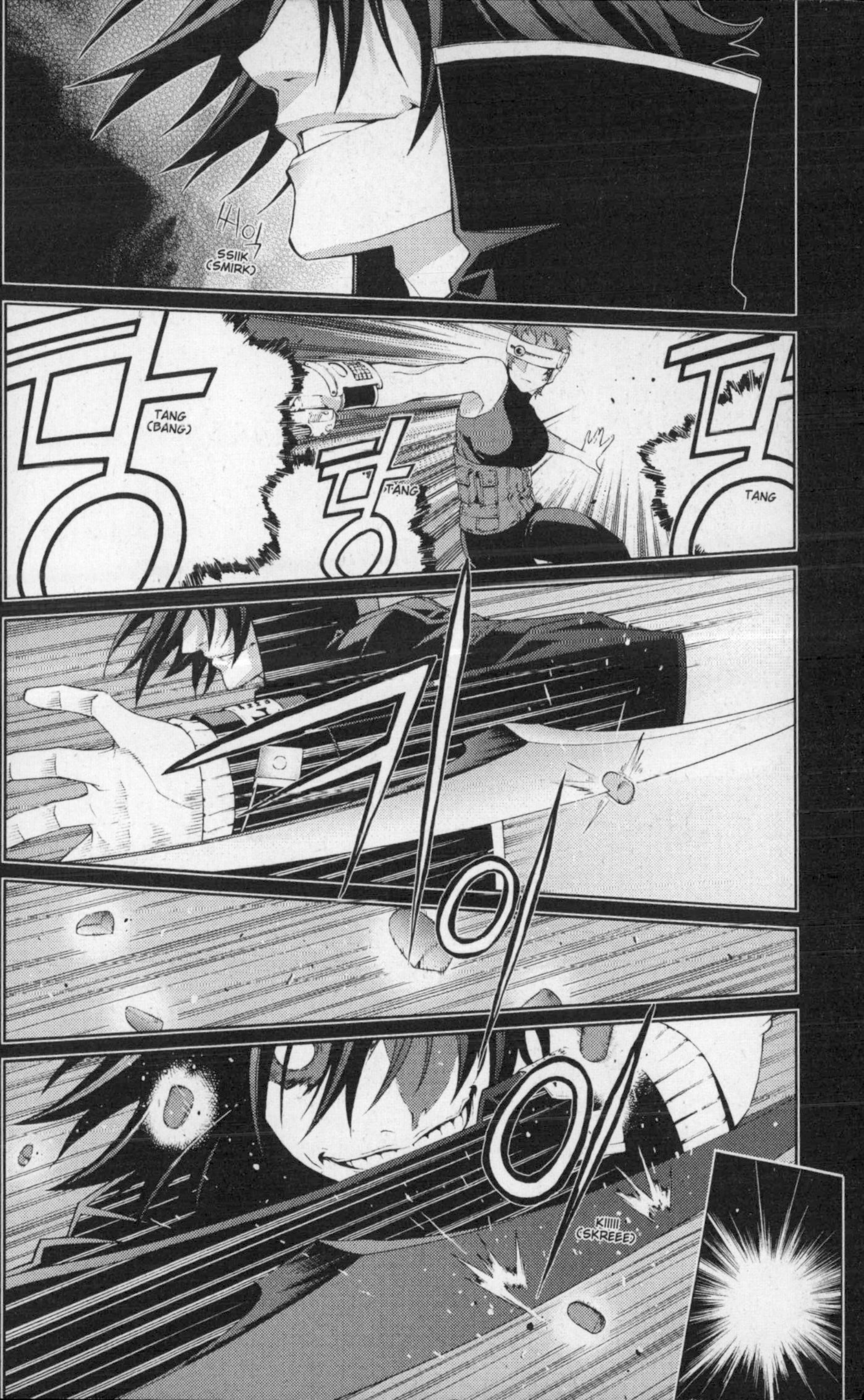

씨익
SSIIK (SMIRK)
탕
TANG (BANG)
탕
TANG
탕
TANG
KIIII (SKREEE)

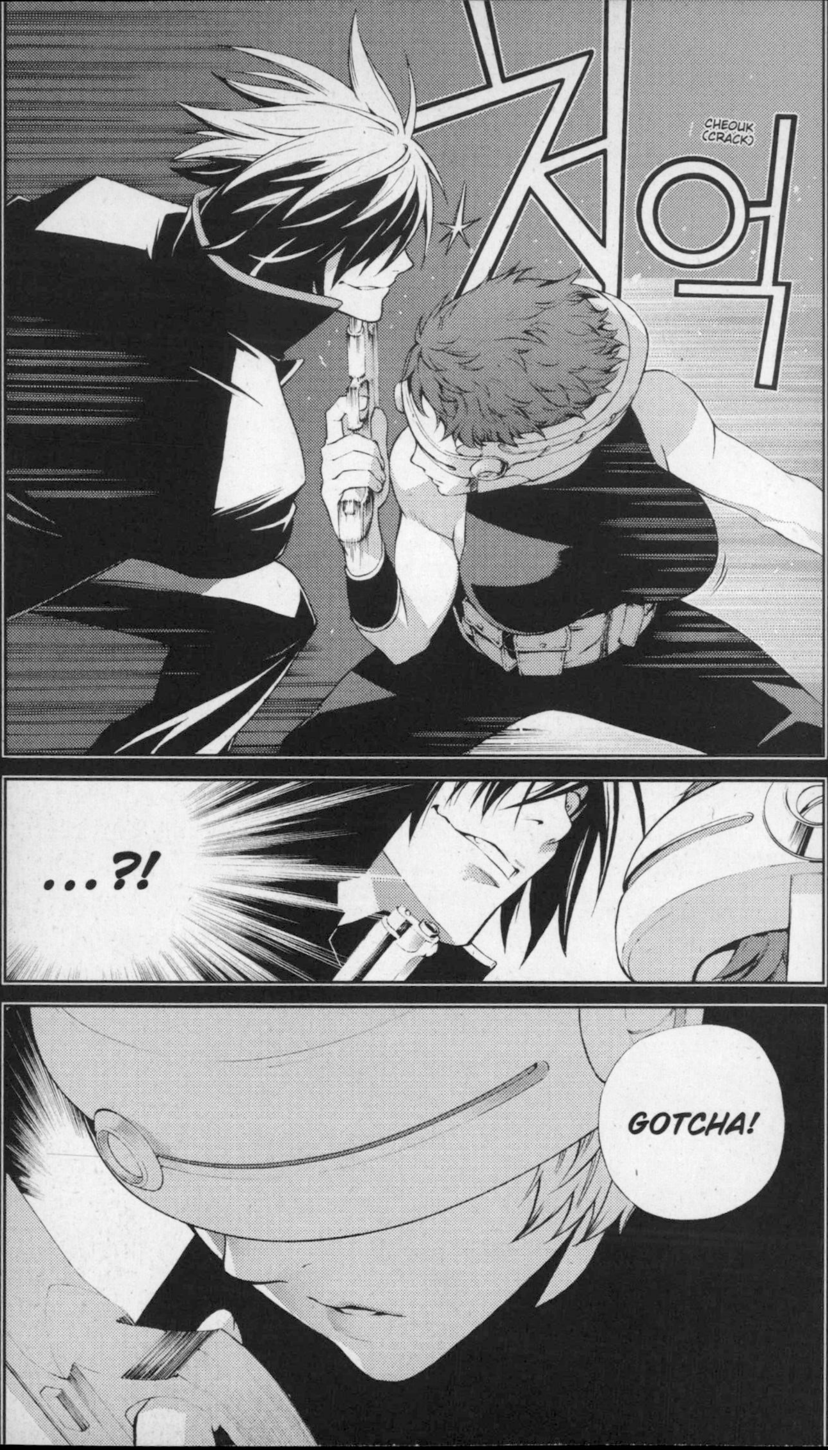
CHEOUK (CRACK)
...?!
GOTCHA!

VIOLENCE 23. FLASHBACK II

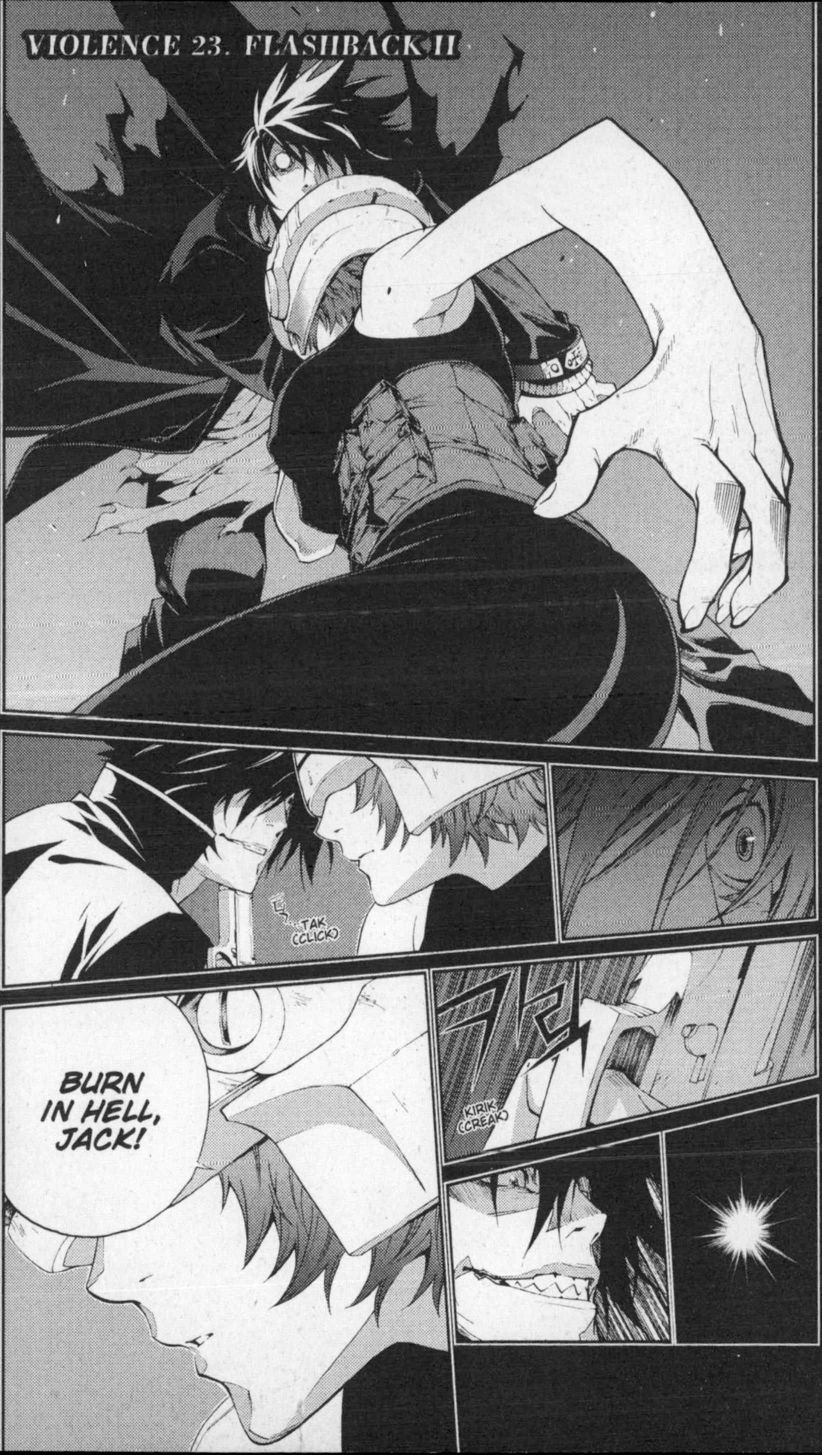
TAK
(CLICK)
BURN IN HELL, JACK!
KIRIK
(CREAK)

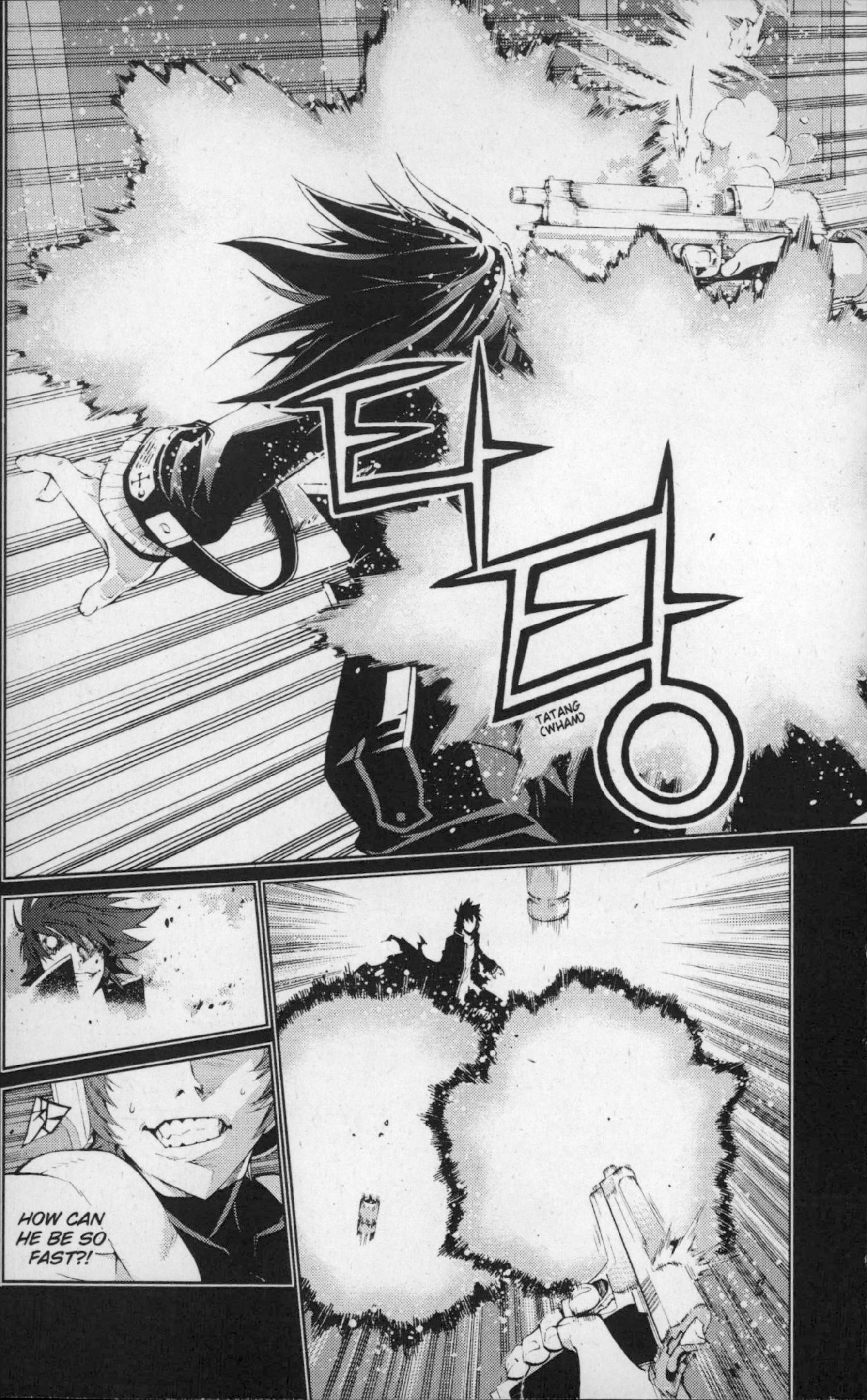
TATANG
(WHAM)
HOW CAN
HE BE SO
FAST?!

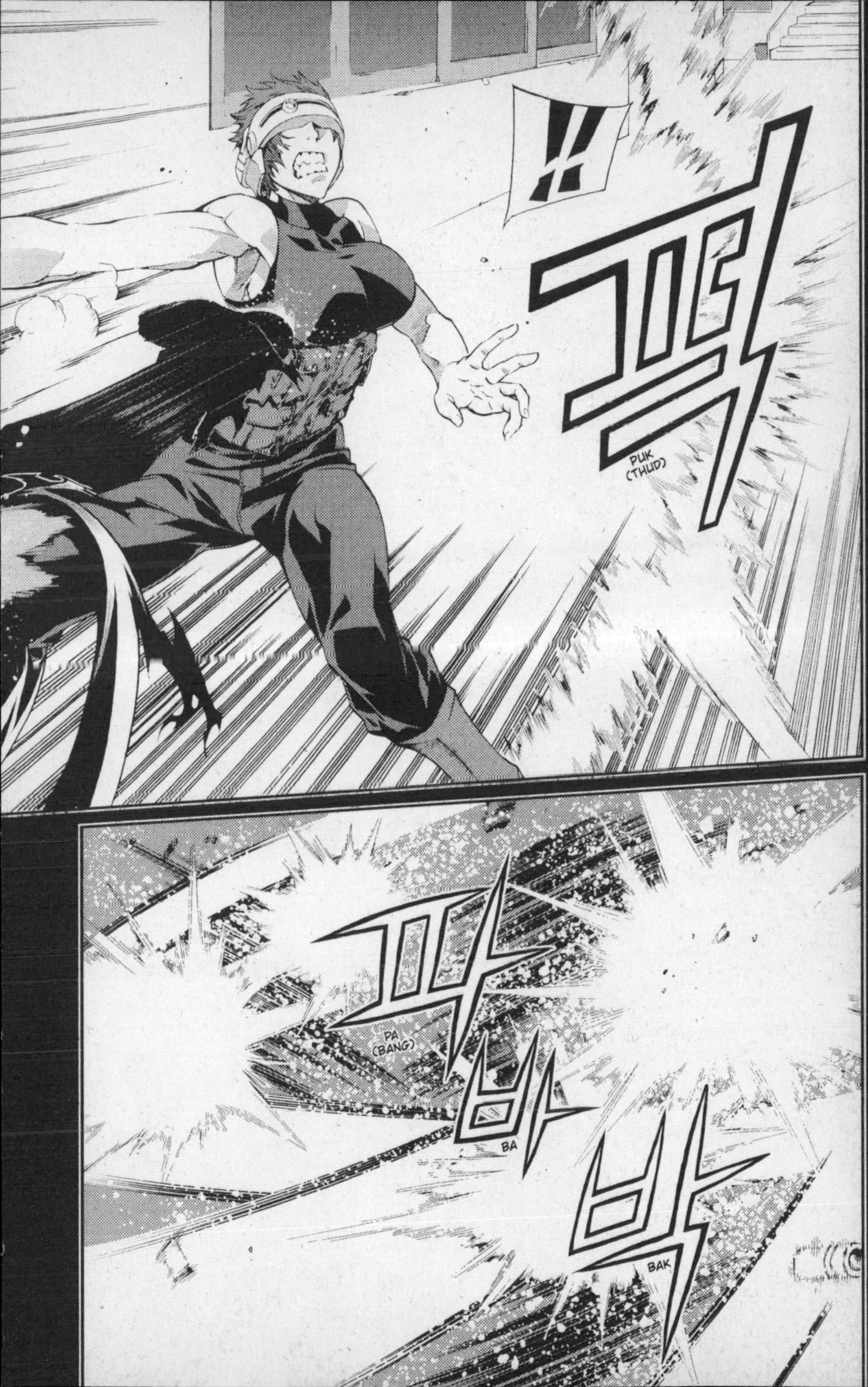
!!
퍽
PUK
(THUD)
파
PA
(BANG)
바
BA
박
BAK

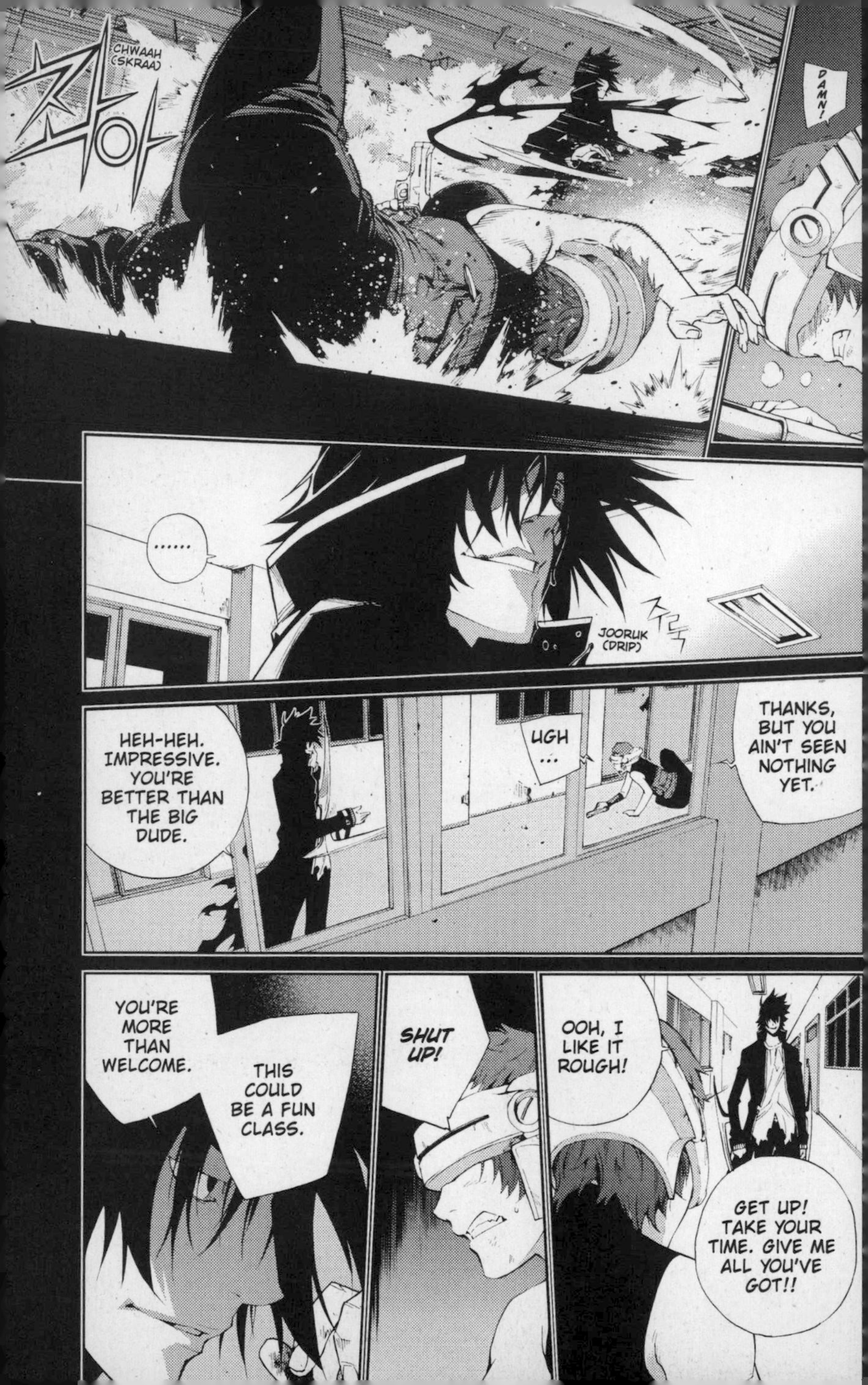

CHWAAH (SKRAA)
DAMN!
......
JOORUK (DRIP)
HEH-HEH. IMPRESSIVE. YOU'RE BETTER THAN THE BIG DUDE.
UGH ...
THANKS, BUT YOU AIN'T SEEN NOTHING YET.
YOU'RE MORE THAN WELCOME.
THIS COULD BE A FUN CLASS.
SHUT UP!
OOH, I LIKE IT ROUGH!
GET UP! TAKE YOUR TIME. GIVE ME ALL YOU'VE GOT!!

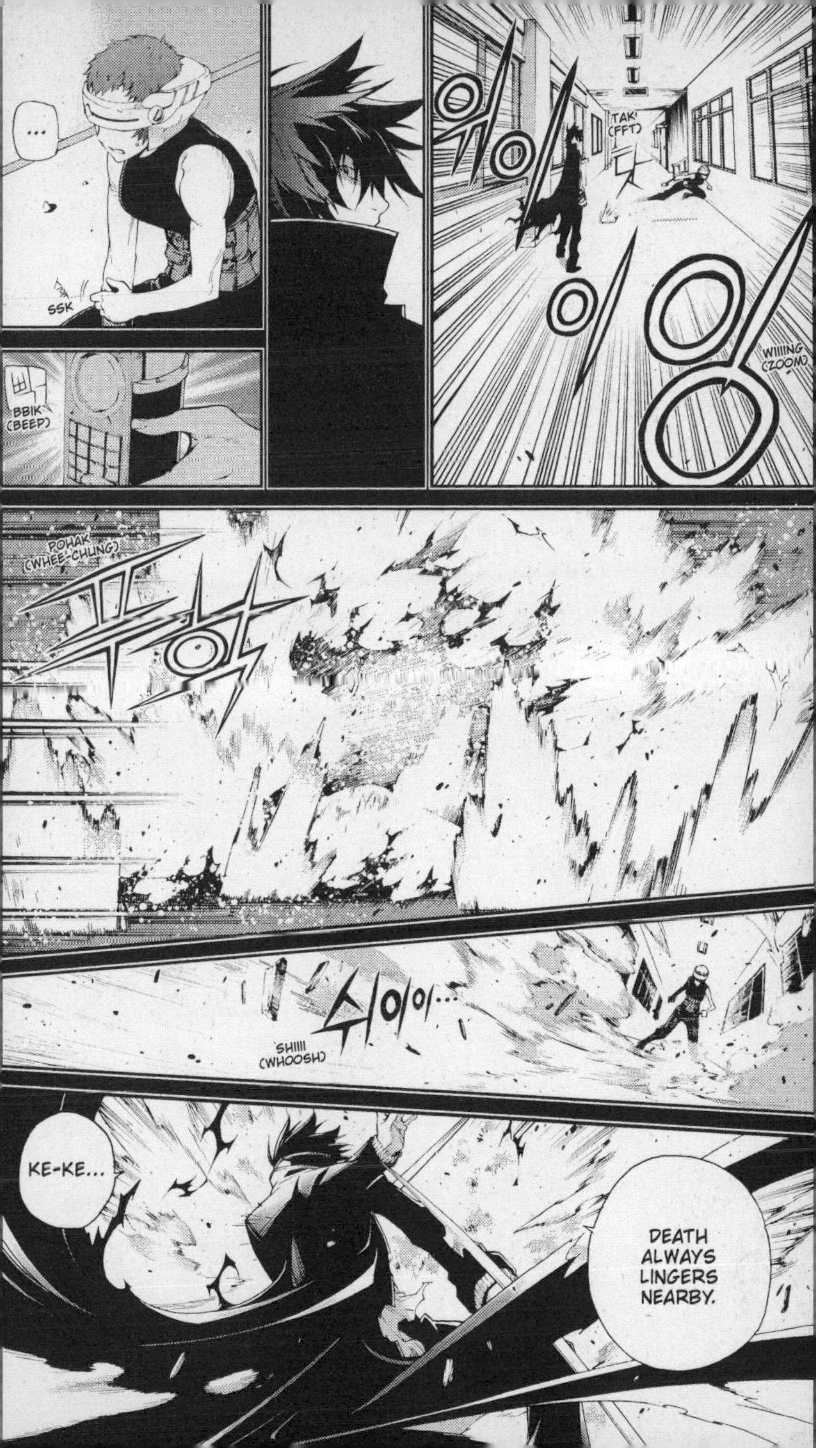
...
SSK
BBIK (BEEP)
TAK (FFT)
WIIING (ZOOM)
POHAK (WHEE-CHUNG)
SHIIII (WHOOSH)
KE-KE...
DEATH ALWAYS LINGERS NEARBY.

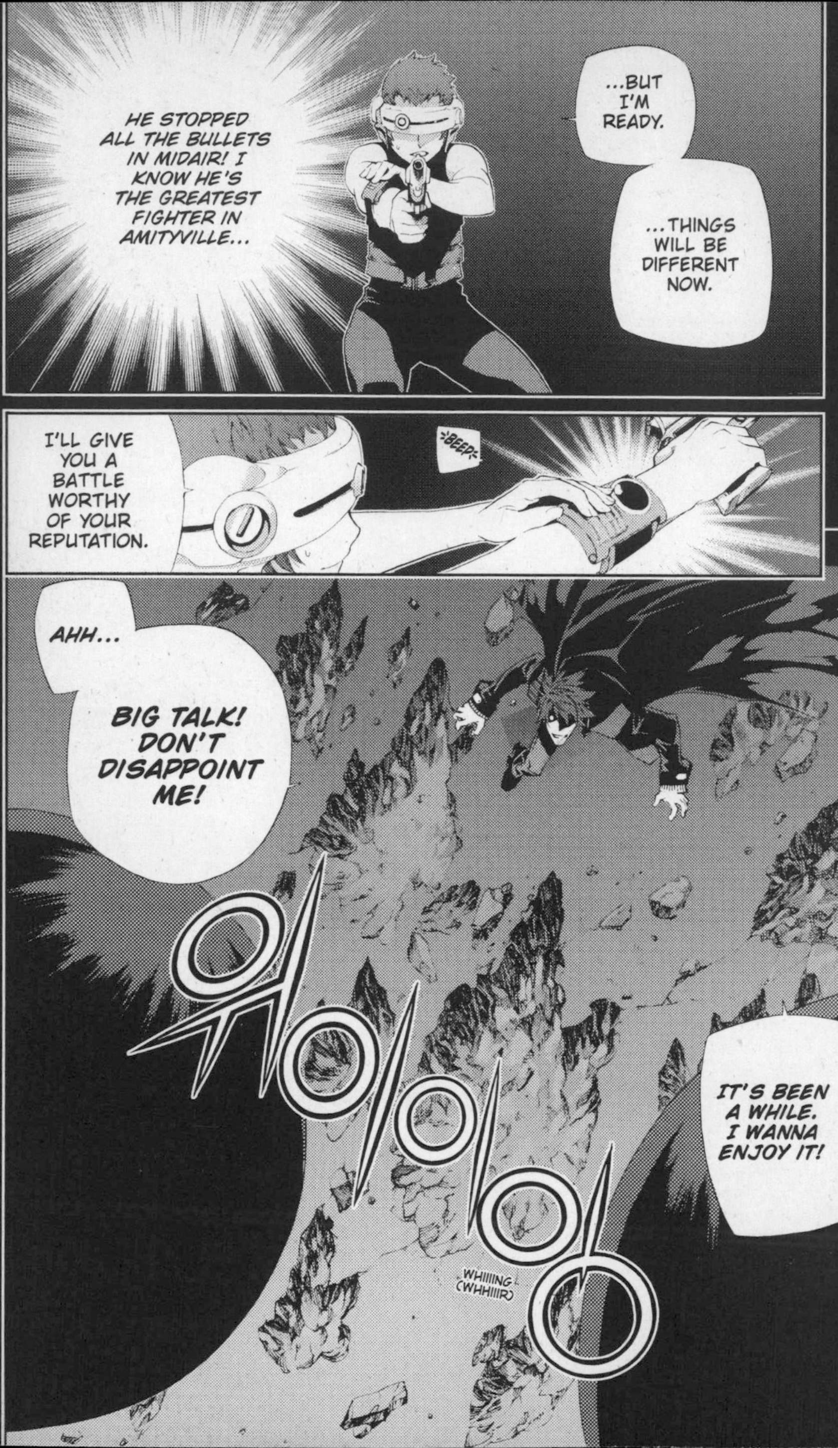
HE STOPPED ALL THE BULLETS IN MIDAIR! I KNOW HE'S THE GREATEST FIGHTER IN AMITYVILLE...
...BUT I'M READY.
...THINGS WILL BE DIFFERENT NOW.
I'LL GIVE YOU A BATTLE WORTHY OF YOUR REPUTATION.
BEEP
AHH...
BIG TALK! DON'T DISAPPOINT ME!
IT'S BEEN A WHILE. I WANNA ENJOY IT!
WHIIIING (WHHIIIR)

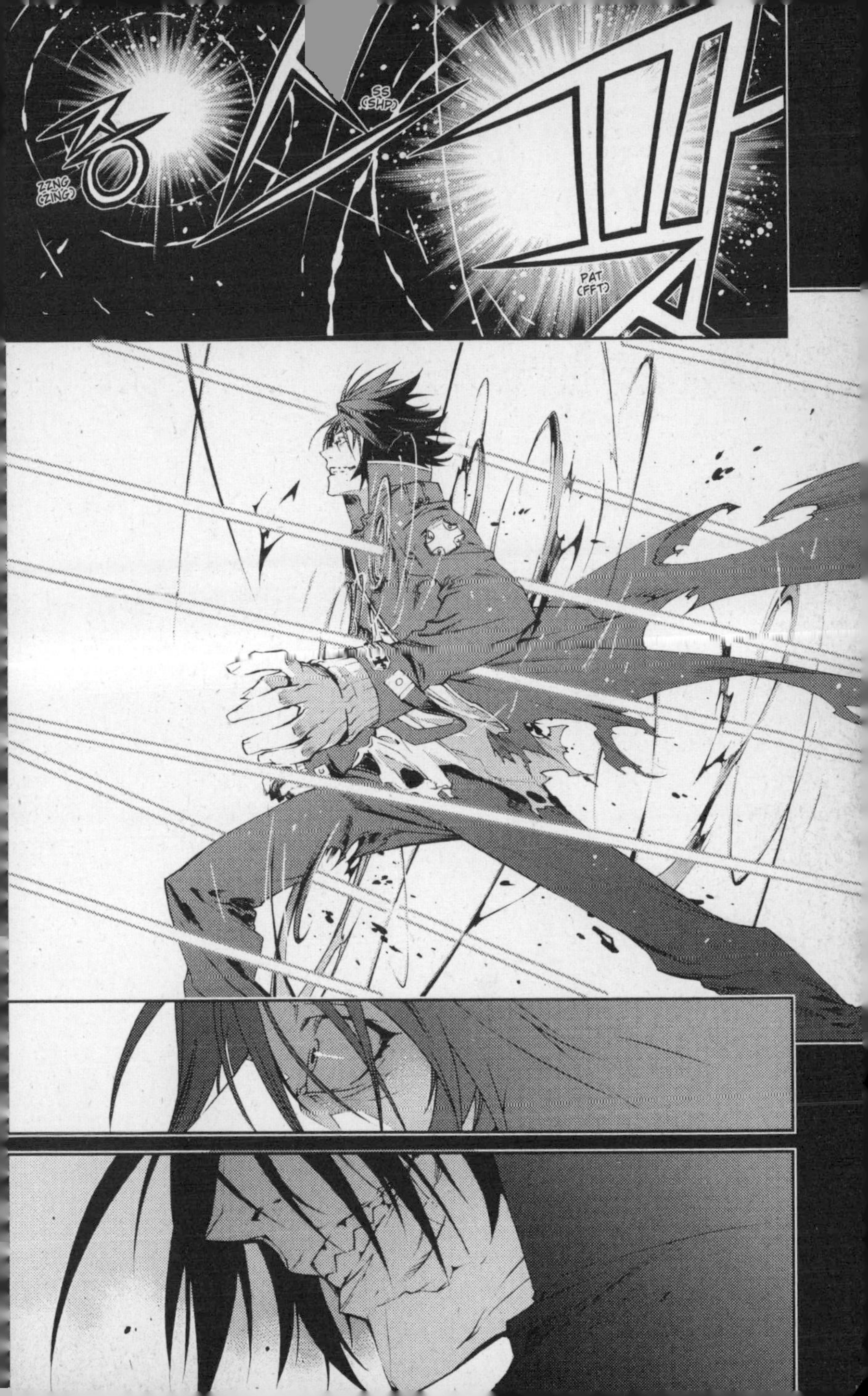
ZZNG (ZING)
SS (SHP)
PAT (FFT)

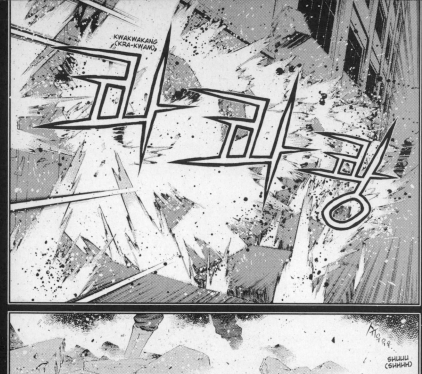

KWAKWAKANG
(KRA-KWAM)

SHUUU
(SHHHH)

아이영
WHIING
(WHIR)

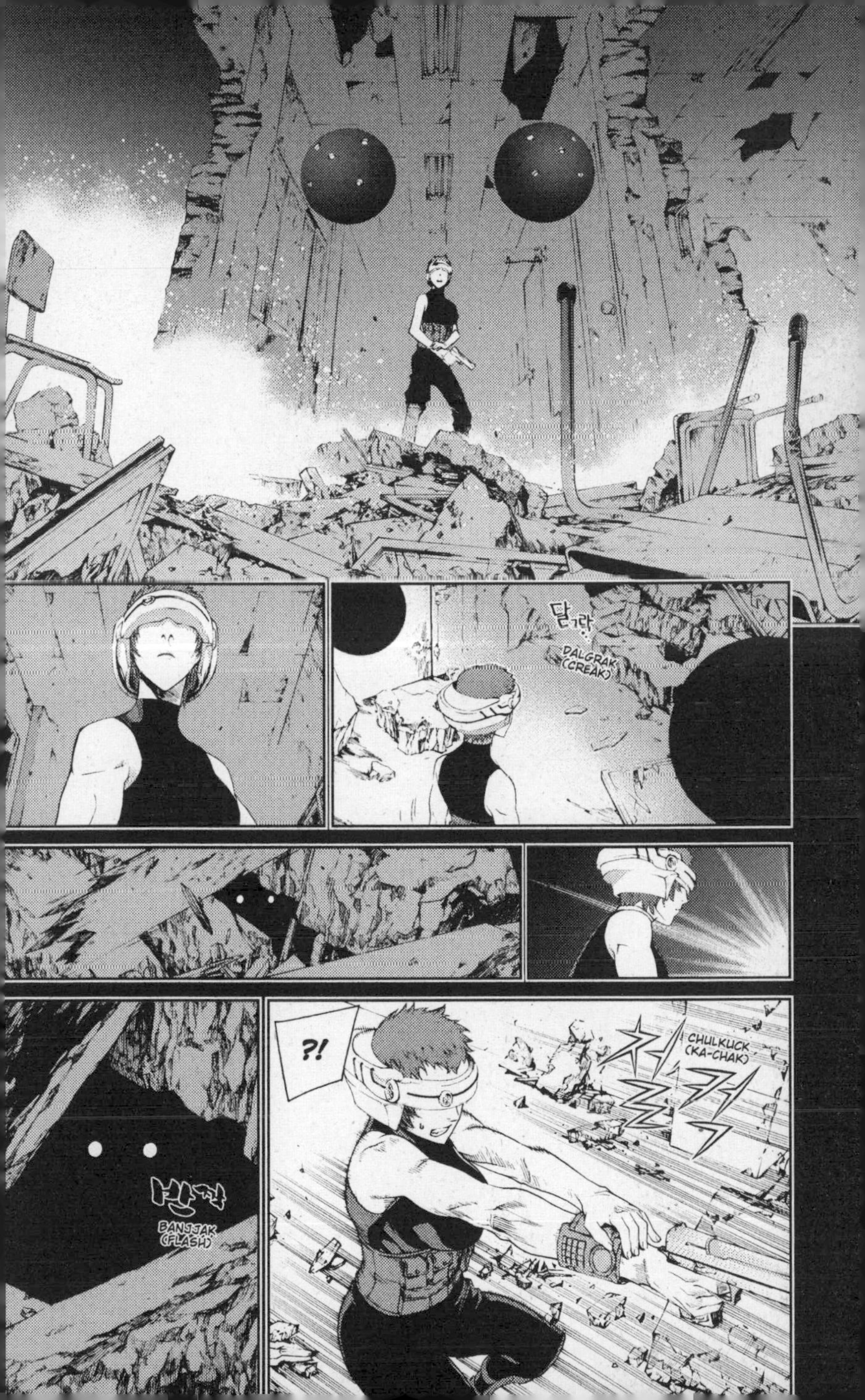
달그락
DALGRAK (CREAK)
반짝
BANJJAK (FLASH)
?!
CHULKUCK (KA-CHAK)

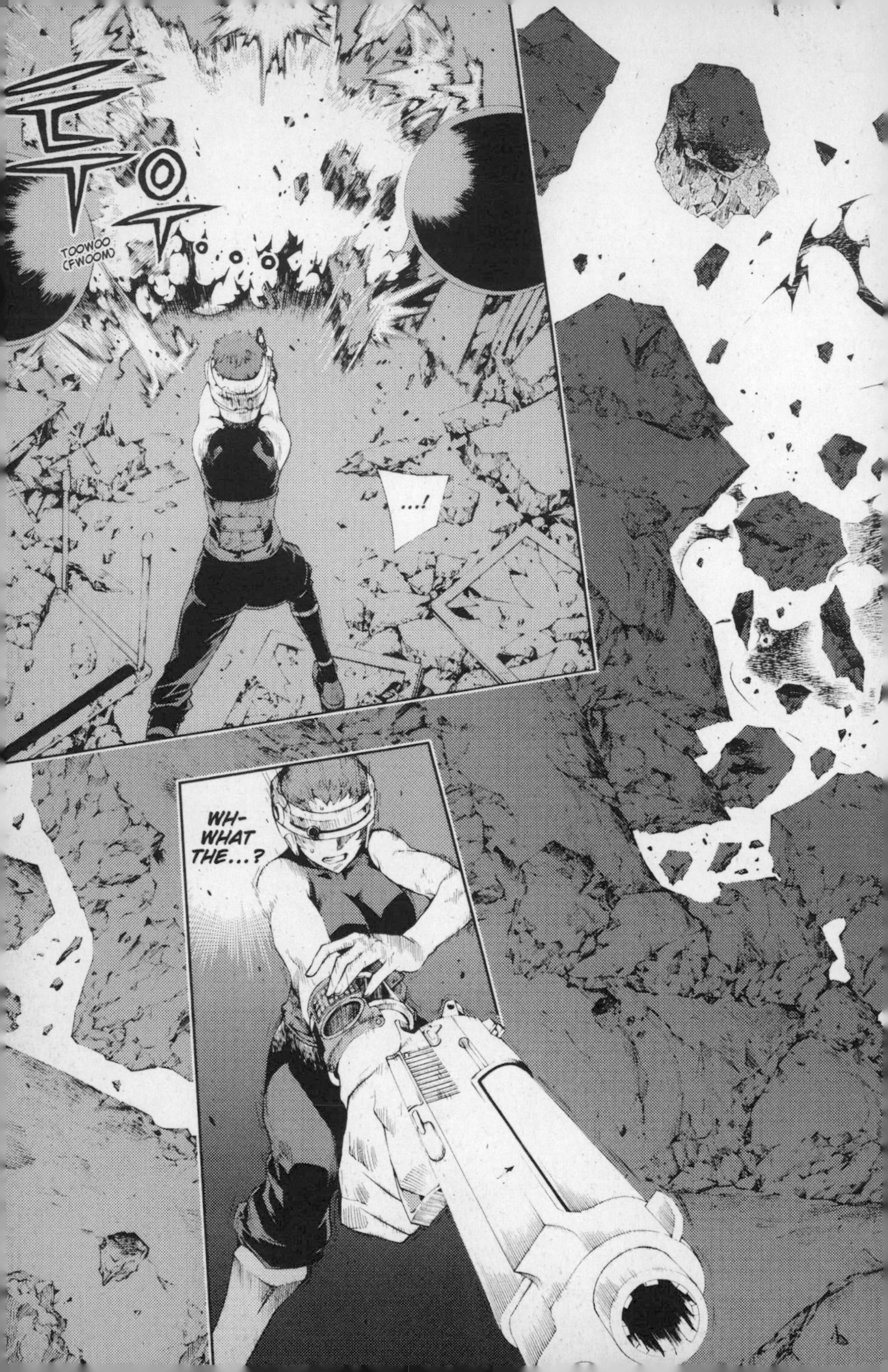
TOOWOO
(FWOOM)
...!
WH-
WHAT
THE...?

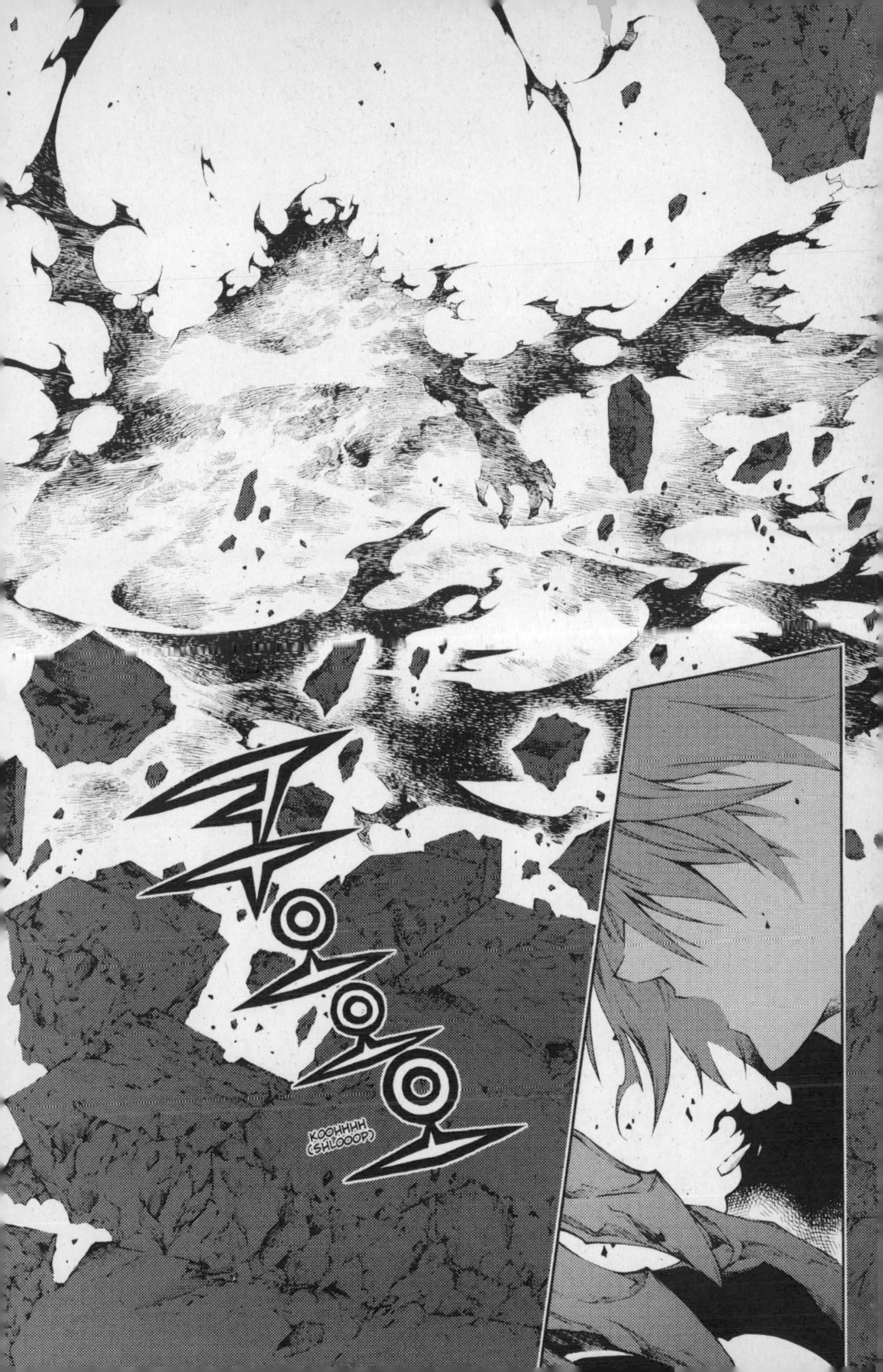
KOOHHHH
(SHLOOOP)

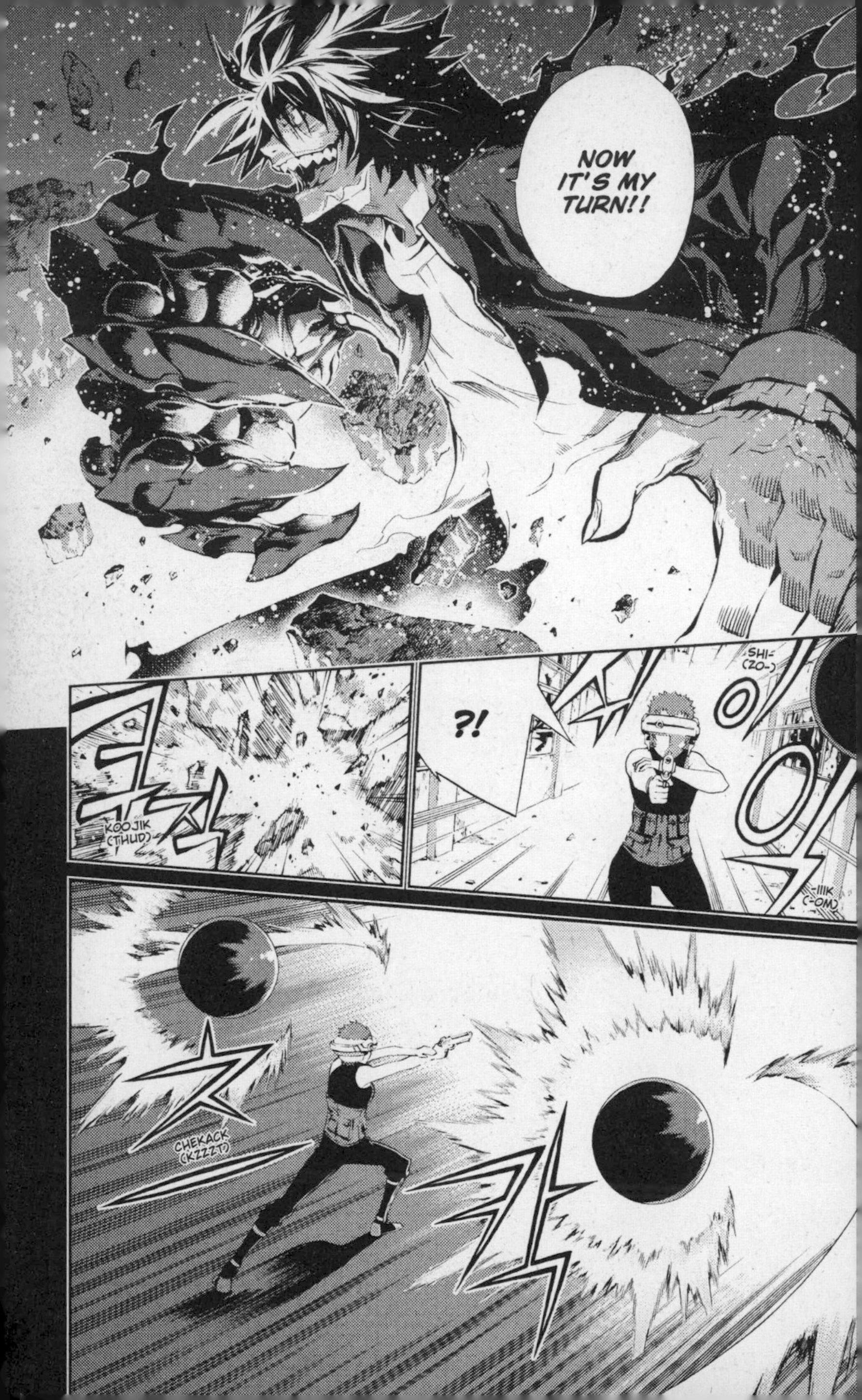
NOW IT'S MY TURN!!
KOOJIK (THUD)
?!
SHI- (ZO-)
-IIIK (-OM)
CHEKACK (KZZZT)

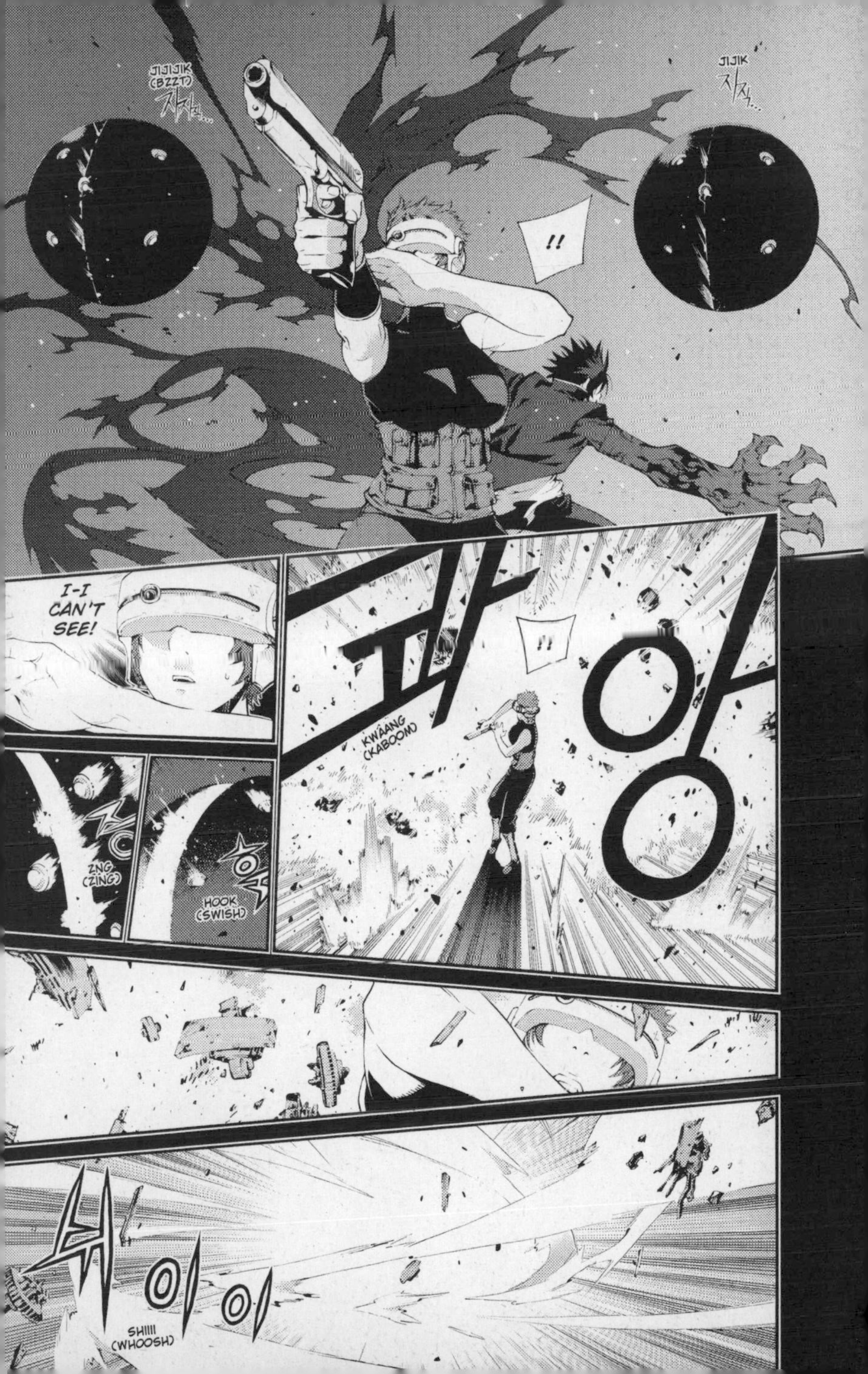
JIJIJIK (BZZT)
!!
JIJIK
I-I CAN'T SEE!
ZNG (ZING)
HOOK (SWISH)
!!
KWAANG (KABOOM)
SHIIII (WHOOSH)

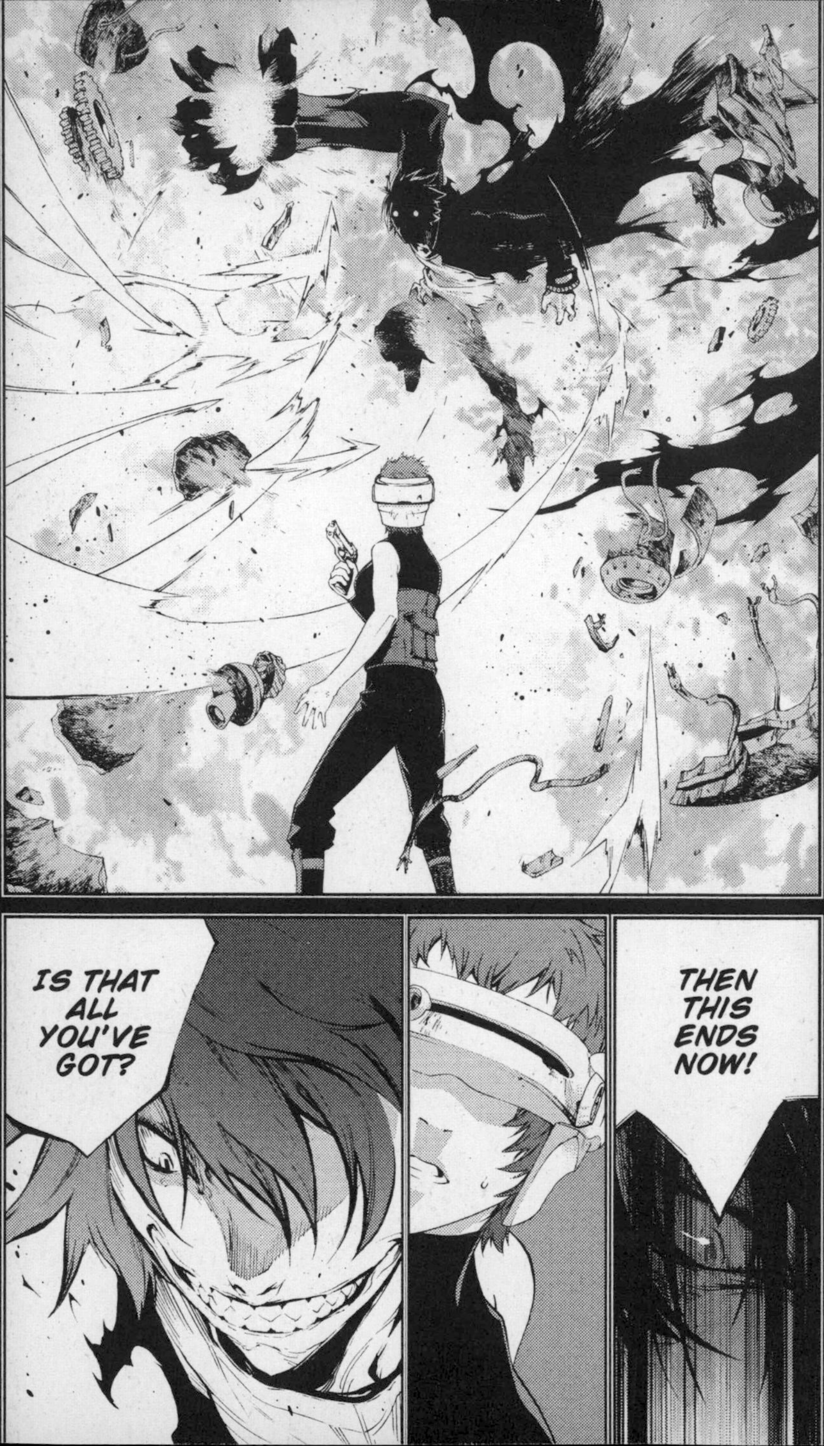
IS THAT ALL YOU'VE GOT?
THEN THIS ENDS NOW!

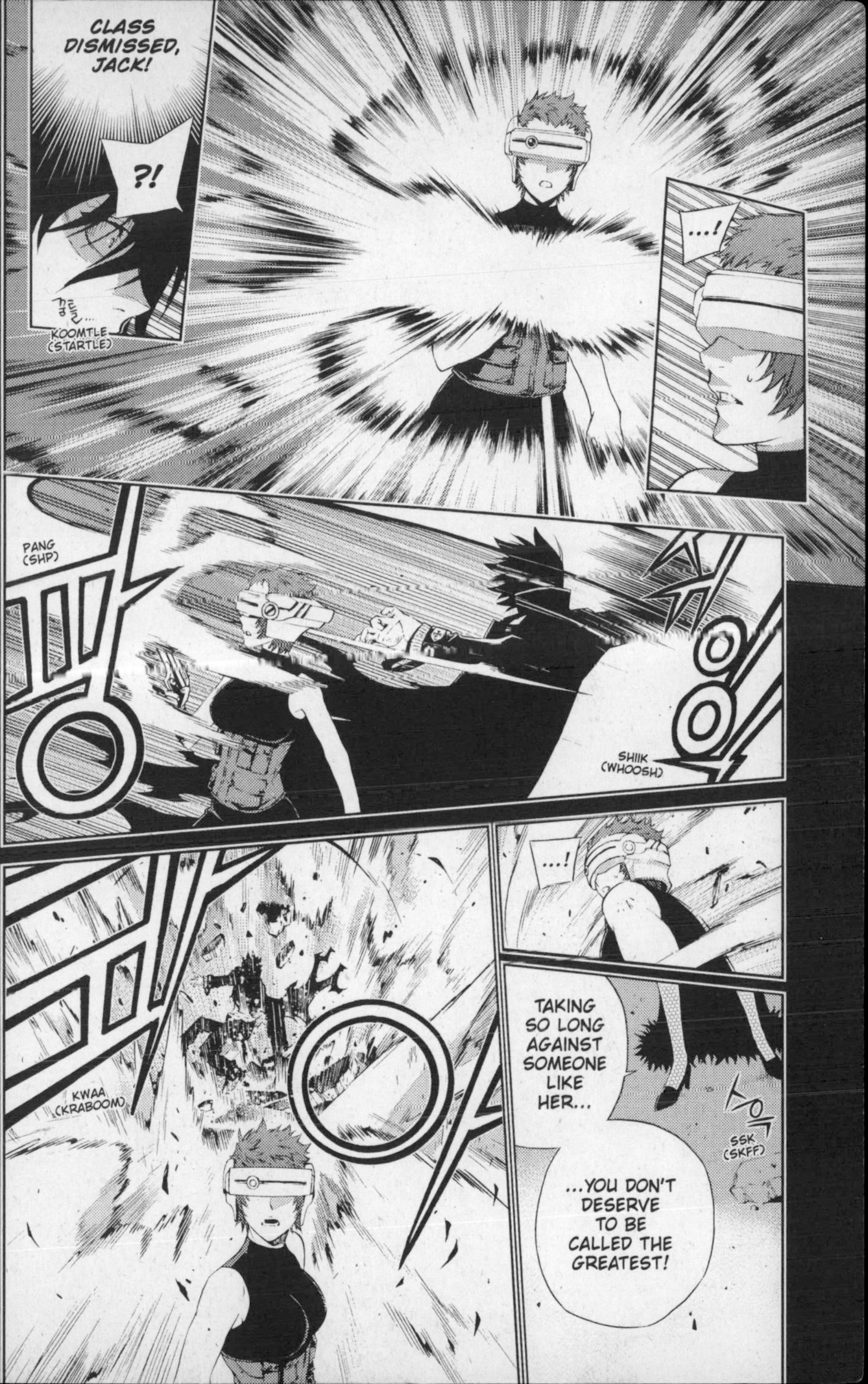
CLASS DISMISSED, JACK!
?!
KOOMTLE (STARTLE)
...!
PANG (SHP)
SHIIK (WHOOSH)
KWAA (KRABOOM)
...!
TAKING SO LONG AGAINST SOMEONE LIKE HER...
...YOU DON'T DESERVE TO BE CALLED THE GREATEST!
SSK (SKFF)

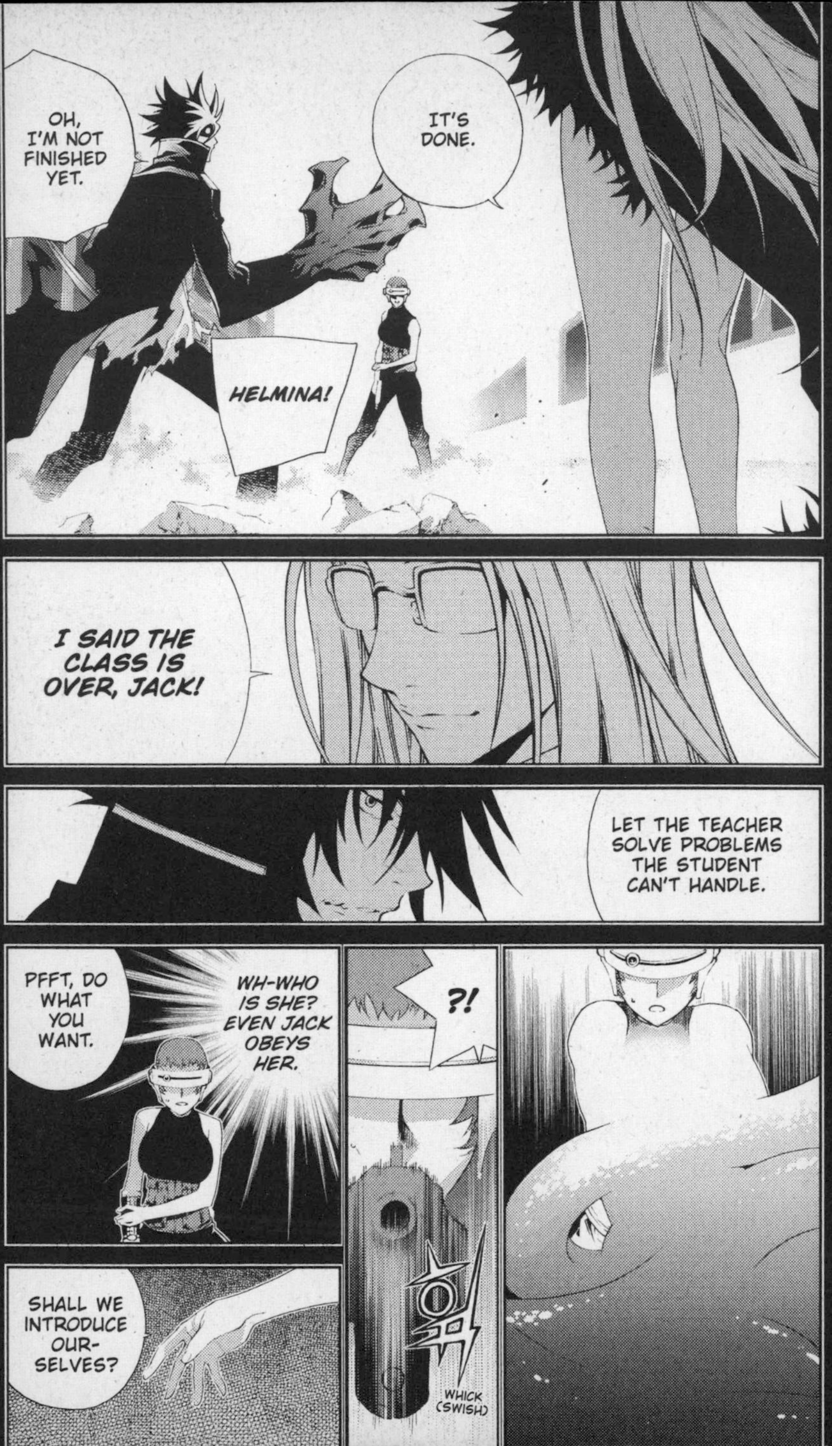
OH, I'M NOT FINISHED YET.
IT'S DONE.
HELMINA!
I SAID THE CLASS IS OVER, JACK!
LET THE TEACHER SOLVE PROBLEMS THE STUDENT CAN'T HANDLE.
PFFT, DO WHAT YOU WANT.
WH-WHO IS SHE? EVEN JACK OBEYS HER.
SHALL WE INTRODUCE OUR-SELVES?
?!
WHICK (SWISH)

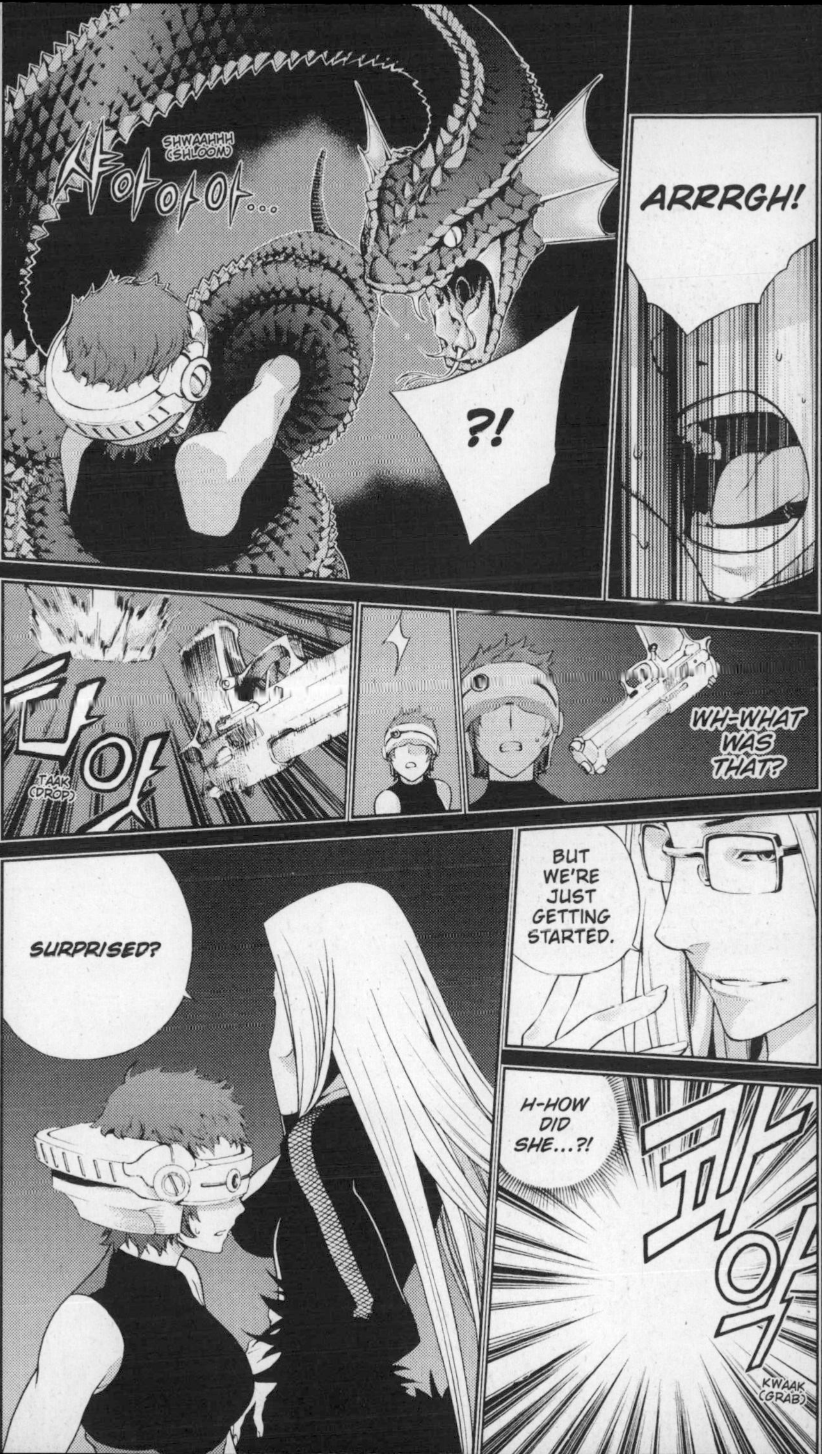
샤아아아아...
SHWAAHHH (SHLOOM)
?!
ARRRGH!
TAAK (DROP)
WH-WHAT WAS THAT?
SURPRISED?
BUT WE'RE JUST GETTING STARTED.
H-HOW DID SHE...?!
KWAAK (GRAB)

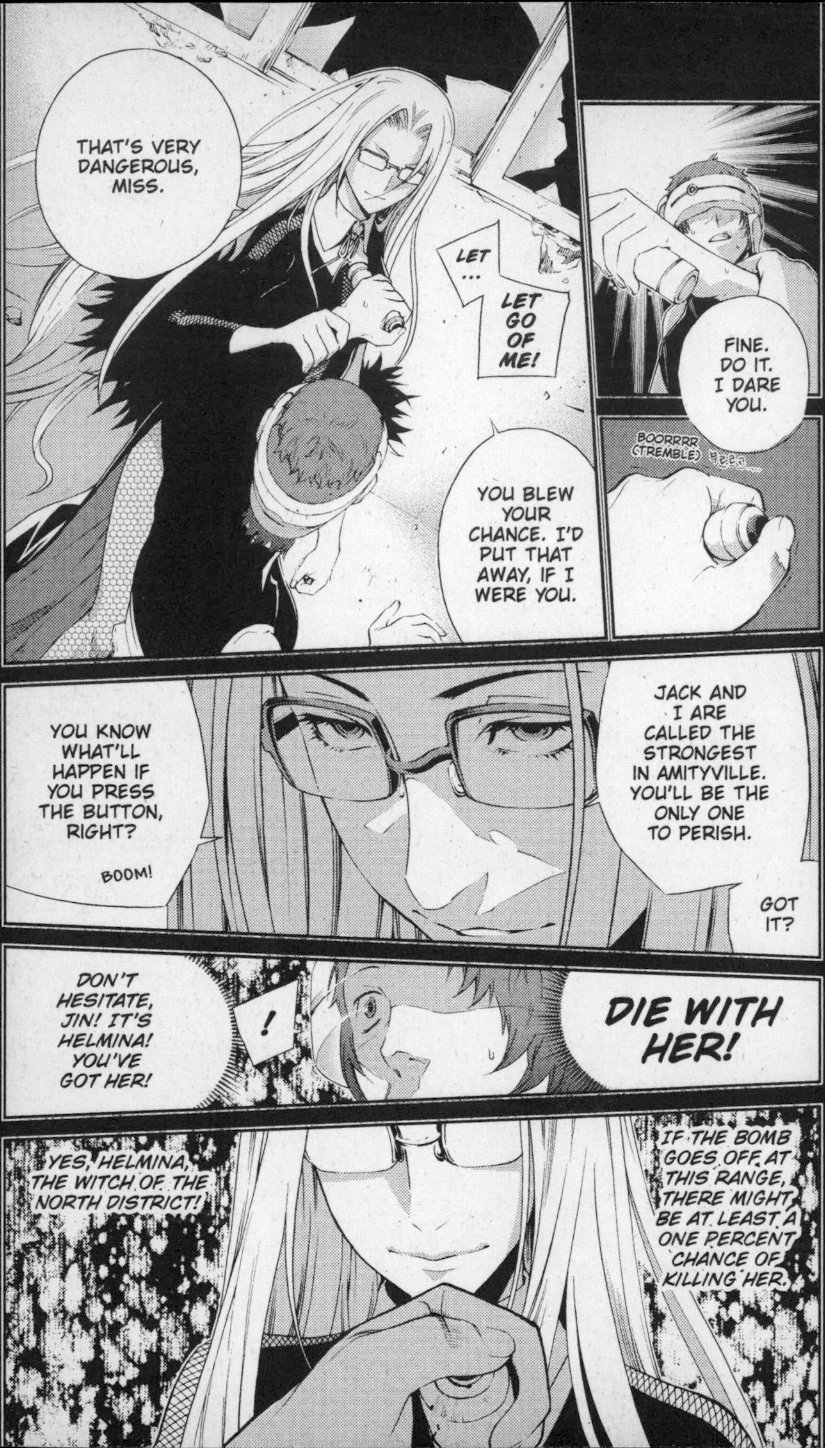
THAT'S VERY DANGEROUS, MISS.
LET... LET GO OF ME!
YOU BLEW YOUR CHANCE. I'D PUT THAT AWAY, IF I WERE YOU.
FINE. DO IT. I DARE YOU.
BOORRRR (TREMBLE)
YOU KNOW WHAT'LL HAPPEN IF YOU PRESS THE BUTTON, RIGHT?
BOOM!
JACK AND I ARE CALLED THE STRONGEST IN AMITYVILLE. YOU'LL BE THE ONLY ONE TO PERISH.
GOT IT?
DON'T HESITATE, JIN! IT'S HELMINA! YOU'VE GOT HER!
!
DIE WITH HER!
YES, HELMINA, THE WITCH OF THE NORTH DISTRICT!
IF THE BOMB GOES OFF AT THIS RANGE, THERE MIGHT BE AT LEAST A ONE PERCENT CHANCE OF KILLING HER.

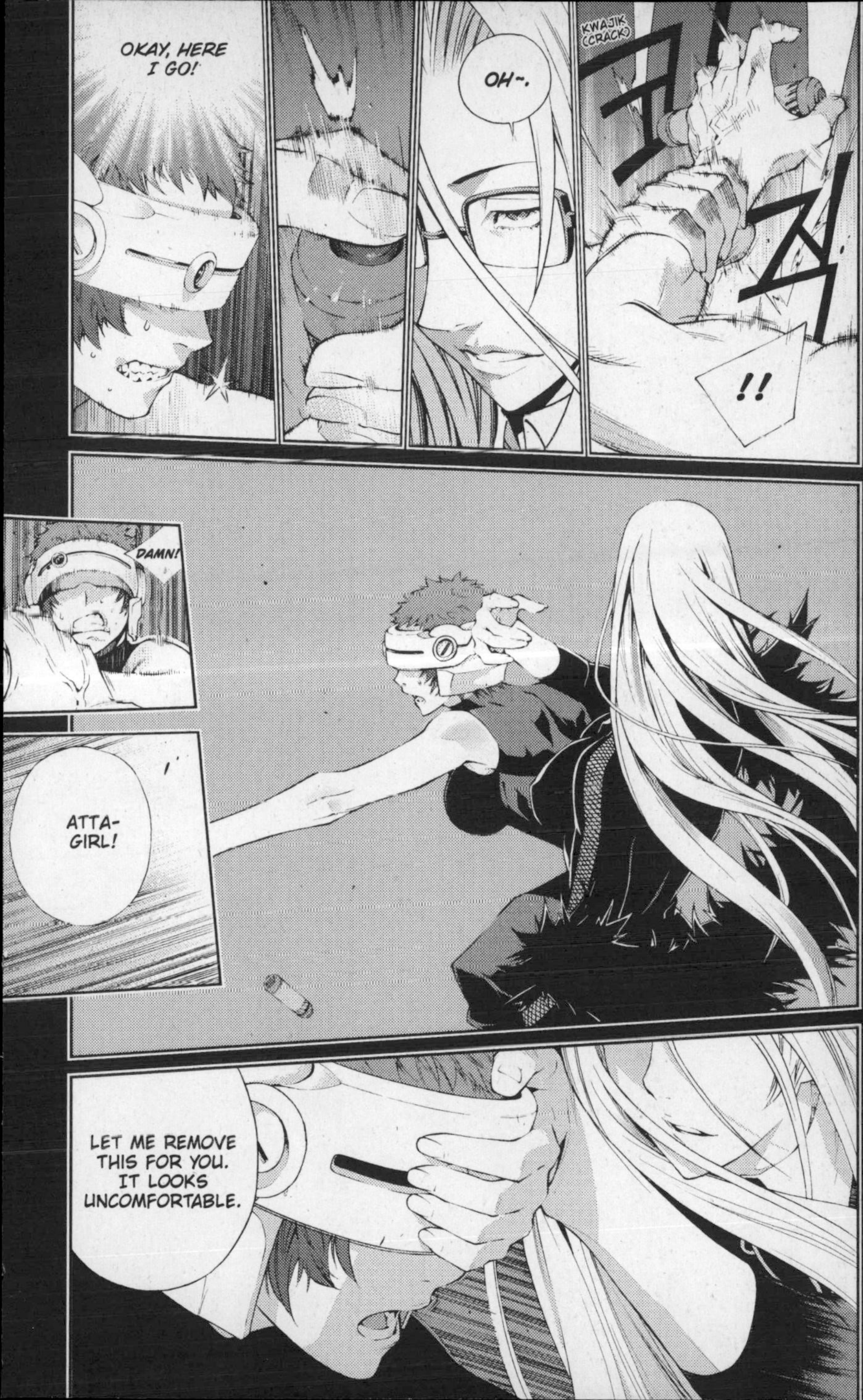
OKAY, HERE I GO!
OH~.
KWAJIK (CRACK)
!!
DAMN!
ATTA-GIRL!
LET ME REMOVE THIS FOR YOU. IT LOOKS UNCOMFORTABLE.

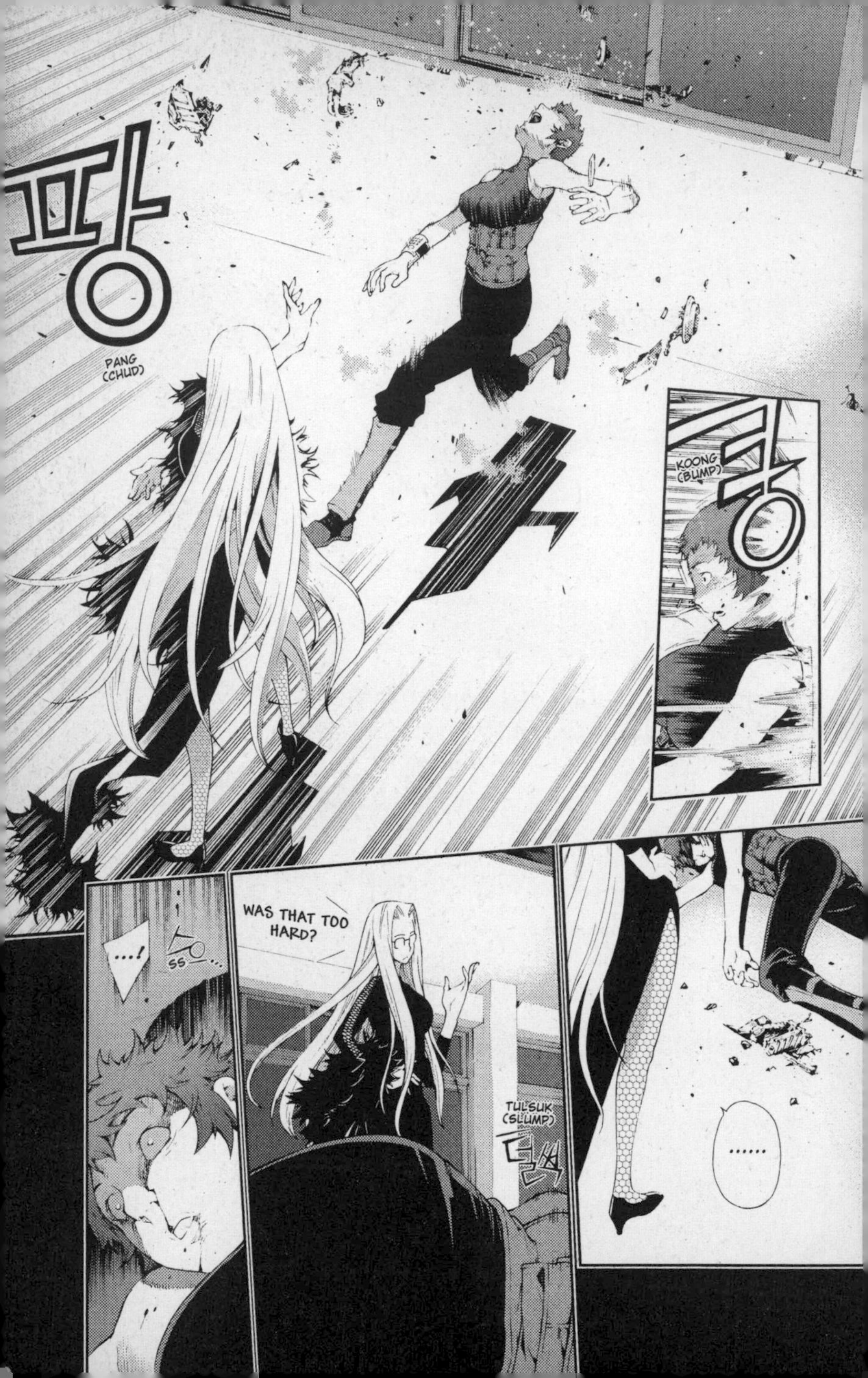
PANG
(CHUD)
KOONG
(BUMP)
...!
SS...
WAS THAT TOO HARD?
TULSUK
(SLUMP)
......

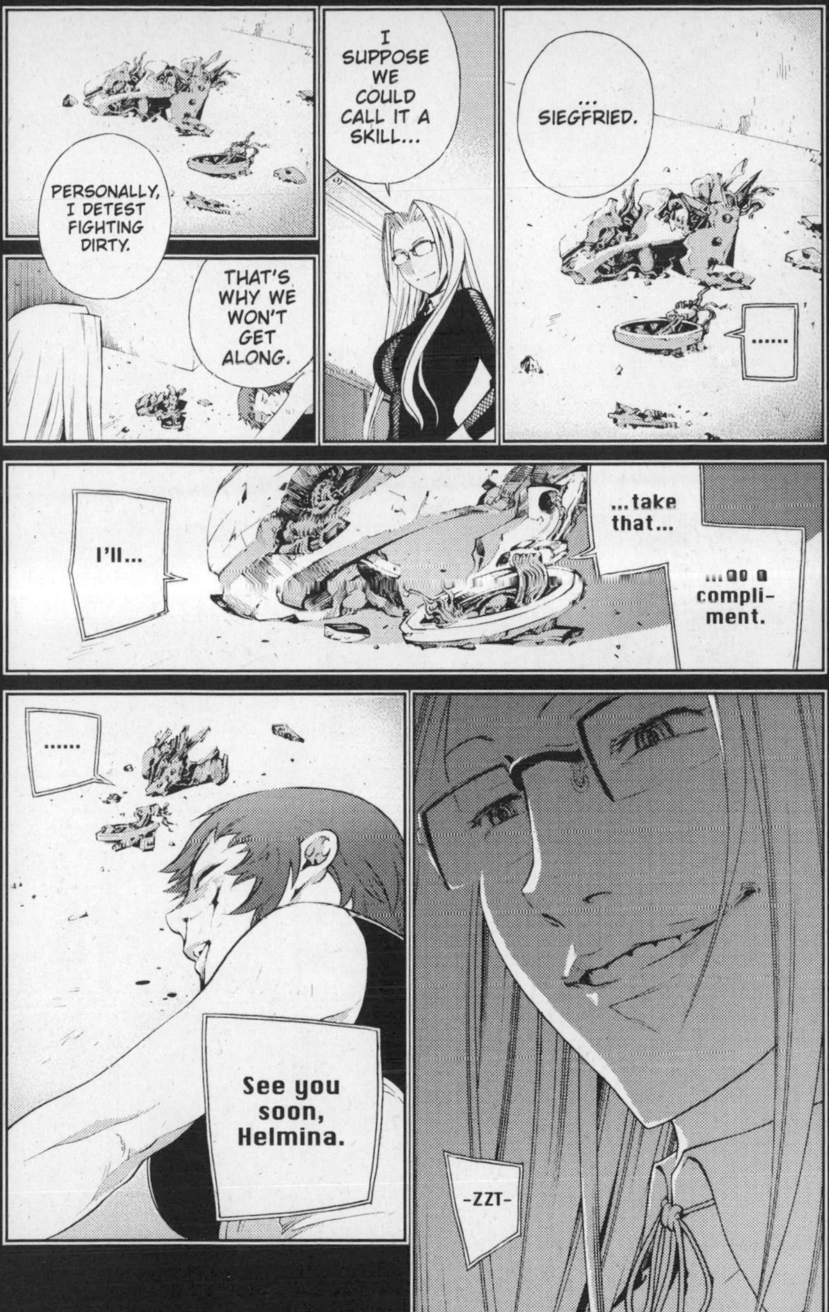
PERSONALLY, I DETEST FIGHTING DIRTY.
THAT'S WHY WE WON'T GET ALONG.
I SUPPOSE WE COULD CALL IT A SKILL...
... SIEGFRIED.
......
I'll...
...take that...
compliment.
......
See you soon, Helmina.
-ZZT-

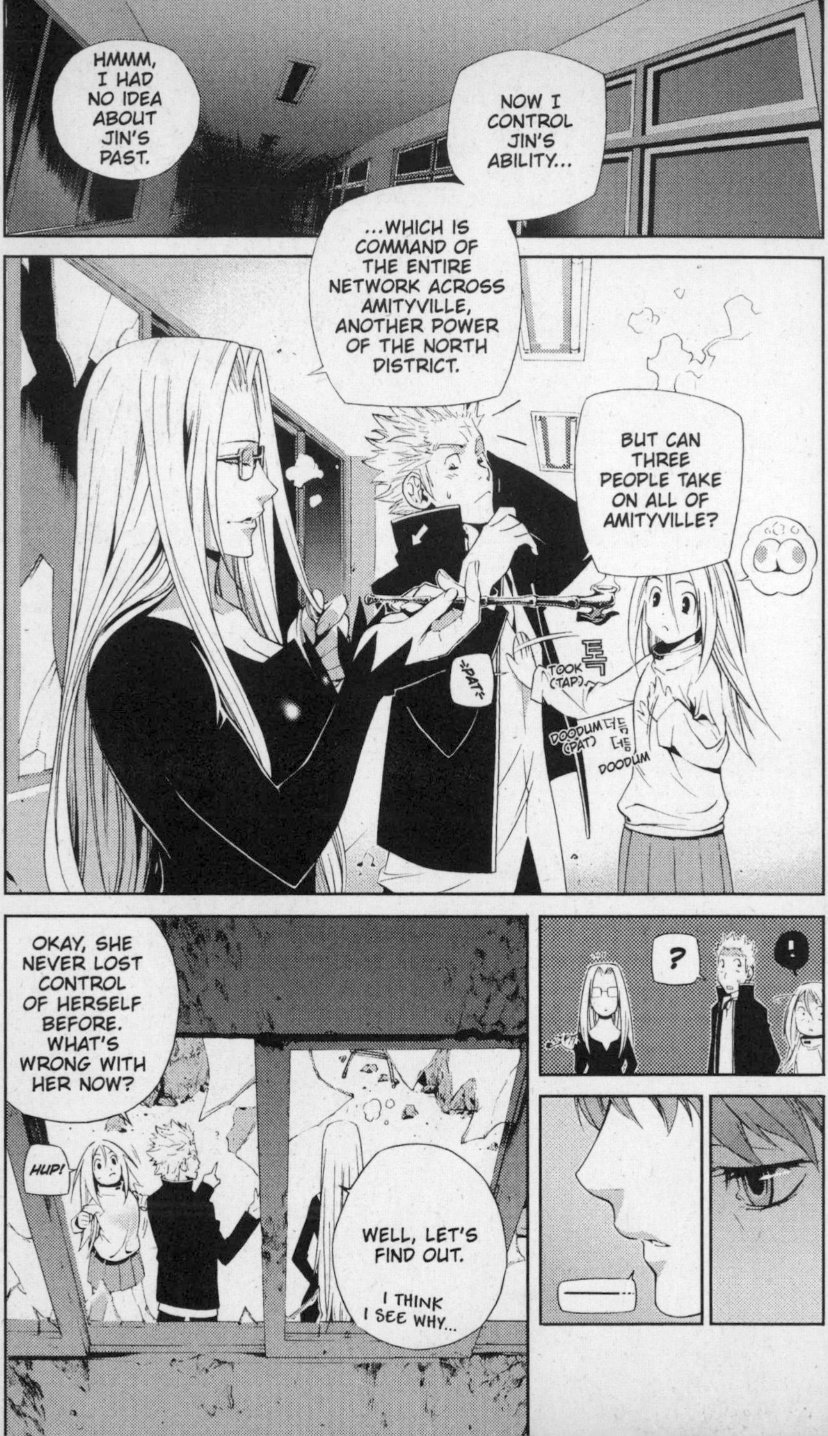

HMMM, I HAD NO IDEA ABOUT JIN'S PAST.
NOW I CONTROL JIN'S ABILITY...
...WHICH IS COMMAND OF THE ENTIRE NETWORK ACROSS AMITYVILLE, ANOTHER POWER OF THE NORTH DISTRICT.
BUT CAN THREE PEOPLE TAKE ON ALL OF AMITYVILLE?
PAT
톡
TOOK (TAP)
더듬 DOODUM (PAT)
더듬 DOODUM
OKAY, SHE NEVER LOST CONTROL OF HERSELF BEFORE. WHAT'S WRONG WITH HER NOW?
HUP!
WELL, LET'S FIND OUT.
I THINK I SEE WHY...
?
!
——...

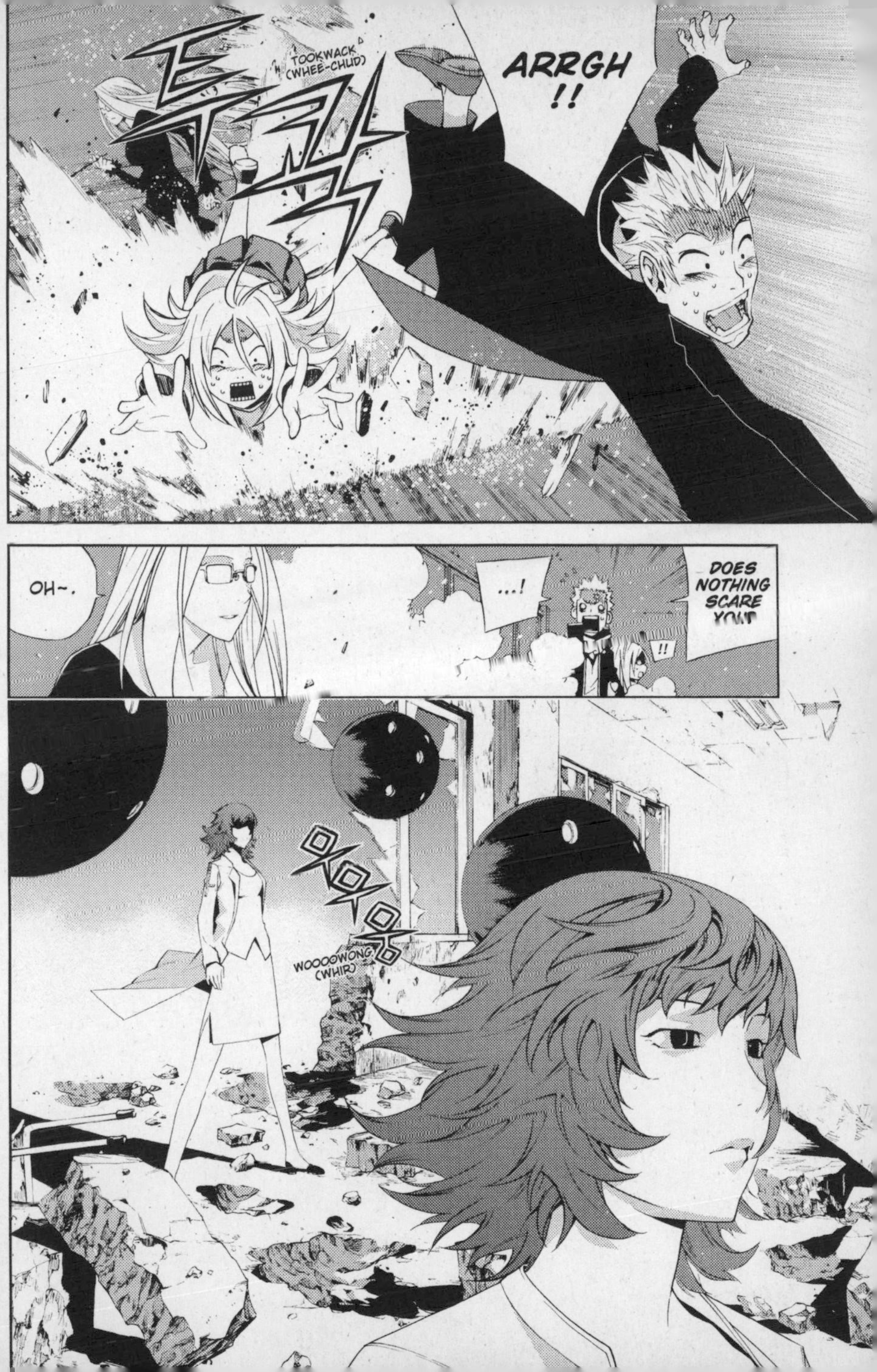
TOOKWACK (WHEE-CHUD)
ARRGH !!
OH~.
...!
!!
DOES NOTHING SCARE YOU
WOOOOWONG (WHIR)

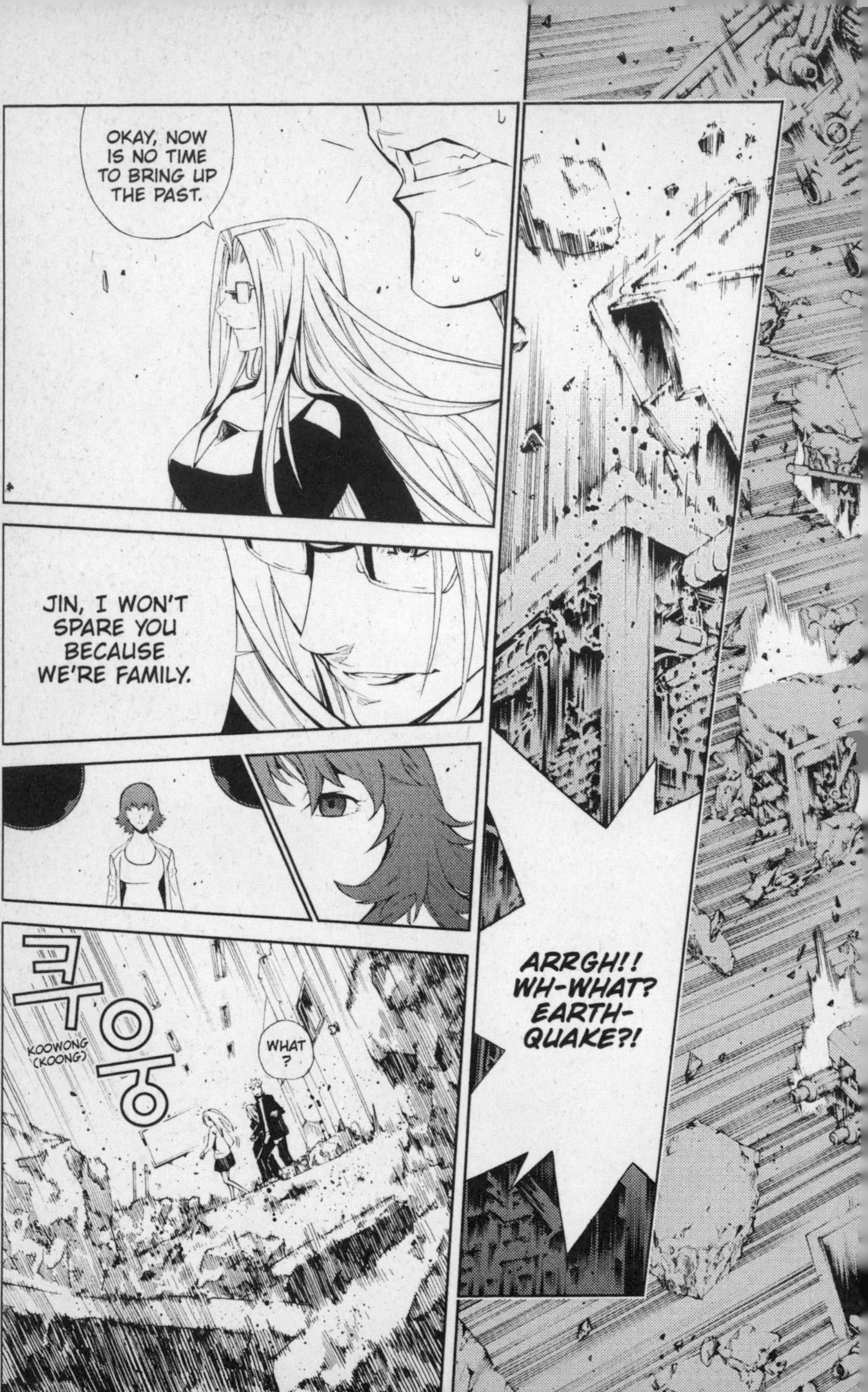
OKAY, NOW IS NO TIME TO BRING UP THE PAST.
JIN, I WON'T SPARE YOU BECAUSE WE'RE FAMILY.
KOOWONG (KOONG)
WHAT?
ARRGH!! WH-WHAT? EARTH-QUAKE?!

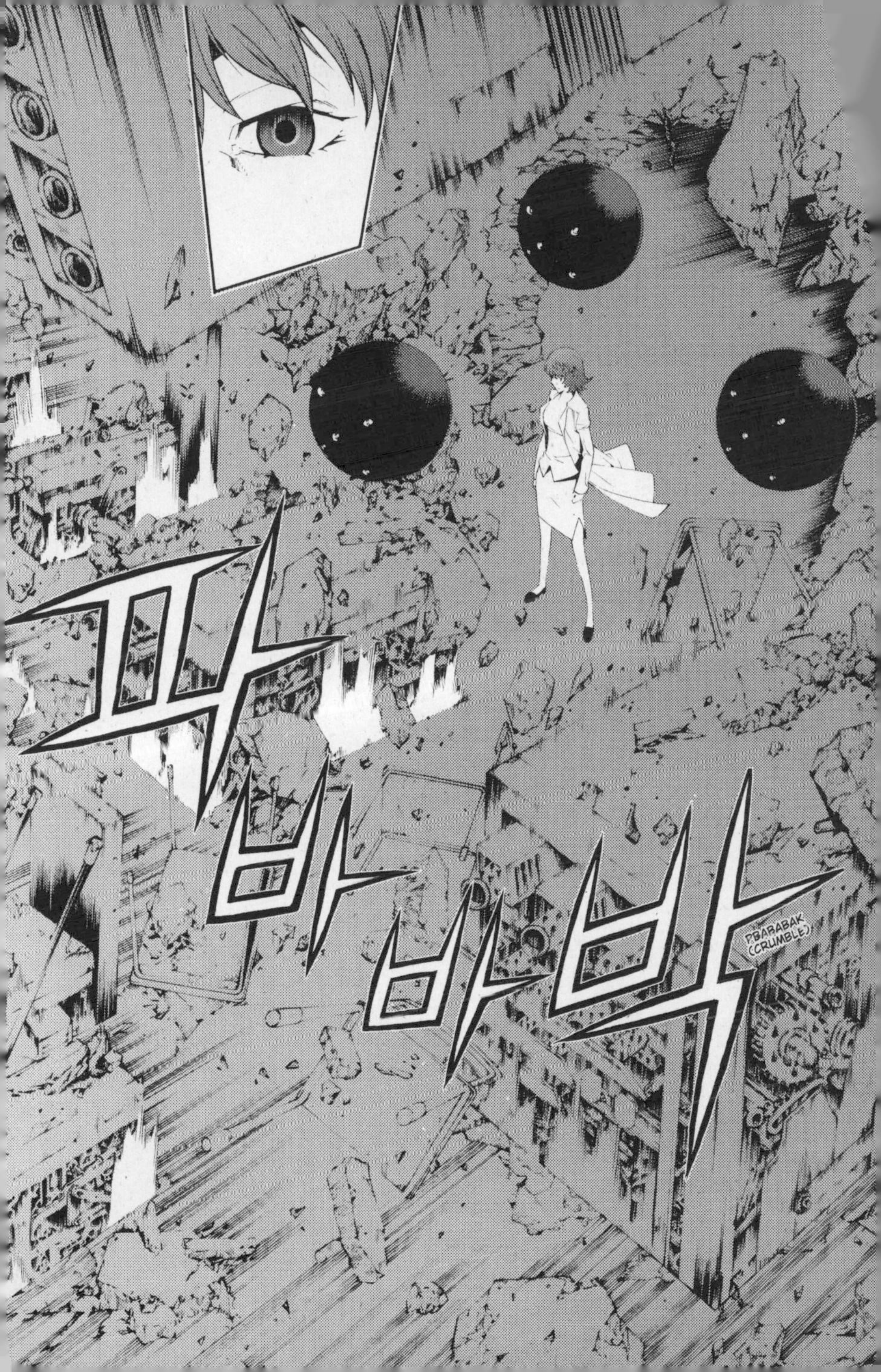
파바박
P'BABABAK
(CRUMBLE)

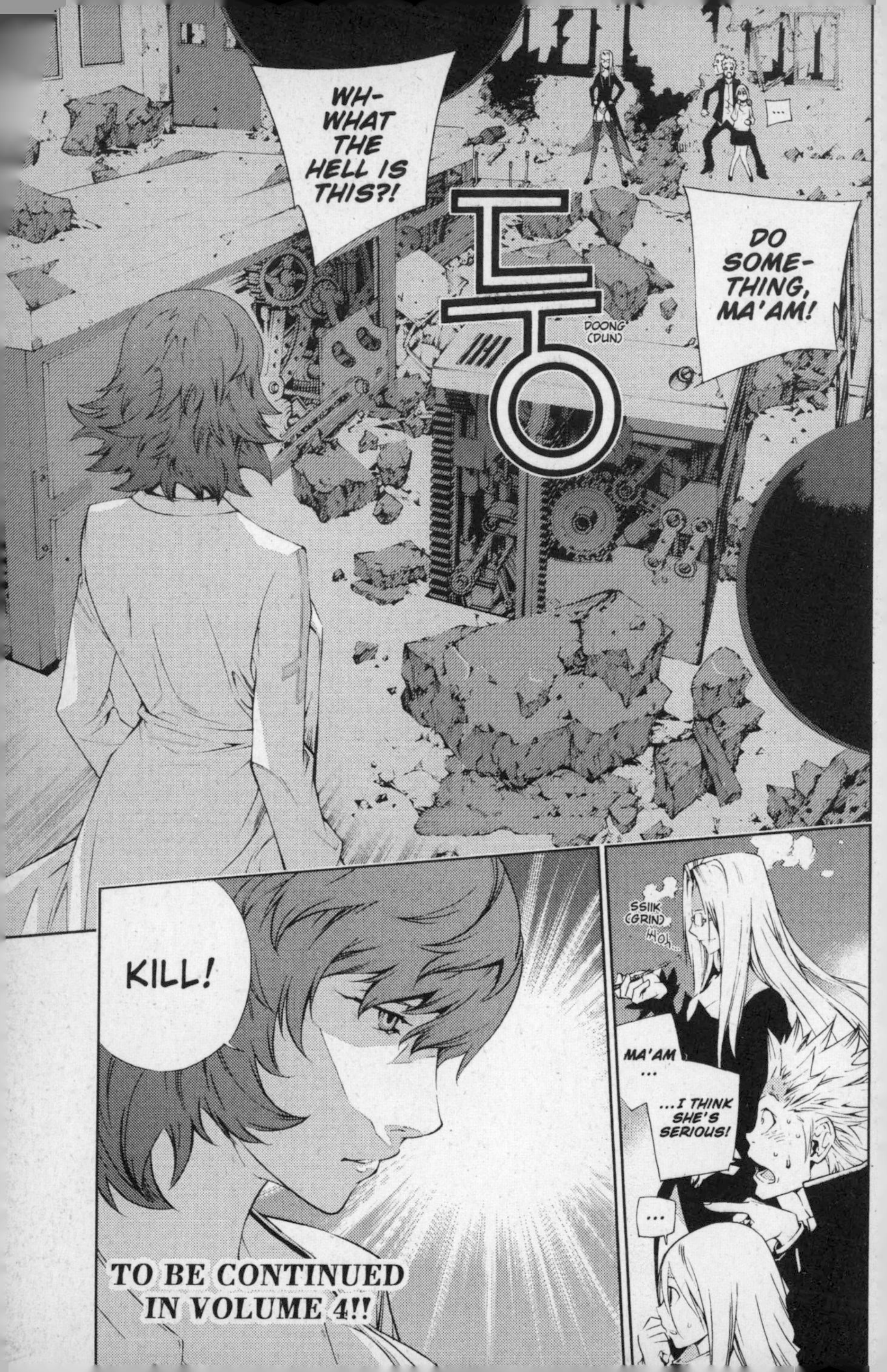

WH-WHAT THE HELL IS THIS?!
DOONG (DUN)
...
DO SOMETHING, MA'AM!
KILL!
TO BE CONTINUED IN VOLUME 4!!
SSIIK (GRIN)
MA'AM ...
...I THINK SHE'S SERIOUS!
...

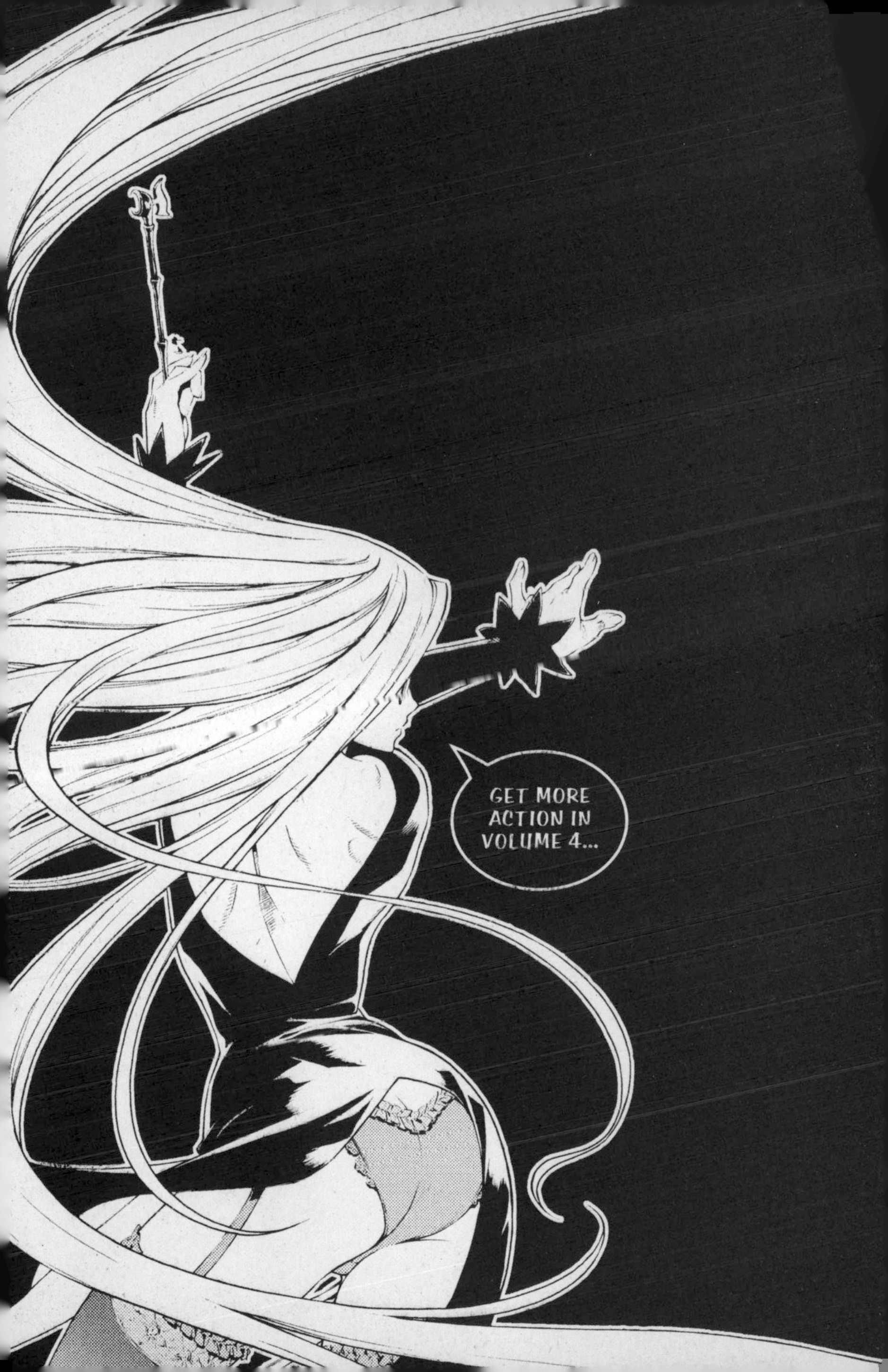
GET MORE ACTION IN VOLUME 4...

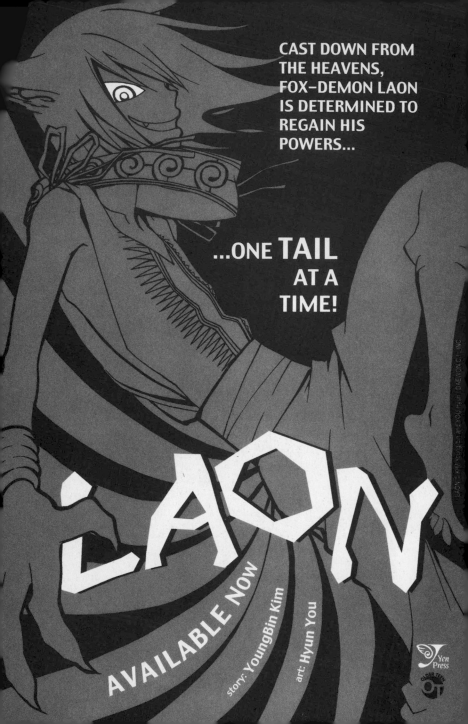

CAST DOWN FROM
THE HEAVENS,
FOX-DEMON LAON
IS DETERMINED TO
REGAIN HIS
POWERS...

...ONE **TAIL**
AT A
TIME!

LAON

AVAILABLE NOW

story: YoungBin Kim

art: Hyun You

LAON © KIM YoungBin and YOU Hyun / DAEWON.C.I. INC

Yen Press

OLDER TEEN
OT

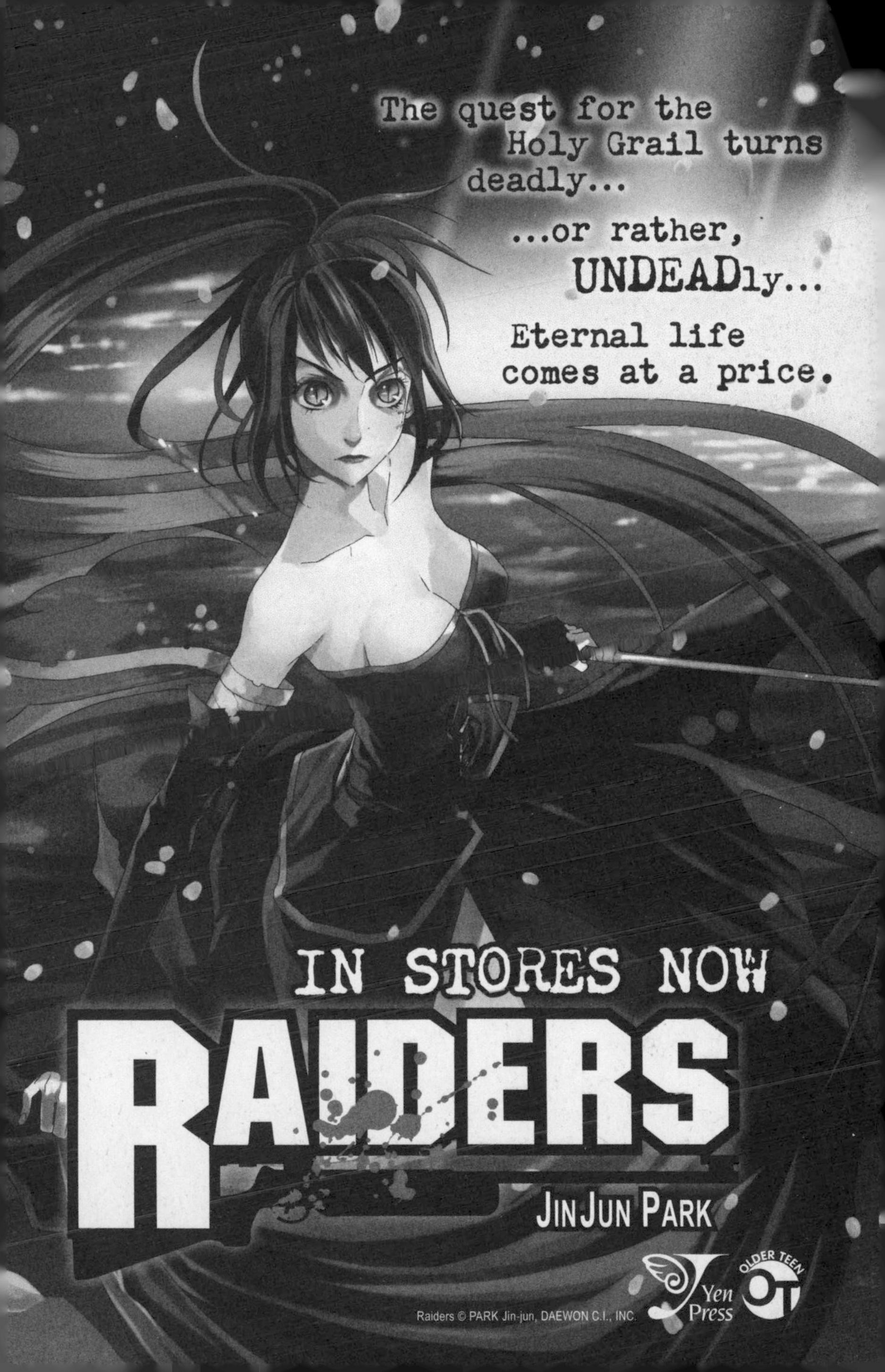

The quest for the Holy Grail turns deadly...
...or rather, UNDEADly...
Eternal life comes at a price.
IN STORES NOW
RAIDERS
JIN JUN PARK
Yen Press
OLDER TEEN OT
Raiders © PARK Jin-jun, DAEWON C.I., INC.

To become the ultimate weapon, one boy must eat the souls of 99 humans...

...and one witch.

Maka is a scythe meister, working to perfect her demon scythe until it is good enough to become Death's Weapon—the weapon used by Shinigami-sama, the spirit of Death himself. And if that isn't strange enough, her scythe also has the power to change form—into a human-looking boy!

Yen Press

Yen Press is an imprint of
Hachette Book Group

www.yenpress.com

VOLUME 3 IN STORES NOW

Soul Eater ©Atsushi Ohkubo/SQUARE ENIX

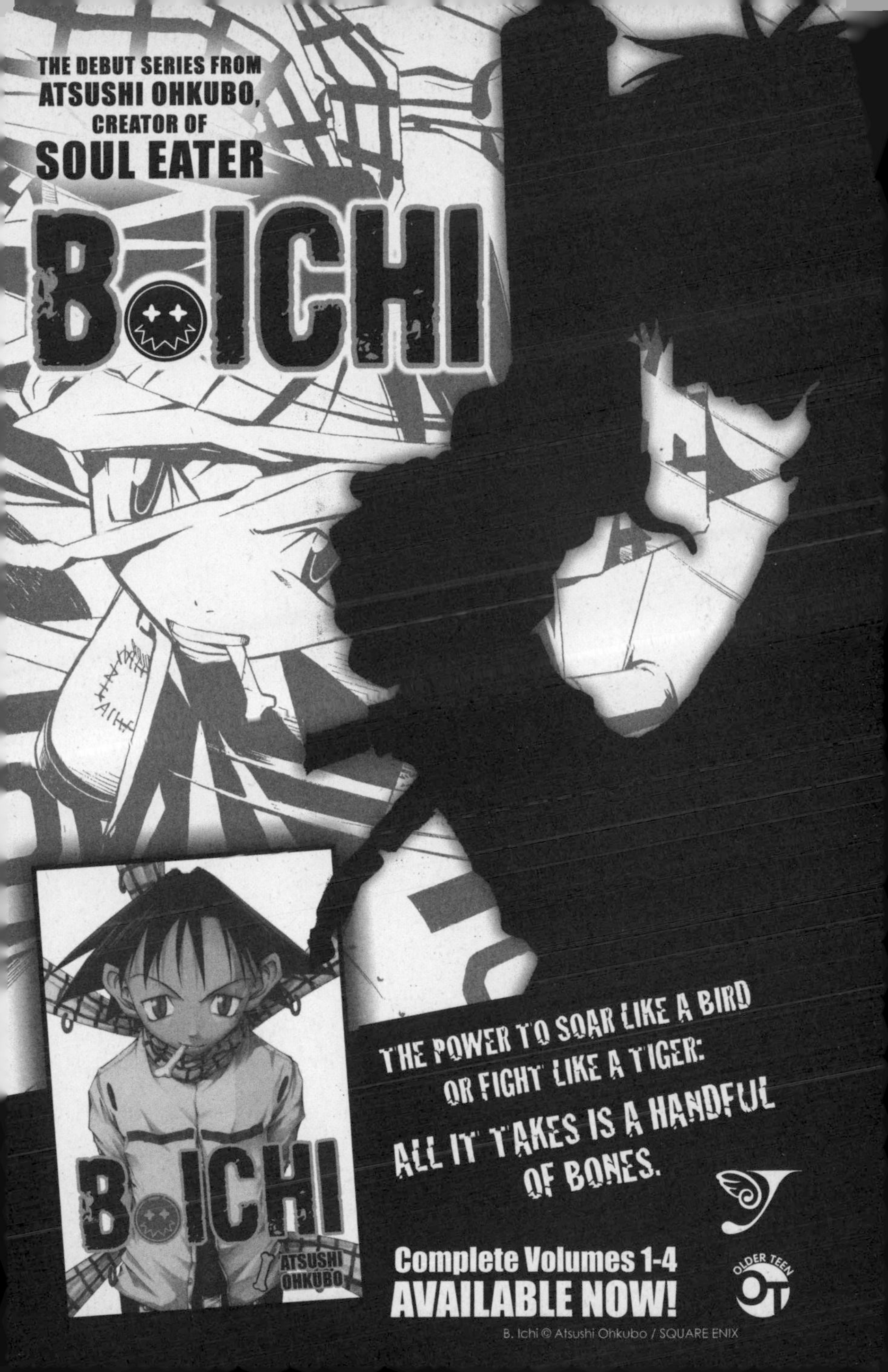
THE DEBUT SERIES FROM ATSUSHI OHKUBO, CREATOR OF SOUL EATER
B. ICHI
B. ICHI
ATSUSHI OHKUBO
THE POWER TO SOAR LIKE A BIRD OR FIGHT LIKE A TIGER:
ALL IT TAKES IS A HANDFUL OF BONES.
Complete Volumes 1-4
AVAILABLE NOW!
OLDER TEEN
OT
B. Ichi © Atsushi Ohkubo / SQUARE ENIX

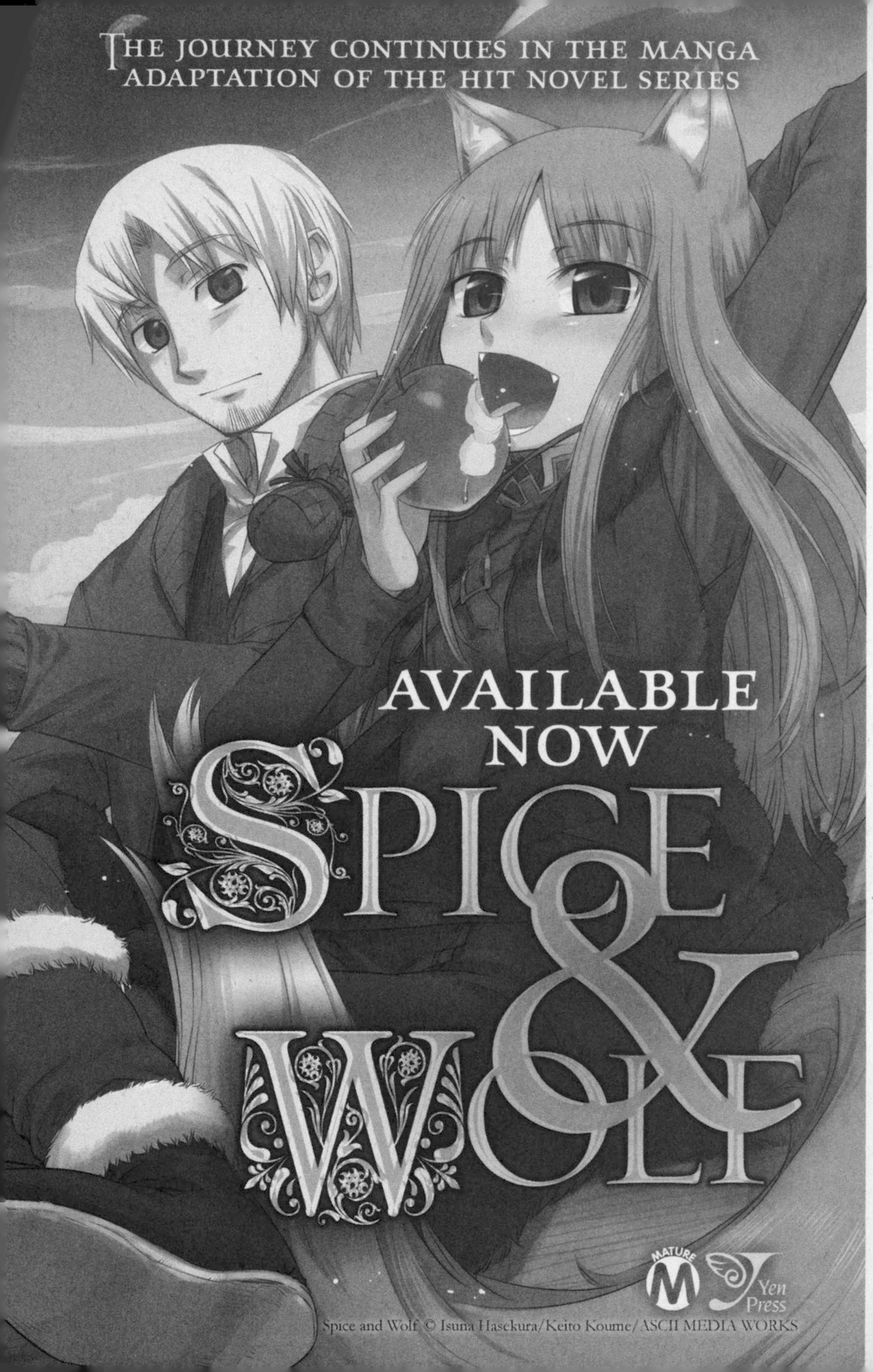
THE JOURNEY CONTINUES IN THE MANGA ADAPTATION OF THE HIT NOVEL SERIES
AVAILABLE NOW
SPICE & WOLF
MATURE
Yen Press
Spice and Wolf © Isuna Hasekura/Keito Koume/ASCII MEDIA WORKS

NOW AVAILABLE FROM YEN PRESS

Kieli sees ghosts.
Harvey cannot die.
He will throw
her world into
chaos...
...and become her
one true friend.

STORY BY **Yukako Kabei**
ART BY **Shiori Teshirogi**

KIELI

Kieli © YUKAKO KABEI/ASCII MEDIA WORKS, INC. © SHIORI TESHIROGI/AKITASHOTEN

DEALING WITH THE DEAD IS EVEN WORSE THAN DEALING WITH THE DEVIL!

ZOMBIE-LOAN
BY PEACH-PIT

AVAILABLE NOW.
www.yenpress.com

Yen Press

ZOMBIE-LOAN © PEACH-PIT/SQUARE ENIX
Yen Press is an imprint of Hachette Book Group.

OLDER TEEN
OT

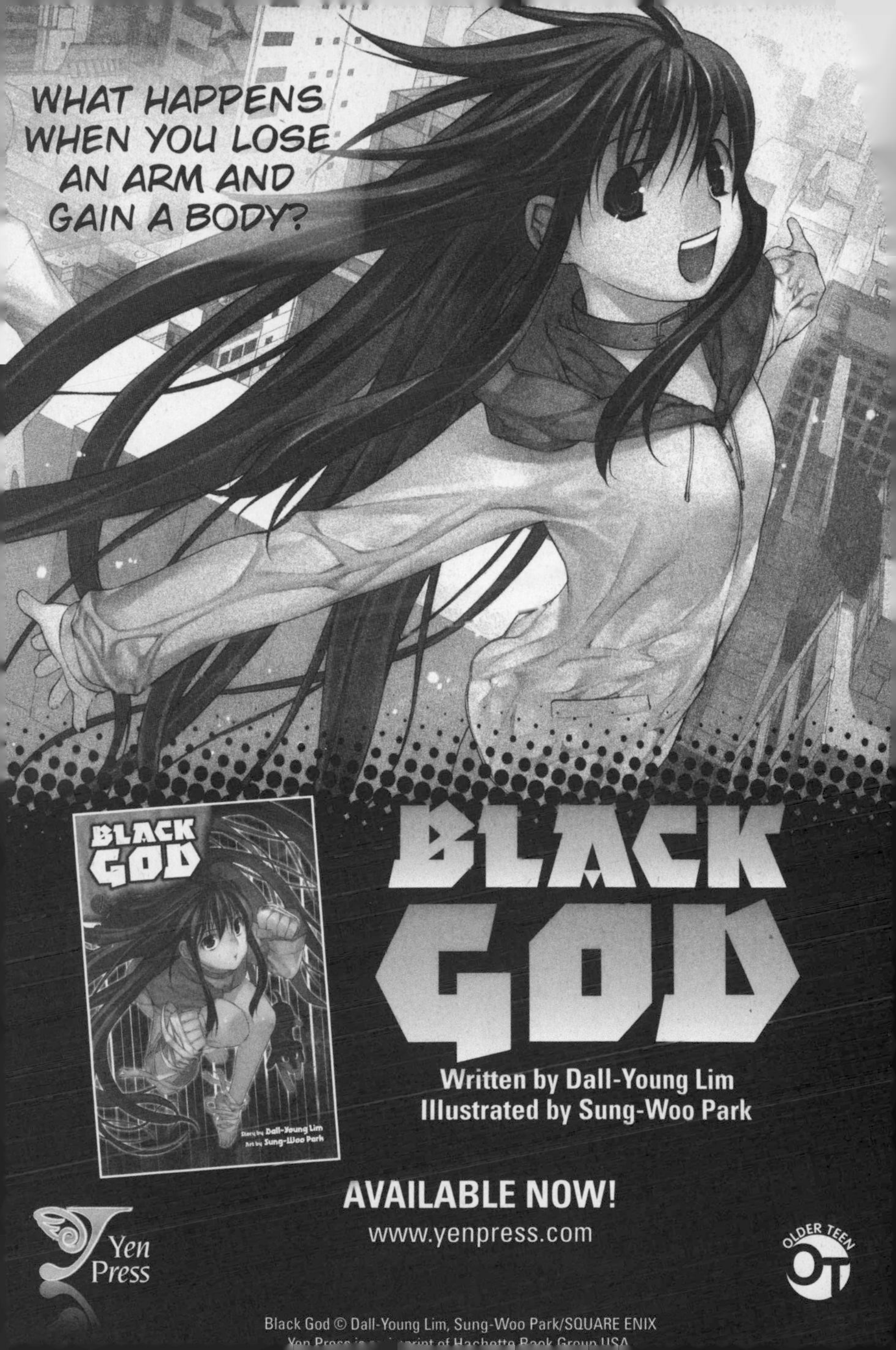
WHAT HAPPENS WHEN YOU LOSE AN ARM AND GAIN A BODY?
BLACK GOD
Story by Dall-Young Lim
Art by Sung-Woo Park
BLACK GOD
Written by Dall-Young Lim
Illustrated by Sung-Woo Park
AVAILABLE NOW!
www.yenpress.com
Yen Press
OLDER TEEN
OT
Black God © Dall-Young Lim, Sung-Woo Park/SQUARE ENIX

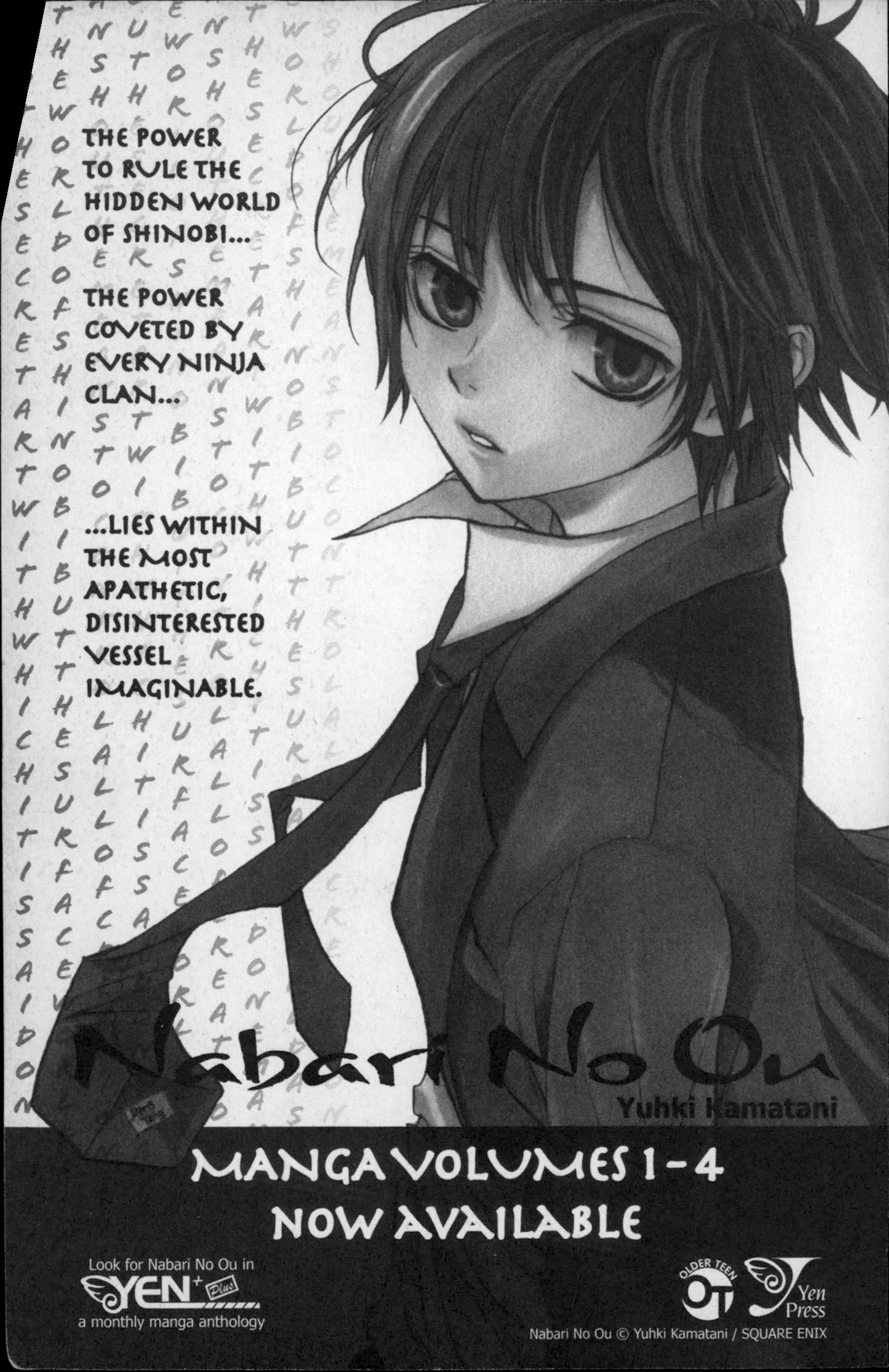
THE POWER TO RULE THE HIDDEN WORLD OF SHINOBI...
THE POWER COVETED BY EVERY NINJA CLAN...
...LIES WITHIN THE MOST APATHETIC, DISINTERESTED VESSEL IMAGINABLE.
Nabari No Ou
Yuhki Kamatani
MANGA VOLUMES 1-4
NOW AVAILABLE
Look for Nabari No Ou in
YEN+ Plus
a monthly manga anthology
OLDER TEEN OT
Yen Press
Nabari No Ou © Yuhki Kamatani / SQUARE ENIX

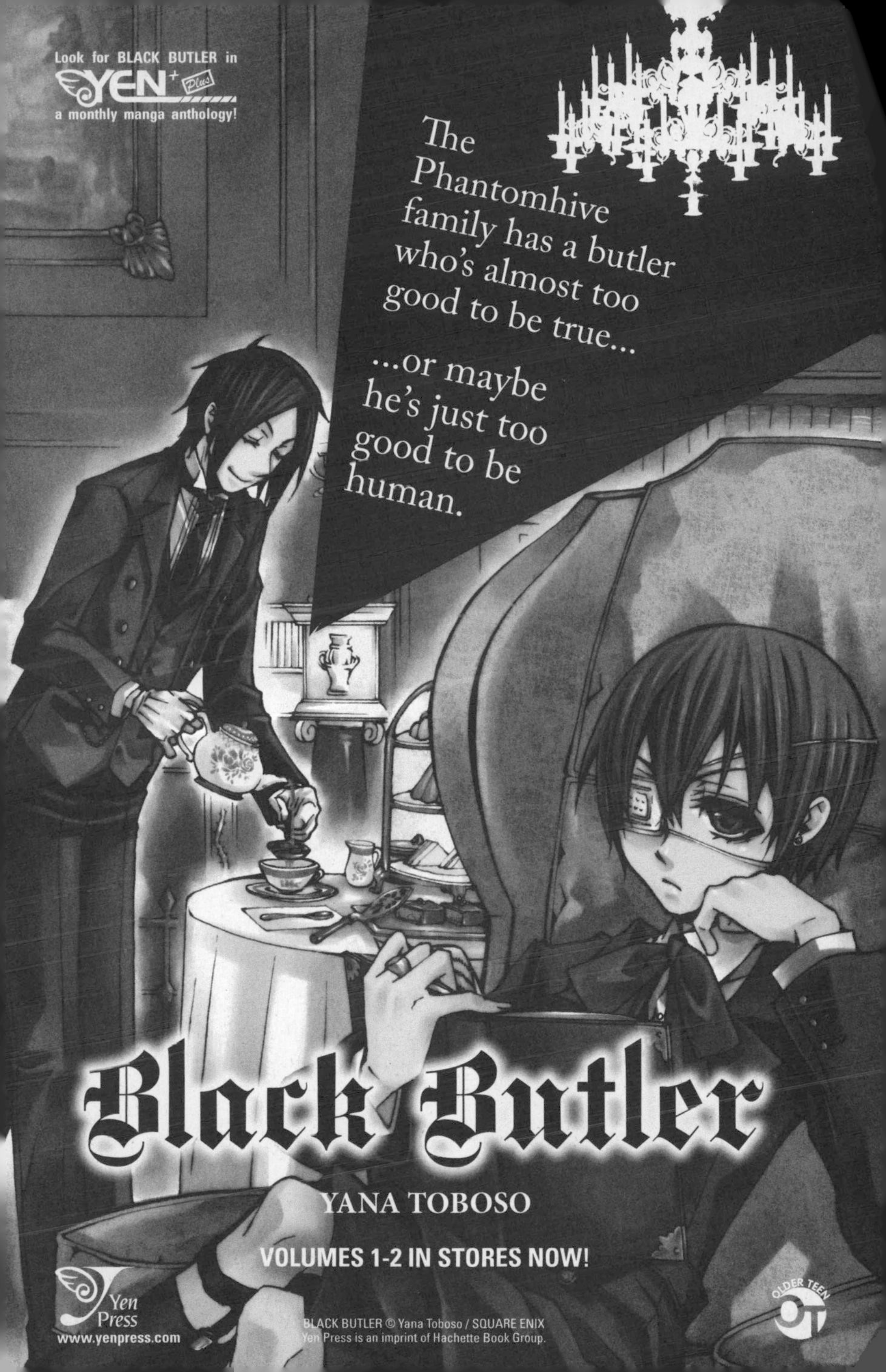
Look for BLACK BUTLER in
YEN+ Plus
a monthly manga anthology!
The Phantomhive family has a butler who's almost too good to be true...
...or maybe he's just too good to be human.
Black Butler
YANA TOBOSO
VOLUMES 1-2 IN STORES NOW!
Yen Press
www.yenpress.com
BLACK BUTLER © Yana Toboso / SQUARE ENIX
Yen Press is an imprint of Hachette Book Group.
OLDER TEEN
OT

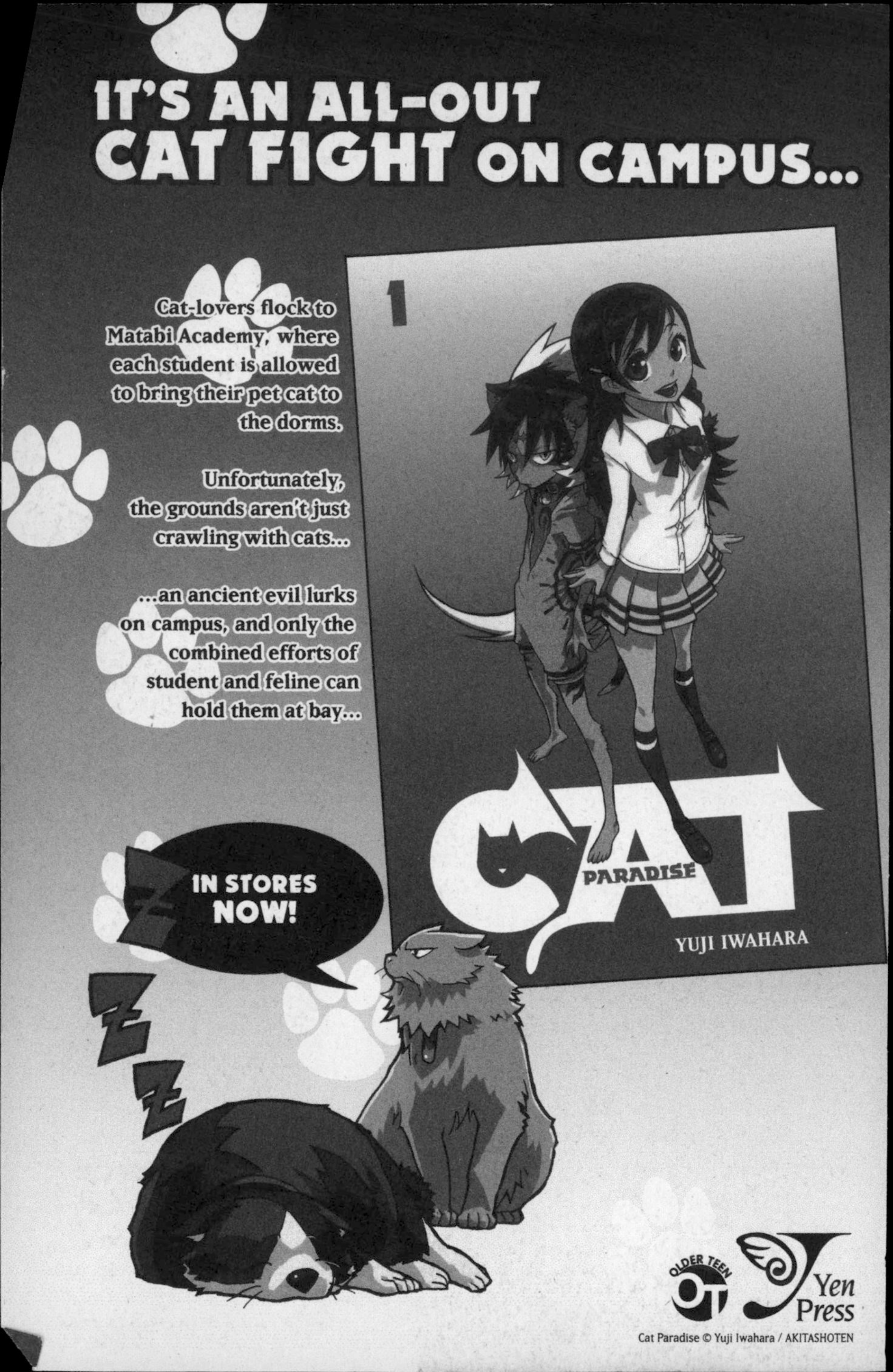
IT'S AN ALL-OUT
CAT FIGHT ON CAMPUS...
Cat-lovers flock to Matabi Academy, where each student is allowed to bring their pet cat to the dorms.
Unfortunately, the grounds aren't just crawling with cats...
...an ancient evil lurks on campus, and only the combined efforts of student and feline can hold them at bay...
1
CAT PARADISE
YUJI IWAHARA
IN STORES NOW!
OLDER TEEN OT
Yen Press
Cat Paradise © Yuji Iwahara / AKITASHOTEN

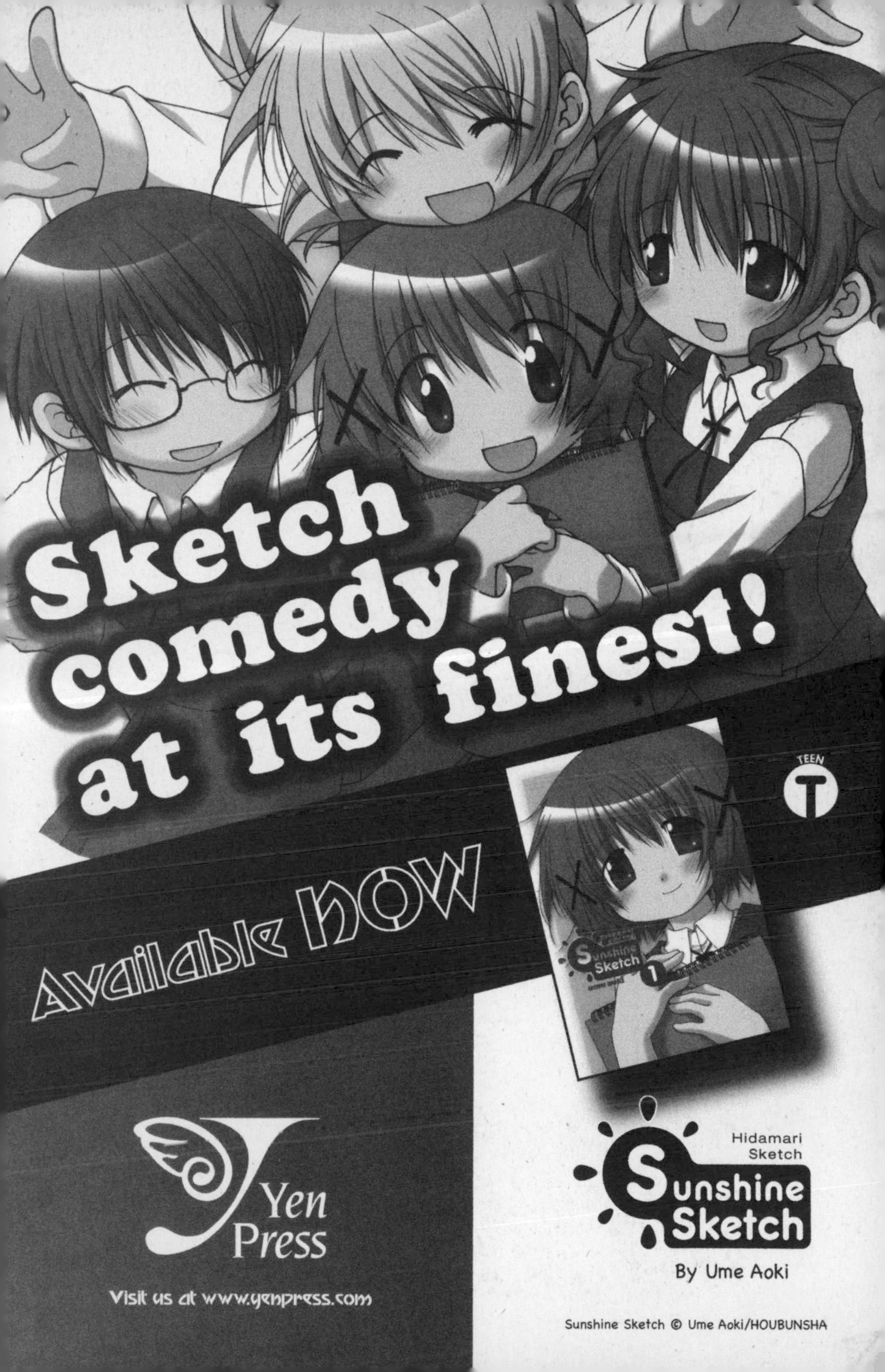
Sketch comedy at its finest!
TEEN
T
Available NOW
Yen Press
Visit us at www.yenpress.com
Hidamari Sketch
Sunshine Sketch
By Ume Aoki
Sunshine Sketch © Ume Aoki/HOUBUNSHA

Hello! This is YOTSUBA!

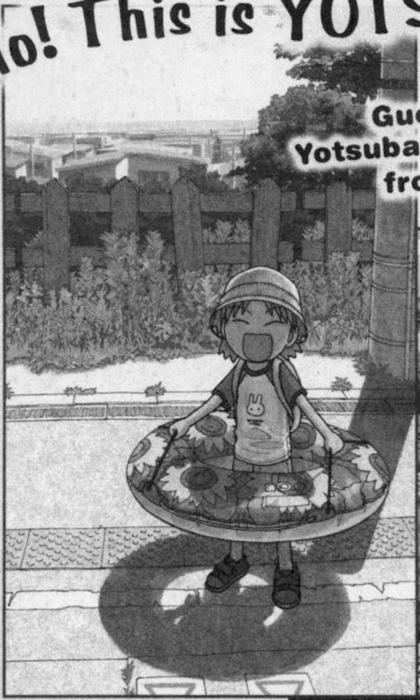

Guess what? Guess what?
Yotsuba and Daddy just moved here
from waaaay over there!

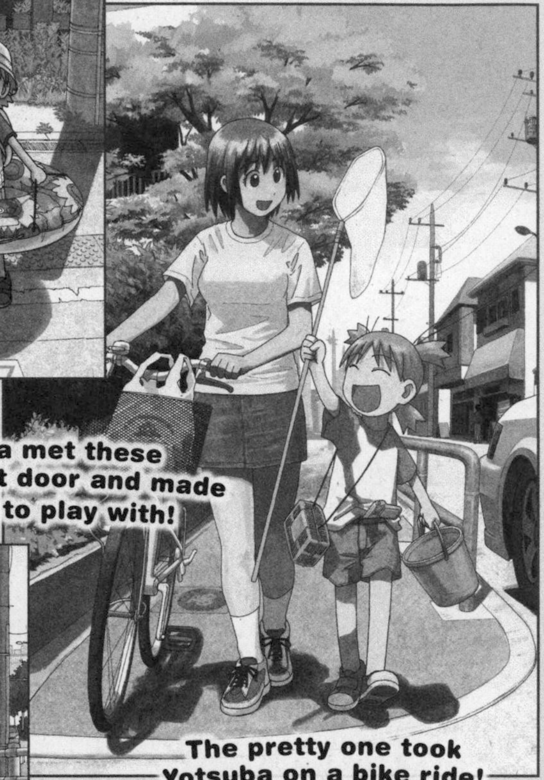

And Yotsuba met these
nice people next door and made
new friends to play with!

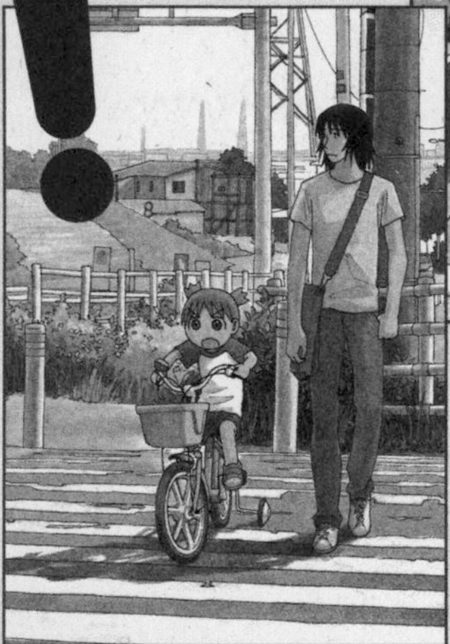

The pretty one took
Yotsuba on a bike ride!
(Whoooa! There was a big hill!)

And Ena's a good drawer!
(Almost as good as Yotsuba!)

And their mom always
gives Yotsuba ice cream!
(Yummy!)

And...
And...
OHHHH!

ENJOY EVERYTHING.

YOU SHOULD COME PLAY WITH YOTSUBA TOO!

**Join Yotsuba as she delights in the
things many of us take for granted in
this Eisner-nominated series.**

VOLUMES 1-8
AVAILABLE NOW!

Visit our website at www.yenpress.com.

Yotsuba&! © Kiyohiko Azuma / YOTUBA SUTAZIO

JACK FROST ③

JINHO KO

Translation: JiEun Park
English Adaptation: Arthur Dela Cruz

Lettering: Jose Macasocol, Jr.

Jack Frost Vol. 3 © 2008 JinHo Ko. All rights reserved. First published in Korea in 2008 by Haksan Publishing Co., Ltd. English translation rights in U.S.A., Canada, UK, and Republic of Ireland arranged with Haksan Publishing Co., Ltd.

English translation © 2010 Hachette Book Group, Inc.

All rights reserved. Except as permitted under the U.S. Copyright Act of 1976, no part of this publication may be reproduced, distributed, or transmitted in any form or by any means, or stored in a database or retrieval system, without the prior written permission of the publisher.

The characters and events in this book are fictitious. Any similarity to real persons, living or dead, is coincidental and not intended by the author.

Yen Press
Hachette Book Group
237 Park Avenue, New York, NY 10017

www.HachetteBookGroup.com
www.YenPress.com

Yen Press is an imprint of Hachette Book Group, Inc.
The Yen Press name and logo are trademarks of Hachette Book Group, Inc.

First Yen Press Edition: July 2010

ISBN: 978-0-316-07786-6

10 9 8 7 6 5 4 3 2 1

BVG

Printed in the United States of America

SKOKIE PUBLIC LIBRARY